New Perspectives on

MICROSOFT® WINDOWS® XP

Introductory

JUNE JAMRICH PARSONS

DAN OJA

JOAN & PATRICK CAREY
Carey Associates

LISA RUFFOLO

**COURSE
TECHNOLOGY**

THOMSON LEARNING

Australia • Canada • Mexico • Singapore • Spain • United Kingdom • United States

New Perspectives on Microsoft® Windows® XP—Introductory
is published by Course Technology.

Managing Editor:
Greg Donald

Senior Editor:
Donna Gridley

Senior Product Manager:
Kathy Finnegan

Product Manager:
Melissa Hathaway

Technology Product Manager:
Amanda Young

Editorial Assistant:
Jessica Engstrom

Marketing Manager:
Sean Teare

Developmental Editor:
Kim Crowley

Production Editor:
Kristen Guevara

Composition:
GEX Publishing Services

Text Designer:
Meral Dabcovich

Cover Designer:
Efrat Reis

Preface

Course Technology is the world leader in information technology education. The New Perspectives Series is an integral part of Course Technology's success. Visit our Web site to see a whole new perspective on teaching and learning solutions.

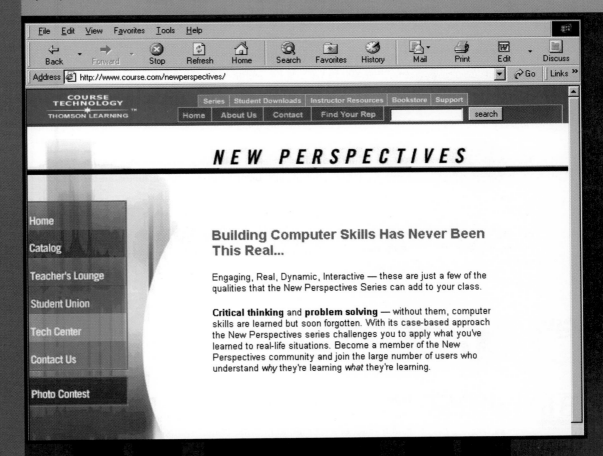

New Perspectives—Building Computer Skills Has Never Been This Real

Why New Perspectives will work for you.

Critical thinking and **problem solving**—without them, computer skills are learned but soon forgotten. With its **case-based** approach, the New Perspectives Series challenges students to apply what they've learned to real-life situations. Become a member of the New Perspectives community and watch your students not only **master** computer skills, but also **retain** and carry this **knowledge** into the world.

New Perspectives catalog
Our online catalog is never out of date! Go to the Catalog button on our Web site to check out our available titles, request a desk copy, download a book preview, or locate online files.

Complete system of offerings
Whether you're looking for a Brief book, an Advanced book, or something in between, we've got you covered. Go to the Catalog button on our Web site to find the level of coverage that's right for you.

Instructor materials
We have all the tools you need—data files, solution files, figure files, a sample syllabus, and ExamView, our powerful testing software package.

How well do your students know Microsoft Office?
Find out with performance-based testing software that measures your students' proficiency in the application. Click the Tech Center button to learn more.

Get certified
If you want to get certified, we have the titles for you. Find out more by clicking the Teacher's Lounge button.

Interested in online learning?
Enhance your course with any one of our online learning platforms. Go to the Teacher's Lounge to find the platform that's right for you.

Your link to the future is at
www.course.com/NewPerspectives

What you need to know about this book.

- Student Online Companion takes students to the Web for additional work.

- ExamView testing software gives you the option of generating a printed test, LAN-based test, or test over the Internet.

- New Perspectives Labs provide students with self-paced practice on computer-related topics.

- Students will appreciate the contemporary, realistic scenarios that place them in the context of a computer lab and a distance learning course.

- The step-by-step instructions and screen illustrations guide students as they tour the Windows XP desktop, practice using the mouse, and explore Windows XP online Help.

- Students will gain confidence with Windows XP by working with files and folders in both My Computer and Windows Explorer, personalizing the Windows environment, bringing the Web to their desktops, and searching for information.

- This text provides a comprehensive overview of working with Windows XP. It moves quickly and is suitable for both beginning students and experienced students, who can use it as a review.

CASE	TROUBLE?	SESSION 1.1	QUICK CHECK	RW
Tutorial Case Each tutorial begins with a problem presented in a case that is meaningful to students. The case sets the scene to help students understand what they will do in the tutorial.	**TROUBLE? Paragraphs** These paragraphs anticipate the mistakes or problems that students may have and help them continue with the tutorial.	**Sessions** Each tutorial is divided into sessions designed to be completed in about 45 minutes each. Students should take as much time as they need and take a break between sessions.	**Quick Check Questions** Each session concludes with conceptual Quick Check questions that test students' understanding of what they learned in the session.	**Reference Windows** Reference Windows are succinct summaries of the most important tasks covered in a tutorial. They preview actions students will perform in the steps to follow.

TABLE OF CONTENTS

Acknowledgments

Many thanks to everyone on the New Perspectives team for their guidance, insight, and good humor, including Greg Donald, Jessica Engstrom, and Kristen Guevara. Special thanks to Kathy Finnegan, whose common sense and dedication to the reader informs this book, and Kim Crowley, who approached each draft with freshness and improved the book with every edit. I also appreciate the careful work of Harris Bierhoff, Quality Assurance tester, and Risa Blair, Hilda Wirth Federico, and Eric Johnston, who reviewed these tutorials. Special thanks to June Parsons, Dan Oja, and Joan and Patrick Carey, on whose previous work this book is based.

—Lisa Ruffolo

New Perspectives on

MICROSOFT®
WINDOWS XP

Read This Before You Begin

To the Student

Data Disks

To complete the Level I tutorials, Review Assignments, and Projects, you need three Data Disks. Your instructor will either provide you with the Data Disks or ask you to make your own.

If you are making your own Data Disks, you will need **three** blank, formatted high-density disks. You will need to copy a set of files and/or folders from a file server, standalone computer, or the Web onto your disks. Your instructor will tell you which computer, drive letter, and folders contain the files you need. You could also download the files by going to www.course.com and following the instructions on the screen.

The information below shows you the Data Disks you need so that you will have enough disk space to complete all the tutorials, Review Assignments, and Projects:

Data Disk 1
Write this on the disk label:
Windows XP Tutorial 2 Data Disk

Data Disk 2
Write this on the disk label:
Windows XP Disk 1 Data Disk Copy

Data Disk 3
Write this on the disk label:
Windows XP Tutorial 2, Assignment 4

When you begin each tutorial, Review Assignment, or Project, be sure you are using the correct Data Disk. Refer to the "File Finder" chart at the back of this text for more detailed information on which files are used in which tutorials. See the inside front or inside back cover of this book for more information on Data Disk files, or ask your instructor or technical support person for assistance.

Course Labs

The Windows XP Level I tutorials feature three interactive Course Labs to help you understand how to use a keyboard and a mouse, and how to work with files. There are Lab Assignments at the end of Tutorial 1 and Tutorial 2 that relate to these Labs.

To start a Lab, click the **Start** button on the Windows taskbar, point to **Programs**, point to **Course Labs**, point to **New Perspectives Course Labs**, and then click the name of the Lab you want to use.

Using Your Own Computer

If you are going to work through this book using your own computer, you need:

- ■ **Computer System** Microsoft Windows XP must be installed on your computer. This book assumes a typical installation of Microsoft Windows XP Professional.

- ■ **Data Disks** You will not be able to complete the tutorials or exercises in this book using your own computer until you have your Data Disks.

- ■ **Course Labs** See your instructor or technical support person to obtain the Course Lab software for use on your own computer.

Visit Our World Wide Web Site

Additional materials designed especially for you are available on the World Wide Web.
Go to www.course.com/NewPerspectives.

To the Instructor

The Data Disk Files and Course Labs are available on the Instructor's Resource Kit for this title. Follow the instructions in the Help file on the CD-ROM to install the programs to your network or standalone computer. For information on creating Data Disks or the Course Labs, see the "To the Student" section above.

You are granted a license to copy the Data Files and Course Labs to any computer or computer network used by students who have purchased this book.

EXPLORING THE BASICS

Investigating the Windows XP Operating System

OBJECTIVES

In this tutorial you will:

- Start and shut down Windows XP

- Identify the objects on the Windows XP desktop

- Practice mouse functions

- Run software programs, switch between them, and close them

- Identify and use the controls in a window

- Use Windows XP controls, such as menus, toolbars, list boxes, scroll bars, option buttons, tabs, and check boxes

- Explore Windows XP Help

LABS

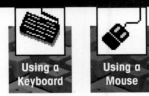

Using a Keyboard   Using a Mouse

Your First Day at the Computer

You walk into the computer lab and sit down at a desk. There are computers in front of you, and you find yourself staring dubiously at the screen. Where to start? As if in answer to your question, your friend Steve Laslow appears.

"You start with the operating system," says Steve. Noticing your puzzled look, Steve explains that the **operating system** is software that helps the computer carry out operating tasks, such as displaying information on the computer screen and saving data on disks. (Software refers to the **programs**, or **applications**, that a computer uses to perform tasks.) Your computer uses the **Microsoft Windows XP** operating system—**Windows XP** for short.

Steve explains that much of the software created for use with Windows XP shares the same look and works the same way. This similarity in design means that once you have learned to use one Windows program, such as Microsoft Word (a word-processing program), you are well on your way to understanding how to use other Windows programs. Windows XP allows you to use more than one program at a time, so you can easily switch between your word-processing program and your address book program, for example. Windows XP also makes it very easy to access the **Internet**, the worldwide collection of computers connected to one another to enable communication. All in all, Windows XP makes your computer an effective and easy-to-use productivity tool.

In this tutorial you will start Microsoft Windows XP and practice some basic computer skills.

SESSION 1.1

In this session, you will learn some basic Windows terminology. You will use a pointing device, start and close a program, and switch between programs that are running at the same time.

Starting Windows XP

Using a Keyboard

Windows XP automatically starts when you turn on your computer. Depending on the way your computer is set up, you might be asked to enter your username and password.

To start Windows XP:

1. Turn on your computer. After a moment, Windows XP starts and displays the Windows XP Welcome screen.

   TROUBLE? If you are asked to select an operating system, do not take action. Windows XP should start automatically after a designated number of seconds. If it does not, ask your instructor or technical support person for help.

   TROUBLE? If this is the first time you have started your computer with Windows XP, messages might appear on your screen informing you that Windows is setting up components of your computer. Wait until the Welcome screen appears, and then continue with Step 2.

2. On the Welcome screen, click your user name. The Windows XP screen appears, as shown in Figure 1-1.

   TROUBLE? If your user name does not appear on the Welcome screen, ask your instructor which name you should click.

   TROUBLE? If prompted to do so, type your assigned user name, press the Tab key, type your password, and then click OK or press the Enter key to continue.

Figure 1-1	THE WINDOWS XP DESKTOP

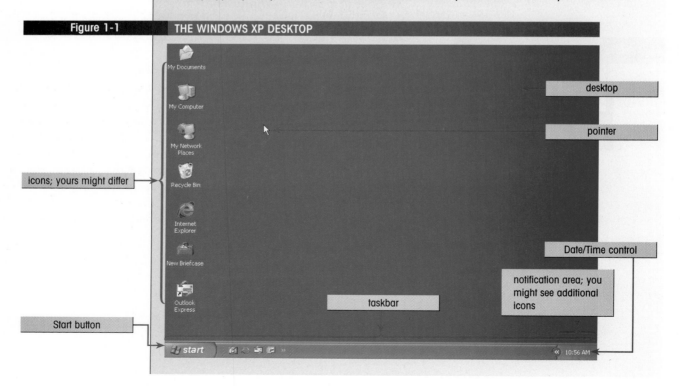

3. Look at your screen and locate the objects labeled in Figure 1-1. The objects on your screen might appear larger or smaller than those in Figure 1-1, depending on your monitor's settings. Figure 1-2 describes the function of each of these objects.

Figure 1-2	ELEMENTS OF THE WINDOWS XP DESKTOP	

ELEMENT	DESCRIPTION
Icon	A small picture that represents an object available to your computer
Pointer	A small object, such as an arrow, that moves on the screen when you move the mouse
Desktop	Your workplace on the screen
Date/Time control	Shows the current date and time and lets you set the clock
Taskbar	Contains buttons that give you quick access to common tools and the programs currently running
Start button	Provides access to Windows XP programs, documents, and information on the Internet
Notification area	Displays icons corresponding to services running in the background, such as an Internet connection

TROUBLE? One default setting for your computer might be to use a screen saver, a program that causes the monitor to go blank or to display an animated design after a specified amount of idle time. If a blank screen or animated design replaces the Window XP desktop, you can press any key or move the mouse to restore the Windows XP desktop.

The Windows XP desktop uses a **graphical user interface** (**GUI**, pronounced "gooey"), which displays **icons**, or pictures of familiar objects, such as file folders and documents, to represent items stored on your computer, such as programs and files. Windows XP gets its name from the rectangular work areas, called "windows," that appear on your screen as you work. No windows should be open right now. You will learn more about windows in Session 1.2.

The Windows XP Desktop

In Windows terminology, the area that appears on your screen when Windows XP starts represents a **desktop**—a workspace for projects and the tools that you need to manipulate your projects. When you first start a computer, it uses **default settings**, those preset by the operating system. The default desktop you see after you first install Windows XP, for example, might have a plain blue background. However, Microsoft designed Windows XP so that you can easily change the appearance of the desktop. You can, for example, change color, or add patterns, images, and text to the desktop background.

Many organizations design customized desktops for their computers. Figure 1-1 shows the default Windows XP desktop. Figure 1-3 shows two other examples of desktops, one designed for a business, North Pole Novelties, and one designed for a school, the University of Colorado. Although your desktop might not look exactly like any of the examples in Figure 1-1 or Figure 1-3, you should be able to locate similar objects on your screen.

Figure 1-3   CUSTOMIZED DESKTOPS

desktop designed for a business   desktop designed for a university

Using a Pointing Device

Using a Mouse

A **pointing device** helps you interact with objects on your computer screen. Pointing devices come in many shapes and sizes; some are designed to ensure that your hand won't tire while using them. Some attach directly to your computer via a cable, whereas others function like a TV remote control and allow you to access your computer without being right next to it. Figure 1-4 shows examples of common pointing devices.

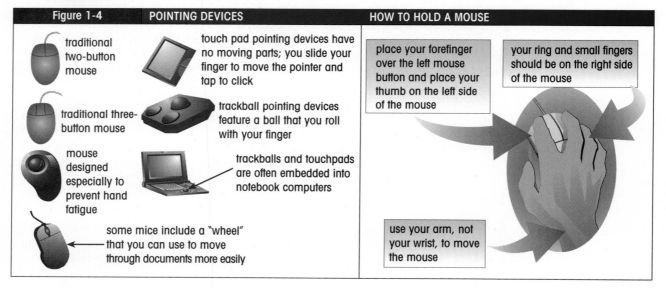

Figure 1-4   POINTING DEVICES   HOW TO HOLD A MOUSE

traditional two-button mouse

touch pad pointing devices have no moving parts; you slide your finger to move the pointer and tap to click

place your forefinger over the left mouse button and place your thumb on the left side of the mouse

your ring and small fingers should be on the right side of the mouse

traditional three-button mouse

trackball pointing devices feature a ball that you roll with your finger

mouse designed especially to prevent hand fatigue

trackballs and touchpads are often embedded into notebook computers

use your arm, not your wrist, to move the mouse

some mice include a "wheel" that you can use to move through documents more easily

The most common pointing device is called a **mouse**, so this book uses that term. If you are using a different pointing device, such as a trackball, substitute that device whenever you see the term *mouse*. Because Windows XP uses a GUI, you need to know how to use the mouse to manipulate the objects on the screen. In this session, you will learn about pointing and clicking. In Session 1.2, you will learn how to use the mouse to move objects.

You can also interact with objects by using the keyboard; however, the mouse is more convenient for most tasks, so the tutorials in this book assume that you are using one.

Pointing

You use a pointing device to move the mouse pointer over objects on the desktop. The pointer is usually shaped like an arrow, although the pointer will change shape depending on its location and on the tasks you are performing. Most computer users place the mouse on a **mouse pad**, a flat piece of rubber that helps the mouse move smoothly. As you move the mouse on the mouse pad, the pointer on the screen moves in a corresponding direction.

You begin most Windows operations by positioning the pointer over a specific part of the screen. This is called **pointing**.

To move the pointer:

1. Position your right index finger over the left mouse button, as shown in Figure 1-4, but don't click yet. Lightly grasp the sides of the mouse with your thumb and little finger.

   TROUBLE? If you want to use the mouse with your left hand, ask your instructor or technical support person to help you use the Control Panel to swap the functions of the left and right mouse buttons. Be sure to find out how to change back to the right-handed mouse setting, so that you can reset the mouse each time you are finished in the lab.

2. Place the mouse on the mouse pad, and then move the mouse. Watch the movement of the pointer.

   TROUBLE? If you run out of room to move your mouse, lift the mouse and place it in the middle of the mouse pad. Notice that the pointer does not move when the mouse is not in contact with the mouse pad or another surface.

When you position the mouse pointer over certain objects, such as the objects on the taskbar, tips appear. These tips are called **ScreenTips**, and tell you the purpose or function of the object to which you are pointing.

To view ScreenTips:

1. Use the mouse to point to the **Start** button start on the taskbar. After a few seconds, you see the ScreenTip "Click here to begin," as shown in Figure 1-5.

Figure 1-5 VIEWING SCREENTIPS

ScreenTip

pointer

2. Point to the time displayed in the notification area at the right end of the taskbar. Notice that a ScreenTip for today's date (or the date to which your computer's time clock is set) appears.

Clicking

Clicking refers to pressing a mouse button and immediately releasing it. Clicking sends a signal to your computer that you want to perform an action on the object you click. In Windows XP you perform most actions with the left mouse button. If you are told to click an object, position the mouse pointer on it and click the left mouse button, unless instructed otherwise.

When you click the Start button, the Start menu opens. A **menu** is a list of options that you can use to complete tasks. The **Start menu** provides you with access to programs, documents, and much more. Try clicking the Start button to open the Start menu.

To open the Start menu:

1. Point to the **Start** button ⟨ start ⟩ on the taskbar.

2. Click the left mouse button. The Start menu opens. Notice the arrow ▶ following the All Programs option on the Start menu. This arrow indicates that you can view additional choices by navigating to a **submenu**, a menu extending from the main menu. See Figure 1-6.

Figure 1-6	START MENU

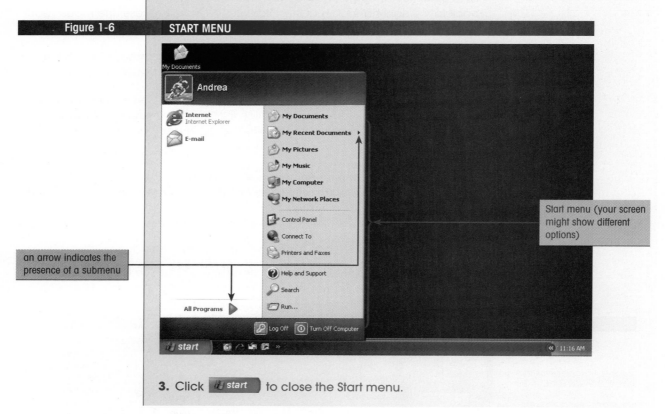

an arrow indicates the presence of a submenu

Start menu (your screen might show different options)

3. Click ⟨ start ⟩ to close the Start menu.

Next you'll learn how to select items on a submenu.

Selecting

In Windows XP, you point to and then click an object to **select** it. You need to select an object to work with it. Windows XP shows you which object is selected by highlighting it, usually by changing the object's color, putting a box around it, or making the object appear to be pushed in, as shown in Figure 1-7.

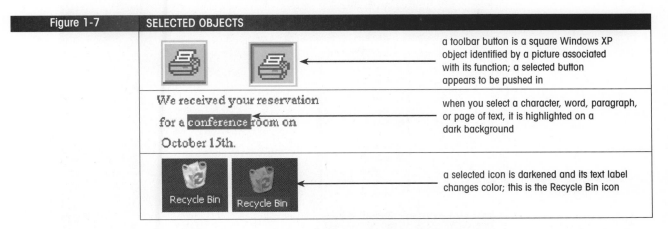

Figure 1-7	SELECTED OBJECTS

a toolbar button is a square Windows XP object identified by a picture associated with its function; a selected button appears to be pushed in

when you select a character, word, paragraph, or page of text, it is highlighted on a dark background

a selected icon is darkened and its text label changes color; this is the Recycle Bin icon

In Windows XP, depending on your computer's settings, you can select certain objects by pointing to them and others by clicking them. Try pointing to the All Programs option on the Start menu to open the All Programs submenu.

To select an option on a menu:

1. Click the **Start** button [🏁 start] on the taskbar, and notice how it appears to be pushed in, indicating that it is selected.

2. Point to (but don't click) **All Programs** on the Start menu. When you first point to the All Programs option, it is highlighted to indicate it is selected. After a short pause, the All Programs submenu opens. See Figure 1-8.

   TROUBLE? If a submenu other than the All Programs menu opens, you pointed to the wrong option. Move the mouse so that the pointer points to All Programs.

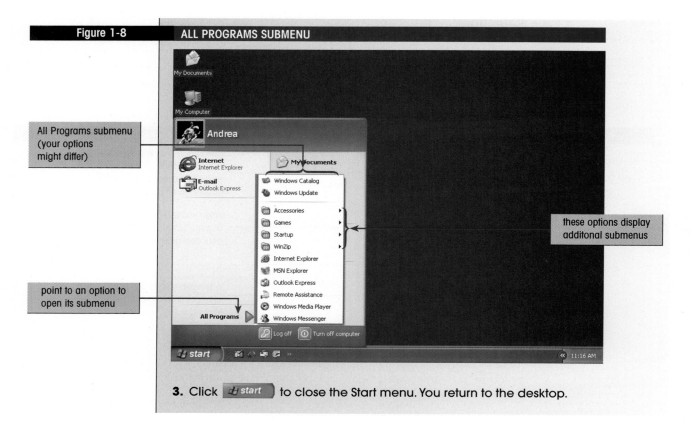

Figure 1-8   ALL PROGRAMS SUBMENU

All Programs submenu
(your options
might differ)

these options display
additonal submenus

point to an option to
open its submenu

3. Click **⟨ start⟩** to close the Start menu. You return to the desktop.

Double-Clicking

In addition to clicking an object to select it, you can double-click an object to open or start the item associated to it. For example, you can double-click a folder icon to open the folder and see its contents. Or you can double-click a program icon to start the program. Double-clicking means to click the mouse button twice in quick succession.

You can practice double-clicking now by opening the My Documents folder. **My Documents** is your personal folder, a convenient place to store documents, graphics, and other work.

To open the My Documents folder:

1. Click and then point to the **My Documents** icon on the desktop. After a few moments, a ScreenTip appears describing the My Documents folder.

TROUBLE? If you don't see the icons for My Computer or My Documents, you can add them to the desktop. Click Start, click Control Panel, click Switch to Category New, if necessary, click Appearance and Themes, and then click Change the desktop background. In the Desktop Items dialog box, click to insert checks in the boxes for My Computer and My Documents to add these icons to the desktop. You can also add icons for My Network Places and Internet Explorer. Click OK to close each dialog box.

2. Click the left mouse button twice quickly to double-click the **My Documents** icon. The My Documents window opens, as shown in Figure 1-9.

Figure 1-9   **CONTENTS OF THE MY DOCUMENTS FOLDER**

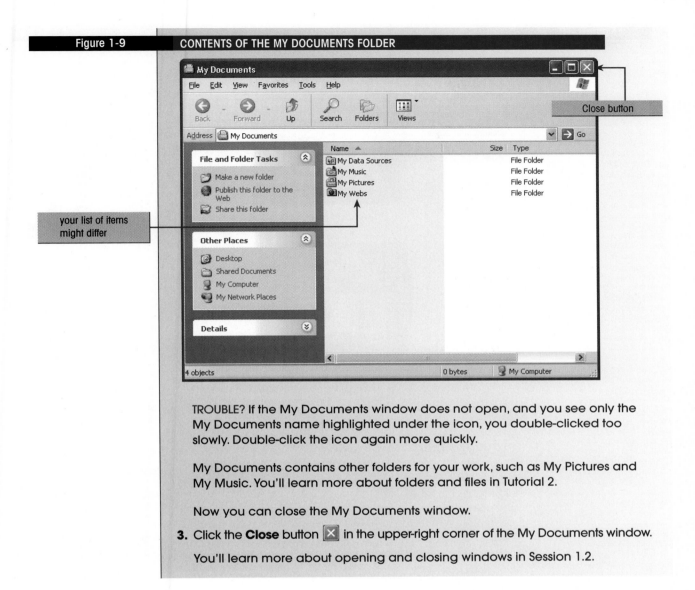

TROUBLE? If the My Documents window does not open, and you see only the My Documents name highlighted under the icon, you double-clicked too slowly. Double-click the icon again more quickly.

My Documents contains other folders for your work, such as My Pictures and My Music. You'll learn more about folders and files in Tutorial 2.

Now you can close the My Documents window.

3. Click the **Close** button ⊠ in the upper-right corner of the My Documents window.

You'll learn more about opening and closing windows in Session 1.2.

Right-Clicking

Pointing devices were originally designed with a single button, so the term "clicking" had only one meaning: you pressed that button. Innovations in technology, however, led to the addition of a second and even a third button (and more recently, options such as a wheel) that expanded the pointing device's capabilities. More recent programs—especially those designed for Windows XP—take advantage of additional buttons, especially the right button. However, the term "clicking" continues to refer to the left button; clicking an object with the *right* button is called **right-clicking**.

In Windows XP, right-clicking both selects an object and opens its **shortcut menu**, which is a list of options directly related to the object that you right-clicked. You can right-click practically any object—the Start button, a desktop icon, the taskbar, and even the desktop itself—to view options associated with that object. For example, the illustration in the top portion of Figure 1-10 shows what happens when you click the Start button with the left mouse button to open the Start menu. Clicking the Start button with the right button, however, opens the Start button's shortcut menu, as shown in the second illustration.

Figure 1-10   **CLICKING WITH THE LEFT AND RIGHT MOUSE BUTTONS**

clicking Start button with left mouse button opens Start menu

click with left mouse button

clicking Start button with right mouse button opens shortcut menu

Open
Explore
Search...
Properties

Open All Users
Explore All Users

click with right mouse button

Try right-clicking to open the shortcut menu for the Start button.

To right-click an object:

1. Position the pointer over the Start button ⊞ start on the taskbar.

2. Right-click ⊞ start to open the Start button's shortcut menu. This menu offers a list of options available to the Start menu.

TROUBLE? If you are using a trackball or a mouse with three buttons or a wheel, make sure you click the button on the far right, not the one in the middle.

TROUBLE? Your menu may look slightly different from the one in Figure 1-11. Different computers often have different options and commands.

Figure 1-11   **START BUTTON SHORTCUT MENU**

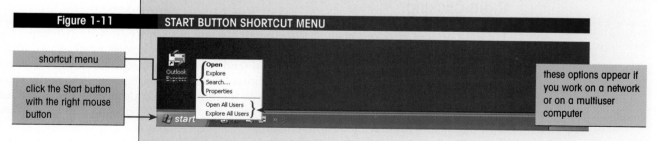

shortcut menu

click the Start button with the right mouse button

Open
Explore
Search...
Properties
Open All Users
Explore All Users

these options appear if you work on a network or on a multiuser computer

3. Press the **Esc** key to close the shortcut menu. You again return to the desktop.

Starting and Closing a Program

To use a program, such as a word-processing program, you must first start it. With Windows XP you start a program by clicking the Start button and then locating and clicking the program's name in the submenus.

The Reference Window below explains how to start a program. Don't do the steps in the Reference Window now; they are for your reference later.

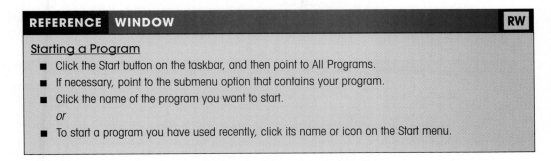

REFERENCE WINDOW RW

Starting a Program

- Click the Start button on the taskbar, and then point to All Programs.
- If necessary, point to the submenu option that contains your program.
- Click the name of the program you want to start.
  or
- To start a program you have used recently, click its name or icon on the Start menu.

Windows XP includes an easy-to-use word-processing program called WordPad. Suppose you want to start the WordPad program and use it to write a letter or report. You open Windows XP programs from the Start menu. Programs are usually located on the All Programs submenu or on one of its submenus. To start WordPad, for example, you navigate to the All Programs and Accessories submenus.

To start the WordPad program from the Start menu:

1. Click the **Start** button ⟳ start on the taskbar to open the Start menu.

2. Point to **All Programs** to display the All Programs submenu.

3. Point to **Accessories**. Another submenu opens. Figure 1-12 shows the open menus.

| Figure 1-12 | START MENU AND RELATED SUBMENUS |

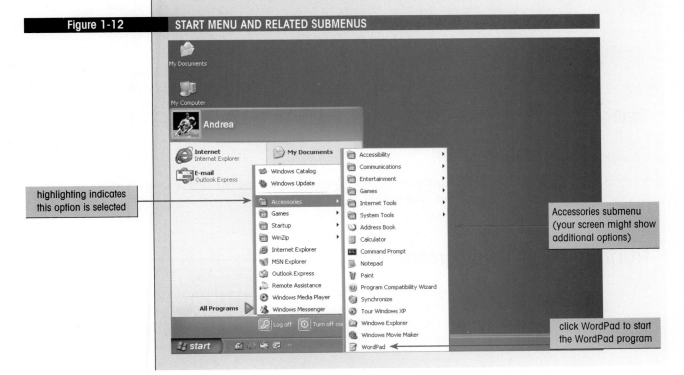

highlighting indicates this option is selected

Accessories submenu (your screen might show additional options)

click WordPad to start the WordPad program

TROUBLE? If a different menu opens, you might have moved the mouse too slowly so that a different submenu opened. Move the pointer back to the All Programs option, and then move the pointer up or down to point to Accessories. Once you're more comfortable moving the mouse, you'll find that you can eliminate this problem by moving the mouse quickly.

4. Click **WordPad** on the Accessories submenu. The WordPad program window opens, as shown in Figure 1-13. Depending on your computer settings, the WordPad program window may fill the entire screen. You will learn how to manipulate windows in Session 1.2.

Figure 1-13   THE WORDPAD PROGRAM WINDOW

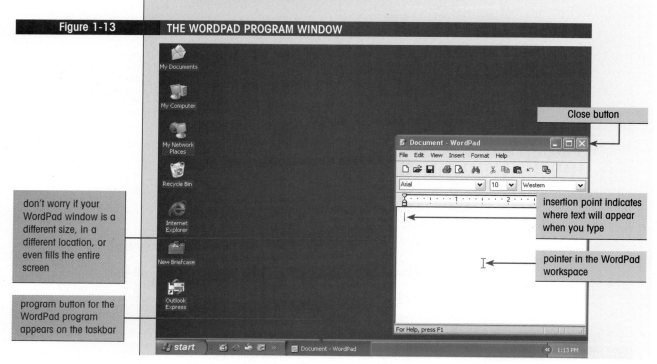

Close button

don't worry if your WordPad window is a different size, in a different location, or even fills the entire screen

program button for the WordPad program appears on the taskbar

insertion point indicates where text will appear when you type

pointer in the WordPad workspace

When you start a program, it is said to be **open** or **running**. A **program button** appears on the taskbar for each open program. You click a program button to switch between open programs. When you finish using a program, you can click the Close button located in the upper-right corner of the program window.

To exit the WordPad program:

1. Click the **Close** button ☒ on the WordPad title bar. You return to the Windows XP desktop.

Running Multiple Programs

One of the most useful features of Windows XP is its ability to run multiple programs at the same time. This feature, known as **multitasking**, allows you to work on more than one project at a time and switch quickly between projects. For example, you can start WordPad and leave it running while you then start the Paint program.

To run WordPad and Paint at the same time:

1. Start WordPad again and then click the **Start** button *start* .

2. Point to **All Programs** and then point to **Accessories**.

3. Click **Paint**. The Paint program window opens, as shown in Figure 1-14. Now two programs are running at the same time.

Figure 1-14	THE PAINT PROGRAM

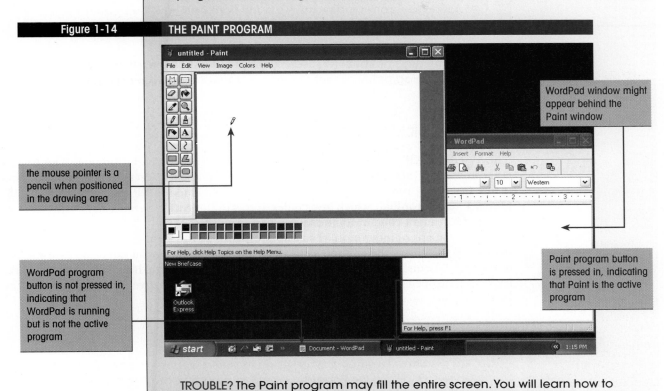

the mouse pointer is a pencil when positioned in the drawing area

WordPad program button is not pressed in, indicating that WordPad is running but is not the active program

WordPad window might appear behind the Paint window

Paint program button is pressed in, indicating that Paint is the active program

TROUBLE? The Paint program may fill the entire screen. You will learn how to manipulate windows in Session 1.2.

What happened to WordPad? The WordPad program button is still on the taskbar, indicating that WordPad is still running even if you cannot see its program window. Try to imagine that the WordPad program window is stacked behind the Paint program window, as illustrated in Figure 1-15. Paint is the active program because it is the one with which you are currently working.

Figure 1-15	PROJECTS STACKED ON A DESK

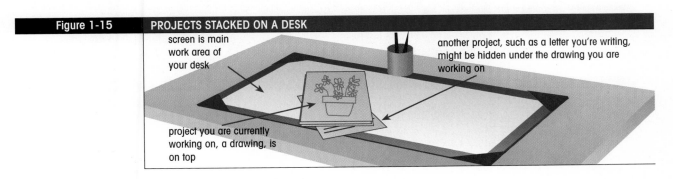

screen is main work area of your desk

another project, such as a letter you're writing, might be hidden under the drawing you are working on

project you are currently working on, a drawing, is on top

Switching Between Programs

The easiest way to switch between programs is to use the program buttons on the taskbar.

To switch between WordPad and Paint:

1. Click the program button labeled **Document - WordPad** on the taskbar. The WordPad program window moves to the front, and now the Document - WordPad button looks as if it has been pushed in, indicating that it is the active program.

2. Click the program button labeled **untitled - Paint** on the taskbar to switch to the Paint program. The Paint program is again the active program.

Using the Quick Launch Toolbar

The Windows XP taskbar displays buttons for programs currently running. The taskbar also can contain **toolbars**, sets of buttons that give single-click access to programs or documents that aren't running or open. For example, the Windows XP taskbar can display the **Quick Launch toolbar**, which gives quick access to Internet programs and to the desktop. Your taskbar might contain additional toolbars or none at all.

When you are running more than one program but you want to return to the desktop, perhaps to use one of the desktop icons, such as My Computer, you can do so by using one of the Quick Launch toolbar buttons. Clicking the Show Desktop button returns you to the desktop. The open programs are not closed; they are simply inactive and reduced to buttons on the taskbar.

To return to the desktop:

1. Click the **Show Desktop** button 🗗 on the Quick Launch toolbar. The desktop displays, and both the Paint and WordPad programs are temporarily inactive. See Figure 1-16.

   TROUBLE? If the Quick Launch toolbar is not visible on your taskbar, right-click the taskbar, point to Toolbars, and then click Quick Launch. Then try Step 1 again.

| Figure 1-16 | ACCESSING THE DESKTOP |

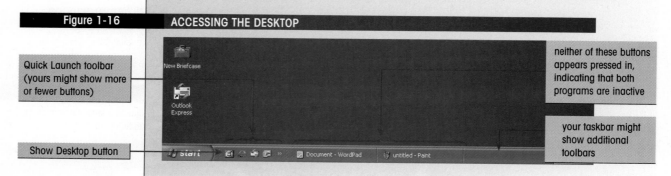

Quick Launch toolbar (yours might show more or fewer buttons)

Show Desktop button

neither of these buttons appears pressed in, indicating that both programs are inactive

your taskbar might show additional toolbars

Closing Inactive Programs from the Taskbar

You should always close a program when you finish using it. Each program uses computer resources, such as memory, so Windows XP works more efficiently when only the programs you need are open. You've already seen how to close an open program using the Close button on the title bar of the program window. You can also close a program, whether active or inactive, by using the shortcut menu associated with the program button on the taskbar.

To close WordPad and Paint using the program button shortcut menus:

1. Right-click the **untitled – Paint** button on the taskbar. Remember that to right-click something, you click it with the right mouse button. The shortcut menu for the Paint program button opens. See Figure 1-17.

| Figure 1-17 | PROGRAM BUTTON SHORTCUT MENU |

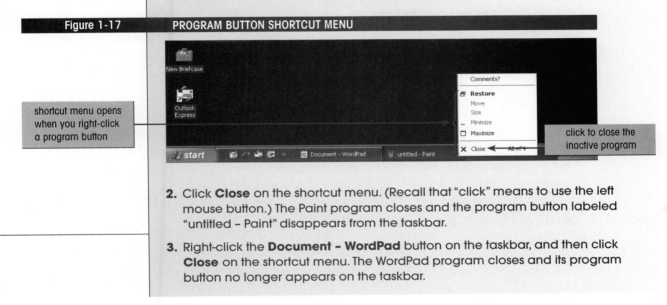

shortcut menu opens when you right-click a program button

click to close the inactive program

2. Click **Close** on the shortcut menu. (Recall that "click" means to use the left mouse button.) The Paint program closes and the program button labeled "untitled – Paint" disappears from the taskbar.

3. Right-click the **Document – WordPad** button on the taskbar, and then click **Close** on the shortcut menu. The WordPad program closes and its program button no longer appears on the taskbar.

Shutting Down Windows XP

You should always shut down Windows XP before you turn off your computer. If you turn off your computer without shutting it down correctly, you might lose data and damage your files.

Typically you will use the Turn Off Computer option on the Start menu when you want to turn off your computer. However, your school might prefer that you select the Log Off option on the Start menu. This option logs you off of Windows XP but leaves the computer on, allowing another user to log on without restarting the computer. Check with your instructor or technical support person for the preferred method at your lab.

To shut down Windows XP:

1. Click the **Start** button ![start] on the taskbar.

2. Click **Turn Off Computer**, located at the bottom of the menu. The Turn Off Computer dialog box opens. See Figure 1-18.

TROUBLE? If you are supposed to log off rather than shut down, click Log Off instead and follow your school's logoff procedure.

Figure 1-18	SHUTTING DOWN THE COMPUTER

Turn Off Computer

click to shut down
Windows

Stand By   Turn Off   Restart

Cancel

3. Click the **Turn Off** button.

4. Wait until you see a message indicating that it is safe to turn off your computer. If your lab procedure includes switching off your computer after shutting it down, do so now; otherwise leave the computer running. Some computers turn themselves off automatically.

In this session, you have started Windows XP, become familiar with the desktop, and learned how to use the mouse to select menu items. In the next session, you will learn how to work with windows.

Session 1.1 QUICK CHECK

1. What is the purpose of the taskbar?

2. The _____ feature of Windows XP allows you to run more than one program at a time.

3. The _____ is a list of options that provides you with access to programs, documents, submenus, and more.

4. What should you do if you are trying to move the pointer to the left edge of your screen, but your mouse bumps into the keyboard?

5. Even if you cannot see an open program on your desktop, the program might be running. How can you tell if a program is running?

6. Why should you close each program when you finish using it?

7. Why should you shut down Windows XP before you turn off your computer?

SESSION 1.2

In this session you will manipulate windows using controls that are available in Windows XP. You will move a window, and you will also change the size and shape of a window. You will use program menus, toolbars, and controls, such as list boxes and scroll bars, available in windows and dialog boxes. Also in this session, you will use Windows XP Help to gain access to program-related information and tasks.

Anatomy of a Window

Recall from Session 1.1 that when you run a program in Windows XP, the program appears in a window. A **window** is a rectangular area of the screen that contains a program, text, graphics, or data. "Windows," spelled with an uppercase "W," is the name of the Microsoft operating system. The word "window" with a lowercase "w" refers to one of the rectangular areas on the screen. A window also contains **controls**, which are graphical or textual objects used for manipulating the window and for using the program. Figure 1-19 describes the controls you are likely to see in most windows.

Figure 1-19	WINDOW CONTROLS
CONTROL	**DESCRIPTION**
Menu bar	Contains the titles of menus, such as File, Edit, and Help
Sizing buttons	Let you enlarge, shrink, or close a window
Status bar	Provides you with messages relevant to the task you are performing
Title bar	Contains the window title and basic window control buttons
Toolbar	Contains buttons that provide you with shortcuts to common menu commands
Window title	Identifies the program and document contained in the window
Workspace	Part of the window you use to enter your work—to enter text, draw pictures, set up calculations, and so on

The WordPad program is a good example of a typical window. Start WordPad and identify its window controls.

To look at the window controls in WordPad:

1. Make sure that Windows XP is running and the Windows XP desktop is displayed.

2. Start WordPad.

   TROUBLE? To start WordPad, click the Start button, point to All Programs, point to Accessories, and then click WordPad.

3. On your screen, identify the controls that are labeled in Figure 1-20. Your WordPad program window may fill the entire screen or differ in size. You'll learn to change window size shortly.

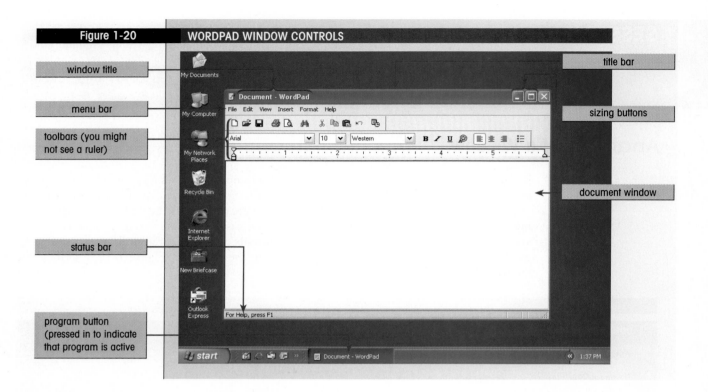

Figure 1-20   WORDPAD WINDOW CONTROLS

window title

menu bar

toolbars (you might not see a ruler)

status bar

program button (pressed in to indicate that program is active

title bar

sizing buttons

document window

Manipulating a Window

On the right side of the title bar are three buttons. You are already familiar with the Close button. The Minimize button, the first of the three buttons, hides a window so that only its program button is visible on the taskbar. The other button changes name and function depending on the status of the window. (It either maximizes the window or restores it to a predefined size.) Figure 1-21 shows how these buttons work.

Figure 1-21   WINDOW BUTTONS

If your screen looks like this...   **and you click this button...**   **your screen will change to this:**

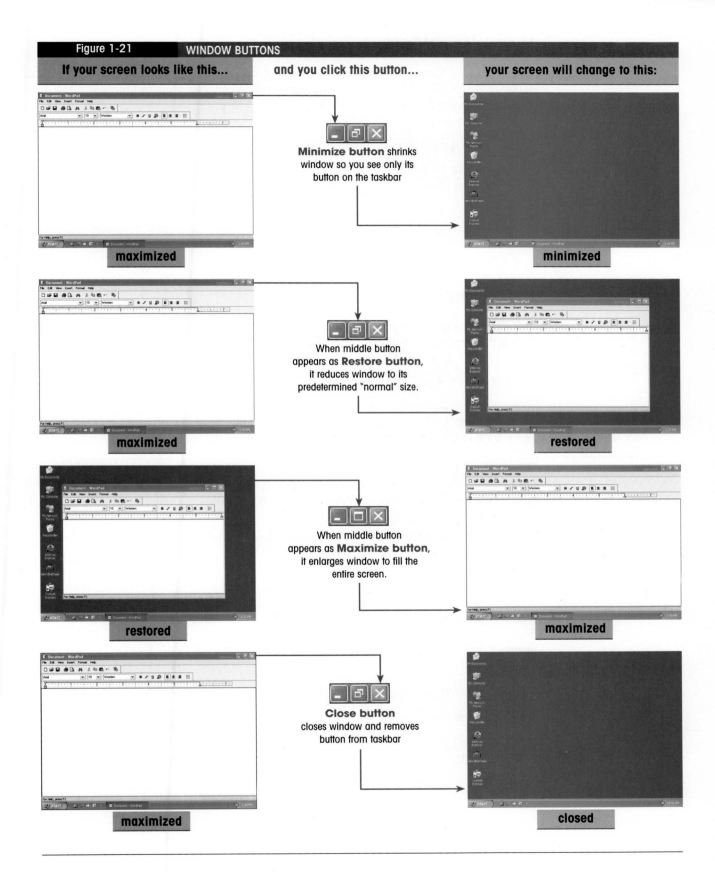

Minimize button shrinks window so you see only its button on the taskbar

maximized   minimized

When middle button appears as **Restore button**, it reduces window to its predetermined "normal" size.

maximized   restored

When middle button appears as **Maximize button**, it enlarges window to fill the entire screen.

restored   maximized

Close button closes window and removes button from taskbar

maximized   closed

Minimizing a Window

The Minimize button hides a window so that only the program button on the taskbar remains visible. You can use the Minimize button when you want to hide a window temporarily but keep the program running.

To minimize the WordPad window:

1. Click the **Minimize** button 🔲 on the WordPad title bar. The WordPad window reduces so that only the Document - WordPad button on the taskbar is visible.

   TROUBLE? If you accidentally clicked the Close button and closed the WordPad program window, use the Start button to start WordPad again, and then repeat Step 1.

Redisplaying a Window

You can redisplay a minimized window by clicking the program's button on the taskbar. When you redisplay a window, it becomes the active window.

To redisplay the WordPad window:

1. Click the **Document - WordPad** button on the taskbar. The WordPad window is restored to its previous size. The Document - WordPad button looks pushed in— a visual clue that WordPad is now the active window.

   The taskbar button provides another means of switching between a window's minimized and active states.

2. Click the **Document – WordPad** button on the taskbar again to minimize the window.

3. Click the **Document – WordPad** button once more to redisplay the window.

Maximizing a Window

The Maximize button enlarges a window so that it fills the entire screen. You will probably do most of your work using maximized windows because they allow you to see more of your program and data.

To maximize the WordPad window:

1. Click the **Maximize** button 🔲 on the WordPad title bar.

   TROUBLE? If the window is already maximized, it will fill the entire screen, and the Maximize button won't appear. Instead, you'll see the Restore button 🔲. Skip Step 1.

Restoring a Window

The Restore button reduces the window so that it is smaller than the entire screen. This feature is useful if you want to see more than one window at a time. Also, because the window is smaller, you can move the window to another location on the screen or change the dimensions of the window.

To restore a window:

1. Click the **Restore** button 🗗 on the WordPad title bar. Notice that once a window is restored, 🗗 changes to the Maximize button 🔲.

Moving a Window

You can use the mouse to move a window to a new position on the screen. When you click an object and then press and hold down the mouse button while moving the mouse, you are **dragging** the object. You can move an object on the screen by dragging it to a new location. If you want to move a window, you drag the window by its title bar. You cannot move a maximized window.

To drag the WordPad window to a new location:

1. Position the mouse pointer on the WordPad title bar.

2. Press and hold down the left mouse button, and then move the mouse up or down a little to drag the window. The window moves as you move the mouse.

3. Position the window anywhere on the desktop, and then release the left mouse button. The WordPad window appears in the new location.

4. Drag the WordPad window to the upper-left corner of the desktop.

Changing the Size of a Window

You can also use the mouse to change the size of a window. Notice the sizing handle 📐 at the lower-right corner of the window. The **sizing handle** provides a visible control for changing the size of a window.

To change the size of the WordPad window:

1. Position the pointer over the sizing handle 📐. The pointer changes to ↘. See Figure 1-22.

Figure 1-22   PREPARING TO RESIZE A WINDOW

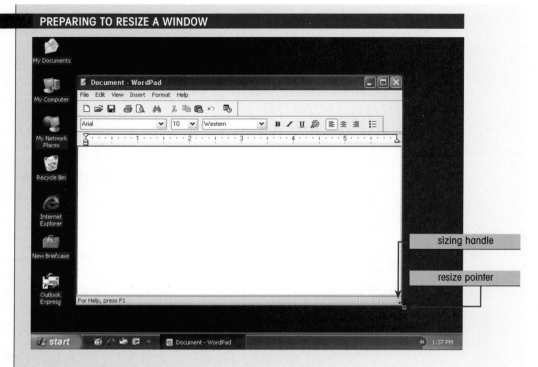

2. Press and hold down the mouse button, and then drag the sizing handle down and to the right.

3. Release the mouse button. Now the window is larger.

4. Practice using the sizing handle to make the WordPad window larger or smaller, and then maximize the WordPad window.

You can also drag the window borders left, right, up, or down to change a window's size.

Using Program Menus

Most Windows programs use menus to organize the program's features and available functions. The menu bar is typically located at the top of the program window and shows the names of the menus, such as File, Edit, and Help. Windows XP menus are relatively standard—most programs designed for Windows include similar menus. Learning new programs is easy because you can make a pretty good guess about which menu contains the task you want to perform.

Selecting Options from a Menu

When you click any menu name, the choices for that menu appear below the menu bar. These choices are referred to as **menu items** or **commands**. To select a menu item, you click it. For example, the File menu, a standard menu in most Windows programs, contains the items and commands typically related to working with a file: creating, opening, saving, and printing.

To select the Page Setup menu command from the File menu:

1. Click **File** on the WordPad menu bar to open the File menu. See Figure 1-23.

Figure 1-23	FILE MENU

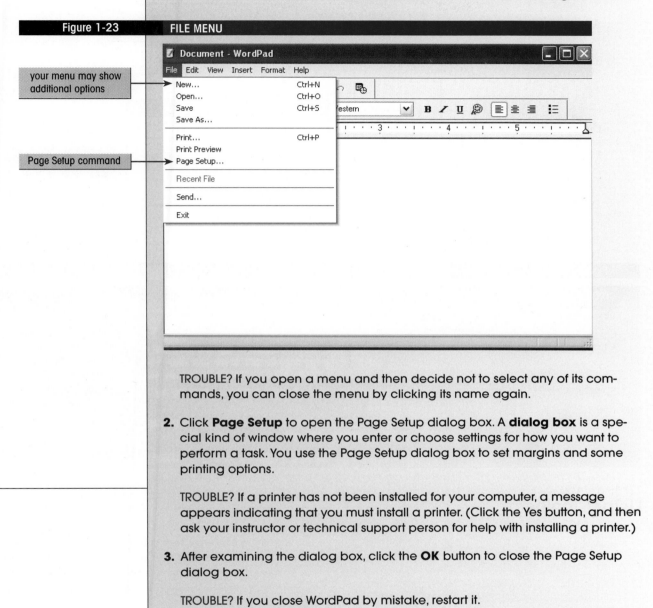

your menu may show additional options

Page Setup command

TROUBLE? If you open a menu and then decide not to select any of its commands, you can close the menu by clicking its name again.

2. Click **Page Setup** to open the Page Setup dialog box. A **dialog box** is a special kind of window where you enter or choose settings for how you want to perform a task. You use the Page Setup dialog box to set margins and some printing options.

TROUBLE? If a printer has not been installed for your computer, a message appears indicating that you must install a printer. (Click the Yes button, and then ask your instructor or technical support person for help with installing a printer.)

3. After examining the dialog box, click the **OK** button to close the Page Setup dialog box.

TROUBLE? If you close WordPad by mistake, restart it.

Not all menu items and commands immediately carry out an action—some show submenus or ask you for more information about what you want to do. The menu gives you visual hints about what to expect when you select an item. These hints are sometimes referred to as **menu conventions**. Figure 1-24 shows examples of these menu conventions.

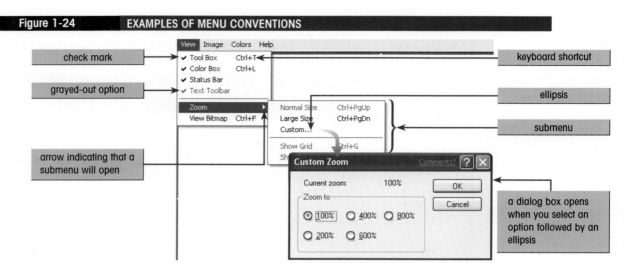

Figure 1-24   **EXAMPLES OF MENU CONVENTIONS**

Figure 1-25 describes the Windows XP menu conventions.

Figure 1-25	**MENU CONVENTIONS**
CONVENTION	**DESCRIPTION**
Check mark	Indicates a toggle, or "on-off" switch (like a light switch) that is either checked (turned on) or not checked (turned off).
Ellipsis	Three dots that indicate you must make additional selections after you select that option. Options without dots do not require additional choices—they take effect as soon as you click them. If an option is followed by an ellipsis, a dialog box opens that allows you to enter specifications for how you want a task carried out.
Triangular arrow	Indicates the presence of a submenu. When you point at a menu option that has a triangular arrow, a submenu automatically appears.
Grayed-out option	Option that is not currently available. For example, a graphics program might display the Text Toolbar option in gray if there is no text in the graphic to work with.
Keyboard shortcut	A key or combination of keys that you can press to select the menu option without actually opening the menu.

Using Toolbars

Although you can usually perform all program commands by using menus, you also have one-click access to frequently used commands on the toolbars in the program window. You can quickly access common commands using the buttons on the toolbars. As task-related menu items and commands provided on menus, the buttons on a toolbar are also grouped and organized by tasks.

In Session 1.1 you learned that Windows XP programs often display ScreenTips, which indicate the purpose and function of a window component, for example, a button. Explore the WordPad toolbar buttons by looking at their ScreenTips.

To determine the names and descriptions of the buttons on the WordPad toolbar:

1. Position the pointer over any button on the toolbar, for example, the Print Preview button 🔍. After a short pause, the ScreenTip for the button appears below the button, and a description of the button appears in the status bar just above the Start button. See Figure 1-26.

| Figure 1-26 | **TOOLBAR BUTTON AIDS** |

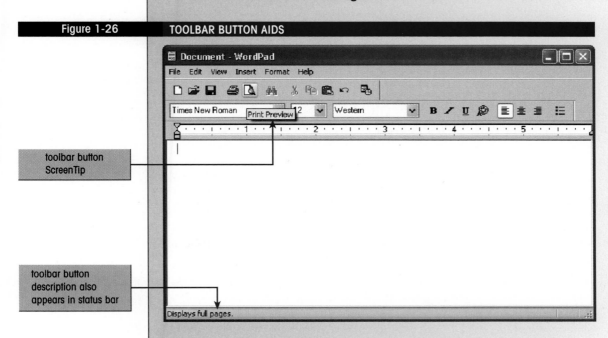

toolbar button ScreenTip

toolbar button description also appears in status bar

2. Move the pointer to each button on the toolbar to display its name and purpose.

To perform a command, you select the toolbar button by clicking it. When you pointed to each button on the WordPad toolbar, you found one called the Undo button. Clicking the Undo button reverses the effects of your last action.

To use the Undo button on the toolbar:

1. Type your name in the WordPad window.

2. Click the **Undo** button 🔙 on the toolbar. WordPad reverses your last action by removing your name from the WordPad window.

Using List Boxes and Scroll Bars

As you might guess from its name, a **list box** displays a list of available choices from which you can select. In WordPad, you can choose a date and time format from the Available formats list box in the Date/Time dialog box. List box controls usually include arrow buttons, a scroll bar, and a scroll box.

To use a list box in the Date/Time dialog box:

1. Click the **Date/Time** button 🖼 on the toolbar to open the Date and Time dia-log box. See Figure 1-27.

Figure 1-27   DATE AND TIME DIALOG BOX

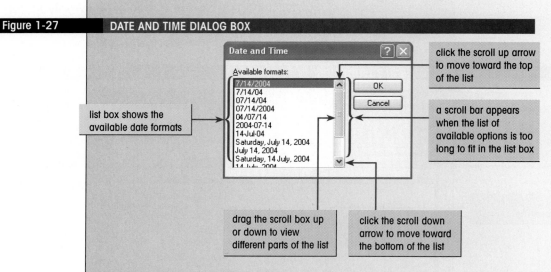

list box shows the available date formats

click the scroll up arrow to move toward the top of the list

a scroll bar appears when the list of available options is too long to fit in the list box

drag the scroll box up or down to view different parts of the list

click the scroll down arrow to move toward the bottom of the list

2. To scroll down the list, click the **scroll down arrow** button until you see the bot-tom of the list.

3. Drag the **scroll box** to the top of the scroll bar. Notice how the list scrolls back to the beginning.

TROUBLE? To drag the scroll box up, point to the scroll box, press and hold down the mouse button, and then move the mouse up.

4. Find a date format similar to "July 14, 2004" in the Available formats list box, and then click that date format to select it.

5. Click the **OK** button to close the Date and Time dialog box. The current date is inserted in your document.

A list box is helpful because it includes only options that are appropriate for your current task. For example, you can select only dates and times in the available formats from the list box in the Date and Time dialog box—no matter which format you choose, WordPad will recognize it. Sometimes, however, a list might not include every possible option, so it lets you type the option you want to select. In this case, the list box includes a **list arrow** on its right side. You can click the list arrow to view options and then select one, or you can type appropriate text.

Buttons can also have list arrows. The list arrow indicates that there is more than one option for that button. Rather than crowding the window with lots of buttons, one for each possible option, including a list arrow on a button organizes its options logically and com-pactly. Toolbars often include list boxes and buttons with list arrows. For example, the Font Size list box on the WordPad toolbar includes a list arrow. To select an option other than the one shown in the list box or on the button, you click the list arrow and then click the option that you want to use.

To select a new font size from the Font Size list box:

1. Click the **list arrow** for the Font Size list box 10 ▾ on the toolbar. See Figure 1-28.

Figure 1-28   **FONT SIZE LIST ARROW**

list box

click the Font Size list arrow to display the available font sizes

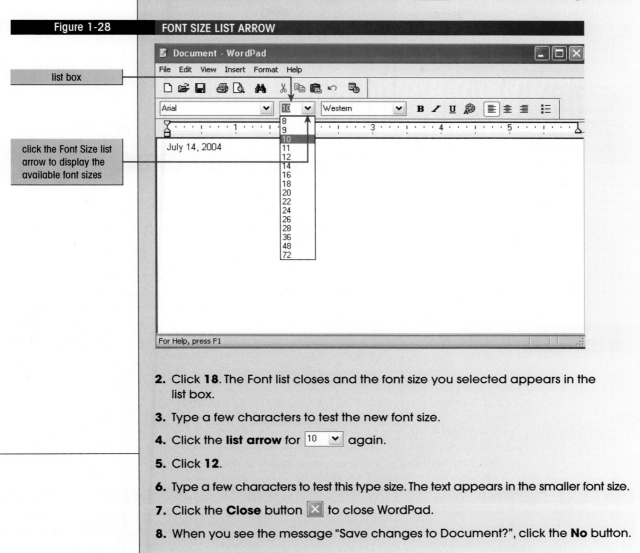

2. Click **18**. The Font list closes and the font size you selected appears in the list box.

3. Type a few characters to test the new font size.

4. Click the **list arrow** for 10 ▾ again.

5. Click **12**.

6. Type a few characters to test this type size. The text appears in the smaller font size.

7. Click the **Close** button ⊠ to close WordPad.

8. When you see the message "Save changes to Document?", click the **No** button.

Using **Dialog Box Controls**

Recall that when you select a menu command or item followed by an ellipsis, a dialog box opens that allows you to provide more information about how a program should carry out a task. Some dialog boxes group different kinds of information into bordered rectangular areas called **panes**. Within these panes, you will usually find tabs, option buttons, check boxes, and other controls that the program uses to collect information about how you want it to perform a task. Figure 1-29 displays examples of common dialog box controls.

Figure 1-29	EXAMPLES OF DIALOG BOX CONTROL

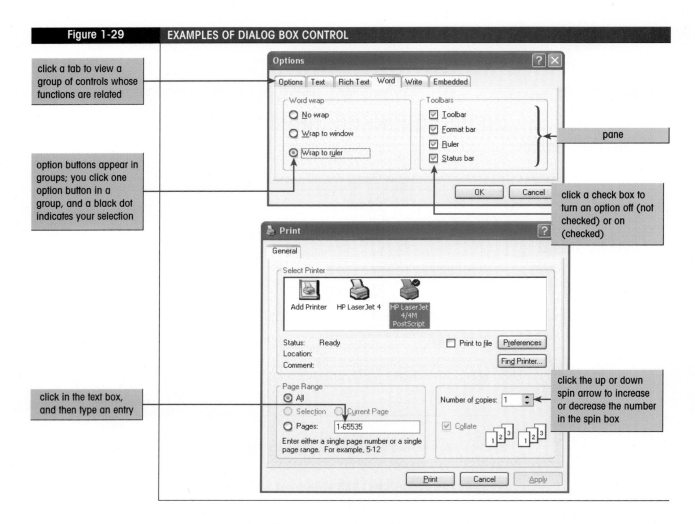

click a tab to view a group of controls whose functions are related

option buttons appear in groups; you click one option button in a group, and a black dot indicates your selection

pane

click a check box to turn an option off (not checked) or on (checked)

click in the text box, and then type an entry

click the up or down spin arrow to increase or decrease the number in the spin box

Figure 1-30 describes these common dialog box controls.

Figure 1-30	DESCRIPTION OF DIALOG BOX CONTROLS
CONTROL	**DESCRIPTION**
Tabs	Modeled after the tabs on file folders, tab controls are often used as containers for other Windows XP controls such as list boxes, option buttons, and check boxes. Click the appropriate tabs to view different pages of information or choices.
Option buttons	Also called radio buttons, option buttons allow you to select a single option from among one or more options.
Check boxes	Click a check box to select or deselect it; when it is selected, a check mark appears, indicating that the option is turned on; when deselected, the check box is blank and the option is off. When check boxes appear in groups, you can select or deselect as many as you want; they are not mutually exclusive, as option buttons are.
Spin boxes	Allow you to scroll easily through a set of numbers to choose the setting you want
Text boxes	Boxes into which you type additional information

Using Help

Windows XP **Help** provides on-screen information about the program you are using. Help for the Windows XP operating system is available by clicking the Start button on the taskbar, and then selecting Help and Support from the Start menu. If you want Help for a particular program, such as WordPad, you must first start the program and then click Help on the program's menu bar.

When you start Help for Windows XP, a Windows Help and Support Center window opens, giving you access to Help files stored on your computer as well as Help information stored on Microsoft's Web site. If you are not connected to the Web, you only have access to the Help files stored on your computer.

To start Windows XP Help:

1. Click the **Start** button [*start*] on the taskbar.

2. Click **Help and Support**. The Help and Support Center window opens. See Figure 1-31.

   TROUBLE? If the Help and Support window does not display the information you see in Figure 1-31, click the Home icon on the navigation bar to view Help contents. The navigation bar is located at the top of the window.

Figure 1-31	WINDOWS XP HELP AND SUPPORT CENTER WINDOW

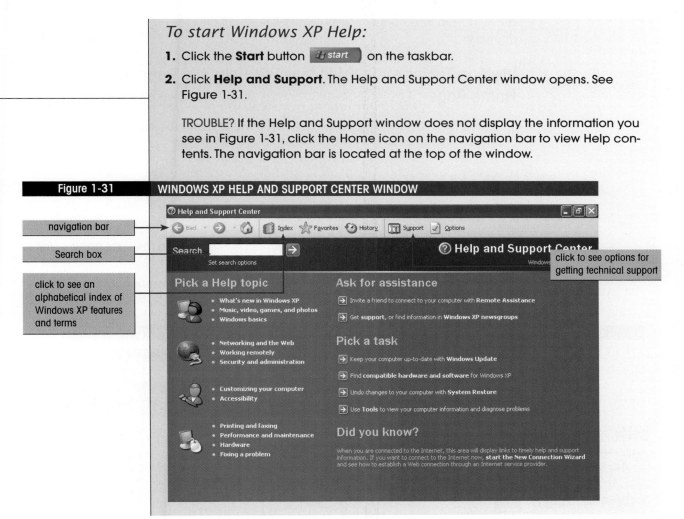

The Windows XP Help and Support window organizes the vast amount of help and support information into **pages**. These six pages of information—the Home, Index, Favorites, History, Support, and Options pages—are designed to aid users in locating help on a particular topic quickly. To open one of these pages, click its icon on the navigation bar. The **Home page** lists common tasks under the heading "Pick a Help topic" in the left pane on the page. Click a task to see detailed information or instructions about that task in the right pane of the page. The right pane of the Home page lists common tasks, tips, and ways you can ask for assistance. For example, you can contact a support professional or download the latest version of Windows XP. The **Index** page displays an alphabetical list of all the Help topics from which you can choose. The **Favorites** page shows Help topics you've added to your Favorites list. To add a topic to the Favorites list, open the topic, and then click the

Favorites button on the Help window. The **History** page lists links you've recently selected in Help. The **Support** page includes links that you can click to connect to the Microsoft Web site, if possible, for additional assistance. The **Options** page provides ways you can customize Help. For example, you can change the appearance of the navigation bar.

If you cannot find the topic you want listed on any of the six Help and Support Services pages, the word that you are using for a feature or topic might differ from the word that Windows XP uses. You can use the **Search box** to search for all keywords contained in the Help pages, not just the topic titles. In the Search box, you can type any word or phrase, click the Start Searching button, and Windows XP lists all the Help topics that contain that word or phrase.

Viewing Topics on the Windows XP Help and Support Center Home Page

Windows XP Help includes instructions on using Help itself. You can learn how to find a Help topic by using the Help and Support Center Home page.

To use the Help and Support Center Home page:

1. On the Home page, click **Windows basics**. A list of topics related to using Windows XP appears in the left pane of the Help and Support Center window.

2. Click **Tips for using Help**. A list of Help topics appears in the right pane of the Help window.

3. Click **Change fonts in Help and Support Center**. The instructions appear in the right pane of the Help and Support Center window, as shown in Figure 1-32.

Figure 1-32   FINDING A HELP TOPIC ON THE HOME PAGE

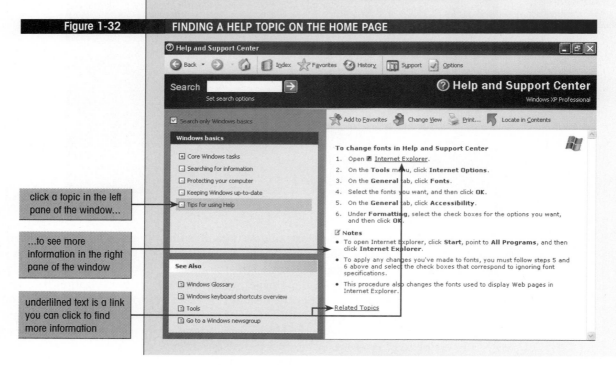

click a topic in the left pane of the window...

...to see more information in the right pane of the window

underlilned text is a link you can click to find more information

Besides listing the pages in the Help and Support Center window, the navigation bar contains two buttons—the Back button ◀ and the Forward button ▶. You use these buttons to navigate the pages you've already opened. You'll use the Back button next to return to the previous page you viewed. Once you do, you activate the Forward button, which you can click to go to the next page of those you've opened.

4. Click the **Back** button ◀. You return to the Tips for using Help page.

Selecting a Topic from the Index

The Index page allows you to jump to a Help topic by selecting a topic from an indexed list. For example, you can use the Index page to learn how to arrange open windows on your desktop.

To find a Help topic using the Index page:

1. On the navigation bar, click **Index** 📖. A long list of indexed Help topics displays in the left pane.

2. Drag the **scroll box** down to view additional topics in the list box.

You can quickly jump to any part of the list by typing the first few characters of a word or phrase in the box that appears above the Index list.

3. If necessary, click in the **Type in the keyword to find** text box above the Index list, and then type **windows**. As you type each character in the word, the list of Index topic scrolls and eventually displays topics that relate to windows.

4. Under the "windows and panes on your computer screen" topic, click the topic **reducing windows to taskbar buttons**, and then click the **Display** button. When there is just one topic, it appears immediately in the right pane; otherwise, the Topics Found window opens, listing all topics indexed under the entry that interests you.

The information you requested displays in the right pane. See Figure 1-33. Notice this topic has two underlined phrases, "taskbar" and "Related Topics." You can click underlined words or phrases to view definitions or additional information.

Figure 1-33   USING THE INDEX TO LOCATE INFORMATION

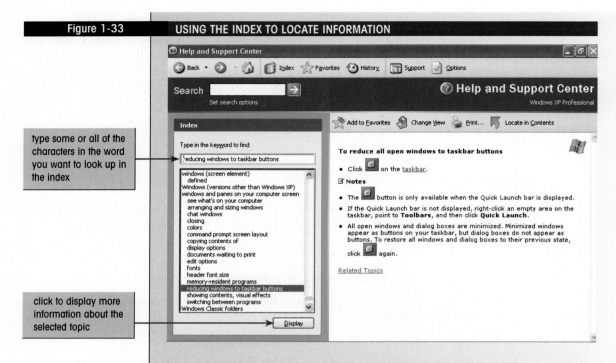

type some or all of the characters in the word you want to look up in the index

click to display more information about the selected topic

5. Click the underlined phrase **taskbar**. A ScreenTip shows the definition of "taskbar." See Figure 1-34.

Figure 1-34   VIEWING ADDITIONAL INFORMATION

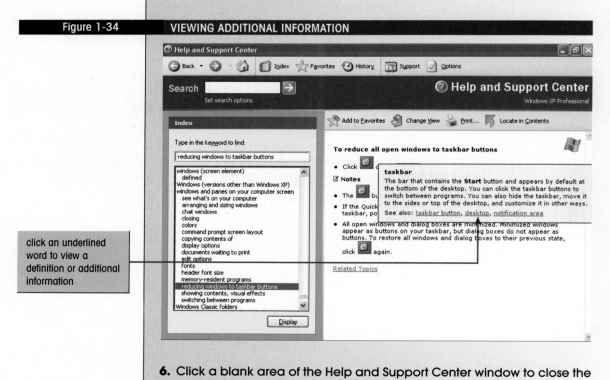

click an underlined word to view a definition or additional information

6. Click a blank area of the Help and Support Center window to close the ScreenTip.

If you have an Internet connection, you can use another Help page, Support, to contact Microsoft Support or get in touch with other users of Windows XP. The Support page works like the Home page. To get support on a particular feature, you click a support option and then click the topic for which you need help. Continue clicking topics, if necessary, until you get help from a Microsoft support person or an experienced Windows XP user.

Searching the Help Pages

If you can't find the topic you need by using the Home or Index pages, or if you want to quickly find Help pages related to a particular topic, you can use the Search box. Suppose you want to know how to exit Windows XP, but you don't know if Windows refers to this as exiting, quitting, closing, or shutting down. You can search the Help pages to find just the right topic.

To search the Help pages for information on exiting Windows XP:

1. Click in the Search box. A blinking insertion point appears.

2. Type **shutdown** and then click the **Start Searching** button ➡. A list of Help pages containing the word "shutdown" displays in the left pane of the Help and Support window. The ones listed under Suggested Topics are topics where "shutdown" has been assigned as a keyword—meaning the topics have to do with shutting something down.

3. Click the **Full-text Search Matches** button. The text of these topics includes the word *shutdown*.

4. Click the **Suggested Topics** button, and then click **Turn off the computer**. A Help topic displays in the right pane of the Help and Support Center window, as shown in Figure 1-35.

Figure 1-35	USING SEARCH TO FIND A HELP PAGE

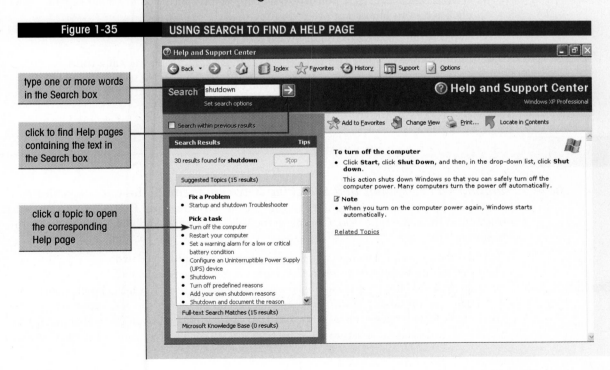

type one or more words in the Search box

click to find Help pages containing the text in the Search box

click a topic to open the corresponding Help page

If the text of this topic were longer than the Help and Support Center window, you could use the scroll bar to read all the text.

5. Click the **Close** button ☒ to close the Help and Support Center window.

Now that you know how Windows XP Help works, don't forget to use it! Use Help when you need to perform a new task or when you forget how to complete a procedure.

You've finished the tutorial, and as you shut down Windows XP, Steve returns from class. You take a moment to tell him all you've learned: you know how to start and close programs and how to use multiple programs at the same time. You have learned how to work with windows and the controls they employ. Finally, you've learned how to get help when you need it. Steve congratulates you and comments that you are well on your way to mastering the fundamentals of using the Windows XP operating system.

Session 1.2 QUICK CHECK

1. What is the difference between the title bar and a toolbar?

2. Provide the name and purpose of each button:
  a. ▣   **b.** ▢   **c.** ▣   **d.** ☒

3. Explain each of the following menu conventions:
  a. Ellipsis (...)
  b. Grayed-out
  c. ▶
  d. ✔

4. A (n) _____ consists of a group of buttons, each of which provides one-click access to important program functions.

5. What is the purpose of the scroll bar?

6. Option buttons allow you to select _____ option(s) at a time.

7. To learn how to perform new tasks, you can use _____ .

REVIEW ASSIGNMENTS

Case 1. Running Two Programs and Switching Between Them In this tutorial you learned how to run more than one program at a time, using WordPad and Paint. You can run other programs at the same time, too. Complete the following steps, and write your answers to Questions b through f:

  a. Start the computer. Enter your username and password if prompted to do so.
  b. Click the Start button. How many menu options are on the Start menu?

Explore
  c. Run the Calculator program located on the Accessories menu. How many program buttons are now on the taskbar? (Don't count toolbar buttons or items in the notification area.)
  d. Run the Paint program and maximize the Paint window. How many programs are running now?
  e. Switch to Calculator. What are two visual clues that tell you that Calculator is the active program?

Explore

    f. Multiply 576 by 1457 using the Calculator accessory. (*Hint*: Click the numbers and arithmetic operators on the Calculator keypad.) What is the result?

    g. Close Calculator and then close Paint.

Explore

Case 2. WordPad Help In Tutorial 1 you learned how to use Windows XP Help. Just about every Windows XP program has a Help feature. Many computer users can learn to use a program just by using Help. To use Help, you start the program and then click the Help menu at the top of the program window. Try using WordPad Help:

    a. Start WordPad.

    b. Click Help on the menu bar, and then click Help Topics.

    c. The Index tab in WordPad Help works like the Index page in Windows XP Help. Using the Index tab in WordPad Help, write out your answers to Questions 1 through 4.

      1. How do you create a bulleted list?

      2. How do you set the page margins in a document?

      3. How do you undo a mistake?

      4. How do you change the font style of a block of text?

    d. Close Help and then close WordPad.

Case 3. The Index Page versus the Search Box You might have heard that Windows XP makes it possible to speak to your computer and have it carry out your voice commands. This feature is called **speech recognition**. You could browse through the Help and Support Home page, although you might not know where to look to find information about speech recognition. You could also use the Index page to search through the indexed entries. Or you could use the Search box to find all Help topics that mention speech recognition.

    a. Start Windows XP Help and use the Index page to find information about the topic of speech recognition. How many topics are listed? What is their primary subject matter?

    b. Use the Search box to find information about the topic of speech recognition. How many topics are listed?

    c. Write a paragraph comparing the two lists of topics. You don't have to view them all, but in your paragraph, indicate which tab seems to yield more information. Close the Help and Support Center window.

Case 4. Discover Windows XP Windows XP Help lets you access articles that provide more detailed information about common features or introduce new features. You can find and read an article about one new feature Windows XP offers—playing music and making music CDs on your computer.

    a. Start Windows XP Help, open the Home page, click What's new in Windows XP, and then click Windows XP Articles: Walkthrough ways to use your PC.

    b. Click Walkthrough: Making Music.

    c. Read the Getting Started page. Note that the box in the upper-left corner of the window lists the contents of the article. Each topic is a link you can click to go to another page in the article.

    d. Click the links in the contents box, and then answer the following questions using the information you find:

      1. How can you listen to music using Windows XP?

      2. What is a playlist? What is the first step you take to create one?

      3. What is the advantage of listening to the Internet radio?

    e. Close Help and then close WordPad.

PROJECTS

1. Many types of pointing devices are on the market today. Research the types of available devices. Consider what devices are appropriate for these situations: desktop or laptop computers, connected or remote devices, and ergonomic or standard designs. (Look up the term *ergonomic*.)

   To locate information, use up-to-date computer books, trade computer magazines (such as *PC Computing* and *PC Magazine*), or the Internet (if you know how). Your instructor might suggest specific resources you can use. Write a one-page report describing the types of devices available, the differing needs of users, special features that make pointing devices more useful, price comparisons. Finally, indicate what you would choose if you needed to buy a pointing device.

2. Locate information about the release of Windows XP, using the resources available to you, either through your library or the Internet (if you know how). Trade computer magazines are an excellent source of information about software. Read several articles about Windows XP, and then write a one-page essay discussing the features that seem most important to the people who evaluate the software. If you find reviews of the software, mention the features to which reviewers had the strongest reaction, pro or con.

3. **Upgrading** is the process of placing a more recent version of a product onto your computer. When Windows XP first came out, people had to decide whether they wanted to upgrade their computers to Windows XP. Interview at least three people you know who are well-informed Windows computer users. Ask them whether they use Windows XP or an older version of Windows. If they use an older version, ask why they chose not to upgrade. If they use Windows XP, ask why they chose to upgrade. Ask such questions as:

   a. What features convinced you to upgrade or made you decide to wait?
   b. What role did the price of the upgrade play?
   c. Would you or did you have to purchase new hardware to make the upgrade? How did this affect your decision?
   d. If you did upgrade, are you happy with that decision? If you didn't, do you intend to upgrade in the near future? Why or why not?
      Write a single-page essay summarizing what you learned from these interviews about making the decision to upgrade.

4. Choose a topic you'd like to research using the Windows XP online Help system. Look for information on your topic using the Help and Support Home page, Index page, and Search box. Once you find all the information you can, compare the three methods (Home page, Index page, Search box) of looking for information. Write a paragraph that discusses which method proved most useful. Did you reach the same information topics using all three methods? In a second paragraph, summarize what you learned about your topic. Finally, in a third paragraph, indicate under what circumstances you'd use which method.

LAB ASSIGNMENTS

Using a Keyboard To become an effective computer user, you must be familiar with your primary input device—the keyboard. See the Read This Before You Begin page for information on installing and starting the lab.

1. The Steps for the Using a Keyboard Lab provides you with a structured introduction to the keyboard's layout and the functions of special computer keys. Click the Steps button and begin the steps. As you work through the Steps, answer all of the Quick Check questions that appear. When you complete the steps, you will see a Summary Report of your performance on the Quick Checks. Follow the directions on the screen to print the Summary Report.

2. You can develop your typing skills using the typing tutor in Explore. Start the typing tutor in Explore. Take the typing test and print your results.

3. In Explore, try to increase your typing speed by 10 words per minute. For example, if you currently type 20 words per minute, your goal is 30 words per minute. Practice each typing lesson until you see a message indicating that you can proceed to the next lesson. Create a Practice Record, as shown here, to keep track of how much you practice. When you reach your goal, print the results of a typing test to verify your results.

Practice Record

Name:

Section:

Start Date: Start Typing Speed: wpm

End Date: End Typing Speed: wpm

Lesson #:   Date Practiced/Time Practiced

Using a Mouse A mouse is a standard input device on most of today's computers. You need to know how to use a mouse to manipulate graphical user interfaces and to use the rest of the Labs. See the Read This Before You Begin page for information on installing and starting the lab.

1. The Steps for the Using a Mouse Lab show you how to click, double-click, and drag objects using the mouse. Click the Steps button and begin the steps. As you work through the steps, answer all Quick Check questions that appear. When you complete the steps, you will see a Summary Report of your performance on the Quick Checks. Follow the directions on the screen to print the Summary Report.

2. In Explore, create a poster to demonstrate your ability to use a mouse and to control a Windows program. To create a poster for an upcoming sports event, select a graphic, type the caption for the poster, and then select a font, font styles, and a border. Print your completed poster.

QUICK CHECK ANSWERS

Session 1.1

1. The taskbar contains buttons that give you access to commands and programs.

2. multitasking

3. Start menu

4. Lift up the mouse and move it to the right.

5. Its button appears on the taskbar.

6. to conserve computer resources such as memory

7. to ensure you don't lose data and damage your files

Session 1.2

1. The title bar identifies the window and contains window controls; toolbars contain buttons that provide you with shortcuts to common menu commands.

2.   a. The Minimize button shrinks the window so you see its button on the taskbar.
   b. The Maximize button enlarges the window to fill the entire screen.
   c. The Restore button reduces the window to a predetermined size.
   d. The Close button closes the window and removes the program button from the taskbar.

3.   a. Ellipsis indicates a dialog box will open.
   b. Grayed out indicates that the option is not currently available.
   c. Arrow indicates that a submenu will open.
   d. Check mark indicates a toggle option.

4. toolbar

5. Scroll bars appear when the contents of a box or window are too long to fit; you drag the scroll box to view different parts of the contents.

6. one

7. online Help

OBJECTIVES

In this tutorial you will:

- Format a disk
- Enter, select, insert, and delete text
- Create and save a file
- Open, edit, and print a file
- View the list of files on your Data Disk and change view options
- Navigate a hierarchy of folders
- Move, copy, delete, and rename a file
- Make a copy of your Data Disk

LAB

Using Files

WORKING WITH FILES

Creating, Saving, and Managing Files

CASE

Distance Learning

You recently purchased a computer to gain new skills and stay competitive in the job market. You hope to use the computer to enroll in a few distance learning courses. **Distance learning** is formalized education that typically takes place using a computer and the Internet, replacing normal classroom interaction with modern communications technology. Distance learning instructors often make their course material available on the **World Wide Web**, also called the **Web**. The Web is a network of **Web pages**, which are electronic documents stored on the Internet that people can access and explore using **hyperlinks**. Hyperlinks are text or graphical elements embedded in the Web pages. You click the hyperlinks in a Web page to navigate to related Web pages and **Web sites**, computers connected to the Internet that store collections of Web pages.

Your computer came with the Windows XP operating system already installed. Your friend Shannon suggests that before you enroll in any online course, you should become more comfortable with your computer and with Windows XP. Knowing how to save, locate, and organize your files will make the time you spend working with your computer much more productive. A **file** is a collection of data that has a name and is stored on a computer. Once you create a file, you can open it, edit its contents, print it, and save it again—usually using the same program you used to create it.

In this tutorial, you will learn how to perform some basic tasks in Windows XP programs, such as formatting a disk and working with text and files. You will also learn how to view information on your computer in different ways. Finally, you'll spend time learning how to organize your files.

SESSION 2.1

In Session 2.1 you will format a disk so you can store files on it. You will create, save, open, and print a file. You will learn more about the difference between the insertion point and the mouse pointer. You also will learn the basic skills for working with text, such as entering, selecting, inserting, and deleting text. For the steps in this tutorial, you will need two blank 3½" disks.

Formatting a Disk

Before you can save files on a disk, the disk must be formatted. When the computer **formats** a disk, the magnetic particles on the disk's surface are arranged so data can be stored on the disk. Today, many disks are sold preformatted and can be used right out of the box. However, if you purchase an unformatted disk or if you have an old disk you want to completely erase and reuse, you can format the disk using the Windows XP Format command. This command is available through the **My Computer window**, a feature of Windows XP that you use to view, organize, and access the programs, files, and drives on your computer. You open My Computer by using its icon on the desktop. You'll learn more about the My Computer window in Session 2.2.

The following steps explain how to format a 3½" high-density disk using drive A. Your instructor will explain how to revise the instructions given in these steps if the procedure is different for your lab equipment.

Make sure you are using a blank disk (or one that contains data you no longer need) before you perform these steps.

To format a disk:

1. Start Windows XP and log on using your user name, if necessary.

2. Write your name on the label of a 3½-inch disk, and then insert your disk in drive A. See Figure 2-1.

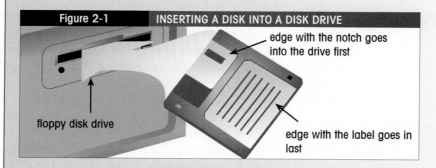

| Figure 2-1 | INSERTING A DISK INTO A DISK DRIVE |

edge with the notch goes into the drive first

floppy disk drive

edge with the label goes in last

TROUBLE? If your disk does not fit in drive A, put it in drive B, and then substitute drive B for drive A in all of the steps for the rest of the tutorial.

3. Double-click the **My Computer** icon on the desktop. See Figure 2-2. The My Computer window on your screen might be maximized.

TROUBLE? If you see a list of items instead of icons like those in Figure 2-2, click View on the My Computer menu bar, and then click Tiles. Your toolbar may not exactly match the one in Figure 2-2; it may have fewer or more buttons.

Figure 2-2   MY COMPUTER WINDOW

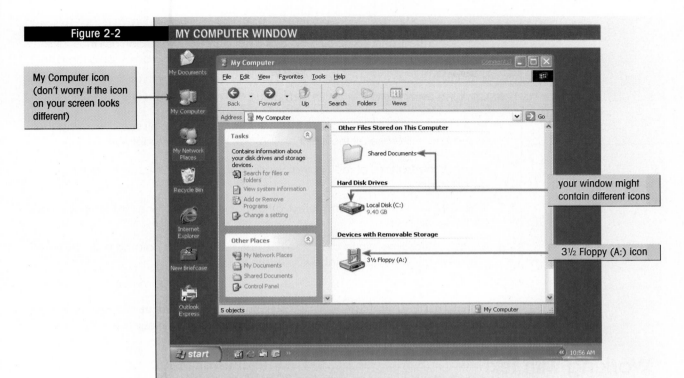

My Computer icon (don't worry if the icon on your screen looks different)

your window might contain different icons

3½ Floppy (A:) icon

4. Right-click the **3½ Floppy (A:)** icon to open its shortcut menu, and then click **Format**. The Format 3½ Floppy (A:) dialog box opens. See Figure 2-3.

Figure 2-3   FORMATTING A FLOPPY DISK

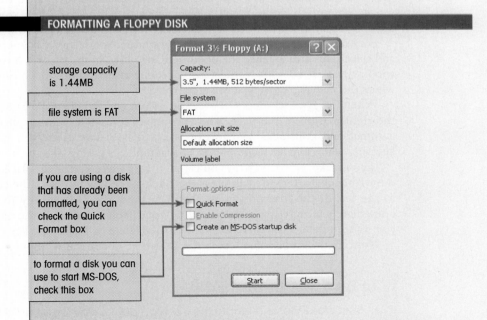

storage capacity is 1.44MB

file system is FAT

if you are using a disk that has already been formatted, you can check the Quick Format box

to format a disk you can use to start MS-DOS, check this box

5. Make sure your dialog box settings match those in Figure 2-3. These settings describe a disk's characteristics and format options. The capacity of a floppy disk indicates how much data it can hold—a 3½-inch floppy disk can hold 1.44MB of data. By default, Windows XP uses the FAT (File Allocation Table) file system for floppy disks. A **file system** is the way files are organized on the disk. Windows XP supports other file systems such as FAT32 and NTFS. Selecting a file system, allocation unit size, volume label, and creating an MS-DOS startup disk are advanced topics, so you can accept the defaults for these options. If you have a disk that has been previously formatted, and you're sure the disk is not damaged, you can use the Quick Format option. In this instance, you will do a full format, so this box should remain unchecked.

6. Click the **Start** button to begin formatting the disk.

   TROUBLE? If you are using a disk that contains data, you will see a warning that formatting will erase all the data on the disk. Click OK to continue.

   A bar at the bottom of the Format window shows you how the formatting is progressing.

7. When the formatting is completed, a Format Complete message box appears. Click the **OK** button.

8. Click the **Close** button to close the Format 3½ Floppy (A:) dialog box, and then close the My Computer window to return to the desktop.

Now that you have formatted a disk, you can create a document and save it as a file on your disk. To create a document, you first need to learn how to enter text into a document.

Working with Text

To accomplish many computing tasks, you need to type text where text is required, whether it is in a document or in a text box. Entering text involves first learning how to place the mouse pointer so the text will appear where you want it. Then you can insert new text between existing words or sentences, select text, and delete text.

For example, when you start WordPad, a white area will appear below the menu bar, toolbars, and ruler. This area is called the **document window**. In the upper-left corner of the document window, there is a flashing vertical bar, called the **insertion point**. The insertion point indicates where the characters you type will appear.

When you type sentences of text, you do not need to press the Enter key when you reach the right margin of the page. Most programs contain a feature called **word wrap**, which automatically continues your text on the next line. Therefore, you should press the Enter key only when you have completed a paragraph.

If you make a typing error, you can use the Delete key or the Backspace key. If you type the wrong character, you can press the **Backspace key** to delete the character immediately to the left of the insertion point. You can press the **Delete key** to delete the character immediately to the right of the insertion point. You can also use the mouse to select the text you want to delete and then press either the Delete or Backspace key.

Now you will type some text in the WordPad document window.

To type text in WordPad:

1. Start WordPad and locate the insertion point in the WordPad document window.

   TROUBLE? If the WordPad window does not fill the screen, click the Maximize button ▣ on the WordPad title bar.

   TROUBLE? If you cannot find the insertion point, move the ⌶ pointer over the WordPad window and then click the mouse button. The insertion point will appear in the upper-left corner of the document window.

2. Type your name, just as you would on a typewriter, pressing the Shift key as you type uppercase letters and using the spacebar to enter spaces.

3. Press the **Enter** key to end the current paragraph and to move the insertion point down to the next line.

4. Type the following sentences, watching what happens when the insertion point reaches the right margin of the page:

This is a sample typed in WordPad. See what happens when the insertion point reaches the right edge of the page. Note how the text wraps automatically to the next line.

TROUBLE? If you make a mistake, delete the incorrect character(s) using the Backspace key or Delete key. Then type the correct character(s).

TROUBLE? If your text doesn't wrap, your screen might be set up to display more information than the screen used for the figures in this tutorial, or your WordPad program might not be set to use Word Wrap. To set the Word Wrap option, click View on the menu bar, click Options, click the Rich Text tab in the Options dialog box, click the Wrap to window option button, and then click the OK button.

The Insertion Point Versus the Pointer

The insertion point is not the same as the pointer. When the pointer is in the document window, the pointer is called the **I-beam pointer**. Figure 2-4 explains the difference between the insertion point and the I-beam pointer.

Figure 2-4	THE INSERTION POINT VS. THE POINTER

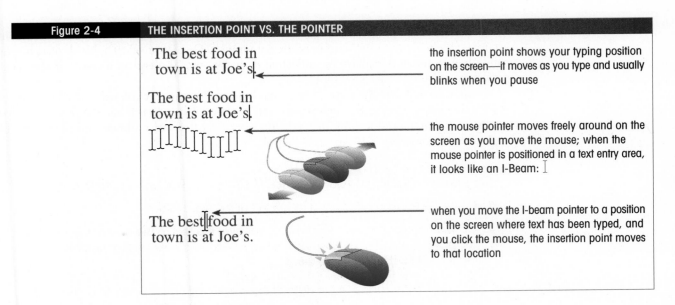

The best food in
town is at Joe's.

the insertion point shows your typing position on the screen—it moves as you type and usually blinks when you pause

The best food in
town is at Joe's.

the mouse pointer moves freely around on the screen as you move the mouse; when the mouse pointer is positioned in a text entry area, it looks like an I-Beam: I

The best food in
town is at Joe's.

when you move the I-beam pointer to a position on the screen where text has been typed, and you click the mouse, the insertion point moves to that location

When you enter text, the insertion point moves as you type. If you want to enter text in a location other than where the insertion point is positioned, you can use the pointer to move the insertion point to a different location. Move the I-beam pointer to where you want to type, and then click. The insertion point moves to where you clicked. In most programs, the insertion point blinks so you can locate it easily on a screen filled with text.

Try moving the insertion point to different locations in the sample text in the WordPad document window.

To move the insertion point to a new location in the sample text:

1. Locate the insertion point and the I-beam pointer in the WordPad document window. The insertion point should be at the end of the sentence you typed in the last set of steps. The easiest way to find the I-beam pointer is to move your mouse gently until you see the pointer. The pointer will look like ▷ until you move it into the document window; then the pointer will change to Ⅰ.

2. Use your mouse to move the I-beam pointer just to the left of the word "sample," and then click. The insertion point should now be just to the left of the "s" in the word "sample."

   TROUBLE? If you have trouble clicking just to the left of the "s," try clicking in the word and then using the left arrow key to move the insertion point one character at a time.

3. Move the I-beam pointer to a blank area near the bottom of the document window, and then click. Notice the insertion point does not jump to the location of the I-beam pointer. Instead the insertion point jumps to the end of the last sentence or to the point in the bottom line directly above where you clicked. The insertion point can move only within existing text. In most programs, the insertion point cannot be moved out of the existing text.

Selecting Text

Many text-editing operations are performed on a **block of text**, which is one or more consecutive characters, words, sentences, or paragraphs. Once you select a block of text, you can delete it, move it, replace it, underline it, and so on. To deselect a block of text, click anywhere outside the selected block.

If you want to delete the phrase "See what happens" in the text you just typed and replace it with the phrase "You can watch word wrap in action," you do not have to delete the first phrase one character at a time. Instead, you can select the entire phrase and then type the replacement phrase.

To select and replace the block of text "See what happens":

1. Move the I-beam pointer just to the left of the word "See."

2. Click and then drag the I-beam pointer over the text to the end of the word "happens." The phrase "See what happens" should now be highlighted, indicating it is selected. See Figure 2-5.

   TROUBLE? If the space to the right of the word "happens" is also selected, that means your computer is set up to select spaces in addition to words. You can continue with Step 3.

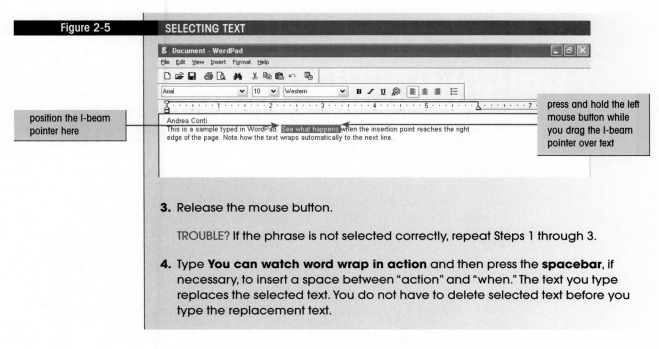

Figure 2-5   **SELECTING TEXT**

position the I-beam pointer here

press and hold the left mouse button while you drag the I-beam pointer over text

3. Release the mouse button.

TROUBLE? If the phrase is not selected correctly, repeat Steps 1 through 3.

4. Type **You can watch word wrap in action** and then press the **spacebar**, if necessary, to insert a space between "action" and "when." The text you type replaces the selected text. You do not have to delete selected text before you type the replacement text.

In addition to replacing existing text with new material, you can also insert text into an existing block of text.

Inserting Text

Windows XP programs usually operate in **insert mode**—when you type a new character, the characters to the right of the insertion point automatically move over to make room.

Insert the word "page" before the word "typed" in the sample text.

To insert text:

1. Position the insertion point just before the word "typed".

2. Type **page** and then press the **spacebar**. The letters in the first line are pushed to the right to make room for the new characters. When you insert text and a word is pushed past the right margin, the word wrap feature moves the word down to the beginning of the next line.

Now that you have practiced typing, you can save the file.

Saving a File

As you type text, it is held temporarily in the computer's memory and is erased when you turn off or restart the computer. For permanent storage, you need to save your work on a disk. In the computer lab, you will probably save your work on a floppy disk in drive A.

When you save a file, you must give it a name, which then becomes its **filename**. Windows XP allows you to use up to 255 characters in a filename—this gives you plenty of room to name your file accurately so that you'll know the contents of the file just by looking at the filename. You can use spaces and certain punctuation symbols in your filenames. You cannot use the symbols \ / ? : * " < > | in a filename, but other symbols such as & ; - and $ are allowed.

When naming a file, you should also consider whether you might use your files on a computer that is running older programs. Programs designed for the Windows 3.1 or DOS operating systems (which were created before 1995) require that filenames have eight characters or less and no spaces. When you save a file with a long filename in Windows XP, Windows XP also creates an eight-character filename that can be used by older programs. The eight-character filename is created from the first six nonspace characters in the long filename, with the addition of a tilde (~) and a number. For example, the filename Car Sales for 2004 would be converted to Carsal~1.

Most filenames have an extension. An **extension** (a set of no more than three characters at the end of a filename, separated from the filename by a period) is used by the operating system to identify and categorize the files by their file types. The characters also indicate the program in which the file was created. In the filename Car Sales for 2004.doc, for example, the file extension "doc" identifies the file as one created with Microsoft Word. You might also have a file called Car Sales for 2004.xls—the "xls" extension identifies the file as one created in Microsoft Excel, a spreadsheet program. When pronouncing filenames with extensions, say "dot" for the period, so that you pronounce the filename Resume.doc as "Resume dot doc."

You usually do not need to add an extension to a filename because the program that you use to create the file adds the file extension automatically. Also, Windows XP keeps track of extensions, but not all computers are set to display extensions. The steps in these tutorials refer to files using the filename without its extension. So if you see the filename Practice Text in the steps, but "Practice Text.doc" on your screen, both names refer to the same file. Also, you do not have to use lowercase and uppercase letters consistently when naming files. Usually the operating system doesn't distinguish between them. Be aware, however, that some programs are case-sensitive—that is, they check for case in filenames.

Now you can save the document you typed.

To start saving your document:

1. Click the **Save** button 🖫 on the toolbar. The Save As dialog box opens, as shown in Figure 2-6.

Figure 2-6	SAVING A FILE

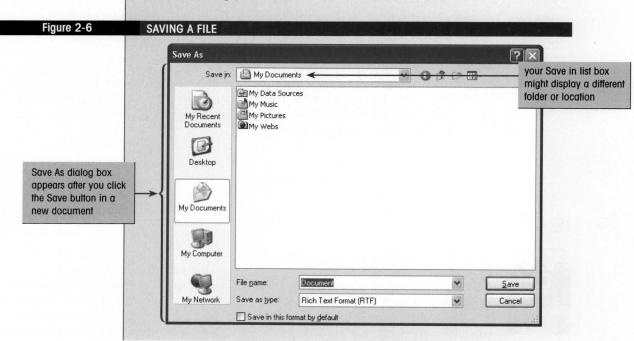

your Save in list box might display a different folder or location

Save As dialog box appears after you click the Save button in a new document

You use the Save As dialog box to specify where you want to save your file (on the hard disk or on a floppy disk, in a folder or not, and so on). Before going further with the process of saving a file, examine some of the features of the Save As dialog box so that you learn to save your files exactly where you want them.

Specifying the File Location

In the Save As dialog box, Windows XP provides the **Places Bar**, a list of important locations on your computer. When you click the different icons in the Places Bar, the contents of those locations will be displayed in the white area of the Save As dialog box. You can then save your document directly to those locations. Figure 2-7 identifies the icons in the Places Bar and gives their function.

Figure 2-7	ICONS IN THE PLACES BAR

ICON	DESCRIPTION
My Recent Documents	Displays a list of recently opened files, folders, and objects
Desktop	Displays a list of files, folders, and objects on the Windows XP desktop
My Documents	Displays a list of files, folders, and objects in the My Documents folder
My Computer	Displays a list of files, folders, and objects in the My Computer window
My Network Places	Displays a list of computers and folders available on the network

To see this in action, try displaying different locations in the Save As dialog box.

To use the Places Bar:

1. Click the **Desktop** icon in the Places Bar.

2. The Save As dialog box now displays the contents of the Windows XP desktop. See Figure 2-8.

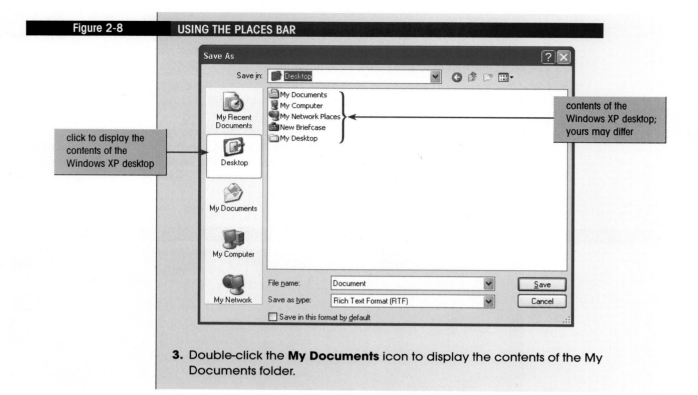

| Figure 2-8 | USING THE PLACES BAR |

click to display the contents of the Windows XP desktop

contents of the Windows XP desktop; yours may differ

3. Double-click the **My Documents** icon to display the contents of the My Documents folder.

Once you've clicked an icon in the Places Bar, you can open any file displayed in that location, and you can save a file in that location. The Places Bar doesn't have an icon for every location on your computer, however. The Save in list box (located at the top of the dialog box) does. Use the Save in list box now to save your document on your floppy disk.

To use the Save in list box:

1. Click the **Save in** list arrow to display a list of drives.

2. Click **3½ Floppy (A:)**.

Now that you've specified where you want to save your file, you can specify a name and type for the file.

Specifying the File Name and Type

After choosing the location for your document, you have to specify the name of the file. You should also specify (or at least check) the file's format. A file's **format** determines what type of information you can place in the document, the document's appearance, and what kind of programs can work with the document. You can save a WordPad document in one of four file formats: Rich Text Format (RTF), Text, Text for MS-DOS, and Unicode Text. In addition, you can open a document in the Word for Windows 6.0 or Windows Write formats. The Word, Write, and RTF formats allow you to create documents with text that can use boldfaced or italicized fonts as well as documents containing graphic images and scanned photos. However, only word-processing programs like WordPad or Microsoft Word can work with those files. The four text formats allow only simple text with no graphics or special formatting, but such documents are readable by a wider range of programs. The default format for WordPad documents is RTF, but you can change that, as you'll see shortly.

Continue saving the document, using the name "Practice Text" and the file type Text Document.

To finish saving your document:

1. Select the text **Document** in the File name text box, and then type **Practice Text.** The new text replaces "Document."

2. Click the **Save as type** list arrow, and then click **Text Document** in the list. See Figure 2-9.

Figure 2-9	COMPLETED SAVE AS DIALOG BOX

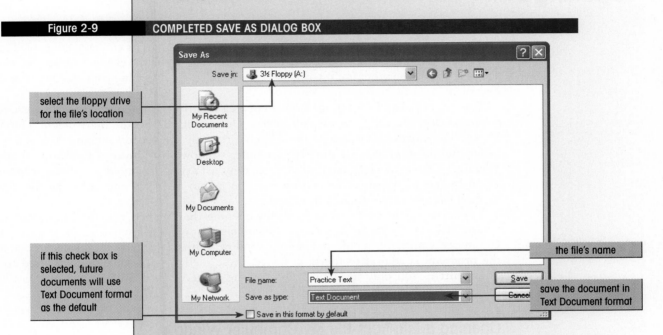

select the floppy drive for the file's location

if this check box is selected, future documents will use Text Document format as the default

the file's name

save the document in Text Document format

3. Click the **Save** button in the lower-right corner of the dialog box.

4. If you are asked whether you are sure that you want to save the document in this format, click the **Yes** button.

Your file is saved on your Data Disk, and the document title, "Practice Text," appears in the WordPad title bar.

Note that after you save the file, the document appears a little different. What has changed? By saving the document in Text Document format rather than RTF, you've changed the format of the document slightly. One change is that the text is wrapped differently in Text Document format. A Text Document file does not wrap text when it reaches the right margin.

What if you try to close WordPad before you save your file? Windows XP will display a message—"Save changes to document?" If you answer "Yes," Windows XP will display the Save As dialog box so you can give the document a name. If you answer "No," Windows XP will close WordPad without saving the document. Any changes you made to the document will be lost. Unless you are absolutely sure you don't need to keep the work you just did, answer "Yes."

After you save a file, you can work on another document or close WordPad. Because you have already saved your Practice Text document, you'll continue this tutorial by closing WordPad.

> *To close WordPad:*
>
> **1.** Click the **Close** button ☒ to close the WordPad window.

Opening a File

Now that you have saved and closed the Practice Text file, suppose you now want to revise it. To revise a file you must first open it. When you open a file, its contents are copied into the computer's memory. If you revise the file, you need to save the changes before you close the file or close the program. If you close a revised file without saving your changes, you will lose them.

You can use one of several methods to open a file. If you have opened the file recently, you can select the file from the My Recent Documents list on the Start menu. The My Recent Documents list contains the 15 most recently opened documents. You can also locate and open a file using the My Computer window (or **Windows Explorer**, another Windows XP file management tool). Or you can start a program and then use the program's Open button (or Open command on the File menu) to locate and open the file. Each method has advantages and disadvantages.

Using one of the first two methods for opening the Practice Text file simply requires you to click the file in the My Recent Documents list or locate and select it from the My Computer window or Windows Explorer window. With these methods, the document, not the program, is central to the task; hence, these methods are sometimes referred to as **docucentric**. You only need to remember the name of your file—you do not need to remember which program you used to create it.

Opening a File from the My Computer Window

You can open a file by selecting it from the My Computer window or Windows Explorer window. Windows XP uses the file extension (whether it is displayed or not) to determine which program to start so you can work with the file. Windows XP starts the program and then opens the file. The advantage of this method is simplicity. The disadvantage is that Windows XP might not start the program you expect. For example, when you select Practice Text, you might expect Windows XP to start WordPad because you used WordPad to create it. Depending on the programs installed on your computer system, however, Windows XP might start Notepad or Microsoft Word instead. Notepad works with simple text files, such as those that have a .txt extension, and Word works with a wide range of documents that can include formatting, graphics, and other elements. Word files have a .doc extension. Using any word-processing program to open a text file is not usually a problem. Although the program might not be the one you expect, you can still use it to revise your file.

> *To open the Practice Text file by selecting it from My Computer:*
>
> **1.** Double-click the **My Computer** icon on the desktop to open the My Computer window.
>
> **2.** Double-click the **3½ Floppy (A:)** icon in the My Computer window.

3. Double-click the **Practice Text** file icon. Windows XP starts Notepad and then opens the Practice Text file. You could edit the document at this point, but instead, you'll close all the windows on your desktop so you can try another method for opening files.

   TROUBLE? If Windows XP starts Microsoft Word or another word-processing program instead of NotePad, continue with Step 4.

4. Close all open windows on the desktop.

Windows XP opened Practice Text in Notepad because you saved it as a text document—and Windows is usually setup to open text documents with Notepad. If you want to be sure to edit Practice Text in WordPad, first open WordPad and then use the Open button. You will try that next.

Opening a File from Within a Program

The advantage of opening a file from within a program is that you can specify the program you want to use to modify the file—WordPad, in this case. This method, however, involves more steps than the method you tried previously.

You can take advantage of the Places bar to reduce the number of steps it takes to open a file from within a program. Recall that the Places Bar contains the My Recent Documents icon, which when clicked, provides a list of recently opened files. One of the most recently opened files was the Practice Text file, so you should be able to open it using this method.

Open the Practice Text file using the Open button in WordPad.

To open a list of recent files and then save a WordPad document:

1. Start **WordPad** and maximize the WordPad window.

2. Click the **Open** button 🗁 on the toolbar.

3. In the Open dialog box, click **My Recent Documents** in the Places bar.

The Practice Text file doesn't appear in the list. Why not? Look at the Files of Type list box. The selected entry is "Rich Text Format (rtf)". What this means is that the only files listed in the Open dialog box are those saved as Rich Text files—they all have an .rtf file extension. Limiting the types of files displayed frees you from having to deal with the clutter of unwanted or irrelevant files. The downside is that unless you're aware of how the Open dialog box will filter the list of files, you may mistakenly think that the file you're looking for doesn't exist. You can change how the Open dialog box filters this file list. Try this now by changing the filter to show only .txt documents.

To change the types of files displayed:

1. Click the **Files of type** list arrow. Note that WordPad can open files with a .doc or .wri extension, in addition to the file types it can save. Click **Text Documents (*.txt)**. The Practice Text file now appears in the list.

2. Click **Practice Text** in the list box. See Figure 2-10.

Figure 2-10	SELECTING THE FILE

list only files in Text Documents format

3. Click the **Open** button. The document opens in the WordPad window. Note that you could also open the Practice Text file by double-clicking its name in the file list.

   Saving the file as a Text Document did not preserve the word wrap. To restore word wrap, you can save the file in the Rich Text Format.

4. Click **File** on the menu bar, and then click **Save As**. You use the Save As command when you want to save the current file with a different name, file type, or location.

5. Click the **Save as type** list arrow, and then click **Rich Text Format (RTF)**.

6. Click the **Save** button. A message appears indicating that a file named Practice Text already exists in the selected location. You want to replace this file with one in the RTF format.

7. Click the **Yes** button. The word wrap in the Practice Text document is restored.

Now that you have opened and saved the Practice Text file as an RTF file, you can print it.

Printing a Document

Windows XP provides easy access to the printers connected to your computer. You can choose which printer to use, you can control how the document is printed, and you can control the order in which documents print. You also can preview your document before printing it to see how it will appear when it is printed.

Previewing Your Document Before Printing

Before you send a document to the printer, you should always preview it using Print Preview. **Print Preview** shows your document exactly as it will appear when printed on paper. You can check your page layout so you don't waste paper printing a document that is not quite the way you want it.

Preview and print the Practice Text document. Your instructor might supply you with additional instructions for printing in your lab.

To preview the Practice Text document:

1. Click the **Print Preview** button 🔍 on the WordPad toolbar.

   TROUBLE? If an error message appears, printing capabilities might not be set up on your computer. Ask your instructor or technical support person for help, or skip this set of steps.

2. Look at your document in the Print Preview window. Before you print the document, you should make sure the font, margins, and other document features are the way you want them.

   TROUBLE? If the document does not look the way you want it to, click the Close button, edit the document, and then click the Print Preview button again.

   TROUBLE? If you can't read the document text on screen, click the Zoom In button as many times as necessary to read the text.

3. Click the **Close** button on the Print Preview toolbar to close Print Preview, and return to the document.

Now that you've verified that the document looks the way you want, you can print it.

Sending Your Document to the Printer

There are three ways to send your document to the printer. One way is to click the Print button 🖨 on your program's toolbar. This method will send the document directly to your printer—you do not need to take any further action. It's the quickest and easiest way to print a document, although it does not allow you to change settings such as margins and number of copies. What if you have access to more than one printer? In that case, Windows XP sends the document to the default printer, the one set up to handle your print tasks.

If you want to select a different printer or control how the printer prints your document, you can select the Print command from the File menu. Selecting the Print command opens the Print dialog box, allowing you to choose which printer to use and how that printer will print the document.

You can also print your document directly from the Print Preview window by clicking the Print button on the Print Preview toolbar. Clicking the Print button in Print Preview also opens the Print dialog box so you can verify or change settings.

Print the Practice Text document using the File menu.

To print the document using the Print command on the File menu:

1. Click **File** on the menu bar, and then click **Print**. The Print dialog box opens, as shown in Figure 2-11.

Figure 2-11   PRINTING A FILE

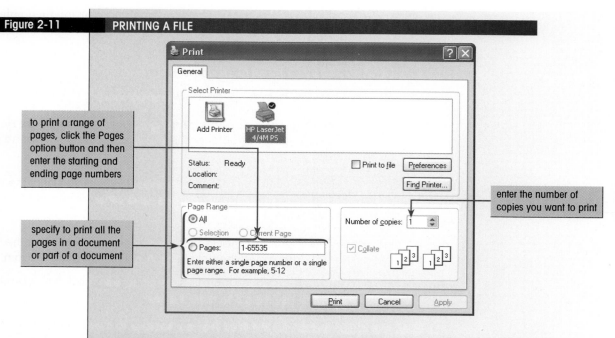

to print a range of pages, click the Pages option button and then enter the starting and ending page numbers

specify to print all the pages in a document or part of a document

enter the number of copies you want to print

2. Make sure your Print dialog box shows the Print range set to **All** and the number of copies set to **1**.

3. Click the **Print** button to print your document.

TROUBLE? If your document does not print, make sure the printer is turned on and contains paper. If your document still doesn't print, ask your instructor or technical support person for help.

4. Close WordPad.

TROUBLE? If you see the message "Save changes to Document?", click the No button.

You've now learned how to create, save, open, and print word-processed files—essential skills for students in distance learning courses that rely on word-processed reports transmitted across the Internet. Shannon assures you that the techniques you've just learned apply to most Windows XP programs.

Session 2.1 QUICK CHECK

1. A(n) _____ is a collection of data that has a name and is stored on a disk or other storage medium.

2. _____ erases the data on a disk and arranges the magnetic particles on the disk's surface so the disk can store data.

3. True or False: When you move the mouse pointer over a text entry area, the pointer's shape changes to an I-beam I.

4. What shows you where each character you type will appear?

5. _____ automatically moves text down to the beginning of the next line when you reach the right margin.

6. How do you select a block of text?

7. In the filename New Equipment.doc, doc is a(n) _____.

SESSION 2.2

In this session you will change the settings in the My Computer window to control its appearance and the appearance of desktop objects. You will use My Computer to manage the files on your Data Disk; view information about the files on your disk; organize the files into folders; and move, delete, copy, and rename files.

Using My Computer

The My Computer icon on the desktop represents your computer, its storage devices, printers, and other objects. The My Computer icon opens the My Computer window, which contains an icon for each of the storage devices on your computer, as shown in Figure 2-12. These icons appear in the right pane of the My Computer window. On most computer systems, the My Computer window also has a left pane, which shows icons and links to other resources. You'll learn more about the left pane shortly.

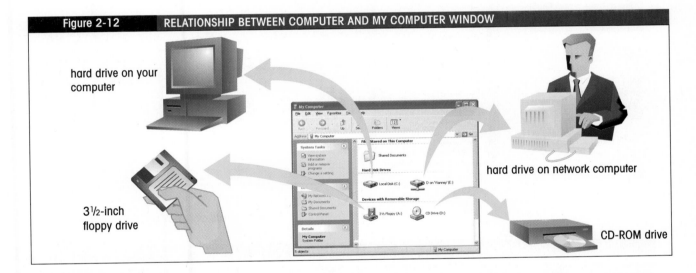

Figure 2-12   RELATIONSHIP BETWEEN COMPUTER AND MY COMPUTER WINDOW

hard drive on your computer

3½-inch floppy drive

hard drive on network computer

CD-ROM drive

Each storage device you have access to on your computer has a letter associated with it. The first floppy drive on a computer is usually designated as drive A. (If you add a second floppy drive, it is usually designated as drive B.) The first hard drive is usually designated drive C. (If you add additional hard drives, they are usually designated as D, E, and so on.) If you have a CD or DVD drive, it will usually have the next letter in the alphabetic sequence. If you have access to hard drives located on other computers in a network, those drives will sometimes (although not always) have letters associated with them as well. In the example shown in Figure 2-12, the network drive has the drive letter E.

You can use the My Computer window to keep track of where your files are stored and to organize your files. In this session, you will move and delete files on your Data Disk, which is assumed to be located in drive A. If you use your own computer at home or work, you will probably store your files on drive C instead of drive A. However, in a school lab environment you usually don't know which computer you will use, so you need to carry your files with you on a floppy disk that you can use in drive A on any computer. In this session, therefore, you will learn how to work with the files on drive A. Most of what you learn will also work on your home or work computer when you use drive C (or other drives).

Now you'll open the My Computer window.

To explore the contents of your Data Disk using the My Computer window:

1. Make sure your Data Disk is in the floppy drive. If necessary, remove the disk you formatted—the one that contains only the Practice Text file—and then insert your Data Disk in the floppy drive.

2. Open the My Computer window. See Figure 2-13.

Figure 2-13	MY COMPUTER WINDOW

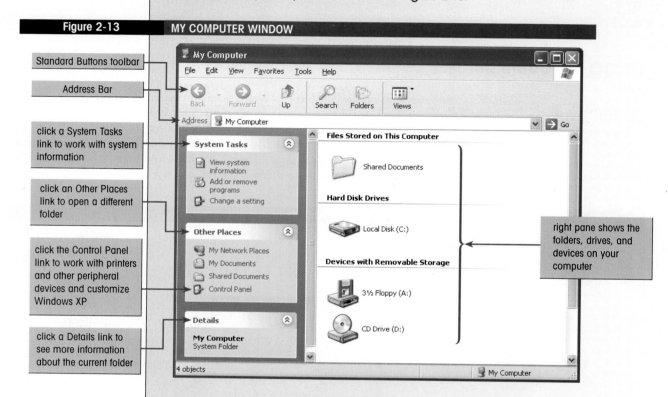

Standard Buttons toolbar

Address Bar

click a System Tasks link to work with system information

click an Other Places link to open a different folder

click the Control Panel link to work with printers and other peripheral devices and customize Windows XP

click a Details link to see more information about the current folder

right pane shows the folders, drives, and devices on your computer

Figure 2-14 identifies and describes the elements of the My Computer window.

Figure 2-14	ELEMENTS OF THE MY COMPUTER WINDOW

ELEMENT	DESCRIPTION
System Tasks	Click a System Tasks link to view system information, such as the capacity of your hard drive, add or remove programs, or change a system setting.
Other Places	Click an Other Places link to open the My Documents or Shared Documents folder or the Network Places or Control Panel Window.
Control Panel	Click this link to view or change your computer settings.
Details	If you are viewing the contents of a folder, click a Details link to see more information about the folder or device, such as its size and the date it was created on.
Right pane	Shows the folders, drives, and devices on your computer; double-click an icon to open the object.
Standard Buttons toolbar	Contains buttons for performing common tasks, such as navigating your computer or changing the icon view.
Address Bar	Shows the name and location of the current device or folder; you can enter a different location in the Address Bar to open a different folder or other object.

3. Double-click the **3½ Floppy (A:)** icon. A window opens showing the contents of drive A; maximize this window if necessary. See Figure 2-15.

| Figure 2-15 | CONTENTS OF DATA DISK |

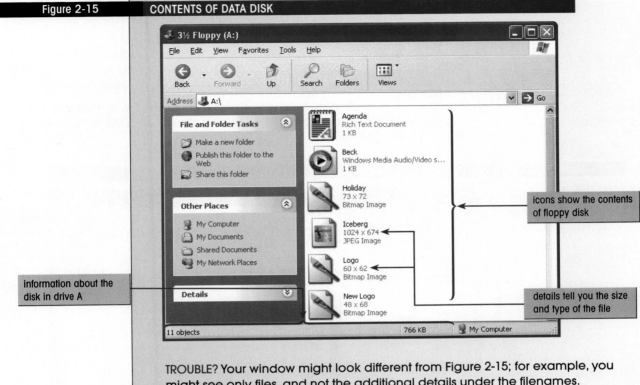

TROUBLE? Your window might look different from Figure 2-15; for example, you might see only files, and not the additional details under the filenames.

TROUBLE? If you see a list of filenames instead of icons, click View on the menu bar, and then click Tiles.

TROUBLE? If you do not see the status bar, click New on the menu bar, and then click Status Bar.

Changing the Appearance of the My Computer Window

Windows XP offers several options that control how toolbars, icons, and buttons appear in the My Computer window. To make the My Computer window look the same as it does in the figures in this book, you need to ensure three things: that only the Standard and Address toolbars are visible; that files and other objects appear as Tiles, which displays files as large icons, and that the configuration of Windows XP uses the default setting. Setting your computer to match the figures makes it easier for you to follow the steps in these tutorials.

Controlling the Toolbar Display

The My Computer window, in addition to featuring a Standard toolbar, allows you to display the same toolbars that can appear on the Windows XP taskbar, such as the Address toolbar or the Links toolbar. You can use these toolbars to access the Web from the My Computer window. In this tutorial, however, you need to see only the Address and Standard Buttons toolbars.

To display only the Address and Standard Buttons toolbars:

1. Click **View** on the menu bar, and then point to **Toolbars**. The Standard Buttons and Address Bar commands on the Toolbars submenu should be checked, indicating that they are displayed in the My Computers window. The Links option should not be checked.

2. If the Standard Buttons or Address Bar commands *are not checked*, click the command to select it. Or if the Links option *is checked*, click it to deselect it. Note that you must display the Toolbars submenu to select or deselect each option.

3. If necessary, click **View** on the menu bar, and then point to **Toolbars** to verify that your Toolbars submenu and the toolbars displayed in the My Computer Window look like Figure 2-16.

| Figure 2-16 | CHECKING VIEW OPTIONS |

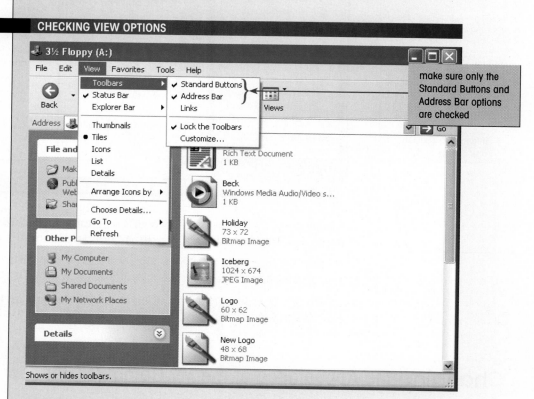

TROUBLE? If the check marks on the Toolbars submenu are distributed differently than in Figure 2-16, repeat Steps 1 and 2 until the correct options are selected.

TROUBLE? If your toolbars' arrangement differs from that shown in Figure 2-16 (for example, both the Standard Buttons and Address toolbars are on the same line or the Standard Buttons toolbar is above the Address toolbar), you can easily rearrange them. To move a toolbar, first make sure it is unlocked. Click View on the menu bar, point to Toolbars, and then click Lock the Toolbar to uncheck this command. Then drag the vertical bar at the far left of the toolbar left, right, up, or down.

TROUBLE? If there are no labels included on the toolbar buttons, click View on the menu bar, point to Toolbars, click Customize, click the Text options list arrow in the Customize Toolbar dialog box, click Show text labels, and then click the Close button.

4. Press the **Esc** key to close the Toolbars menu.

Changing the Icon Display

Windows XP provides five ways to view the contents of a disk—Thumbnails, Tiles, Icons, List, and Details. Figure 2-17 shows examples of these five styles.

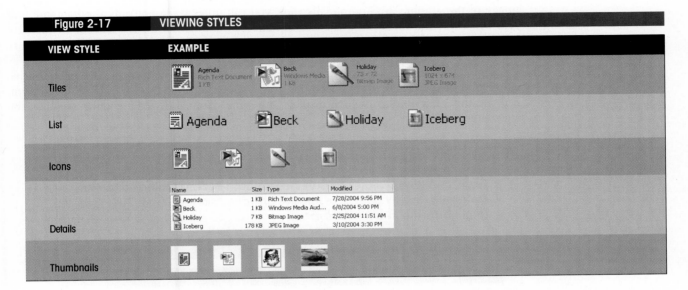

| Figure 2-17 | VIEWING STYLES |

VIEW STYLE	EXAMPLE
Tiles	Agenda — Rich Text Document 1 KB · Beck — Windows Media 1 KB · Holiday — 73 x 72 Bitmap Image · Iceberg — 1024 x 674 JPEG Image
List	Agenda · Beck · Holiday · Iceberg
Icons	(icons)
Details	Name / Size / Type / Modified · Agenda 1 KB Rich Text Document 7/28/2004 9:56 PM · Beck 1 KB Windows Media Aud... 6/8/2004 5:00 PM · Holiday 7 KB Bitmap Image 2/25/2004 11:51 AM · Iceberg 178 KB JPEG Image 3/10/2004 3:30 PM
Thumbnails	(thumbnails)

The default view, **Tiles view**, displays a large icon, title, file type, and file size for each file. The icon provides a visual cue to the type of file, as shown in Figure 2-18. You also can find this same information with the smaller icons displayed in the **Icons** and **List views**, but in less screen space. In Icons and List views, you can see more files and folders at one time, which is helpful when you have many files in one location.

| Figure 2-18 | TYPICAL ICONS IN WINDOWS XP |

FILE AND FOLDER ICONS

Text documents that you can open using the Notepad accessory are represented by notepad icons.

Graphic image documents that you can open using the Paint accessory are represented by drawing instruments.

Word-processed documents that you can open using the WordPad accessory are represented by a formatted notepad icon, unless your computer designates a different word-processing program to open files created with WordPad.

Word-processed documents that you can open using a program such as Microsoft Word are represented by formatted document icons.

Files created by programs that Windows does not recognize are represented by the Windows logo.

A folder icon represents folders.

Certain folders created by Windows XP have a special icon design related to the folder's purpose.

PROGRAM ICONS

Icons for programs usually depict an object related to the function of the program. For example, an icon that looks like a calculator represents the Calculator accessory.

Non-Windows programs are represented by the icon of a blank window.

All of the three icon views (Tiles, Icons, and List) help you quickly identify a file and its type, but what if you want more information about a set of files? **Details view** shows more information than the other three views. Details view shows the file icon, filename, file size, program used to create the file, and the date and time the file was created or last modified.

If you have graphic files, you can use **Thumbnails view**, which displays a small preview image of the graphic. In Thumbnails view, you can quickly see not only the filename, but also which picture or drawing the file contains. Thumbnails view is great for browsing a large collection of graphic files, but switching to this view can be time-consuming because Windows XP must first create all the preview images.

To practice switching from one view to another, start by displaying the contents of drive A in Details view. So far, you've used the View menu to change the window view. Now you can use the Views button, which displays the same commands for changing views as the View menu.

To view a detailed list of files:

1. Click the **Views** button 🔲 ▾ on the Standard Buttons toolbar, and then click **Details** to display details for the files on your disk. See Figure 2-19. Your files might be listed in a different order.

Figure 2-19	DETAILS VIEW

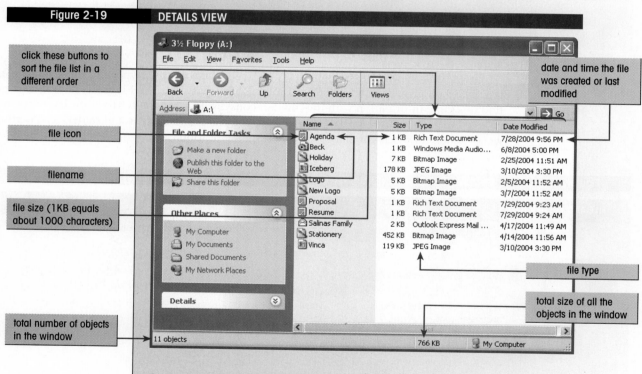

2. Look at the file sizes. Which files are the largest?

3. Look at the Type column. Which file is an Outlook Express Mail Message?

One of the advantages of Details view is that you can sort the file list by filename, size, type, or date. This helps if you're working with a large file list and you're trying to find a specific file.

To sort the file list by type:

1. Click the **Type** button at the top of the list of files. The files are now sorted in alphabetical order by type, starting with the Bitmap Image files and ending with the Windows XP Audio/Visual Media file.

   If you were looking for all the .rtf files (those created with WordPad, for example), sorting by type would be useful because the .rtf files would all be grouped together under "R" for Rich Text Format.

2. Click the **Type** button again. The sort order is reversed, with the Windows XP Audio/Visual Media file now at the top of the list.

3. Click the **Name** button at the top of the file list. The files are now sorted in alphabetical order by filename.

Now that you have looked at the file details, you can switch back to Tiles view.

To switch to Tiles view:

1. Click the **Views** button ⊞ ˇ on the Standard Buttons toolbar, and then click **Tiles** to return to the Tiles view.

Restoring the My Computer Default Settings

Windows XP provides other options for working with your files and windows. These options fall into two general categories: Classic style and Web style. **Classic style** lets you interact with windows and files using techniques from earlier versions of the Windows operating system. **Web style** lets you work with windows and files in the same way you work with Web pages on the World Wide Web. For example, to open a file in Classic style, you can double-click the file icon or the filename, or you can click the file icon or filename once and press the Enter key. To open a file in Web style, you would point to a file icon until the pointer changed to ⬆, and then you would click the file icon once. The filenames would also appear underlined, indicating you can click once to open them. Underlined text is usually called a **hyperlink** or just **link**. You can also create your own style, choosing elements of both the Classic and Web styles, and add customized features of your own.

Try switching to the Web style to see how it works in the My Computer window. Then, to maintain consistency and make sure your screens match the ones in this tutorial, you'll return to the default style—the one Windows XP uses when it's initially installed. No matter what changes you make to the setup of Windows XP, you can always revert to the default style.

To switch to the Web style and back to the default style:

1. Click **Tools** on the menu bar, and then click **Folder Options**.

2. If necessary, click the **General** tab in the Folder Options dialog box. The General sheet includes options for working with files and windows.

3. In the Click items as follows section, click the **Single-click to open an item (point to select)** option button. When you select this option button, the Underline icon titles consistent with my browser option button is also selected. This means that filenames will always be underlined to indicate that you can click to open them.

4. Click the **OK** button. The filenames in the My Computer window are underlined as hyperlinks.

5. In the My Computer window, point to the **Agenda** icon. The icon is highlighted, indicating it is selected, and after a few moments, a ScreenTip appears. See Figure 2-20.

MY COMPUTER WINDOW IN WEB STYLE

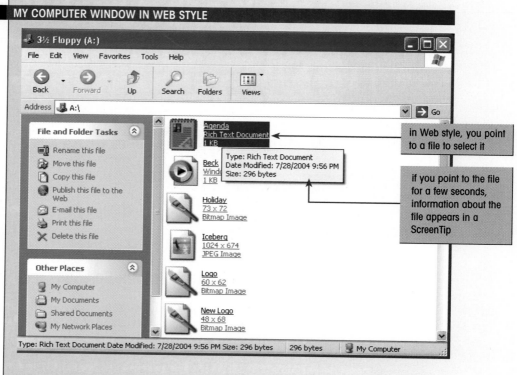

In Web style, when you move the pointer over an icon or underlined text, it appears as a hand 🖑, indicating the icon or text is a hyperlink. In Classic style, when you point to an icon or filename, the pointer is a selection arrow ▷.

6. To restore the default style, click **Tools** on the menu bar, and then click **Folder Options**.

7. Click the **Restore Defaults** button in the Folder Options dialog box.

8. Click the **View** tab. The View tab includes options that control the appearance of files and other objects. You need to make sure these options are set to their default settings as well.

9. Click the **Restore Defaults** button.

10. Click the **OK** button to close the Folder Options dialog box.

Working with Folders and Directories

Up to now, you've done a little work with files and windows, but before going further, you should look at some of the terminology used to describe these tasks. Any location where you can store files on a computer is called a **directory**. The main directory of a disk is sometimes called the **root directory**, or the **top-level directory**. All of the files on your Data Disk are currently in the root directory of your floppy disk.

If too many files are stored in a directory, the directory list becomes very long and difficult to manage. You can divide a directory into **subdirectories**, also called **folders**. The number of files for each folder then becomes much fewer and easier to manage. A folder within a folder is called a **subfolder**. The folder that contains another folder is called the **parent folder**.

Windows XP arranges all of these objects—root directory, folders, subfolders, and files—in a **hierarchy**. The hierarchy begins with your desktop and extends down to each subfolder. Figure 2-21 shows part of a typical hierarchy of Windows XP objects.

Figure 2-21	PART OF A TYPICAL HIERARCHY OF WINDOWS XP OBJECTS

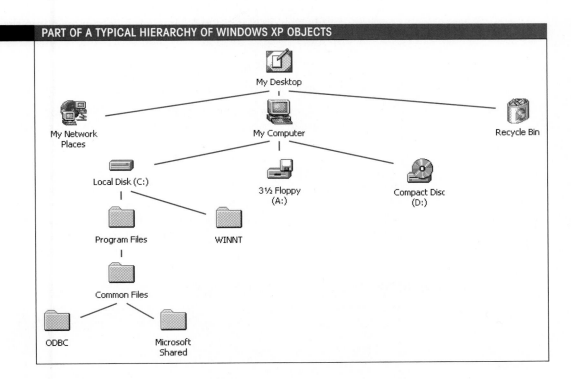

Creating a Folder

You've already seen folder icons in the windows you've opened. Now you'll create your own folder called Practice to hold your documents. This time, you can work in Icons view so you can see all the files on the Data Disk.

To create a Practice folder:

1. Click the **Views** button ▦ ˇ on the Standard Buttons toolbar, and then click **Icons**.

2. Click **File** on the menu bar, and then point to **New** to display the submenu.

3. Click **Folder**. A folder icon with the label "New Folder" appears in the My Computer window.

4. Type **Practice** as the name of the folder.

   TROUBLE? If nothing happens when you type the folder name, it's possible that the folder name is no longer selected. Right-click the new folder, click Rename on the shortcut menu, and then repeat Step 4.

5. Press the **Enter** key. The new folder is now named "Practice" and is the selected item on your Data Disk.

6. Click a blank area next to the Practice folder to deselect it.

Navigating Through the Windows XP Hierarchy

Now that you've created a folder, how do you move into it? You've learned that to view the contents of a file, you open it. To move into a folder, you open it in the same way.

To view the contents of the Practice folder:

1. Double-click the **Practice** folder. The Practice folder opens.

Because the folder doesn't contain any files, there's nothing listed in the right pane of the My Computer window. You'll change that shortly.

You've learned that to navigate through your computer, you open My Computer and then click the icons representing the objects you want to explore, such as folders and files. But what if you want to move back to the root directory? The Standard Buttons toolbar, which stays the same regardless of which folder or object is open, includes buttons that help you navigate the hierarchy of drives, directories, folders, subfolders, and other objects in your computer. Figure 2-22 summarizes the navigation buttons on the Standard Buttons toolbar.

Figure 2-22		NAVIGATION BUTTONS
BUTTON	**ICON**	**DESCRIPTION**
Back	⬅	Returns you to the folder, drive, directory, or object you were most recently viewing. The button is active only when you have viewed more than one window in the current session.
Forward	➡	Reverses the effect of the Back button.
Up	⬆	Moves you up one level in the hierarchy of directories, drives, folders, and other objects on your computer.

You can return to your floppy's root directory by using the Back or Up buttons. Try both of these techniques now.

To move up to the root directory:

1. Click the **Back** button ⬅ on the Standard Buttons toolbar. Windows XP opens the previous window, in this case, the root directory of your Data Disk.

2. Click the **Forward** button ➡ on the Standard Buttons toolbar. The Forward button reverses the effect of the Back button and takes you to the Practice folder.

3. Click the **Up** button ⬆ on the Standard Buttons toolbar. You move up one level in the hierarchy of Windows XP objects, to the root directory of the Data Disk.

Another way of moving around in the Windows XP hierarchy is through the Address Bar. By clicking the Address Bar list arrow, you can view a list of the objects in the top part of the Windows XP hierarchy, as illustrated in Figure 2-23. This gives you a quick way of moving to the top without navigating through the intermediate levels.

Figure 2-23 **A HIERARCHY OF OBJECTS IN THE ADDRESS LIST BOX**

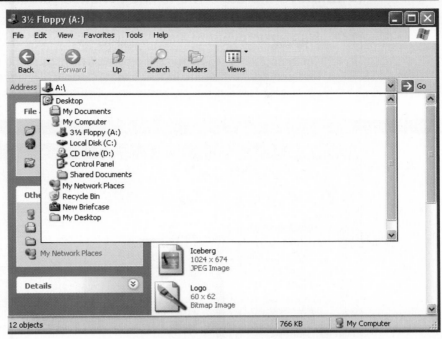

Now that you know how to move around your computer's hierarchy, you can practice manipulating files. The more organized the hierarchy of your computer, the easier it is to find the files you need.

Working with Files

As you've seen, the Practice folder doesn't contain any files. To add files to a folder or drive, you can move a file from one place to another or copy a file so you have duplicates in two locations. After you copy a file, you might want to rename it—that way, you won't confuse it with the original file. If you no longer use a file, you can delete it from your disk. You should periodically delete files you no longer need, so your folders and disks don't get too full and slow the performance of your system.

My Computer simplifies these tasks because you can move, copy, rename, and delete files using the My Computer window. Next, you will use My Computer to place a file from the root directory in the Practice folder.

Moving and Copying a File

If you want to place a file in a folder from another location, you can either move the file or copy it. **Moving** a file removes it from its current location and places it in a new location you specify. **Copying** leaves the file in its current location and places a copy in the new location. Windows XP provides several techniques for moving and copying files. One way is to make sure that both the current and the new location are visible on your screen and then hold down the right mouse button and drag the file from the old location to the new location. A menu appears, including options to move or copy the selected file to the new location. The advantage to this technique is that it is clear whether you are moving or copying a file. Try this technique now by moving the Logo file to the Practice folder.

To move the Logo file to the Practice folder:

1. Point to the **Logo** file in the root directory of your Data Disk, and then press and hold the *right* mouse button.

2. With the right mouse button still pressed down, drag the **Logo** file to the Practice folder. When the Practice folder icon is highlighted, release the button. A shortcut menu appears, as shown in Figure 2-24.

Figure 2-24   MOVING A FILE

3. Click **Move Here** on the shortcut menu with the left mouse button. The Logo file is removed from the window showing the files in the root directory.

   TROUBLE? If you release the mouse button by mistake before dragging the Logo file to the Practice folder, the Logo shortcut menu opens. Press the Esc key, and then repeat Steps 1 through 3.

4. Double-click the **Practice** folder. The Logo file now appears in the Practice folder.

You can also copy a file from one folder to another, or from one disk to another. When you copy a file, you create an exact duplicate of a file in whatever disk or folder you specify. To copy a file from one folder to another on your floppy disk, you use the same procedure as for moving a file, except that you select Copy Here on the shortcut menu. Try copying the Agenda file into the Practice folder.

To copy the Agenda file into the Practice folder:

1. Click the **Up** button 🡑 on the Standard Buttons toolbar. The root directory of your Data Disk is displayed.

2. Using the right mouse button, drag the **Agenda** file into the Practice folder.

> **3.** Using the left mouse button, click **Copy Here** on the shortcut menu. Notice this time the file is not removed from the root directory because you copied the file.
>
> **4.** Double-click the **Practice** folder. A copy of the Agenda file now appears in the Practice folder.

Note that the Move Here command was also on the shortcut menu. In fact, the command was in boldface, indicating that it is the default command whenever you drag a document from one location to another on the same drive. This means that if you were to drag a file from one location to another on the same drive using the left mouse button (instead of the right), the file would be moved and not copied.

Renaming a File

Sometimes you decide to give a file a different name to clarify the file's contents. You can easily rename a file by using the Rename command on the file's shortcut menu.

Practice this technique by renaming the Agenda file to give it a more descriptive filename.

> ### *To rename the Agenda file:*
>
> **1.** Make sure the right pane is set to Tiles view. If necessary, click the **Views** button ▦ ˇ on the Standard Buttons toolbar, and then click **Tiles**.
>
> **2.** Right-click the **Agenda** icon.
>
> **3.** Click **Rename** on the shortcut menu. The filename is highlighted and a box appears around it.
>
> **4.** Type **Practice Agenda** and press the **Enter** key. The file now appears with the new name.
>
> TROUBLE? If you make a mistake while typing and you haven't pressed the Enter key yet, you can press the Backspace key until you delete the mistake, and then complete Step 3. If you've already pressed the Enter key, repeat Steps 1 through 3 to rename the file again.

Deleting a File or Folder

You should periodically delete files you no longer need so that your folders and disks don't get cluttered. In My Computer, you delete a file or folder by deleting its icon. Be careful when you delete a folder, because you also delete all the files it contains! When you delete a file from a hard drive on your computer, the filename is deleted from the directory but the file contents are held in the Recycle Bin. The **Recycle Bin** is an area on your hard drive that holds deleted files until you remove them permanently; an icon on the desktop allows you easy access to the Recycle Bin. If you change your mind and want to retrieve a file deleted from your hard drive, you can recover it by using the Recycle Bin. However, after you empty the Recycle Bin, you can no longer recover the files that were in it.

When you delete a file from a floppy disk or another disk on your network, it does not go into the Recycle Bin. Instead, it is deleted as soon as its icon disappears—and you can't recover it.

Try deleting the Practice Agenda file from your Data Disk. Because this file is on the floppy disk and not on the hard disk, it will not go into the Recycle Bin. If you change your mind, you won't be able to recover it.

To delete the Practice Agenda file:

1. Right-click the **Practice Agenda** file icon.

2. Click **Delete** on the shortcut menu.

   A message box appears, Windows XP asking if you're sure you want to delete this file.

3. Click the **Yes** button.

4. Click the **Close** button [X] to close the My Computer window.

Another way of deleting a file is to drag its icon to the Recycle Bin on the desktop. Be aware that if you're dragging a file from your floppy disk or network drive, the file will *not* be placed in the Recycle Bin—it will be permanently deleted.

Other Copying and Moving Techniques

As you become more familiar with Windows XP, you will probably settle on the copying and moving technique you like best. Figure 2-25 describes some of the other ways of moving and copying files.

Figure 2-25	METHODS FOR MOVING AND COPYING FILES	
METHOD	**TO MOVE**	**TO COPY**
Cut, copy and paste	Select the file icon. Click Edit on the menu bar, and then click Cut. Move to the new location. Click Edit and then click Paste.	Select the file icon. Click Edit on the menu bar, and then click Copy. Move to the new location. Click Edit and then click Paste.
Drag and drop	Click the file icon. Drag and drop the icon to the new location.	Click the file icon. Hold down the Ctrl key, and drag and drop the icon to the new location.
Right-click, drag and drop	With the right mouse button pressed down, drag the file icon to the new location. Release the mouse button, and click Move Here on the shortcut menu.	With the right mouse button pressed down, drag the file icon to the new location. Release the mouse button, and click Copy Here on the shorcut menu.
Move to folder and copy to folder	Click the file icon. Click Edit on the menu bar, and then click Move to Folder. Select the new location in the Browse for Folder dialog box.	Click the file icon. Click Edit on the menu bar, and then click Copy to Folder. Select the new location in the Browse for Folder dialog box.

The techniques shown in Figure 2-25 are primarily for document (data) files. Because a program might not work correctly if moved to a new location, the techniques for moving program files are slightly different. See the Windows XP online Help for more information on moving or copying a program file.

Copying an Entire Floppy Disk

You can have trouble accessing the data on your floppy disk if the disk is damaged, is exposed to magnetic fields, or picks up a computer virus. To avoid losing all your data, you should always make a copy of your floppy disk.

If you wanted to make a copy of a videotape, your VCR would need two tape drives. You might wonder, therefore, how your computer can make a copy of your disk if you have only one floppy disk drive. Figure 2-26 illustrates how the computer uses only one disk drive to make a copy of a disk.

Figure 2-26	USING ONE DISK DRIVE TO COPY A DISK

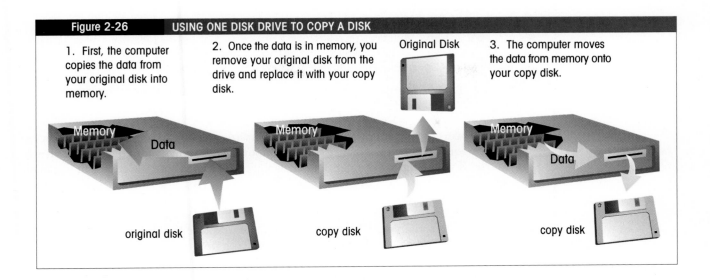

1. First, the computer copies the data from your original disk into memory.

2. Once the data is in memory, you remove your original disk from the drive and replace it with your copy disk.

3. The computer moves the data from memory onto your copy disk.

Original Disk

Memory

Data

Memory

Memory

Data

original disk

copy disk

copy disk

REFERENCE WINDOW   RW

Copying a Disk
- Insert the disk you want to copy in drive A.
- In My Computer, right-click the 3½ Floppy (A:) icon, and then click Copy Disk.
- Click Start to begin the copy process.
- When prompted, remove the disk you want to copy, place your second disk in drive A, and then click OK.

If you have an extra floppy disk, you can make a copy of your Data Disk now. Make sure you copy the disk regularly so that as you work through the tutorials in the book the disk stays updated.

To copy your Data Disk:

1. Write your name and "Windows XP Disk 1 Data Disk Copy" on the label of a blank, formatted disk.

   TROUBLE? If you aren't sure the disk is blank, place it in the disk drive and open the 3½ Floppy (A:) window to view its contents. If the disk contains files you need, get a different disk. If it contains files you don't need, you could format the disk now, using the steps you learned at the beginning of this tutorial.

2. Make sure your original Data Disk is in drive A, and then open and maximize the My Computer window.

3. Right-click the **3½ Floppy (A:)** icon, and then click **Copy Disk**. The Copy Disk dialog box opens.

4. Click the **Start** button to begin the copy process.

5. When the message "Insert the disk you want to copy from (source disk)" appears, click **OK**. Windows XP reads the disk in drive A and stores its contents in memory.

6. Click the **OK** button. When the copy is completed, you will see the message "Copy completed successfully."

7. Click the **Close** button to close the Copy Disk dialog box.

8. Close the My Computer window, and then remove your disk from the drive.

As you finish copying your disk, Shannon emphasizes the importance of making copies of your files frequently, so you won't risk losing important documents for your distance learning course. If your original Data Disk were damaged, you could use the copy you just made to access the files.

Keeping copies of your files is so important that Windows XP includes with it a program called **Backup** that automates the process of duplicating and storing data. In the Projects at the end of the tutorial you'll have an opportunity to explore the difference between what you just did in copying a disk and the way in which a program such as the Windows XP Backup program helps you safeguard data.

Session 2.2 QUICK CHECK

1. If you want to find out about the storage devices and printers connected to your computer, what Windows XP window can you open?

2. If you have only one floppy disk drive on your computer, the letter _____ usually identifies it.

3. The letter C typically designates the _____ drive of a computer.

4. What information does Details view supply about a list of folders and files?

5. The main directory of a disk is referred to as the _____ directory.

6. True or False: You can divide a directory into folders.

7. If you have one floppy disk drive and two floppy disks, can you copy the files on one floppy disk to the other?

REVIEW ASSIGNMENTS

1. **Opening, Editing, and Printing a Document** In this tutorial you learned how to create a document using WordPad. You also learned how to save, open, and print a document. Practice these skills by opening the document called **Resume** on your Data Disk. This document is a resume for Jamie Woods. Make the changes shown in Figure 2-27, and then save the document in the Practice folder with the name **Woods Resume** using the Save As command. After you save your revisions, preview and then print the document. Close WordPad.

Figure 2-27

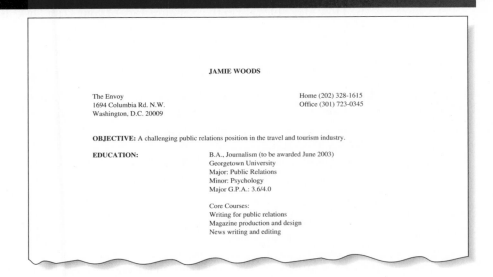

JAMIE WOODS

The Envoy   Home (202) 328-1615
1694 Columbia Rd. N.W.   Office (301) 723-0345
Washington, D.C. 20009

OBJECTIVE: A challenging public relations position in the travel and tourism industry.

EDUCATION: B.A., Journalism (to be awarded June 2003)
                                      Georgetown University
                                      Major: Public Relations
                                      Minor: Psychology
                                      Major G.P.A.: 3.6/4.0

                                      Core Courses:
                                      Writing for public relations
                                      Magazine production and design
                                      News writing and editing

2. **Creating, Saving, and Printing a Letter** Use WordPad to write a one-page letter to a relative or a friend. Save the document in the Practice folder on your Data Disk with the name **Letter**. Use the Print Preview feature to look at the format of your finished letter, then print it, and be sure to sign it. Close WordPad.

3. **Managing Files and Folders** Using the copy of the disk you made at the end of the tutorial, complete Steps a through f below to practice your file-management skills. Then answer Questions 1 through 5 below.

   a. Create a folder called "Documents" on the copy of your Data Disk.
   b. Move the files Agenda, Proposal, and Resume to the Documents folder.
   c. Create a folder called "Park Project."
   d. Move the files New Logo, Stationery, and Vinca to the Park Project folder.
   e. Delete the file called "Logo."
   f. Switch to Details view, and write out your answers to Questions 1 through 5:

      1. What is the largest file in the Park Project folder?

      2. What is the newest file in the Documents folder?

      3. How many files are in the root directory of your Data Disk? (Don't count folders.)

      4. How are the Salinas Family and Iceberg icons different? Judging from the appearance of the icons, what would you guess these two files contain?

      5. Which file in the root directory has the most recent date?

4. **More Practice with Files and Folders** For this assignment, you need a third blank disk. Complete parts a through g below to practice your file-management skills.

   a. Write "Windows XP Tutorial 2 Assignment 4" on the label of the blank disk, and then format the disk if necessary.
   b. Create another copy of your original Data Disk, using the Assignment 4 disk. Refer to the section "Copying an Entire Floppy Disk" in Session 2.2.
   c. Create three folders on the Assignment 4 Data Disk you just created: Documents, Meetings, and Graphics.
   d. Move the files Iceberg, Holiday, Logo, and New Logo to the Graphics folder.
   e. Move the files Resume and Salinas Family to the Documents folder.
   f. Move Agenda and Stationery to the Meetings folder.
   g. Switch to Details view, and write out your answers to Questions 1 through 5.

      1. What is the largest file in the Graphics folder?

      2. How many documents created with a word-processing program are in the root directory? (*Hint*: These documents will appear with the WordPad, Microsoft Word, or some other word-processing icon, depending on what software you have installed.)

      3. What is the newest file or files in the root directory? (Don't include folders.)

      4. How many files in all folders are 5KB in size?

      5. How many files in the root directory are JPEG images? (*Hint*: Look in the Type column to identify JPEG images.)

      6. Do all the files in the Graphics folder have the same icon? What type are they?

Explore

5. **Searching for a File** Windows XP Help includes topics that explain how to search for files on a disk without looking through all the folders. Start Windows Help and use one of the following methods to locate topics on searching for files.

   - On the Home page, click the Windows basics link. On the Windows basics page, click the Searching for information link, and then click the Search for a file or folder topic. In the article, click the Related Topics link, and then click Search for a file or folder.
   - On the Index page, type "files and folders" (no quotation marks) in the Type in the keyword to find text box and then click the Display button. In the list of entries for "files and folders," double-click "searching for." In the Topics found dialog box, double-click "To search for a file or folder."
   - In the Search box, type "searching for files and folders" and then press the Enter key. Click the Search for a file or folder link.

   Read the topic and click the Related Topics link at the end of the topic, if necessary, to answer Questions a through c:

   a. How do you display the Search window?
   b. Do you need to type the entire filename in the Search window to find the file?
   c. What are three file characteristics you can use as Search options?

6. **Help with Managing Files and Folders** In Tutorial 2 you learned how to work with Windows XP files and folders. Use the Index page in Windows XP Help and Support to find an overview of files and folders. Use the Related Topics link to find two procedures for managing files and folders that were not covered in the tutorial. Write out the procedures in your own words, and include the title of the Help page that contains the information.

Explore

7. **Formatting Text** You can use a word processor such as WordPad to **format** text, that is, to change its appearance by using bold, italic, and different fonts, and by applying other features. Using WordPad, type the title and words of one of your favorite songs, and then save the document on your Data Disk with the name **Song**. (Make sure to use your original Data Disk.)

   a. Select the title of the song, click the Center button ▤ on the toolbar, click the Bold button **B**, and then click the Italic button *I*.
   b. Click the list arrow for the Font button on the toolbar, and then select a different font. Repeat this step several times with different fonts until you locate a font that is appropriate for the song.
   c. Experiment with formatting options until you find a look you like for your document. Save and print the final version.

PROJECTS

1. Formatting a floppy disk removes all the data on a disk. Answer the following questions:

   a. What other method did you learn in this tutorial to remove data from a disk?
   b. If you wanted to remove all data from a disk, which method would you use? Why?
   c. What method would you use if you wanted to remove only one file? Why?

2. A friend who is new to computers is trying to learn how to enter text into WordPad. She has just finished typing her first paragraph when she notices a mistake in the first sentence. She can't remember how to fix a mistake, so she asks you for help. Write the set of steps that she should follow.

3. Computer users usually develop habits about how they access their files and programs. Take a minute to practice methods of opening a file, and then evaluate which method you would be most likely to use and why.

   a. Using WordPad, create a document containing the words to a favorite poem, and save it on your Data Disk with the name **Poem**.
   b. Close WordPad and return to the desktop.
   c. Open the document using a *docucentric* approach.
   d. After a successful completion of part c, close the program and reopen the same document using another approach.
   e. Write the steps that you used to complete parts c and d of this assignment. Then write a paragraph discussing which approach is most convenient when you are starting from the desktop, and indicate what habits you would develop if you owned your own computer and used it regularly.

Explore ▷ 4. The My Computer window gives you access to the objects on your computer. In this tutorial you used My Computer to access your floppy drive so you could view the contents of your Data Disk. The My Computer window gives you access to other objects, too. Open My Computer and write a list of the objects you see, including folders. Then double-click each icon and write a two-sentence description of the contents of each window that opens.

Explore

5. In this tutorial you learned how to copy a disk to protect yourself in the event of data loss. If you had your own computer with a 40GB hard drive that was being used to capacity, it would take many 1.44MB floppy disks to copy the contents of the entire hard drive. Is copying a reasonable method to use for protecting the data on your hard disk? Why, or why not?

a. Windows XP includes an accessory called Backup that helps you safeguard your data. Backup doesn't just copy the data, it organizes the data so that it takes up much less space than if you simply copied it. This program might not be installed on your computer, but if it is, try starting it (click the Start button, point to all Programs, point to Accessories, point to System Tools, and then click Backup) and opening the Help files to learn what you can about how it functions. If it is not installed, continue with part b.

b. Look up the topic of backups in a computer concepts textbook or in computer trade magazines. You could also interview experienced computer owners to find out which method they use to protect their data. When you have finished researching the concept of the backup, write a single-page essay that explains the difference between copying and backing up files, and that evaluates which method is preferable for backing up large amounts of data, and why.

LAB ASSIGNMENTS

Using Files In this Lab you manipulate a simulated computer to view what happens in memory and on disk when you create, save, open, revise, and delete files. Understanding what goes on "inside the box" will help you quickly grasp how to perform basic file operations with most application software. See the Read This Before You Begin page for instructions on starting the Using Files Course Lab.

1. Click the Steps button to learn how to use the simulated computer to view the contents of the memory and disk when you perform basic file operations. As you proceed through the Steps, answer all of the Quick Check questions that appear. After you complete the Steps, you will see a Quick Check Summary Report. Follow the instructions on the screen to print this report.

2. Click the Explore button and use the simulated computer to perform the following tasks:
    a. Create a document containing your name and the city in which you were born. Save this document as NAME.
    b. Create another document containing two of your favorite foods. Save this document as FOODS.
    c. Create another file containing your two favorite classes. Call this file CLASSES.
    d. Open the FOOD file and add another one of your favorite foods. Save this file without changing its name.
    e. Open the NAME file. Change this document so it contains your name and the name of your school. Save this as a new document called SCHOOL.
    f. Write down how many files are on the simulated disk and the exact contents of each file.
    g. Delete all the files.

3. In Explore, use the simulated computer to perform the following tasks.
    a. Create a file called MUSIC that contains the name of your favorite CD.
    b. Create another document that contains eight numbers, and call this file LOTTERY.
    c. You didn't win the lottery this week. Revise the contents of the LOTTERY file but save the revision as LOTTERY2.
    d. Revise the MUSIC file so it also contains the name of your favorite musician or composer, and save this file as MUSIC2.
    e. Delete the MUSIC file.
    f. Write down how many files are on the simulated disk and the exact contents of each file.

QUICK CHECK ANSWERS

Session 2.1

1. file
2. Formatting
3. True
4. insertion point
5. word wrap
6. Move the I-beam pointer to the left of the first word you want to select, and then drag the I-beam pointer over the text to the end of the last word you want to select.
7. file extension

Session 2.2

1. My Computer
2. A
3. hard
4. filename, size, type, and date modified
5. root or top-level
6. True
7. yes

New Perspectives on

WINDOWS XP

Read This Before You Begin

To the Student

Data Disks

To complete the Level II tutorials, Review Assignments, and Projects, you need three Data Disks. Your instructor will either provide you with these Data Disks or ask you to make your own.

If you are making your own Data Disks, you will need **three** blank, formatted high-density disks. You will need to copy a set of files and/or folders from a file server, standalone computer, or the Web onto your disks. Your instructor will tell you which computer, drive letter, and folders contain the files you need. You could also download the files by going to **www.course.com** and following the instructions on the screen.

The information below shows you the Data Disks you need so that you will have enough disk space to complete all the tutorials, Review Assignments, and Projects:

Data Disk 1

Write this on the disk label:
Data Disk 1: Windows XP Tutorial 3

Data Disk 2

Write this on the disk label:
Data Disk 2: Windows XP Tutorials 4 and 5

Data Disk 3

Write this on the disk label:
Data Disk 3: Windows XP Tutorial 6

When you begin each tutorial, Review Assignment, or Project, be sure you are using the correct Data Disk. Refer to the "File Finder" chart at the back of this text for more detailed information on which files are used in which tutorials. See the inside front or inside back cover of this book for more information on Data Disk files, or ask your instructor or technical support person for assistance.

Course Labs

The Windows XP Level II tutorials feature an interactive Course Lab to help you understand Internet concepts. There are Lab Assignments at the end of Tutorial 5 that relate to this Lab.

To start a Lab, click the **Start** button on the Windows taskbar, point to **Programs**, point to **Course Labs**, point to **New Perspectives Course Labs**, and then click the name of the Lab you want to use.

Using Your Own Computer

If you are going to work through this book using your own computer, you need:

- **Computer System** Microsoft Windows XP must be installed on your computer. This book assumes a typical installation of Microsoft Windows XP Professional.

- **Data Disks** You will not be able to complete the tutorials or exercises in this book using your own computer until you have your Data Disks.

- **Course Labs** See your instructor or technical support person to obtain the Course Lab software for use on your own computer.

Visit Our World Wide Web Site

Additional materials designed especially for you are available on the World Wide Web.
Go to **www.course.com/NewPerspectives**.

To the Instructor

The Data Disk Files and Course Labs are available on the Instructor's Resource Kit for this title. Follow the instructions in the Help file on the CD-ROM to install the programs to your network or standalone computer. For information on creating Data Disks or the Course Labs, see the "To the Student" section above.

You are granted a license to copy the Data Files and Course Labs to any computer or computer network used by students who have purchased this book.

OBJECTIVES

In this tutorial you will:

- View the structure of folders and files in Windows Explorer

- Select, create, and rename folders in Windows Explorer

- Navigate through devices and folders using navigation buttons

- Select a single file, a group of files, all files, or all files but one in a list of files

- Create a printout showing the structure of folders and files

- Move and copy one or more files from one location to another

- "Quick" format a floppy disk

- View files in the Favorites, Media, History, and Search Companion panes

ORGANIZING
FILES WITH WINDOWS EXPLORER

Structuring Information on a Disk for the Kolbe Climbing School

CASE

Kolbe Climbing School

Bernard Kolbe knew how to climb before he could ride a bike. In college he started what is now one of the most popular guide services in the Front Range, the Kolbe Climbing School, known to locals as "KCS." KCS offers guided climbs in the Front Range area, especially in Rocky Mountain National Park and nearby climbing areas such as Lumpy Ridge. While most clients simply want to learn rock and sport climbing, a few want guides for longer alpine climbs and ice climbing.

Until recently, Bernard maintained mostly paper records of his business activities, with some electronic records stored on the computer he used in college. When he graduated from college, his business took off, and he now has twice as many clients and employees as he did a year ago. In addition, conversations with his insurance agent and accountant have convinced him that he needs to keep more reliable and complete records on his employees, clients, and equipment. He bought a new computer and copied all his business files from his old computer to a floppy disk. Now he's ready to store and maintain these files on his new computer.

Not too long ago, Bernard asked if you could help him organize the KCS files on his floppy disk before he copies them to the new hard disk. You agreed (in exchange for some free climbing lessons) and got to work reviewing and organizing the files on his floppy disk. When Bernard first gave you the disk, all the files were stored together—you couldn't tell which files related to employee guides, for example, unless you opened them. Your first task was to create a folder structure on the disk, with separate folders for guides, clients, and gear.

This morning, you walked into the office and found that Bernard had spent yesterday evening at his new computer creating business files. You realize you need to show him the folder structure you created so he can learn to use it. You point out that an important part of electronic recordkeeping is creating and using a system that makes it easy to find important information. Bernard is willing to learn more (it's too cold to climb anyway), so you pull up a chair and offer to spend some time looking over Bernard's files.

SESSION 3.1

In this session, you will learn how Windows Explorer displays the devices and folders on your computer. Understanding how to manipulate this display is the first step in using Windows Explorer to organize files, which will make you a more productive Windows user. In this tutorial, you will work with files and folders on a floppy disk. If you have your own computer or are in a business environment, you will more likely work with files and folders on a hard disk. You will discover that file management techniques are practically the same for floppy disks and hard disks. For this tutorial, you will need the Windows XP Tutorial 3 Data Disk 1 and one blank 3½-inch disk.

Windows Explorer

Using Windows Explorer is one way to organize files. **Windows Explorer** is a program included with Windows XP that is designed to simplify file management tasks. Through an easy-to-navigate representation of the resources on your computer, Windows Explorer makes it easy to view, move, copy, or delete your files and folders.

If you have used the My Computer window, the Windows Explorer window will be familiar to you. Many of the techniques you use with the My Computer window apply to Windows Explorer—and vice-versa. Both let you display and work with files and folders. By default, however, Windows Explorer also lets you see the hierarchy of all the folders on your computer. Viewing this hierarchy makes it easier to navigate your computer, especially if it contains many files and folders.

The root directory of Bernard's floppy disk contains three folders—Clients, Gear, and Guides—plus the files he hasn't yet organized. You will use Windows Explorer to view the information stored on Bernard's disk.

Starting Windows Explorer

As with other Windows XP programs, you start Windows Explorer using the Start menu.

> ### To start Windows Explorer:
>
> 1. Insert the Windows XP Tutorial 3 Data Disk 1 in drive A, click the **Start** button
>   **start** , point to **All Programs**, point to **Accessories**, and then click **Windows Explorer**. The Windows Explorer window opens, as shown in Figure 3-1.

Figure 3-1	THE WINDOWS EXPLORER WINDOW

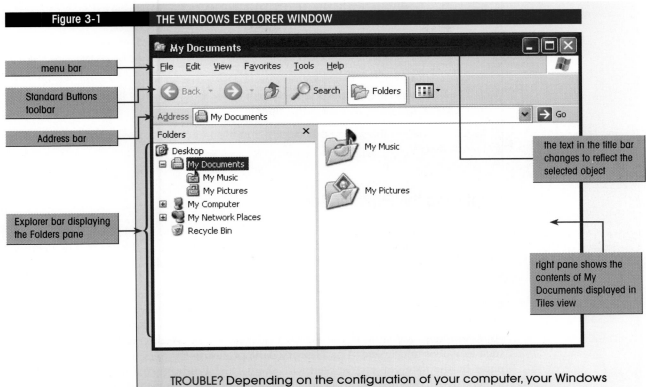

menu bar

Standard Buttons toolbar

Address bar

Explorer bar displaying the Folders pane

the text in the title bar changes to reflect the selected object

right pane shows the contents of My Documents displayed in Tiles view

TROUBLE? Depending on the configuration of your computer, your Windows Explorer window may look slightly different from the one in Figure 3-1.

2. If the Windows Explorer window is not maximized, click the **Maximize** button ▣. Figure 3-2 describes the elements of the Windows Explorer window.

Figure 3-2	THE ELEMENTS OF THE WINDOWS EXPLORER WINDOW

WINDOWS EXPLORER WINDOW ELEMENT	DESCRIPTION
Title bar	Displays the name of the currently selected object in the Windows Explorer window
Menu bar	Contains commands for working with files and folders in the Windows Explorer window
Standard Buttons toolbar	Contains buttons that provide shortcuts to common commands
Address bar	Shows the location of the active folder; you can click the list arrow on the Address bar to select a different location
Explorer bar	Appears in the left pane and can be displayed in one of five ways: as a Search, Favorites, Media, History, or Folders Pane
Folders pane	Shows the folders and files on your computer; one of five panes you can display in the left pane, also called the Explorer bar
Right pane	Shows the contents of the object selected in the left pane

Like the My Computer window, the Windows Explorer window can display the Standard Buttons, Address, and Links toolbars and a status bar. For this tutorial, you need to make sure the window displays the Standard Buttons toolbar, the Address bar, and status bar. Also make sure the Lock toolbars option is selected. To match the figures in this tutorial, you should also display the files in the right pane in Tiles view unless the steps instruct you to use a different view.

To set up the appearance of Windows Explorer:

1. Click **View** on the menu bar, and then point to **Toolbars**. Change the settings, if necessary, so that the Standard Buttons toolbar and the Address bar are the only toolbars displayed.

2. Click **View** on the menu bar and point to **Toolbars** again. If the **Lock the Toolbar** option is not checked, click to select it.

3. Click **View** on the menu bar again, and then click **Tiles** to select this option, if necessary.

Displaying the Explorer Bar

Windows Explorer is divided into two sections called **panes**. The left pane, also called the **Explorer bar**, shows different ways of locating specific files or folders on your computer. The right pane lists the contents of these files and folders (similar to the view of files and folders you had using My Computer in Tutorial 2).

You can display the Explorer bar in one of five ways: as a Search, Favorites, Media, History, or Folders pane. The **Search** pane includes tools to help you search for a particular file or folder on your computer. The **Favorites** pane lists your favorite files and folders on your computer and sites on the World Wide Web. The **Media** pane lists multimedia files, such as videos and music. The **History** pane organizes the files and folders on your computer by the date you last worked with them. The **Folders** pane organizes your files and folders based on their location in the hierarchy of objects on your computer. To move between these different panes, you click the appropriate command on the View menu. You can also quickly open the Search and Folders panes by clicking either the Search button 🔍 or the Folders button 📁 on the Standard Buttons toolbar. Note that the Explorer bar is available in any Windows XP window that displays files and folders. You can, for example, use the Explorer bar in the My Computer window.

You'll start working with Windows Explorer using the Folders pane.

To view the Folders pane:

1. Click **View** on the menu bar, and then point to **Explorer Bar**.

2. If necessary, click **Folders** to check that option; otherwise click a blank area of the screen to close the View menu. Your Windows Explorer window should now resemble Figure 3-3.

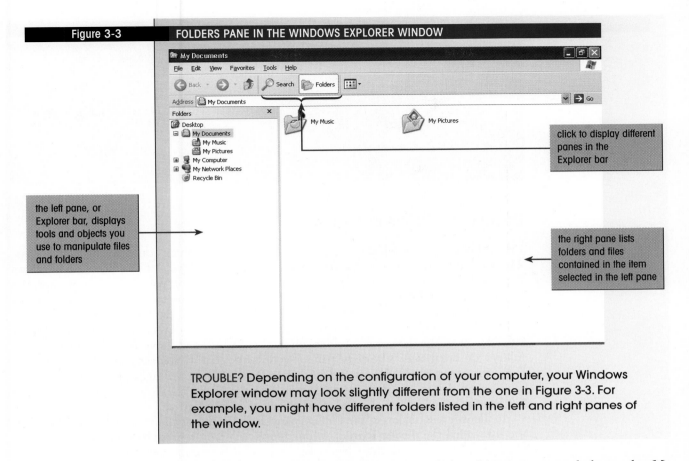

Figure 3-3	FOLDERS PANE IN THE WINDOWS EXPLORER WINDOW

TROUBLE? Depending on the configuration of your computer, your Windows Explorer window may look slightly different from the one in Figure 3-3. For example, you might have different folders listed in the left and right panes of the window.

The Folders pane initially displays a list of the objects on your desktop: the My Documents folder, the My Computer window, the My Network Places window, and the Recycle Bin. If your desktop contains other folders or objects, the pane displays those as well. The right pane of the Windows Explorer window displays the contents of the object selected in the Folders pane. In this case, the My Documents folder is the selected object, and it contains two items—the My Music and My Pictures folders. Therefore, the right pane displays icons for these objects.

Working with the Folders Pane

The Folders pane displays the devices and resources available to your computer. (You may need to scroll the Folders pane to view the complete list of objects.) Each object in the list has a small icon next to it. In this session you will use the Folders pane to explore your computer's contents. Windows Explorer uses the icons shown in Figure 3-4, among others, to represent different types of storage objects.

Figure 3-4 **STORAGE DEVICE ICONS**

ICON	REPRESENTS
	Floppy disk drive
	Hard disk drive on your computer
	CD-ROM drive
	Network disk drive
	Zip drive

Opening an Object in the Folders Pane

Like a file cabinet, a typical storage device on your computer contains files and folders. These folders can contain additional files and one or more levels of subfolders. If Windows Explorer displayed all the storage devices, folders, and files on your computer at once, the list could be very long. Instead, Windows Explorer allows you to open devices and folders only when you want to see what they contain. Otherwise, you can keep them closed.

When the Folders pane is open in the left pane of the Windows Explorer window, it provides a view of the devices and folders on your computer and shows how these devices and folders are organized. The right pane is your work area. If you select a folder in the left pane, for example, the files stored in that folder appear in the right pane. Then you can move, copy, delete, and perform other tasks with the files in the right pane, referring to the left pane to see how your changes affect the overall organization.

To identify the objects in the Folders pane, look for the small icon next to each object in the list, called the **device icon** or **folder icon**; each icon represents a device or folder on your computer. Many of these icons also have a plus box or minus box next to them, which indicates whether the device or folder contains additional folders. The device and folder icons and the plus and minus boxes are controls that you can click to change the display in the Windows Explorer window. You click the plus box to display folders or subfolders, and you click the minus box to hide them. (You can also refer to clicking the plus box as "expanding" the view of the file hierarchy and clicking the minus box as "collapsing" the view of the file hierarchy.) When you click a device or folder icon, its contents appear in the right pane.

You begin assisting Bernard by showing him how you've structured the folders on drive A, which is located in the Windows XP hierarchy beneath the My Computer icon. You explain to him how he can use the plus and minus boxes to open the My Computer icon and then the drive icon for his floppy disk.

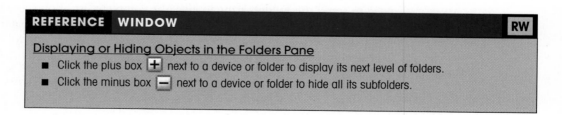

REFERENCE WINDOW **RW**

Displaying or Hiding Objects in the Folders Pane
- Click the plus box ➕ next to a device or folder to display its next level of folders.
- Click the minus box ➖ next to a device or folder to hide all its subfolders.

To display or hide the levels of folders on drive A:

1. Click the **plus box** ➕ to the left of the My Computer icon in the Folders pane.

2. Click ➕ to the left of the 3½ Floppy (A:) device icon. The folders in the root directory of drive A appear in the left pane, and the plus box in front of drive A changes to a minus box ➖. See Figure 3-5.

Figure 3-5	THE FOLDERS PANE DISPLAYING FOLDERS ON DRIVE A

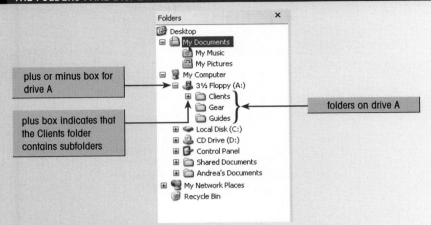

plus or minus box for drive A

plus box indicates that the Clients folder contains subfolders

folders on drive A

TROUBLE? The 3½ Floppy (A:) device icon 🖴 might appear with a different name on your computer. This is the icon representing the device that contains your Data Disk. In the steps in this tutorial, this icon is also called drive A.

TROUBLE? If you initially see a minus box to the left of the device icon for drive A, your drive A folders are already visible in the left pane. You don't need to click the icon in Step 2.

3. Click ➖ to the left of 3½ Floppy (A:). Now the Folders pane shows only drive A; it does not show the folders it contains.

4. Click ➕ to the left of 3½ Floppy (A:) one more time to redisplay the folders on the drive.

When you click the plus box ➕ next to drive A, you do not necessarily see all the folders on the drive. You only see the first level of folders. If one of these folders contains subfolders, a plus box appears next to it. The Clients folder on drive A has a plus box next to it, indicating that it contains subfolders. When you originally created the structure for Bernard's disk, you grouped his clients into Advanced and Basic, and then grouped the Advanced clients by their primary interests—Alpine, Ice, and Sport.

To view the subfolders for Clients:

1. Click ➕ next to the Clients folder. You see that Clients contains two subfolders: Advanced and Basic. Because ➕ appears next to the Advanced folder, you know it contains subfolders as well.

2. Click ➕ next to the Advanced folder. Now you see three additional subfolders: Alpine, Ice, and Sport. See Figure 3-6.

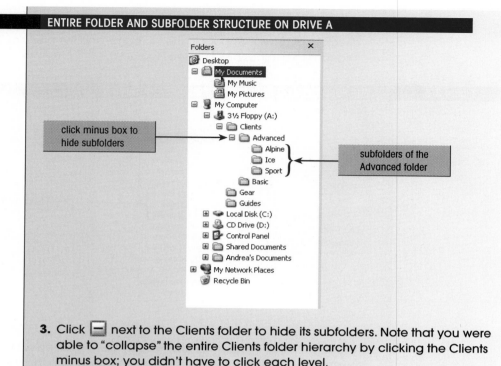

Figure 3-6   ENTIRE FOLDER AND SUBFOLDER STRUCTURE ON DRIVE A

3. Click ☐ next to the Clients folder to hide its subfolders. Note that you were able to "collapse" the entire Clients folder hierarchy by clicking the Clients minus box; you didn't have to click each level.

4. Click ☐ next to the Clients folder again. Note that the entire folder structure appears again—including the subfolders—because the last time you collapsed the Clients folder, you had all its subfolders displayed.

Using the plus and minus boxes does not select a device or folder. As you were clicking the plus and minus boxes next to the folders in drive A, the right pane still displayed the contents of the My Documents folder. To work with a device or folder in the Folders pane, you must first select its name or icon. Once selected, the device or folder appears highlighted, and the right pane displays its contents.

Selecting an Object in the Folders Pane

To select a device or folder, you must click its icon, not its plus or minus box. The selected device or folder is the one the computer uses when you take an action. For example, if you want to create a new folder on drive A, you first need to select drive A in the Folders pane. If you don't first select drive A, the new folder you create will be placed in whatever device or folder is currently selected—it could be a folder on the hard disk or network drive.

You can determine which device or folder is selected in four ways. First, it appears highlighted in the Folders pane, indicating it is selected. Also, its name appears in the Address bar and the title bar of the Windows Explorer window, and finally, its contents appear in the right pane.

You can experiment by selecting drive A and then selecting the Clients folder.

To select devices and folders:

1. Click **3½ Floppy (A:)**. Drive A is highlighted and its name appears in the Address bar and the Windows Explorer title bar. Its contents appear in the right pane.

2. Click **Clients** in the Folders pane. The computer highlights the folder name "Clients" and displays it in the Address bar and the title bar. Its contents appear in the right pane. See Figure 3-7.

Figure 3-7	THE SELECTED DEVICE OR FOLDER IN THE FOLDERS PANE

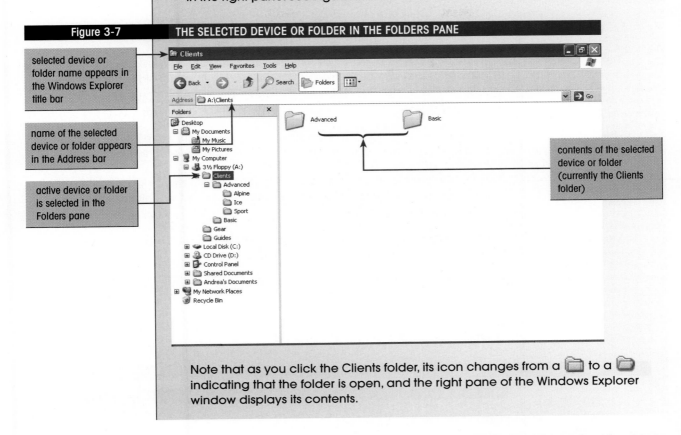

selected device or folder name appears in the Windows Explorer title bar

name of the selected device or folder appears in the Address bar

active device or folder is selected in the Folders pane

contents of the selected device or folder (currently the Clients folder)

Note that as you click the Clients folder, its icon changes from a 🗀 to a 🗁 indicating that the folder is open, and the right pane of the Windows Explorer window displays its contents.

Bernard tracks gear usage for ropes and other types of equipment such as karabiners, belay plates, and so on. His disk already contains a folder named Gear that contains files for each of the KCS ropes. Next, you decide to create two new subfolders within the Gear folder: one for all files having to do with ropes and the other for files having to do with hardware equipment.

Creating a New Folder

You can create a new folder using the New command on the File menu. You just have to make sure that you've first selected the location for the new folder in the Folders pane before creating the new folder.

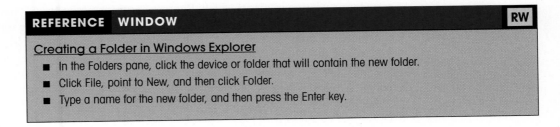

REFERENCE WINDOW   **RW**

Creating a Folder in Windows Explorer
- In the Folders pane, click the device or folder that will contain the new folder.
- Click File, point to New, and then click Folder.
- Type a name for the new folder, and then press the Enter key.

The Clients folder is currently selected. If you create a new folder now, it will become a subfolder of Clients. Because you want to create the two subfolders in the Gear folder, you must first select the Gear folder.

To create the new subfolders within the Gear folder:

1. Click **Gear** in the Folders pane to select it.

2. Click **File** on the menu bar, point to **New**, and then click **Folder**. A folder icon labeled "New Folder" appears in the right pane. The folder name is selected. You can now type an appropriate name for the new folder.

   TROUBLE? If the folder name is not selected, you might have clicked to deselect it. Click the folder and then click it a second time to select the folder name.

3. Type **Hardware** as the title of the new folder, press the **Enter** key and then click a blank area of the right pane. Now create the second subfolder of the Gear folder for all the rope files.

   TROUBLE? If you pressed Enter twice by mistake, Hardware becomes the selected folder. Be sure the Gear folder is still selected.

4. Click **File**, point to **New**, click **Folder**, type **Ropes** as the name of the second folder, and then press the **Enter** key.

5. If necessary, click ⊞ next to the Gear folder in the left pane to see the new folders in the left pane. See Figure 3-8.

| Figure 3-8 | CREATING NEW FOLDERS |

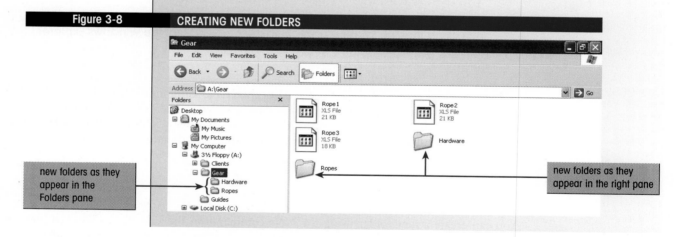

new folders as they appear in the Folders pane

new folders as they appear in the right pane

As you and Bernard go over the current folder structure, you realize that a complete inventory of the KCS gear also includes the harnesses climbers wear to attach themselves to the rope for protection in case they fall. Because harnesses aren't considered hardware, you decide that the harness inventory files should go in the same folder with the ropes. Thus, you need to rename the Ropes folder "Ropes and Harnesses." You rename a folder by right-clicking the folder icon in either the Folders pane or the right pane and then clicking the Rename command on the shortcut menu. You can also rename a folder by selecting the folder, clicking File on the menu bar, and then clicking Rename, or by clicking a folder name twice (more slowly than double-clicking) until a blinking insertion point appears in the folder name, indicating you can edit it. Then, you type the new text and press the Enter key.

To rename the Ropes folder, you'll try the right-clicking method.

To change the name of the Ropes folder:

1. Right-click **Ropes** in the Folders pane.

2. Click **Rename** on the shortcut menu. The folder name is selected and ready for you to rename.

3. Type **Ropes and Harnesses** as the new folder name, and then press the **Enter** key.

The new folder name now appears in both the left and right panes. If you cannot see the full name, you can adjust the width of the Explorer bar. You'll show Bernard how to do this next.

Adjusting the Width of the Explorer Bar

As you create or view more levels of folders, the Explorer bar might not be wide enough to display all the levels of folders in the Folders pane, especially if the folder names are long. As a result, you might not be able to see all the device and folder icons. You can change the width of the Windows Explorer window panes by dragging the dividing bar that separates the two panes.

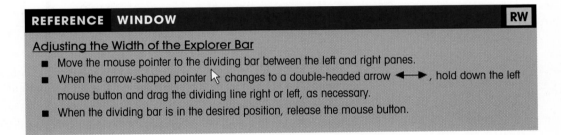

REFERENCE WINDOW   **RW**

Adjusting the Width of the Explorer Bar
- Move the mouse pointer to the dividing bar between the left and right panes.
- When the arrow-shaped pointer ▹ changes to a double-headed arrow ◄──►, hold down the left mouse button and drag the dividing line right or left, as necessary.
- When the dividing bar is in the desired position, release the mouse button.

To increase the width of the Explorer bar:

1. Move the mouse pointer to the vertical dividing bar between the two panes. The ▹ pointer changes to a ◄──► pointer.

2. Hold down the left mouse button while you drag the dividing bar about one-half inch to the right, as shown in Figure 3-9.

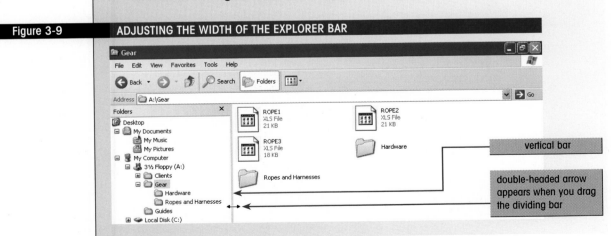

Figure 3-9   **ADJUSTING THE WIDTH OF THE EXPLORER BAR**

3. Release the mouse button. The Explorer bar is now wider and will allow you to see more of the items listed in the Folders pane. The next time you open the Windows Explorer window, the Explorer bar will have the same width.

TROUBLE? If your instructor wants you to return the Explorer bar to its original width, drag the dividing bar about one-half inch to the left when you finish this tutorial.

4. Click the **Close** button ☒ to close the Windows Explorer window. You return to the Windows XP desktop.

You have now shown Bernard how to use Windows Explorer to view the files, folders, and devices on his computer, and how to create new folders for storing files. In the next session, you will show Bernard how the right pane in Windows Explorer can be used to organize the files and folders on his computer.

Session 3.1 QUICK | CHECK

1. _____ is an alternative to using My Computer for file management tasks.

2. The Windows Explorer window is divided into two panes. Describe each pane, using one sentence for each pane.

3. True or False: If you see folders with the same names in both the right and left panes of the Windows Explorer window, the folders are duplicates and you should erase those in the right pane.

4. True or False: The Folders pane displays all the files in a folder.

5. A folder that is contained in another folder is referred to as a(n) _____.

6. You click the _____ to expand the display of folders in the Folders pane.

7. If you want to create a new folder on drive A, what should you first click in the Folders pane?

8. True or False: The Explorer bar exists only in Windows Explorer. You cannot use the Explorer bar in the My Computer window.

SESSION 3.2

In Session 3.2, you will work with the right pane of the Windows Explorer window, which you use to work with the files on your computer. You'll learn how to select multiple files in the right pane. You'll work with different methods of moving and copying files from one location to another. You'll also see how to print a copy of the Windows Explorer window to use as a reference.

Working with Files in the Right Pane of Windows Explorer

Now that you've worked with the Folders pane, it's time to put the right pane of Windows Explorer to use. Recall that the Folders pane shows how your devices and folders are arranged in a hierarchy on your computer. You've already used the Folders pane to create a folder structure for Bernard's files. The left pane, however, doesn't show files. When you want to manipulate files in your devices and folders—to move, copy, rename, or delete them, for example—you work in the right pane. You'll work in the right pane to move Bernard's files into different folders. To do this, you'll learn how to select and work with multiple files using the right pane of the Windows Explorer window.

Working with files listed in the right pane is exactly like working with files listed in the My Computer window or any Windows XP dialog box or window that displays a list of files. You can use the View command to determine the way the right pane displays files and objects, switching from Tiles view to Details or Thumbnails view. You can click the Back ⬅, Forward ➡, and Up ⬆ buttons located on the Standard Buttons toolbar to navigate through the hierarchy of objects in your computer. (When you use these buttons, the view of your computer's contents changes in both the left and right panes.) You can open a file by double-clicking its icon. You can rename a file by right-clicking its icon and choosing the Rename command from the shortcut menu. You also use the same techniques to select files with which to work.

Selecting Multiple Files

You select a file by clicking the file's icon in the right pane of the Windows Explorer window. You can also select multiple files from the right pane, using one of several techniques. Suppose you want to select all the files in a folder or all the folders and files on your floppy disk. You can easily do this using the Select All command on the Edit menu.

To select all of the files in the root directory:

1. Make sure your Data Disk is in drive A, and then start Windows Explorer. Set up Windows Explorer so that the Standard Buttons toolbar, Address bar, and Folders pane are all visible.

2. Locate and click 3½ **Floppy (A)** in the Folders pane to display the contents of the root directory of drive A in the right pane.

3. Click **View** on the menu bar, and then click **Details** to display the file icons in Details view. In this view, you can see the complete contents of your Data Disk, so you'll know at a glance when everything is selected.

4. Click **Edit** on the menu bar, and then click **Select All**. (Note that you also can click Ctrl+A to select all the files in the list.) Windows Explorer highlights the files and folders on drive A to show that they are selected. See Figure 3-10.

Figure 3-10   **SELECTING ALL THE FILES IN A FOLDER**

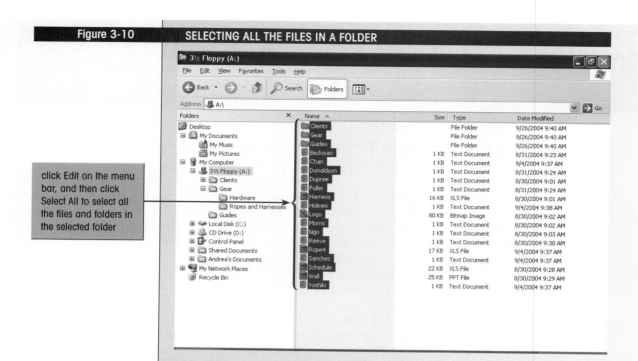

click Edit on the menu bar, and then click Select All to select all the files and folders in the selected folder

5. Deselect the files by clicking any blank area of the window. The highlighting is removed to indicate that no files are currently selected.

What if you want to work with more than one file, but not with all the files in a folder? For example, suppose Bernard wants to delete three of the files in a folder. In Windows Explorer, you can select a group of files in two ways. You can select files listed consecutively using the Shift key, or you can select files scattered throughout the right pane using the Ctrl key. Figure 3-11 shows the two different ways to select a group of files.

Figure 3-11   **TWO WAYS TO SELECT A GROUP OF FILES**

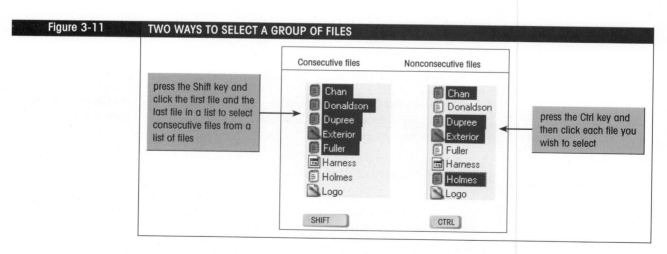

press the Shift key and click the first file and the last file in a list to select consecutive files from a list of files

press the Ctrl key and then click each file you wish to select

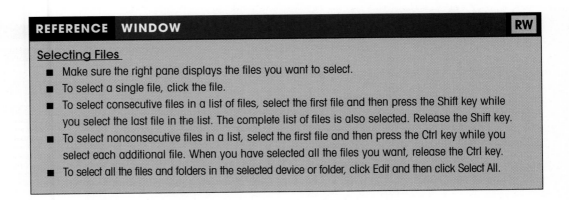

Selecting Files
- Make sure the right pane displays the files you want to select.
- To select a single file, click the file.
- To select consecutive files in a list of files, select the first file and then press the Shift key while you select the last file in the list. The complete list of files is also selected. Release the Shift key.
- To select nonconsecutive files in a list, select the first file and then press the Ctrl key while you select each additional file. When you have selected all the files you want, release the Ctrl key.
- To select all the files and folders in the selected device or folder, click Edit and then click Select All.

First try selecting a set of consecutive files, and then select a set of nonconsecutive files listed within a folder.

To select groups of files:

1. Make sure the right pane displays the root directory of drive A, and then click the **Beckman** file.

2. Press the **Shift** key while you click the **Fuller** file. Release the **Shift** key. The Beckman and Fuller files and all files in between are selected. See Figure 3-12.

Figure 3-12   **SELECTING CONSECUTIVE FILES**

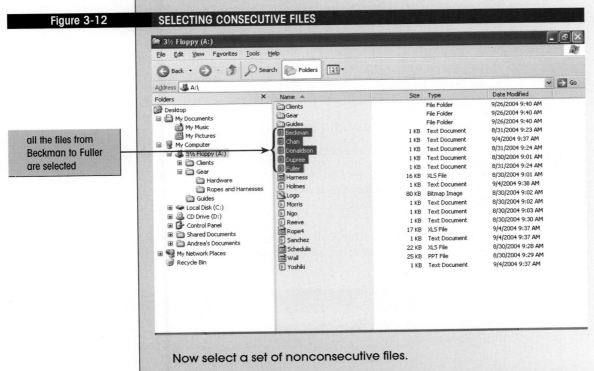

Now select a set of nonconsecutive files.

3. Click the **Reeve** file. Notice that selecting this file automatically deselects any selected files.

4. Press the **Ctrl** key and select the **Morris** file and then the **Sanchez** file. Release the **Ctrl** key. All three files are now selected. See Figure 3-13.

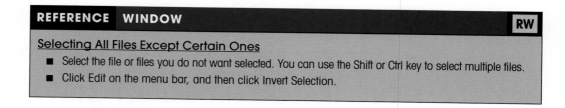

Figure 3-13

SELECTING NONCONSECUTIVE FILES

press the Ctrl key as you click each file

TROUBLE? If you release the Ctrl key by mistake while selecting a set of nonconsecutive files, press it again and select the files you want.

While selecting multiple files with the Ctrl key, you can deselect any file by clicking it again while pressing the Ctrl key. You can also select more files by pressing the Ctrl key again, then selecting the additional files.

To select and deselect additional files:

1. Press the **Ctrl** key and click the **Chan** file to select it. Four files are now selected.

2. Continue to press the **Ctrl** key, and click the **Sanchez** file to deselect it. Release the **Ctrl** key. Now three files are selected: Chan, Morris, and Reeve.

Suppose you want to select all the files in a folder except one. You can use the Invert Selection menu option to select all the files that are not selected.

REFERENCE WINDOW   **RW**

Selecting All Files Except Certain Ones

■ Select the file or files you do not want selected. You can use the Shift or Ctrl key to select multiple files.

■ Click Edit on the menu bar, and then click Invert Selection.

To use Invert Selection to select all files except Dupree:

1. Click the **Dupree** file.

2. Click **Edit** on the menu bar, and then click **Invert Selection**. All the folders and files except Dupree are now selected.

3. Click a blank area to deselect the files on drive A.

You are almost ready to start moving Bernard's files into the appropriate folders. Bernard first wants to identify the files that need to be moved. He wonders if there's a quick way to get a hard copy (that is, a paper copy) of the Windows Explorer window so he can write on it.

Printing the Windows Explorer Window

In Windows XP you can temporarily store an image of your computer screen in memory using the Print Screen key. Then you can start the WordPad program and paste the image into a blank WordPad document. Finally, you can print the document, which will contain an image of your screen. Bernard would like to have a hard copy of the hierarchy of files and folders currently on his floppy disk. You can use the Print Screen key to capture an image of the Windows Explorer window displaying the contents of the disk.

To print the Windows Explorer window:

1. In the Folders pane, click ⊞ next to 3½ Floppy (A:), Clients, Advanced, and Gear as necessary so that all the folders and subfolders on Bernard's disk are visible in the left pane.

2. Press the **Print Screen** key. Although no visual cue appears on screen, an image of the Windows Explorer window is stored in your computer's memory.

TROUBLE? If you cannot locate the Print Screen key, it might be accessible through another key on your keyboard or it might be labeled with an abbreviation such as "PrtScn." Ask your instructor or technical support person for help.

3. Start WordPad.

4. Maximize the WordPad window if necessary, type your name and the date on separate lines at the top of the WordPad window, and then press the **Enter** key twice.

5. Click the **Paste** button 📋 to insert the image of the Windows Explorer window into the document, and then scroll to the top of the document (also scroll left, if necessary). The image of the Windows Explorer window appears in the WordPad document. See Figure 3-14.

| Figure 3-14 | WINDOWS EXPLORER SCREEN IMAGE IN WORDPAD |

image of the
Windows Explorer
window in WordPad

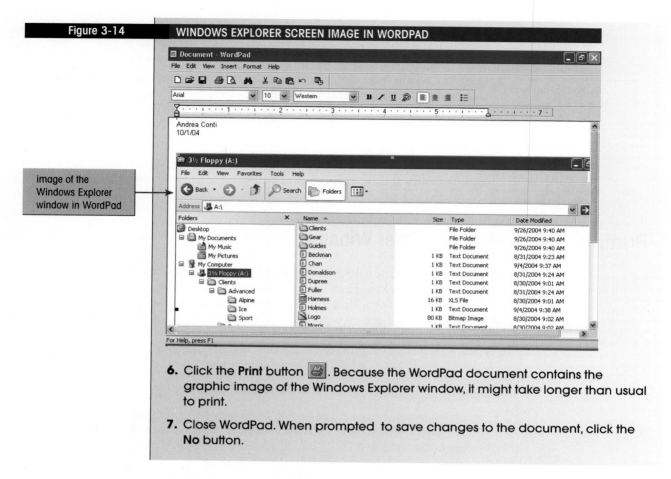

6. Click the **Print** button 🖨. Because the WordPad document contains the graphic image of the Windows Explorer window, it might take longer than usual to print.

7. Close WordPad. When prompted to save changes to the document, click the **No** button.

Bernard annotates the printout of the Windows Explorer window as shown in Figure 3-15. His notes show you which files to move into folders on the root directory.

| Figure 3-15 | BERNARD'S PRINTOUT |

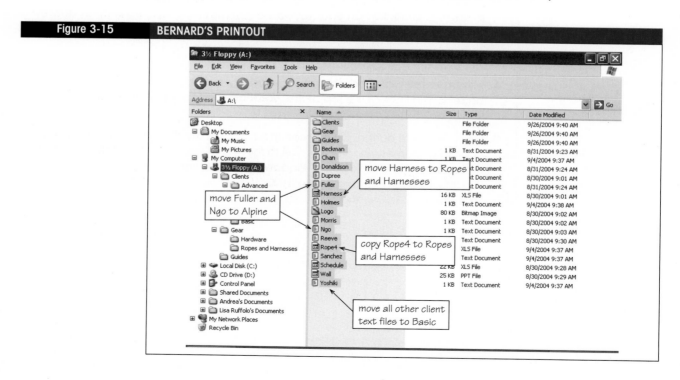

Moving Files in Windows Explorer

You've already had some experience in moving files. You saw in Tutorial 2 how you could right-click an object in My Computer and drag it into a folder on a floppy disk, choosing whether to copy or move the file. Moving files in Windows Explorer is exactly the same, except that you have the added benefit of using the Folders pane to navigate the hierarchy of Windows XP objects while still being able to view the files you are moving in the right pane. Because the Folders pane can display a detailed tree of folders and devices, you can easily move a file to almost any location on your computer.

Bernard has already marked the printout you created to show which files you need to move. You begin by moving the Harness file from the root directory to the Equipment folder.

To move the Harness file:

1. Make sure that the 3½ Floppy (A:) drive is selected in the Folders pane and that the Hardware and the Ropes and Harnesses subfolders of the Gears folder are also visible.

2. Hold down the right mouse button while you drag the **Harness** file icon from the right pane to the **Ropes and Harnesses** folder in the left pane, as shown in Figure 3-16.

Figure 3-16	MOVING A SINGLE FILE USING THE FOLDERS PANE

drag Harness with the right mouse button until the Ropes and Harnesses folder is selected

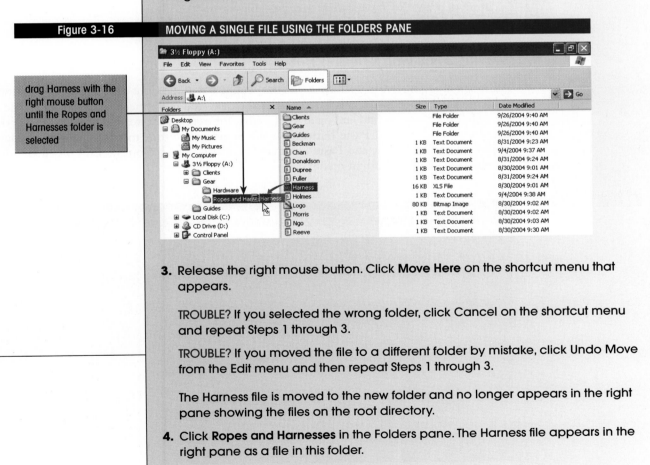

3. Release the right mouse button. Click **Move Here** on the shortcut menu that appears.

   TROUBLE? If you selected the wrong folder, click Cancel on the shortcut menu and repeat Steps 1 through 3.

   TROUBLE? If you moved the file to a different folder by mistake, click Undo Move from the Edit menu and then repeat Steps 1 through 3.

   The Harness file is moved to the new folder and no longer appears in the right pane showing the files on the root directory.

4. Click **Ropes and Harnesses** in the Folders pane. The Harness file appears in the right pane as a file in this folder.

Bernard recently purchased a fourth rope, and he is tracking its use in the file named Rope4. He wants a copy of the Rope4 file in the Ropes and Harnesses folder. You can also drag with the right mouse button to copy files.

To copy the Rope4 file into the Ropes folder:

1. Click **3½ Floppy (A:)** in the Folders pane to display the files in the root directory in the right pane.

2. Hold down the right mouse button while you drag the **Rope4** icon from the root directory to the **Ropes and Harnesses** folder.

3. Make sure the Ropes and Harnesses folder is selected, and then release the right mouse button.

4. Click **Copy Here** on the shortcut menu. Rope4 is copied from the root directory to the Ropes and Harnesses folder. Notice that Rope4 is still listed in the right pane for drive A because you copied the file rather than moved it.

5. Click **Ropes and Harnesses** in the Folders pane, and notice that Rope4 now appears in this folder along with the Harness file.

Bernard wants to move the three rope files from the Gear folder to the Ropes and Harnesses folder. You can do this next using the cut-and-paste technique.

Moving Files with Cut and Paste

Although dragging works well when you can see the file in the right pane and its destination folder in the Folders pane, this is not always the case. You might need to navigate the folders in left pane first to find and open a subfolder, for example. Instead of dragging, you can use the Cut, Copy, and Paste buttons on the Standard Buttons toolbar to move or copy objects. The Cut, Copy, and Paste commands are also available on the Edit menu and on the selected objects' shortcut menus.

REFERENCE WINDOW   **RW**

<u>Moving or Copying Files with Cut, Copy, and Paste</u>
- Select the file or files you want to copy or move.
- Click the Cut command on the Edit menu to move the files, or click the Copy command on the Edit menu to copy the selected file(s).
- Select the device or folder in which you want to place the copied or cut files.
- Click Edit on the menu bar, and then click the Paste command.
  or
- Select the file or files you want to copy or move.
- Right-click the selected file or files.
- Click the Cut command on the shortcut menu to move the files, or click the Copy command on the shortcut menu to copy the files.
- Right-click the device or folder into which you want to place the copied or cut files.
- Click the Paste command on the shortcut menu.

The rope files Bernard wants to move are listed consecutively, so you should use the Shift key to select these three files and move them as a group. You can then use the Cut and Paste commands to move the files.

To move the rope files to the Ropes and Harnesses folder:

1. Click the **Gear** folder in the left pane to select the Gear folder and view the other rope files, which also need to be moved into the Ropes and Harnesses folder. Switch to Details view, if necessary.

2. Select the three rope files, **Rope1**, **Rope2**, and **Rope3**.

3. Click **Edit** on the menu bar, and then click **Cut**.

4. Click the **Ropes and Harnesses** folder in the Folders pane.

5. Click **Edit** on the menu bar, and then click **Paste** to move the files to the Ropes and Harnesses folder. The Ropes and Harnesses folder now contains Harness, Rope1, Rope2, Rope3, and Rope4.

If you cut or copy a file or set of files but then neglect to paste them into a destination folder, you won't lose the files. Windows Explorer doesn't actually carry out the cut or copy until you paste. It stores the files on the Clipboard and in their original location until you finish moving or copying the files. If you close Windows Explorer without pasting a file, the file remains in its original position.

Using the Move To Folder and Copy To Folder Commands

Now that you've organized Bernard's gear files, it's time to look at the new client files he added. Mark Fuller and George Ngo are interested exclusively in alpine climbing, so you'll move the Fuller and Ngo client files into the Alpine folder. If you want to move these files without navigating many folders and subfolders in the Folders pane, you can do so with the Move To Folder and Copy To Folder commands. These commands open a dialog box you can use to navigate directly to the folder where you want to move or copy the files.

REFERENCE WINDOW   RW

Moving or Copying Files with the Move To Folder and Copy To Folder Commands

- Select the file or files you want to move.
- Click Edit on the menu bar, and then click Move To Folder.
- In the Move Items dialog box, locate and click the folder to which you want to move the files.
- Click the Move button.
  or
- Select the file or files you want to copy.
- Click Edit on the menu bar, and then click Copy To Folder.
- In the Copy Items dialog box, locate and click the folder to which you want to copy the files.
- Click the Copy button.

Try this technique now by moving the Fuller and Ngo files into the Alpine folder.

To move files using the Move To command:

1. Click **3½ Floppy (A:)** in the Folders pane to display the files on the floppy disk's root directory. Switch to Details view, if necessary.

2. Select the **Fuller** and **Ngo** files.

3. Click **Edit** on the menu bar, and then click **Move To Folder**.

The Move Items dialog box opens and displays the hierarchy of objects and folders on your computer.

4. If necessary, click ⊞ next to the My Computer icon to display the contents of that object.

5. Move through the rest of the hierarchy of objects by clicking ⊞ next to the 3½ Floppy (A:) icon and then clicking the ⊞ boxes next to the Clients and the Advanced folders.

6. Click the **Alpine** folder to select it. The Move Items dialog box should look like the one shown in Figure 3-17.

| Figure 3-17 | MOVING FILES USING THE MOVE TO FOLDER COMMAND |

if you click the Make New Folder button, you can create a new folder and then move files into that folder

7. Click the **Move** button to move the files into the Alpine folder. The Move Items dialog box closes, and you return to the Windows Explorer window.

8. Locate and click **Alpine** in the Folders pane to confirm that the Ngo and Fuller files have been moved to that location. (There should now be five files.)

You need to move the remaining client files from the root directory into the Basic folder. You can combine some of the methods you have already learned to complete this task most efficiently.

Moving Files of Similar Type

If you are working in Details view, you'll see that the client files (the ones with people's names) are all text files. If you arrange these files by type, they'll all be next to each other, so you can select them as a group and move them together to the Basic folder. You'll use the technique of cutting and pasting to accomplish this task.

To move a group of related files to a new folder:

1. Click 3½ **Floppy (A:)** in the left pane to display the files of the floppy drive's root directory in the right pane.

2. If necessary, switch to Details view.

3. Click the **Type** button at the top of the file list. The client text files are now grouped together.

   TROUBLE? The Type button is at the top of the third column under the Address Bar in the right pane.

4. Select the **Beckman** and **Yoshiki** text files and all the files in between.

5. Right-click the selected files, click **Cut** on the shortcut menu, right-click **Basic** in the Folders pane, and then click **Paste** on the shortcut menu. The files move from the root directory into the Basic folder.

Bernard's disk is now reorganized, with the appropriate files in the Gear and Client folders.

Moving or Copying Files Between Drives

So far all the moving and copying you've done has been within a single drive—the floppy drive. Often you will want to move or copy files from one drive to another, for example, from your floppy drive to your hard disk, or from one floppy drive to another. You can do this using the same techniques you've learned so far: dragging with the right mouse button, using cut and paste, and so forth.

Bernard has one more file on his disk he needs to move—a PowerPoint file named Wall. This file contains a slide presentation for the local Parks and Recreation Department, proposing the construction of an indoor climbing wall. Bernard needs to fine-tune this presentation and also wants you to review it and make suggestions. Bernard wants to work with the file on his hard disk and also wants you to have a copy to work with on your home computer.

Moving Files from the Floppy to the Hard Disk

In addition to using Windows Explorer to copy and move files between folders, you can also use this tool to move and copy files from different devices on your computer, such as from the floppy disk to the hard disk. So that Bernard can work with the Wall file on his hard disk, you will show him how to move the file from his floppy disk to his hard disk. Also, you notice that none of the current KCS folders—Clients, Gear, or Guides—is appropriate for storing the climbing presentation. As you move Bernard's Wall file to the hard disk, you also will create a new folder named "Presentations."

To move a file from a floppy disk to a new folder on the hard disk:

1. If necessary, scroll the left pane to display the icon for drive C.

2. Click **My Documents** in the Folders pane.

3. Click **File** on the menu bar, point to **New**, and then click **Folder** to create a new folder in the My Documents folder.

TROUBLE? If a message warns you that you cannot create a folder on drive C, you might be working on a computer that restricts hard disk access. Ask your instructor or technical support person about other options for working on a hard disk, and read through the rest of this section to learn how you would work on a hard disk if you had the opportunity.

4. Type **Presentations** as the name of the new folder, and then press the **Enter** key.

TROUBLE? If there is already a Presentations folder on the hard disk, you must specify a different name. Use the name "Presentation" with your initials, such as "PresentationJP." Substitute this folder name for the Presentations folder for the rest of this tutorial.

5. Click **3½ Floppy (A:)** in the Folders pane (you might have to scroll to see it) to display its contents in the right pane.

6. Right-click the **Wall** file in the right pane.

7. Click **Cut** on the shortcut menu. Locate and then right-click the **Presentations** folder in the Folders pane. (You might have to scroll to see it.)

8. Click **Paste** on the shortcut menu.

9. Click the **Presentations** folder in the Folders pane, if necessary, to ensure that the Wall file was copied onto the hard disk.

Recall that Bernard wants to give you a copy of the Wall file on another floppy disk, so you can take it home and review it. To do this, you will need one 3½-inch floppy disk that is either blank or contains files you no longer need.

Preparing a Data Disk with Quick Format

When you want to erase the contents of a floppy disk, you can use the Quick format option rather than the Full format that you use on a new disk. A Quick format takes less time than a Full format because, instead of preparing the entire disk surface, a Quick format erases the file allocation table. The **file allocation table (FAT)** contains information that your operating system uses to track the locations of all the files on the disk. By erasing the FAT, you erase all the information that tells the computer about the files on the disk, and so the disk appears empty to the computer. Note that to delete only a few files from a floppy disk, you don't need to format the disk; you can just select the files (as you'll learn later in this tutorial) and delete them.

To Quick format a disk:

1. Write "Windows XP Tutorial 3 Data Disk—Disk 2" on the label of your disk.

2. Place your disk in drive A.

3. Right-click the 3½ **Floppy (A:)** icon in the Folders pane.

4. Click **Format** on the shortcut menu to open the Format 3½ Floppy (A:) dialog box.

5. Click the **Quick Format** check box, as shown in Figure 3-18.

Figure 3-18	FORMAT DIALOG BOX

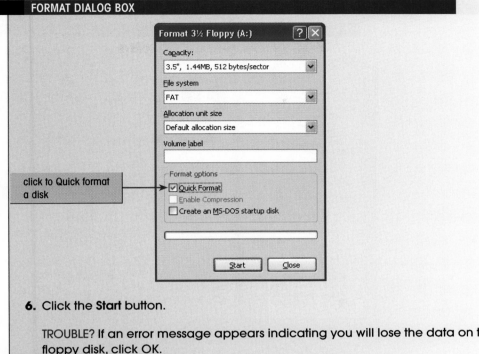

6. Click the **Start** button.

   TROUBLE? If an error message appears indicating you will lose the data on the floppy disk, click OK.

   TROUBLE? If an error message appears indicating your disk capacity might be double-density, click OK, then replace the disk in the drive with a high-density disk, and repeat Steps 3 through 7.

7. Wait a few moments until an information box opens indicating that formatting is complete. Click the **OK** button and then click the **Close** button on the Format 3½ Floppy (A:) dialog box.

You can now copy Bernard's Wall file from the hard disk onto the newly formatted disk.

Copying a File from the Hard Disk to the Floppy Drive

To move a file from the hard disk to the destination disk, you can use the Send To command. The Send To command provides a simple one-click method of sending any file on your computer's hard disk to your floppy drive. (You can also use the Send To command to send files to other locations on your computer, such as the desktop.) Be aware, however, that the Send To command can only send files to the root directory of the floppy drive; you cannot direct a file to a specific folder within the floppy drive.

Now that you've moved the Wall file from Bernard's floppy disk to the hard disk, you can use the Send To command to copy the file to the floppy disk you just formatted.

To copy a file from the hard disk to a floppy disk:

1. Select the **Presentations** folder in the Folders pane of Windows Explorer, if necessary.

2. Right-click the **Wall** file in the right pane, and then point to **Send To** on the shortcut menu. See Figure 3-19.

Figure 3-19	COPY A FILE TO THE FLOPPY DISK WITH THE SEND TO COMMAND

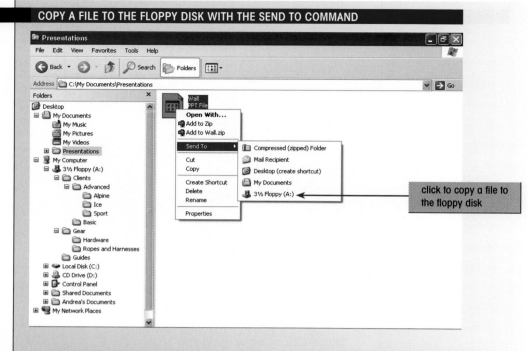

3. Click 3½ **Floppy (A:)** on the shortcut menu. The file should now be copied onto the floppy disk.

4. Click 3½ **Floppy (A:)** in the Folders pane, make sure the Wall file is safely on the disk, and then remove the Data Disk 2 from drive A.

5. Place your Windows XP Tutorial 3 Data Disk 1 back in drive A, click **View** on the menu bar, and then click **Refresh** to view the files on Data Disk 1.

You just showed Bernard how to move a file from a floppy disk to a hard disk and then copy the file to another floppy disk. Suppose you want to copy a file from one floppy disk to another. Most computers have only one floppy disk drive, so you cannot use Windows Explorer to drag a file from one floppy disk to another. If you worked through Tutorial 2, you learned how to copy the contents of one floppy disk to another using the Copy Disk command. However, that technique is useful only if you want to copy *all* the files from one floppy disk to another. To copy one file from a floppy disk to another, you first copy the file from the first floppy disk—the source disk—to a temporary location on the hard disk, and then you insert the second floppy disk—the destination disk—into drive A. Finally, you move the file from the hard disk to the destination floppy disk. You can use this same technique to copy more than one file from one floppy to another. Figure 3-20 shows this procedure.

| Figure 3-20 | COPYING A FILE TO THE HARD DISK AND THEN TO A DIFFERENT FLOPPY DISK |

If you are working in a computer lab, you should delete the Presentations folder to avoid cluttering the hard disk with unnecessary files. You can do so easily by simply removing the Presentations folder from drive C. If you weren't able to move any files to drive C, you can skip these steps.

To delete the Presentations folder from drive C:

1. Right-click the **Presentations** folder in the Folders pane.

2. Click **Delete** on the shortcut menu. The Confirm Folder Delete message box opens.

   TROUBLE? If a message appears telling you that you cannot perform this operation, your system administrator might have restricted user privileges. Continue reading the rest of the instructions to understand the process.

3. Make sure the Confirm Folder Delete message indicates that the Presentations folder will be moved to the Recycle Bin, and then click the Yes button to delete the folder from the hard disk.

   TROUBLE? If a different filename appears in the Confirm Folder Delete dialog box, click the No button and repeat Steps 1 through 3.

4. Click the Close button ☒ to close the Windows Explorer window. You return to the Windows XP desktop.

You look over the structure of folders and files on Bernard's disk and realize that, as his business increases, this structure will become increasingly useful. You've used the power of Windows Explorer to simplify tasks such as locating, moving, copying, and deleting files. You can apply these skills to larger file management challenges when you are using a computer of your own and need to organize and work with the files on your hard disk.

Session 3.2 QUICK CHECK

1. When you select files, you hold down the _____ key to select consecutive files, whereas you hold down the _____ key to select nonconsecutive files.

2. What is the difference between the left pane (the Folders pane) and the right pane in the Windows Explorer window?

3. How can you make a printout of your computer screen?

4. You can move files to a particular folder by using the _____ command on the Edit menu.

5. True or False: Using a hard disk for temporary storage, you can copy a file from one floppy disk to another even if you only have one floppy disk drive in your computer.

6. If you want to copy a file from your hard disk directly to the root directory of your floppy disk (without navigating the hierarchy of Windows XP objects), what command can you use?

SESSION 3.3

In this session, you'll learn how to use the Favorites, Media, History, and Search Companion panes in Windows Explorer. You'll learn how to add files to your Favorites list and view multimedia files in the Media pane. You'll view a list of recently opened files with the History pane and then search for a file you opened recently using the Search Companion pane.

Working with the Favorites Pane

If you want quick access to files and folders, such as those you use often, you can add them to the Favorites pane. Then you can open the Favorites pane in the Windows Explorer window and click a folder in the Favorites pane to see its contents in the right pane, or click a file in the Favorites pane to open the file. For example, if you frequently work with a to-do list file in a subfolder, you could add the to-do list to the Favorites pane. Instead of navigating from one folder to another until you find the to-do list, you can open the Favorites pane and then click the to-do list file to open it.

The Favorites pane is only an organizational tool. Unlike the Folders pane, which reflects the structure of the folders on your computer, the Favorites pane lists only links to files and folders, not the actual location of files and folders themselves. When you add a file to the Favorites pane, a link to the file is actually what appears in the Favorites pane; the file itself remains in its original location.

You can also organize the Favorites pane to make it easier to work with, especially if it lists many files. You can create a folder in the Favorites pane and then group the links to files within it.

Bernard is planning to devote some time next week to creating a spring schedule for Alpine climbing expeditions. You ask him to identify the folders and files he'll work with most often as he prepares the schedule. Then you will add links to these items in the Favorites pane of the Windows Explorer window.

Adding a Folder to the Favorites Pane

To add a folder to the Favorites pane, you open the folder in Windows Explorer, click Favorites on the menu bar, and then click Add to Favorites. After you open the folder, you can also open the Favorites pane, and then click the Add to Favorites button in the Favorites pane.

Bernard wants the Favorites pane to include a link to the Alpine folder. As he creates his schedule for spring climbing expeditions, he will reference this folder often because it contains files for clients who are most likely to participate. The Alpine folder is a subfolder of the Advanced folder, which is contained in the Clients folder. Adding the Alpine folder to the Favorites pane means Bernard can open the folder without navigating three levels of folders.

You explain to Bernard that you'll navigate to the Alpine folder first and then open the Favorites pane to get familiar with it. Then you'll use the Add to Favorites button to add the Alpine folder link to the Favorites pane.

To add a folder to the Favorites pane:

1. Make sure your Data Disk 1 is in the appropriate drive, and then open Windows Explorer.

2. Use the Folders pane to navigate to the Alpine folder on your Data Disk. Click the **Alpine** folder to see its contents in the right pane.

3. Click **View** on the menu bar, point to **Explorer Bar**, and then click **Favorites**. The Favorites pane opens in the Windows Explorer window, replacing the Folders pane. See Figure 3-21.

Figure 3-21	THE FAVORITES PANE IN THE WINDOWS EXPLORER WINDOW

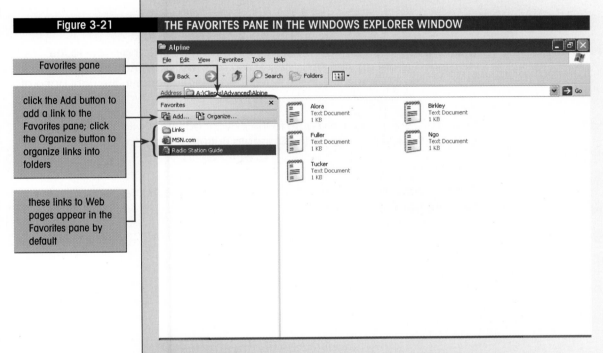

Favorites pane

click the Add button to add a link to the Favorites pane; click the Organize button to organize links into folders

these links to Web pages appear in the Favorites pane by default

Note that the Favorites pane includes links to other objects your computer can access. For example, if you are connected to the Internet, you can click links to open Web pages.

4. In the Favorites pane, click the **Add** button. The Add Favorite dialog box opens with "Alpine" in the Name text box, indicating Windows Explorer will add the Alpine folder to the Favorites pane.

5. Click the **OK** button. The Alpine folder appears in the Favorites pane.

6. To test the new link in the Favorites pane, click the **Up** button 🗗 on the Standard Buttons toolbar until you return to the root directory of your Data Disk. Then click the **Alpine** folder link in the Favorites pane. The right pane of the Windows Explorer window displays the contents of the Alpine folder.

Now that Bernard can quickly access the files in the Alpine folder, he wants the Favorites pane to include links to individual files.

Adding a File to the Favorites Pane

Adding a file to the Favorites pane is different from adding a folder. Instead of opening the Add Favorite dialog box with a menu command or button, you drag one or more files from the right pane of the Windows Explorer window to the Favorites pane.

Emmy Zahn, a corporate trainer, is one of Bernard's clients and an expert Alpine climber. She has offered to accompany him on Spring Alpine expeditions and help train new climbers. Because Bernard will open the Zahn file frequently as he prepares the spring schedule, he wants to include a link to this file in the Favorites pane.

You'll drag the Zahn file from the right pane to add a link to this file in the Favorites pane.

To add a file to the Favorites pane:

1. Click the **Up** button 🗗 on the Standard Buttons toolbar to navigate to the Advanced folder on your Data Disk. Make sure A:\Clients\Advanced appears in the Address bar. The files in the Advanced folder appear in the right pane of the Windows Explorer window.

TROUBLE? If you cannot navigate to the Advanced folder with the 🗗 button, click the Back button ⬅ on the Standard Buttons toolbar to navigate.

2. Select the **Zahn** file.

3. Drag the **Zahn** file to the Favorites pane. A link to the Zahn file appears in the Favorites pane. See Figure 3-22.

Figure 3-22 ADDING FILES TO THE FAVORITES PANE

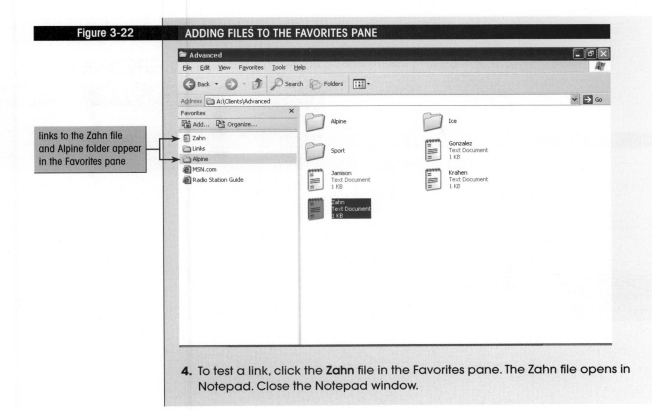

links to the Zahn file and Alpine folder appear in the Favorites pane

4. To test a link, click the **Zahn** file in the Favorites pane. The Zahn file opens in Notepad. Close the Notepad window.

Bernard mentions that he will add a few other files to the Favorites pane as he works on his schedule. You offer to show him how to organize the objects in the Favorites pane to make sure he can find links quickly.

Organizing the Favorites Pane

As you add links in the Favorites pane, you can organize them to make it easier to find the links. Because the Favorites pane is designed to provide quick access to objects such as files and folders, you should organize it logically to keep it uncluttered and easy to use.

To organize the links in the Favorites pane, you can group them in new or existing folders. When you no longer need quick access to a file or folder, you can delete its link from the Favorites pane. When you do, you delete the link only, not the file or folder itself.

You offer to create a folder in the Favorites pane called "Spring Climbs," and then move the links to the Schedule and Zahn files into it. Then Bernard can access those links by clicking the Spring Climbs folder in the Favorites pane.

To organize the Favorites pane:

1. In the Favorites pane, click the **Organize** button. The Organize Favorites dialog box opens. In this dialog box, you can create new folders and move files into the folders in the Favorites pane.

2. In the Organize Favorites dialog box, click the **Create Folder** button.

3. Type **Spring Climbs** as the name of the new folder, and then press the **Enter** key.

4. Select the **Zahn** file and then click the **Move to Folder** button.

5. Click the **Spring Climbs** folder in the Browse folder dialog box, and then click the **OK** button.

6. Click the **Close** button to close the Organize Favorites dialog box. The Spring Climbs folder appears in the Favorites pane.

7. Click the **Spring Climbs** folder to view its contents. See Figure 3-23.

Figure 3-23	ORGANIZING THE FAVORITES PANE

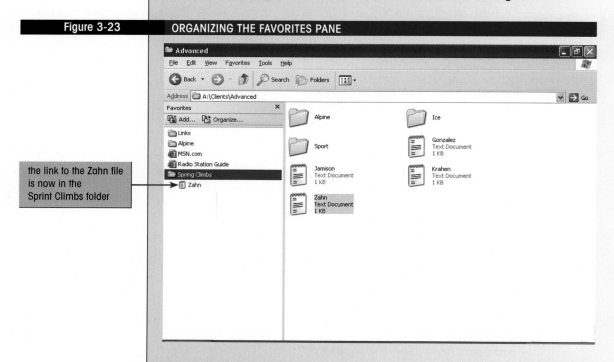

the link to the Zahn file is now in the Sprint Climbs folder

8. Click the **Zahn** file again to make sure you can open it in Notepad. Then close the Notepad window.

Bernard can later use this same technique to move the Alpine folder link to the Spring Climbs folder in the Favorites pane. When he completes his schedule, he can delete the Spring Climbs folder. If you are in a lab environment, you should delete the Spring Climbs and Alpine folders now.

To delete folders from the Favorites pane:

1. In the Favorites pane, click the **Organize** button.

2. In the Organize Favorites dialog box, click the **Spring Climbs** folder.

3. Click the **Delete** button and then click the **Yes** button when prompted to confirm you want to delete the folder.

4. Click **Alpine**, click the **Delete** button, and then click the **Yes** button when prompted to confirm you want to delete the folder.

5. Click the **Close** button to close the Organize Favorites dialog box. The Spring Climbs and Alpine folders no longer appear in the Favorites pane.

The Explorer bar also can display the Media pane. You will work with that pane next.

Working with the Media Pane

You can use the Media pane in the Windows Explorer window to access **multimedia** files, which are files that use sound and images, such as music and video files. Using the Media pane, you can list the multimedia files stored on your computer or on a Web site. Then you can use the Media player to play the files, just as you do with a CD player or VCR. For example, to play a music file, you click the Play button. If you have a sound card and speakers on your computer, the music file plays until it finishes or until you click the Stop button in the Media player.

Bernard wants to find appropriate music to play at the beginning of his presentation to the Parks and Recreation Department. Because he'll show the presentation on a computer, he can play a music file on the hard disk. You suggest he use the Media pane to find music files that come with Windows XP. These are stored in the My Music folder on the hard disk, by default.

To view and play a music file in the Media pane:

1. In Windows Explorer, click **View** on the menu bar, point to **Explorer Bar**, and then click **Media**. The Media pane opens in the Windows Explorer window. See Figure 3-24.

Figure 3-24	OPENING THE MEDIA PANE

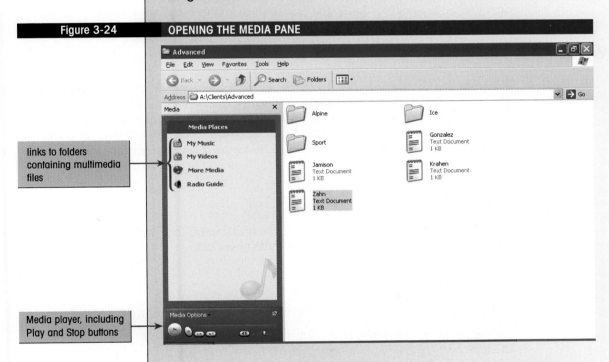

links to folders containing multimedia files

Media player, including Play and Stop buttons

TROUBLE? If a Connection dialog box opens, click the **Work Offline** button so you do not connect to the Internet.

TROUBLE? If the Media pane does not list media folders such as the ones shown in Figure 3-23, locate and open the My Documents folder in the right pane of Windows Explorer, and then double-click the My Music folder. Skip Step 2 and continue with Step 3.

2. Click **My Music** in the Media pane. The contents of the My Music folder appear in the right pane, including the Sample Music icon.

3. Double-click the **Sample Music** icon to access the music files that Windows XP provides by default.

TROUBLE? If the My Music folder on your computer does not include the Sample Music icon, navigate to a folder that contains music files.

4. Click a music file icon, such as **Beethoven's Symphony No. 9 (Scherzo)**, to select it.

5. In the Media pane, click the **Play** button ▸ to play the music file. The file plays through to the end.

TROUBLE? If your computer does not have a sound card, you won't be able to play music files. Close any message dialog boxes that appear. If your computer does not have speakers, you won't be able to hear the music when it plays.

TROUBLE? If the music file plays through to the end and then starts again, the file is set to loop, meaning it will play continuously until you click the Stop button. Click the Stop button ◉ to stop playing the music.

Bernard can use the Beethoven music file to set the mood at the beginning of his presentation. He wonders if Windows Explorer offers any other organizational tools besides the ones you've shown him. You decide to introduce him to the History pane.

Viewing Your File History

Now that you've worked with the Folders, Favorites, and Media panes to organize and open files and folders, you show Bernard the History pane, which displays a history of the files and objects that you've opened recently (within the last three weeks). For example, if Bernard remembers opening a particular file last Tuesday or earlier today, but can't remember the file's location, he might still be able to locate it with the History pane by viewing a list of files opened on those days.

Displaying the History Pane

Like the Folders pane, the History pane is available on the Explorer Bar. You open the History pane using the View command on the menu bar.

To open the History pane:

1. Click **View** on the menu bar, point to **Explorer Bar**, and then click **History**.

Explorer displays the History pane, as shown in Figure 3-25.

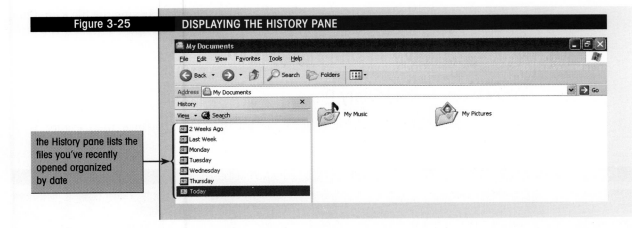

Figure 3-25   DISPLAYING THE HISTORY PANE

the History pane lists the files you've recently opened organized by date

The History pane shows an icon for each of the last few days you've worked with the computer as well as icons for the last three weeks. Each icon displays a list of the files, folders, Web pages, and other objects that were opened during those times. Thus, if Bernard needs to locate the Zahn file that he worked on earlier today, he can do so by opening the Today icon in the History pane. Try this now.

To view files opened earlier today:

1. Click **Today** in the History pane.

   Under the Today icon are the various files and sites Bernard opened today. (Yours might be different.) For example, if he used this computer to access the Web, the Web sites he visited will be listed along with places on his computer, such as the My Computer window. Bernard is interested only in the files he's accessed on his computer.

2. Click the **My Computer** icon listed under Today in the History pane. See Figure 3-26.

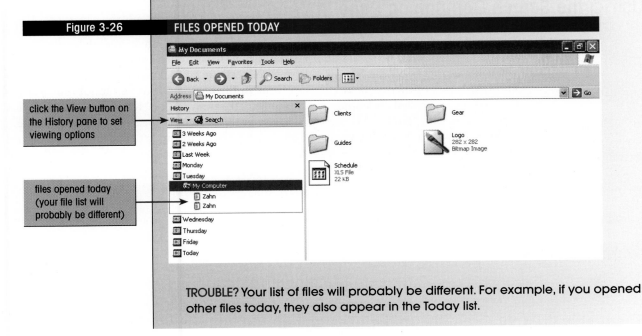

Figure 3-26   FILES OPENED TODAY

click the View button on the History pane to set viewing options

files opened today (your file list will probably be different)

TROUBLE? Your list of files will probably be different. For example, if you opened other files today, they also appear in the Today list.

If Bernard wanted to open one of these files, he could do so by clicking the file icon. One important point: if you or anyone else moved the file since you last opened it, then you cannot open it from the Today list in the History pane—in that case, Windows XP looks for the file in its previous location.

Other Views in the History Pane

You have several choices of how to view the list of recently opened files. Figure 3-27 describes the ways you can view the recent file list.

Figure 3-27	HISTORY PANE VIEWS
VIEW OPTION	**DESCRIPTION**
By Date	View the files by the date that the files were opened (the default)
By Site	View the files according to location
By Most Visited	View the files by the number of times you've opened each file
By Order Visited Today	View the files by the order in which you've opened the files on the current day

Changing the view in the History pane can help you access files more quickly. For example, you opened the Zahn file more than once earlier today. Now Bernard wants to open it again to verify all the classes that Emmy Zahn has taken. He can view the History pane organized by the number of times each file has been opened. To do so, he could click View in the History pane and then click By Most Visited. The Zahn file would probably be near or at the top of that list. Bernard could click the Zahn file icon to open that file directly without having to know where the file is located within the Windows XP hierarchy of objects. The only limitation is that if the file is located on a CD or floppy disk, that disk must be in the corresponding drive before the file can be accessed.

Using the Search Companion Pane in Windows Explorer

Bernard finds the History pane a useful tool for locating the files he's recently worked with. But he wonders what he would do if he didn't know where the file was located, wasn't sure when he last accessed the file, or wasn't certain about a filename. For example, Bernard knows that he's opened a client's file sometime in the last week, but he cannot remember if the filename is spelled "Kranmmer," "Kranmar," "Kranmere," or "Kranmer," although he's sure it starts with "Kran." The best tool to use in this case is the Search Companion pane.

In the Search Companion pane, you can specify the name or part of a name of any file on your computer, and Windows Explorer will then locate the file for you. You show Bernard how to do this with the "Kran" file.

To locate the "Kran" file:

1. Click the **Search** button 🔍 on the Standard Buttons toolbar. Note that you could also click View on the menu bar, and then click Search to open the Search Companion pane. See Figure 3-28.

| Figure 3-28 | SEARCHING FOR FILES IN WINDOWS EXPLORER |

Search Companion pane

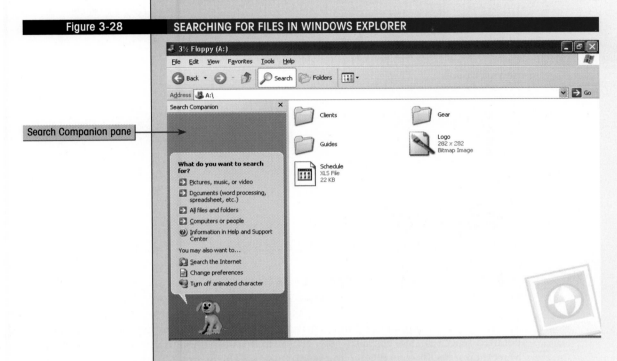

2. Click **All files and folders**.

3. Type **Kran** in the All or part of the file name text box.

    By typing "Kran" you are limiting your search to only files with the text "kran" in their filenames, such as "Kranmer" or "Ckrank". By default, case doesn't matter—typing "kran" is the same as typing "Kran."

4. If necessary, click the **Look in** list arrow and then click **3½ Floppy (A:)** so that Windows XP searches only the files on your Data Disk.

5. Click the **Search** button.

    The Kranmer file is listed in the right pane, as shown in Figure 3-29. This is the file that Bernard is looking for.

Figure 3-29   **LOCATING THE KRANMER FILE**

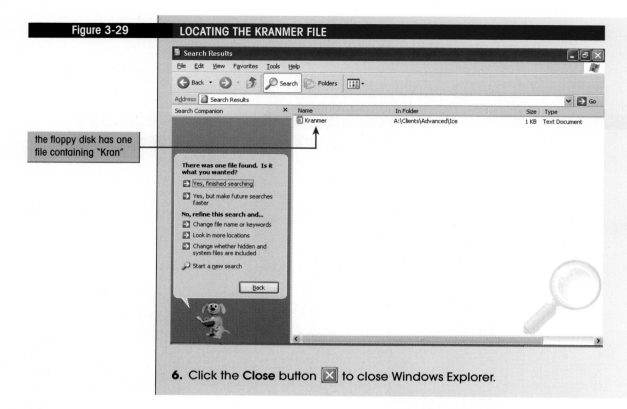

the floppy disk has one file containing "Kran"

6. Click the **Close** button ☒ to close Windows Explorer.

The Search Companion pane is a rich tool containing many features for complex and detailed searches. You can also open the Search Companion as a standalone tool from the Start menu. You'll get a chance to explore more of the Search Companion features in a later tutorial.

You've completed your work with Windows Explorer. You remind Bernard that each of the tools and techniques you've shown him can be used with most of the windows in Windows XP. For example, if he wants to use the History or Favorites panes in the My Computer window, he can do so.

Session 3.3 QUICK CHECK

1. True or False: If you delete a folder in the Favorites pane, you also delete the folder from your computer.

2. Why is it a good idea to organize the objects in the Favorites pane?

3. The Media pane shows the _____ files your computer can access, such as music and video files.

4. True or False: If a file is moved from its original location, the History pane will display the new file location.

5. To display a list of files you worked with earlier in the day, click the _____ icon in the History pane.

6. Under what circumstances would you use the Search Companion pane?

7. True or False: You can use the Search Companion pane to find any file on your computer.

REVIEW ASSIGNMENTS

1. Copying Files to the Hard Disk Bernard wants to place his sport-climbing client files (those in the Sport folder) on the hard disk to work with them on an advertisement campaign. The Sport folder is a subfolder of the Advanced folder, which is itself a subfolder of Clients.

    a. Start Windows Explorer and then create a new folder on the hard disk in the My Documents folder called Advertise.

    b. Copy the files in the Sport folder on your Data Disk to the Advertise folder on the hard disk.

    c. Open the Advertise folder on the hard disk to display the files it contains.

    d. Print the Windows Explorer window from WordPad, including your name and the date on the printout.

    e. Delete the Advertise folder from the hard disk when your printout is completed.

2. Creating a New Folder and Copying Files Bernard now wants a folder that contains all the clients he has because he'd like to mail flyers to all his clients advertising an expedition to the Tetons. (*Hint*: The client files are all text files, so consider viewing the files in the root directory by type. Don't forget that there are also client files in the Clients folder and its subfolders.)

    a. Create a folder called All Clients on the drive A root directory, and then copy any text files from the root directory into the All Clients folder.

    b. Open the Clients folder, open its subfolders one at a time, and then copy the text files from each of those folders into the new All Clients folder.

    c. Print the Exploring screen from WordPad (following the steps in Session 3.2 of this tutorial), showing the contents of the All Clients folder arranged by name. Be sure to include your name and the date on your printout.

    d. Delete the All Clients folder from the floppy disk when your printout is completed.

3. Copying between Floppy Disks Suppose someone who doesn't know how to use Windows Explorer wants to copy the Guides folder from her Data Disk to another floppy disk—but she doesn't want the entire contents of the Data Disk. Try this yourself, and as you go through the procedure, write each step so that this student will be able to follow the steps and make a copy of Guides. Keep in mind that she doesn't know how to use Windows Explorer.

4. Restructuring a Disk

    a. Create a folder called "Tutorial 3" in the My Documents folder on the hard disk. Copy all the folders on the Windows XP Tutorial 3 Data Disk 1 to the Tutorial 3 folder.

    b. Use Quick Format to format any disk that contains files you no longer need. You can use the disk you formatted in Session 3.3 (Disk 2, containing the Wall file).

    c. Copy all the files from the Tutorial 3 folder on your hard disk to the root directory of Disk 2. (Do not store the files on Disk 2 in folders.)

    d. Rearrange the files on the disk so they correspond to Figure 3-30. Delete any files or folders not shown in the figure.

Figure 3-30

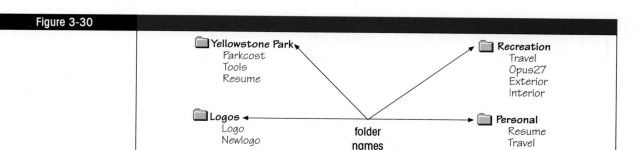

e. Print the Windows Explorer screen from WordPad that shows your new organization and the files in the Yellowstone Park folder arranged by size.

f. Delete the Tutorial 3 folder from the hard disk.

5. *Creating a Folder Structure* When you complete your computer class, you are likely to use a computer for other courses in your major and for general education requirements such as English and math. Think about how you would organize the floppy disk that would hold the files for your courses, and then prepare a disk to contain your files. If you're not a student, prepare a disk using fictitious data.

    a. Make a diagram of this organization.

    b. Use Quick Format to erase any disk containing files you no longer need, such as Disk 2.

    c. Create the folder structure on your Data Disk (even though you don't have any files to place in the folders right now). Use subfolders to help sort files for class projects. (Your composition course, for example, might have a midterm and a final paper.)

    d. Make sure the left pane displays all folders and subfolders, and then paste an image of the Windows Explorer window into WordPad. Be sure to include your name and the date, but don't print anything yet.

    e. Use WordPad to write one or two paragraphs after your name explaining your plan. Your explanation should include information about your major, the courses you plan to take, and how you might use computers in those courses. Print the document when it is finished.

6. *Exploring Your Computer's Devices, Folders, and Files* Answer each of the following questions about the devices, folders, and files on your lab computers. You can find all the answers using the Windows Explorer window. Note that your answers will vary from those of other students because different computers have different devices, folder hierarchies, and files.

    a. What are the names of three folders on drive C?

    b. Which folders on drive C have subfolders? What are the names of two or three of the subfolders?

    c. What is the size of the largest file in the My Documents folder on the hard disk?

    d. Does your computer have a CD drive? If so, what drive letter is assigned to the CD drive?

    e. Does your computer have access to a network storage device? If so, indicate the letter(s) of the network storage device(s).

7. *Separating Program and Data Files* Hard disk management differs from floppy disk management because a hard disk contains programs and data, whereas a floppy disk (unless it is an installation disk that you got from a software company) generally only contains data files. On a hard disk, a good management practice is to keep programs in folders separate from data files. Keeping this in mind, read the following description, draw a sketch of the folder structure described, and then make a sketch of how the current structure could be improved.

The Marquette Chamber of Commerce uses a computer to maintain its membership list and track dues. It also uses the computer for correspondence. All the programs and data used by the Chamber of Commerce are on drive C. The program for the membership database is in a folder called Members. The data file for the membership database is in a subfolder of Members called Member Data. The accounting program used to track income and expenditures is in a folder called Accounting Programs. The data for the current year is in a folder directly under the drive C icon called Accounting Data 2004. The accounting data from 2002 and 2003 is stored in two subfolders of the folder called Accounting Programs. The word-processing program is in a folder called Word. The documents created with Word are stored in the Member Data folder. Finally, Windows XP is stored in a folder called Windows, which has 10 subfolders.

8. *Using the Send To Command* The Send To command provides an efficient way to send files to the root directory of the floppy disk. You also can use this command to send a file on your floppy disk to the My Documents folder on your computer's hard disk. To see how this works, complete the following tasks:

    a. Insert the Windows XP Tutorial 3 Data Disk 1 in the floppy drive of your computer.

    b. Use the Send To command to move the Gonzalez file from the Advanced folder in the Clients folder to the My Documents folder on your hard disk.

    c. Use the Send To command to move the Gonzales file from the My Documents folder back to the root directory of your floppy disk.

    d. Delete the Gonzales file in the My Documents folder.

9. *Using the Favorites, Media, History, and Search Panes* Complete the following tasks and then answer each question about working with the Favorites, Media, History, and Search panes in the Windows Explorer window.

    a. Using the Windows XP Tutorial 3 Data Disk 1, add the Ygo and Tucker files to the Favorites pane, and then organize them in a new folder called "Tutorial 3." Open the Tutorial 3 folder in the Favorites pane, and then create a printout of this screen. Open the Ygo file and then close the Notepad window. Delete the Tutorial 3 folder in the Favorites pane.

    b. Use the Media pane to find at least one multimedia file on your hard disk. What is the size of that file?

    c. Open the History pane and view the files you opened today. Which files are on the list? Use the View button on the History pane to change the view. Which view did you choose? Which files now appear on the list?

    d. Use the Search Companion pane to find the Ramin and Ramirez files on the Data Disk. What did you type to find the files? Where is each located on the Data Disk?

PROJECTS

1. Shortly after graduation, you start working for your aunt and uncle, who own a thriving antique store. They hope to store data about their inventory and business on the computer they recently purchased. They have hired you to accomplish this task. Your Aunt Susan asks you to organize her client files and to prepare some financial statements. Your Uncle Gabe wants you to create customized forms for invoicing and inventory. Two part-time employees, Julia and Abigail, have asked you to help develop documents for advertising. You realize that a folder structure would help to keep things straight.

    a. Quick format a disk, such as Data Disk 2, and then create a folder on it named Antiques.

    b. Create the following subfolders: Customers, Finances, Invoices, Inventory, and Advertising.

   c. In WordPad, create each of the documents listed below and save them in the correct folders on your Data Disk:

     Customers subfolder: Inventory subfolder:
        Harrington   Furniture
        Searls   Art
     Finances subfolder: Advertising subfolder:
        Budget   Anniversary Sale
        Profit and Loss   Winter Clearance
        Balance Sheet
     Invoices subfolder:
        Sales
        Vendors

   d. In Windows Explorer, display the entire Antiques folder hierarchy in the left pane, and display the contents of the Finances subfolder in the right pane. Print an image of the Windows Explorer window showing your file structure.

2. Uncle Gabe decided to have his financial statements prepared by an accountant, so you need to copy the files in the Finances subfolder onto a different disk that you can give to the accountant. Use the folders and files you created in Project 1. You will need a blank floppy disk. You must also be able to access your computer's hard disk to complete this project. Uncle Gabe wants to know how to copy files to a new disk, so as you copy the files, write down in detail what you are doing so he can repeat this procedure by following your directions.

   a. Create a folder in the My Documents folder on your hard disk called Accountant.
   b. Copy the three files in the Finances folder on your Data Disk to the Accountant folder on your hard disk, using the drag technique.
   c. Copy the contents of the Accountant folder to the blank disk, using the copy-and-paste technique.
   d. Delete the Accountant folder from your hard disk.

3. Two of the methods you've learned for moving files between folders are the drag-and-drop method and the cut-and-paste method. Answer the following questions:
   a. Can you think of any situations in which you could not drag to move a file in Windows Explorer?
   b. In such a situation, what should you do instead?
   c. Which method do you prefer? Why?

Explore   4. Windows XP enables users to customize their working environment extensively. For each item, first write the steps you take to make the change, and then comment on the benefits or disadvantages of using the following options in the Windows Explorer window:
   a. Details view or List view
   b. Displaying or hiding the status bar
   c. Displaying or hiding the Folders pane
   d. Switching from the Folders pane to the Favorites pane

QUICK | CHECK ANSWERS

Session 3.1

1. Windows Explorer

2. The left pane displays tools, such as the Folders pane, History pane, and Search pane, used to organize the files on your computer; the right pane displays the contents of the object selected in the right pane.

3. False

4. False

5. subfolder

6. plus box

7. the drive A device icon

8. False

Session 3.2

1. Shift, Ctrl

2. The Folders pane shows how devices and folders are arranged in a hierarchy on a computer, but does not show files. To move, copy, delete, and perform other tasks with files, you work in the right pane.

3. Press the Print Screen key, paste the image into WordPad, and print the WordPad document.

4. Move to Folder

5. True

6. the Send To command

Session 3.3

1. False

2. Because the Favorites pane is designed to provide quick access to objects such as files and folders, you should organize it logically to keep it uncluttered and easy to use.

3. multimedia

4. False

5. Today

6. If you didn't know details about a file, such as where the file is located, when you last accessed the file, or its complete filename, you can use the Search Companion to find the file.

7. True

OBJECTIVES

In this tutorial you will:

- Store a document on the desktop and use the Notepad time-date stamp

- Create and delete shortcuts to a drive, a document, and a printer

- Use the Control Panel to change the desktop appearance

- Configure your taskbar

- Create and modify taskbar toolbars

- Edit your Start menu

PERSONALIZING YOUR WINDOWS ENVIRONMENT

Changing Desktop Settings at Companions, Inc.

CASE

Companions, Inc.

Bow Falls, Arizona, is a popular Sun Belt retirement mecca that is also a college town with several distinguished universities. Beth Yuan, a graduate of Bow Falls University, realized that the unusual mix of ages in her town might be perfectly suited to a business in which college students and recent graduates offer personal care services to retirees. She formed Companions, Inc. to provide older residents with trained assistants who help with housecleaning, home maintenance, and errands. Many of Beth's employees are students at local colleges who like the flexible hours and enjoy spending time with the elderly people. In addition to employees who work directly with clients, Beth has hired office staff, often retirees themselves, who help manage the day-to-day tasks of running a business.

Companions, Inc. uses computers to maintain client records, schedule employees, manage company finances, develop training materials, and create marketing pieces. Beth recently upgraded the office computers to Windows XP. She heard that it's easy to change Windows XP settings to reflect the needs of her office staff. For example, she wants to customize her computers so she and her staff can easily access key documents and computer resources. She would also like the desktop itself to reflect her corporate image. She asks you to help her meet these goals.

SESSION 4.1

In this session, you will learn how to create and store a Notepad document on the desktop and how to "stamp" the document with the time and date. You will create shortcuts to the objects you use most often, including your computer's floppy drive, a document, and a printer. You will learn the difference between document icons and shortcut icons on the desktop, and how to restore your desktop to its original state.

Docucentric Desktops

As you know, when you start Windows XP, the large area you see on your screen is called the desktop. Because the desktop provides your first view of the computer and its contents, it should contain the items you want to access when you start your computer. These items include tools such as My Computer, programs you use often, and key documents. Desktop icons are the most visual and easiest way to access these resources. Figure 4-1 shows the types of icons you can include on the desktop and the objects they represent.

Figure 4-1	TYPES OF DESKTOP ICONS

ICON	DESCRIPTION
	Text document icon
	Shortcut icon
	Floppy drive
	Hard drive
	CD drive
	Printer
	Folder
	System tools

You are already familiar with some icons on your desktop that represent critical tools, such as My Computer and the Recycle Bin. As Figure 4-1 shows, you can place additional icons on the desktop that represent objects you want to access quickly and frequently, such as printers, disk drives, programs, and documents. These icons are **shortcuts**, quick ways to start a program or open a file, folder, or other object without having to go to its permanent location on your computer. Shortcut icons include a small arrow, as in , the shortcut icon for a Notepad document. The small arrow is a reminder that a shortcut icon points to an item that is stored elsewhere on the computer. When you delete a shortcut icon, the file or resource it represents remains in its original location.

Shortcut icons can simplify tasks you perform regularly. For example, you can create a shortcut icon to the floppy drive and then drag files to the shortcut icon to move them to a floppy disk. If you create a shortcut icon for your printer, you can print a file by dragging it to the printer's shortcut icon. You also can create a shortcut icon for a program you use often and then double-click the icon to start the program.

In some cases, instead of creating a shortcut, you might want to store a document right on the desktop. For example, if you move or copy a document often, you could store it on the desktop so you don't have to navigate your computer's file system every time you want to work with the document. Instead, when you want to move or copy the document, you could drag it from the desktop to a shortcut icon for a drive or folder.

When you store a document on the desktop, it appears as a **document icon**. A document icon is similar to a shortcut icon, except it doesn't include the shortcut arrow. For example, ▤ is the document icon for a Notepad document. Document icons represent documents that you create, open, change, and save on the desktop. When you delete a document icon, you send the document to the Recycle Bin.

Desktops that use shortcut icons and document icons to provide immediate access to documents are called **docucentric** desktops.

You offer to help Beth make her desktop more docucentric so she can work more efficiently. She mentions that she wants to create a phone log to track phone calls to her clients and take notes about the services they request. Before an employee visits a client, she wants to copy the phone log to a floppy disk so the employee can update the client notes. She also wants to print the phone log in case the employee wants to take notes during the visit. You'll show Beth how to create a phone log in Notepad and store it on the desktop as a document icon. Then you'll show her how to create shortcut icons for the floppy drive, a document, and the printer.

Creating **and Storing a Document on the Desktop**

You can create a document on the desktop by right-clicking the desktop and then selecting the type of document you want from a list. You also can create a document on Notepad or WordPad, for example, open the Save As dialog box, and then save the document on the desktop. In either case, a document icon appears on the desktop to represent your document. The appearance of the document icon depends on the type of document you create. For example, a Notepad document icon appears as ▤, whereas a WordPad document icon appears as ▨. When you open the document represented by the icon, Windows XP checks the filename extension to determine which program it should start.

REFERENCE WINDOW	**RW**

<u>Creating and Storing a Document on the Desktop</u>
- Right-click an empty area of the desktop, and then point to New on the shortcut menu.
- Click the type of document you want to create.
- Type a name for the document that appears on the desktop as a document icon.

or
- Start the program in which you want to create a document.
- Click File on the menu bar, and then click Save As.
- Click the Save in list arrow, and then click the Desktop icon.
- Type a name for the document, and then click the Save button.

You can use Notepad, an accessory included with Windows XP, to create phone logs and other documents that reflect the current time and date. Notepad, like WordPad, allows you to edit simple text documents, but because it does not include the formatting options provided by WordPad, it is used only for text documents with no formatting. Notepad includes a feature with which you can insert a time-date stamp that automatically inserts the time and date whenever you open the document. Figure 4-2 shows you a Notepad document with automatic time-date stamps.

Figure 4-2	NOTEPAD DOCUMENT WITH TIME-DATE STAMP

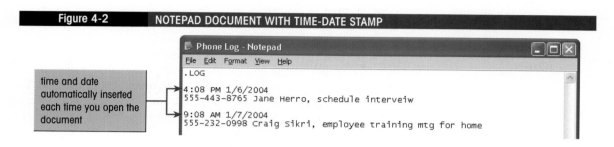

time and date automatically inserted each time you open the document

You suggest that Beth use Notepad to create a Companions, Inc. phone log and store it on her desktop. Then she and her employees can quickly access the phone log by double-clicking its icon on the desktop.

To create a Notepad document on the desktop:

1. Right-click a blank area of the desktop, and then point to **New**. The shortcut menu shown in Figure 4-3 opens.

Figure 4-3	CREATING A NEW TEXT DOCUMENT

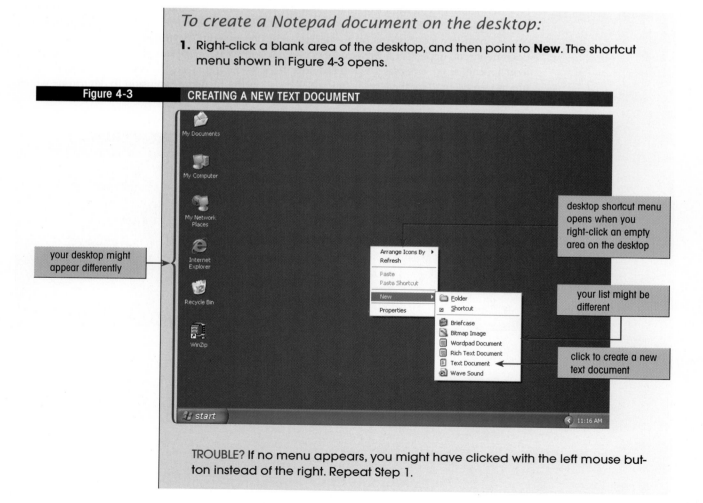

your desktop might appear differently

desktop shortcut menu opens when you right-click an empty area on the desktop

your list might be different

click to create a new text document

TROUBLE? If no menu appears, you might have clicked with the left mouse button instead of the right. Repeat Step 1.

TROUBLE? Your list of options on the New menu may differ from the one shown in Figure 4-3. The document types that appear on the New menu depend on the programs installed on your computer.

TROUBLE? Your monitor settings may differ, causing the objects on your screen to use more or less space than those shown in the figures.

2. Click **Text Document** on the shortcut menu. A document icon for your new text document appears on the desktop. See Figure 4-4. Its default filename, "New Text Document," is selected so you can type an appropriate name for the new file.

| Figure 4-4 | DOCUMENT ICON |

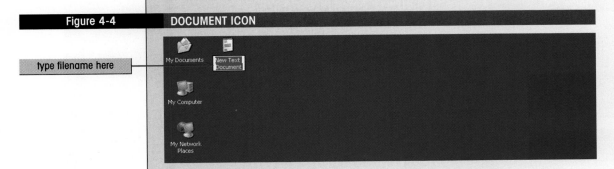

type filename here

TROUBLE? If you receive an error message when you try to create a new document on the desktop, your lab might not allow you to make any changes to the desktop. Ask your instructor which sections of this tutorial you will be able to complete using a lab computer.

3. Type **Phone Log** as the name of your document, and then press the **Enter** key. See Figure 4-5.

| Figure 4-5 | PHONE LOG DOCUMENT ICON |

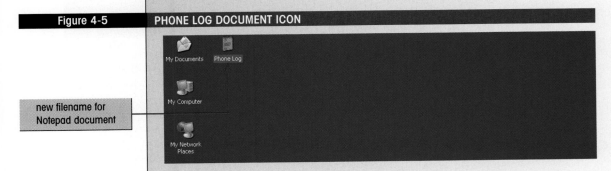

new filename for Notepad document

TROUBLE? If nothing happens when you type the document name, you might have pressed a key or mouse button that deselected the document icon. Right-click the New Text Document icon, click Rename on the shortcut menu, and then type Phone Log.

TROUBLE? If you see a message about changing the filename extension, click the No button, type Phone Log.txt, and then press Enter. Your computer is set to display filename extensions, so you must provide an extension when you create a document on the desktop.

Now that you have created the Phone Log document on the desktop, you can use its icon to open it.

Opening a Document Stored on the Desktop

To open a document that is stored on the desktop, you double-click its icon. Windows XP then starts the appropriate program and opens the document.

To open the Phone Log document:

1. Double-click the **Phone Log** icon on the desktop. Windows XP starts Notepad. See Figure 4-6.

| Figure 4-6 | PHONE LOG DOCUMENT OPENS IN NOTEPAD |

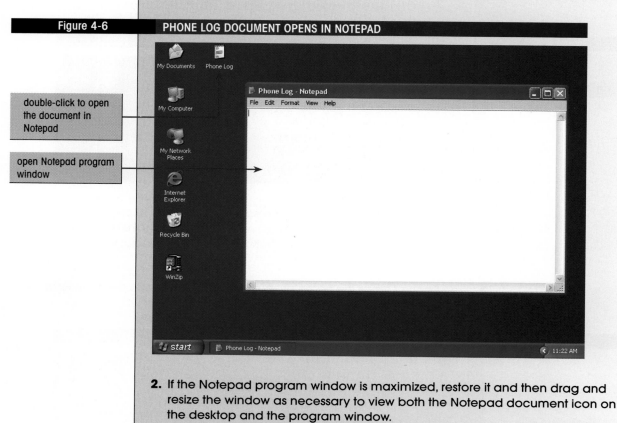

double-click to open the document in Notepad

open Notepad program window

2. If the Notepad program window is maximized, restore it and then drag and resize the window as necessary to view both the Notepad document icon on the desktop and the program window.

Now you can begin adding text to the phone log for Beth.

Creating a LOG File

Notepad automatically inserts the date when you open a document only if the document begins with .LOG, in uppercase letters. Your next step is to create a document with .LOG at the beginning and to enter some text. Then you will save the document and close it, so that the next time you open it, Notepad will automatically enter the time and date for you.

To set up the Phone Log document:

1. Type **.LOG**. Be sure to type the period first and to use uppercase letters. This text indicates that you want Notepad to enter the current time and date every time you open the document.

2. Press the **Enter** key to move the insertion point to the next line, type **Phone Log for**, and then type your name.

3. Press the **Enter** key. Now you are ready to use the Phone Log document to record names, phone numbers, and notes for phone calls you make. The time-date stamp Notepad inserts helps you track the calls by date and time.

4. Save the Phone Log document, and exit Notepad.

Now you will test the Phone Log document to ensure the automatic time-date stamp appears when you open it.

To test the Phone Log document:

1. Double-click the **Phone Log** icon on the desktop to open this document. Make sure your document contains a time-date stamp. See Figure 4-7.

Figure 4-7	TIME-DATE STAMP

typing .LOG in uppercase letters tells Notepad to insert a time-date stamp

time-date stamp; your date might be different

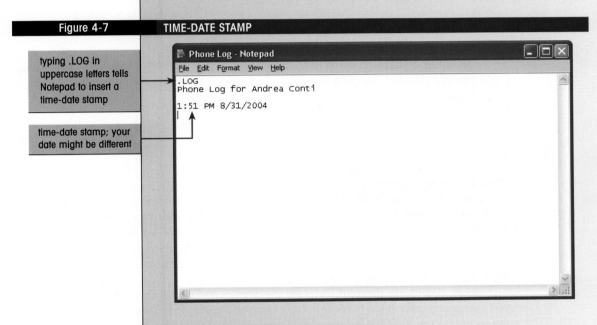

Next, enter your first phone log entry.

2. Click below the time-date stamp if necessary, and then type **941-555-0876 Charlene Maples, prospective client needs household help 5 hrs/week.**

3. Press the **Enter** key. See Figure 4-8.

Figure 4-8	FIRST PHONE LOG ENTRY IN NOTEPAD DOCUMENT

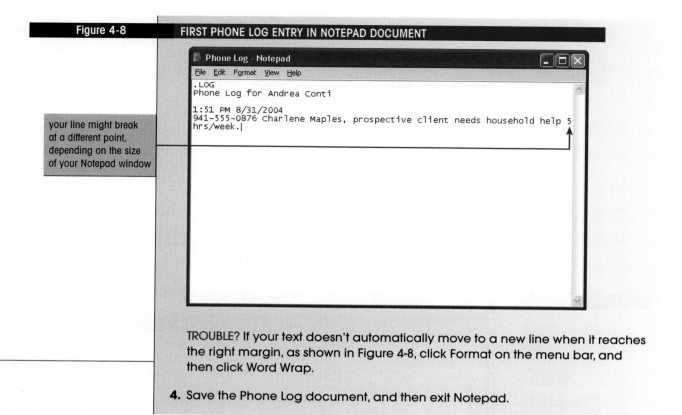

your line might break
at a different point,
depending on the size
of your Notepad window

TROUBLE? If your text doesn't automatically move to a new line when it reaches the right margin, as shown in Figure 4-8, click Format on the menu bar, and then click Word Wrap.

4. Save the Phone Log document, and then exit Notepad.

You have created and edited a document stored on the desktop for easy access. You can also easily access existing documents from the desktop by creating a shortcut icon. A shortcut icon for a document works much the same way as a document icon—you can double-click the shortcut icon to open the document in the appropriate program. However, remember that a shortcut icon only points to the actual document. If you move the icon, for example, you move only the shortcut, not the document itself. One advantage of using shortcut icons is that if your desktop becomes cluttered, you can delete the shortcut icons without affecting the original document.

You can also create shortcut icons for the devices and drives on your computer. This way, you can access your local hard disk, for example, directly from the desktop, instead of having to open Windows Explorer or My Computer, and then navigate to the hard disk.

Using Shortcuts

You can create shortcuts to access drives, documents, files, Web pages, programs, or other computer resources such as a printer. Windows XP provides several ways of creating shortcuts. For example, you can right-click an object and select Create Shortcuts Here on the shortcut menu. Figure 4-9 summarizes the techniques you can use to create shortcuts. The one you choose is a matter of personal preference.

Figure 4-9	METHODS FOR CREATING SHORTCUTS
METHOD	**DESCRIPTION**
Drag	To create a shortcut on the desktop, use My Computer or Windows Explorer to locate the file icon, and then drag the icon to the desktop. For locations other than the desktop, hold down the Alt key as you drag.
Right-drag	Use My Computer or Windows Explorer to locate and select the file icon, hold down the right mouse button, and drag to a new location. Release the mouse button and click Create Shortcuts Here on the shortcut menu.
Right-click, Create Shortcut	Use My Computer or Windows Explorer to locate the file icon, right-click the icon, click Create Shortcut on the shortcut menu, and then drag the shortcut icon to a new location.
Right-click, Send To	To create a shortcut on the desktop, use My Computer or Windows Explorer to locate the file icon, right-click the icon, point to Send To, and then click Desktop (create shortcut).
Copy and paste shortcut	Use My Computer or Windows Explorer to locate and select the file icon. Click Edit on the menu bar, and then click Copy. Move to the new location. Click Edit on the menu bar, and then click Paste.
Create Shortcut command	Use My Computer or Windows Explorer to locate the file icon, Click File on the menu bar, click Create Shortcut, and then drag the shortcut icon to a new location.

Next you will create a shortcut to the floppy drive. You could use any technique listed in Figure 4-9, but you'll use the drag method because it involves the fewest steps.

Creating a Shortcut to a Drive

To create a shortcut to a drive, you can open the My Computer or Windows Explorer window, and then drag the drive icon from the window to the desktop. Windows XP creates a shortcut icon that looks like a hard disk or floppy disk, and includes an appropriate label, such as "Shortcut to 3½ Floppy (A)." When you create a shortcut to your floppy drive, you can double-click the shortcut to view the contents of your Data Disk, or you can move or copy documents to it without having to start Windows Explorer or My Computer.

Beth regularly copies the phone log to a floppy disk and wants to use a shortcut to simplify the task.

To create a shortcut to your floppy drive:

1. Double-click the **My Computer** icon on the desktop. If necessary, resize the My Computer window so you can see an empty area of the desktop. You need to see both the desktop and the My Computer window to drag effectively.

   TROUBLE? If the My Computer icon does not appear on your desktop, click the Start button on the taskbar, and then click My Computer.

2. Press and hold the left mouse button, and then drag the **3½ Floppy (A:) icon** from the My Computer window into an empty area of the desktop.

3. Release the mouse button. A shortcut labeled "Shortcut to 3½ Floppy (A)" now appears on the desktop. (Yours may be in a different location.) See Figure 4-10.

Figure 4-10	SHORTCUT TO DRIVE A

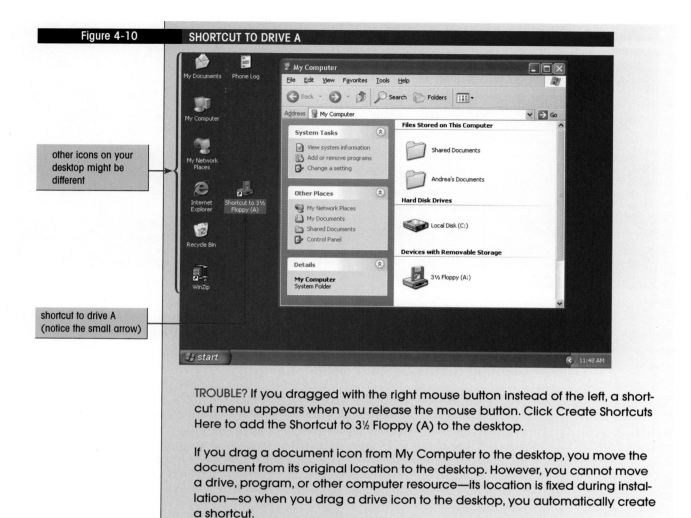

other icons on your
desktop might be
different

shortcut to drive A
(notice the small arrow)

TROUBLE? If you dragged with the right mouse button instead of the left, a shortcut menu appears when you release the mouse button. Click Create Shortcuts
Here to add the Shortcut to 3½ Floppy (A) to the desktop.

If you drag a document icon from My Computer to the desktop, you move the
document from its original location to the desktop. However, you cannot move
a drive, program, or other computer resource—its location is fixed during installation—so when you drag a drive icon to the desktop, you automatically create
a shortcut.

4. Close the My Computer window.

Now use the newly created shortcut to view the contents of your Data Disk in drive A.

To test the 3½ Floppy (A:) shortcut:

1. Make sure your Data Disk is in drive A, and then double-click the **3½ Floppy (A)**
shortcut icon on the desktop. The My Computer window opens, showing the
contents of the disk in your 3½ Floppy (A:) drive.

2. Click the **Close** button ⊠ to close the My Computer window.

Beth often works at her home office, and she'd like to move the phone log to a floppy
disk that she can carry back and forth. To copy the phone log to the floppy disk, you could
drag the document icon to the 3½ Floppy (A:) shortcut icon. To move the log to a floppy
disk, you can use the cut-and-paste method.

To move the document from the desktop to a floppy disk:

1. Right-click the **Phone Log** document icon on the desktop, and then click **Cut** on the shortcut menu.

2. Right-click the **3½ Floppy (A)** shortcut icon on the desktop, and then click **Paste** on the shortcut menu. The Phone Log icon disappears from the desktop, and the Phone Log document is now stored on your floppy disk.

When you moved the document icon to the drive A shortcut, the file itself was moved off your desktop and to the disk in drive A. Beth can now take the disk home with her and use a shortcut to drive A on her desktop there to open the file. You'll show her how to use the shortcut for the floppy drive you just created to access the Phone Log document stored on the floppy disk. (You could also open drive A from My Computer or Windows Explorer, but it is handier to use the drive A shortcut on the desktop.)

To open the Phone Log document using the shortcut to 3½ Floppy (A):

1. Double-click the **3½ Floppy (A)** shortcut icon on the desktop to open the My Computer window displaying the contents of drive A.

   TROUBLE? To switch to Details View, click View, and then click Details.

2. Scroll through the window, if necessary, to locate the Phone Log document on your Data Disk.

   TROUBLE? If you don't see the Phone Log document on your Data Disk, repeat the previous set of steps for moving a document to a floppy disk.

The Phone Log document is now on a floppy disk, as Beth requested; however, it no longer has an icon on the desktop. She realizes that she still might want to open the phone log on the office computer from the desktop. Recall that you can use shortcut icons to provide access to documents stored in other locations on your computer. In the next section, you will show her how to do this.

Creating a Shortcut to a Document

If you want to access the phone log document (now saved on your Data Disk) directly from the desktop, you can create a shortcut that opens the phone log from your Data Disk. Before you can use a shortcut icon that refers to a document on a floppy disk, you must make sure the floppy disk containing the document is in drive A.

You'll show Beth how to create a shortcut to a document using the right-click-and-drag method. (That is, you press and hold the right mouse button as you drag.)

To create a shortcut to the Phone Log document on your Data Disk:

1. Resize the 3½ Floppy (A:) window as necessary to see both the Phone Log icon in the window and a blank area of the desktop. Switch to Details View in the 3½ Floppy (A:) window, if necessary.

2. Press and hold the right mouse button, drag the **Phone Log** icon from the 3½ Floppy (A:) window onto the desktop, and then release the mouse button. A shortcut menu appears listing the tasks you can perform with this document. Note that you can use the shortcut menu to copy or move a document as well as create a shortcut to it.

3. Click **Create Shortcuts Here**.

An icon labeled "Shortcut to Phone Log" now appears on the desktop.

4. Rest your mouse pointer on the Shortcut to Phone Log icon, and note the ScreenTip that appears, indicating the location of the source document (in this case, on the root directory of drive A). See Figure 4-11.

Figure 4-11	CREATING A SHORTCUT TO THE PHONE LOG DOCUMENT ON DRIVE A

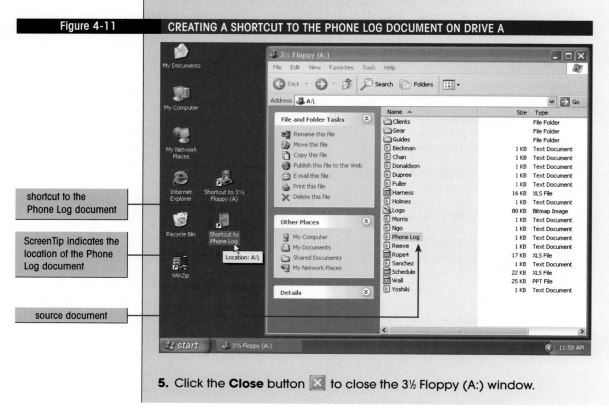

shortcut to the Phone Log document

ScreenTip indicates the location of the Phone Log document

source document

5. Click the **Close** button ☒ to close the 3½ Floppy (A:) window.

Now you can test the shortcut to make sure it opens the Phone Log document.

To test the Phone Log shortcut:

1. Double-click the **Shortcut to Phone Log** icon. Windows XP starts Notepad and then opens the Phone Log document stored on your Data Disk.

2. Type: **941-555-7766 Trinity River Accounting** below the new time-date stamp, and then press the **Enter** key.

3. Click the **Close** button ☒ to close Notepad.

4. Click the **Yes** button to save the changes.

The shortcut icon you just created and tested is different from the Phone Log icon you created at the beginning of this tutorial. That icon was not a shortcut icon, but a document icon representing a document stored on the desktop. The shortcut icon currently on your desktop represents a document located on your Data Disk.

You now have an efficient way to open the phone log and to access your floppy drive. Now you want to add a printer shortcut to the desktop so that Beth's employees can easily print their phone logs and other documents.

Creating a Shortcut to a Printer

You can create a printer shortcut in much the same way as you created a shortcut for the floppy drive: by locating the printer device icon in the Printers and Faxes window and then dragging the icon onto your desktop. You also can use the menu commands in the Printers and Faxes window to create a shortcut to a printer on the desktop. After you create a printer shortcut icon, you can print a document by dragging its icon to the printer shortcut icon on the desktop.

Beth and her employees often print phone logs and other documents before they visit prospective clients. Instead of starting Notepad or another program, opening the Print dialog box, selecting print settings, and then clicking OK, they can print by dragging a document to a printer shortcut icon. You'll show them how to create a printer shortcut using the menu commands in the Printers and Faxes window.

To create a printer shortcut:

1. Click the **Start** button ⟪ start ⟫ on the taskbar, and then click **Printers and Faxes**. The Printers and Faxes window opens. If necessary, resize the window so you can see both the window and a portion of the desktop.

2. Click the icon for the default printer (the one with the ✔) to select it.

   TROUBLE?If you are using a computer that is not connected to a network or printer, you will not be able to complete the steps in this section. Instead, read through the following steps to familiarize yourself with this process.

3. Click **File** on the menu bar, and then click **Create Shortcut**. A message appears, indicating that Windows cannot create a shortcut in the Printers and Faxes window. This is because the Printers and Faxes window shows the actual printers installed to work with your computer; you don't need a shortcut to a printer here. The message also asks if you want to place the shortcut on the desktop instead.

4. Click the **Yes** button. A shortcut icon for the printer you selected appears on the desktop. See Figure 4-12.

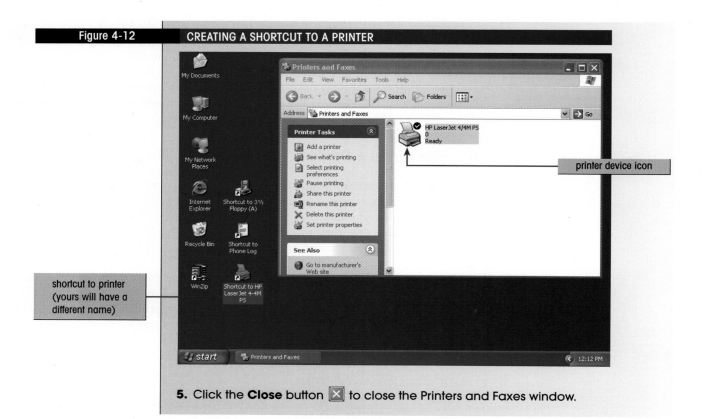

Figure 4-12   CREATING A SHORTCUT TO A PRINTER

printer device icon

shortcut to printer (yours will have a different name)

5. Click the **Close** button ☒ to close the Printers and Faxes window.

Now you can show Beth how to print the Phone Log document on your Data Disk using the printer shortcut icon and the Phone Log document icon.

To print the Phone Log document using the printer shortcut icon:

1. Make sure your Data Disk is in drive A. Using the left mouse button, drag the **Shortcut to Phone Log** icon to the **Shortcut to Printer** icon that you just created on the desktop.

When you release the mouse button, Windows XP opens the Phone Log in Notepad and then prints the Phone Log. Normally Windows XP would simply close the program, but because your document has an automatic time-date stamp, the document is changed every time you open it. Thus, Windows XP asks if you want to save changes to the document before closing it. You don't need to save it because you don't have any new phone entries to log.

2. When prompted to save the changes to the Phone Log document, click the **No** button. Windows XP closes Notepad without saving the document.

If you are working on your own computer, you can leave the printer and drive icons in place, if you think you'll find them useful. Otherwise, you should delete all the shortcuts you created so that the desktop is restored to its original condition for the next user.

Deleting Shortcut Icons

If you delete a document icon, you also delete the document. If you delete a shortcut icon, however, you don't delete the document itself because it is stored elsewhere. You only delete the shortcut that points to the document. For example, if you removed your Data Disk from drive A, the shortcut to the Phone Log would no longer work because the source document would no longer be available.

To delete your shortcuts:

1. Click the **printer** shortcut icon to select it.

2. Press and hold down the **Ctrl** key, then click the **3½ Floppy (A:)** shortcut icon and the **Phone Log** shortcut icon, so that all three icons are highlighted. Make sure no other icons are highlighted. If they are, deselect them by clicking them while you hold down the Ctrl key.

3. Press the **Delete** key.

4. Click the **Yes** button if you are asked if you are sure you want to send these items to the Recycle Bin.

Your desktop is restored to its original appearance. You have learned how to create a docucentric desktop by creating and storing a document icon on the desktop, and by creating desktop shortcuts to a drive, document, and printer. You have also learned the difference between document icons and shortcut icons, and how to remove both from the desktop.

Session 4.1 QUICK | CHECK

1. True or False: On a docucentric desktop, the quickest way to open a document is by locating the program that created the document, starting the program, and then using the Open command to locate and open the document.

2. True or False: You can create a document with an automatic time-date stamp in Notepad by typing "log" at the beginning of the document.

3. What happens if you delete a document icon on the desktop?

4. What happens if you delete a shortcut icon on the desktop?

5. Name three ways you can create a shortcut to the floppy drive on your desktop.

SESSION 4.2

In this session, you'll change the appearance of your desktop by working with a Windows XP tool called Control Panel. You'll experiment with your desktop's background and appearance, enable a screen saver, try different colors to see how they look, and modify desktop settings to explore your monitor's capabilities. As you proceed through this session, check with your instructor or technical support person before you change settings on a school lab computer, and make sure you change them back before you leave.

Using the Control Panel

In Session 4.1, you worked with document and shortcut icons to personalize your desktop. You can also personalize other parts of Windows XP using the Control Panel. The **Control Panel** is a window that contains specialized tools you use to change the way Windows looks and behaves. Some of these tools help you adjust settings that make your computer more fun to use. For example, you can use the Display tool to change the color of your desktop or display a graphic image in the background. You can also use the Sounds and Audio Devices tool to replace standard system sounds with sounds you choose. Other Control Panel tools help you set up Windows so that your computer is easier to use. For example, if you are left-handed, you can use the Mouse tool to switch the mouse buttons so that the button on the right performs the primary functions of selecting and dragging.

All of the Control Panel tools provide access to a dialog box that lets you select or change the **properties**, or characteristics, of an object. For example, to set or change the time of the clock shown on the taskbar, you open the Date/Time Properties dialog box, which you access from Control Panel.

To open the Control Panel:

1. Click the **Start** button start on the taskbar, and then click **Control Panel**. See Figure 4-13.

Figure 4-13   CONTROL PANEL

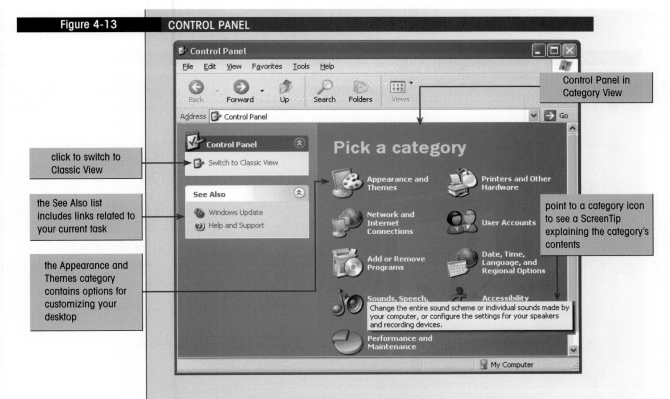

click to switch to
Classic View

the See Also list
includes links related to
your current task

the Appearance and
Themes category
contains options for
customizing your
desktop

Control Panel in
Category View

point to a category icon
to see a ScreenTip
explaining the category's
contents

The Control Panel window opens, showing tasks in the right pane and related links in the left pane. By default, the Control Panel opens in Category View, which groups similar tools into categories.

TROUBLE? If a message appears indicating that the Control Panel is not available, you might be in a computer lab with limited ability for customization. Ask your instructor or technical support person for options.

TROUBLE? If Control Panel opens in Classic View, click Switch to Category View in the left pane of the Control Panel window.

Figure 4-14 describes the Control Panel categories.

Figure 4-14	CONTROL PANEL CATEGORIES
CONTROL PANEL CATEGORY	**DESCRIPTION**
Appearance and Themes	Change the appearance of desktop items, apply a theme or screen saver, or customize the Start menu and taskbar
Network and Inrernet Connections	Connect to the Internet, create a home or small office network, configure network settings to work from home, or change the modem, phone, and Internet settings
Add or Remove Programs	Install and uninstall programs and Windows components
Sounds, Speech, and Audio Devices	Change the sound scheme or individual sounds on your computer and configure the settings for your sound devices
Performance and Maintenance	Schedule maintenance checks, increase the space on your hard disk, or configure energy-saving settings
Printers and Other Hardware	Change the settings for your printer, keyboard, mouse, camera, and other hardware
User Accounts	Change user accounts settings, passwords, and associated pictures (Windows XP Professional only)
Date, Time, Language, and Regional Options	Change the date, time, and time zone, the language you use on your computer, and the format for numbers, currencies, dates, and times
Accessibility Options	Change computer settings for vision, hearing, and mobility

If you are familiar with an earlier version of Windows, such as Windows 2000, and are more comfortable with the view that displays all of the tools individually, you can change to Classic View by clicking the Switch to Classic View link in the left pane. For now, however, you'll continue to explore the Control Panel in Category View.

To open a category and see its related tools, you click the appropriate link. For example, you can open the Appearance and Themes window to change the way the screen looks and behaves, or to set a **theme**, a collection of related colors, images, and effects for the desktop.

To open the Appearance and Themes category:

1. In the right pane of the Control Panel, click **Appearance and Themes**. The Control Panel window displays the tasks and tools related to changing your computer's appearance and setting themes. See Figure 4-15.

Figure 4-15	APPEARANCE AND THEMES OPTIONS IN THE CONTROL PANEL

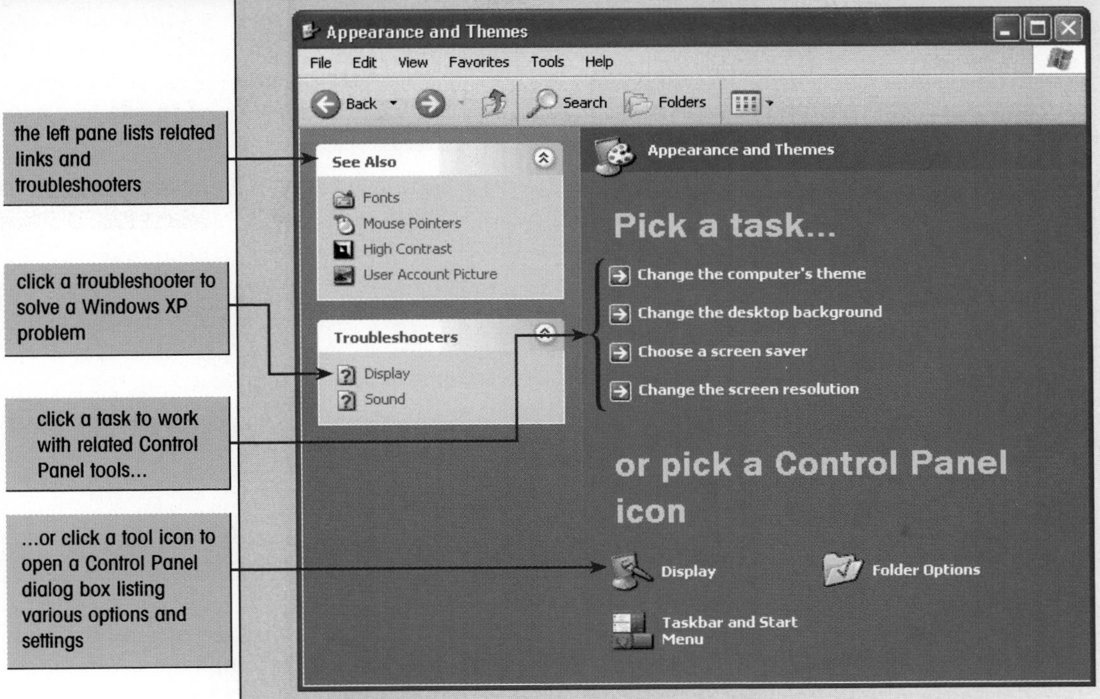

the left pane lists related links and troubleshooters

click a troubleshooter to solve a Windows XP problem

click a task to work with related Control Panel tools...

...or click a tool icon to open a Control Panel dialog box listing various options and settings

Appearance and Themes

File   Edit   View   Favorites   Tools   Help

Back   ·   Search   Folders

See Also
- Fonts
- Mouse Pointers
- High Contrast
- User Account Picture

Troubleshooters
- Display
- Sound

Appearance and Themes

Pick a task...

- Change the computer's theme
- Change the desktop background
- Choose a screen saver
- Change the screen resolution

or pick a Control Panel icon

Display

Folder Options

Taskbar and Start Menu

TROUBLE? Because some tools are optional, your Control Panel might display different tools from the ones shown in Figure 4-15.

The Appearance and Themes window, like the other Control Panel category windows, lists tasks and tools in the right pane and related links in the left pane. To change an element of the desktop, you click the appropriate task in the right pane. For example, when you click the Change the desktop background link, the Display Properties dialog box opens to the Background tab, where you can select or change a desktop background. You can also click the Display tool icon in the right pane to open the Display Properties dialog box to its default tab. The See Also section in the left pane lists links related to the Appearance and Themes tools. The left pane also lists **troubleshooters**, links you can click to solve problems with the display and sound on your computer.

Figure 4-16 lists the options in the Appearance and Themes window and describes their purposes.

Figure 4-16   APPEARANCE AND THEMES OPTIONS

APPEARANCE AND THEMES OPTION	DESCRIPTION
Change the computer's theme	Change the set of colors, images, and other effects for your desktop, or save the current set as a new theme
Change the desktop background	Change the color or background pattern or image of your desktop
Choose a screen saver	Select a moving image to display on the screen after the computer has been idle for a specified amount of time
Change the screen resolution	Change the sharpness of the screen and the quality of the color
Display icon	Open the Display Properties dialog box to change display properties for themes, the desktop background, screen saver, appearance, and other settings
Folder Options	Open the Folder Options dialog box to change the way folders look and behave
Taskbar and Start Menu	Open the Taskbar and Start Menu Properties dialog box to change the way the taskbar and Start menu look and behave
See Also	Set or change properties for fonts, mouse pointers, contrast, or user accounts
Troubleshooters	Open a series of dialog boxes that will help you solve problems with the display and sound on your computer

Beth wants her office computers to reflect the company image of Companions, Inc. She'd like the desktop itself to be more appealing to her and her employees. You suggest she work with the desktop properties to change the desktop background and other elements.

Changing Desktop Properties

In Windows XP, you can think of all the parts of your computer—the operating system, the programs, and the documents—as individual objects. For example, the desktop, taskbar, drives, programs, and documents are all objects. Each object has properties that you can examine and sometimes change to suit your needs and preferences. The desktop has many properties, including its color, its size, and the font it uses. You can change the properties of an object using the Properties command on the shortcut menu or the Control Panel. In this session, you will use Control Panel to change desktop properties.

Changing Your Desktop's Background

You can change the desktop background color, or you can select a graphic to display in the background of your desktop. When you change the background, you are not placing a new object on the desktop; you are simply changing the desktop's appearance.

Beth wants the staff computers in the Companions, Inc. offices to have a corporate look. You and Beth decide to change the desktop color to dark blue, which is one of Companions, Inc.'s corporate colors.

To change the desktop color:

1. In the Appearance and Themes window, click **Change the desktop background**. The Display Properties dialog box opens to the Desktop tab. See Figure 4-17.

Figure 4-17	DESKTOP SETTINGS IN THE DISPLAY PROPERTIES DIALOG BOX

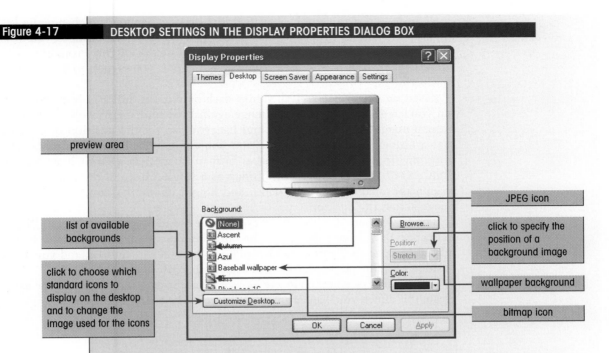

preview area

list of available backgrounds

click to choose which standard icons to display on the desktop and to change the image used for the icons

JPEG icon

click to specify the position of a background image

wallpaper background

bitmap icon

2. Minimize the Appearance and Themes window so you can see the Display Properties dialog box and the desktop at the same time.

3. Note the currently selected background color—you will restore this setting later.

4. If necessary, click **(None)** in the Background list if it is not already selected. The Preview window shows the background as the default color.

5. Click the **Color** list arrow, and then click **dark blue** (row 4, column 2) in the color palette. See Figure 4-18.

Figure 4-18	CHANGING THE COLOR OF THE DESKTOP

Display Properties   ? X

Themes | Desktop | Screen Saver | Appearance | Settings

Background:
- (None)
- Ascent
- Autumn
- Azul
- Baseball wallpaper
- Bliss

Customize Desktop...

Other...

OK   Cancel   Apply

click this color

Right now, dark blue only appears in the Preview window. To change the desktop color but keep the Display Properties dialog box open to make other changes, you would click the Apply button. To change the desktop color and close the Display Properties dialog box, you would click the OK button. Before you do either one, you suggest to Beth that you continue to experiment.

Based on the preview, Beth thinks dark blue looks dull as a background on its own, but you suggest that placing an image against the blue might work well. If you choose a bitmap image from the Background list, you can set the position of the image. Recall that a bitmap image is a graphic that you can edit in Paint or another image-editing program. In the Background list, a bitmap image has a Paint icon ![icon], as shown in Figure 4-17. You can display a bitmap as a single image in the middle of the desktop, stretch the image across the width and height of the desktop, or repeat—or tile—the image across the desktop.

The Background list also includes two kinds of photographic images: JPEG images and wallpaper. Both have a ![icon] icon. The only differences are that wallpaper backgrounds are related to desktop themes, which you'll use later in this tutorial, and you can change the position of wallpaper backgrounds, but not other JPEG images.

Beth wants to see how an image looks if it has the dark blue desktop as its background. To create this effect, you display a bitmap image in the center of the desktop.

To select and position a bitmap image:

1. Scroll the Background list to locate and then click **Prairie Wind**. A pattern of blues and greens fills the preview window. Note that Tile is the default position for this image, so the pattern repeats across the screen.

   TROUBLE? If the Prairie Wind image isn't available, choose a different bitmap image.

2. Click the **Position** list arrow, and then click **Center** to preview a single copy of the Prairie Wind image in the middle of the desktop.

3. Click the **Apply** button to apply this effect to the desktop. See Figure 4-19.

Figure 4-19	PRAIRIE WIND IMAGE POSITIONED IN THE CENTER OF THE DESKTOP

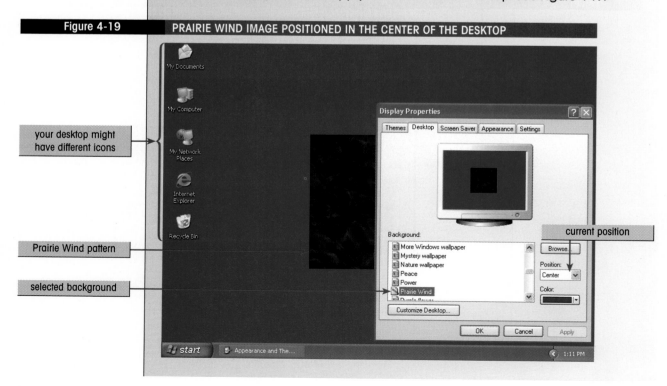

Beth doesn't think the Prairie Wind image fits her company very well. You decide to experiment with other backgrounds. Recall that in the Background list, an image with a JPEG icon indicates a photographic image. You decide to explore these backgrounds. Beth noticed a background named Home and thinks that might be appropriate for her business, which offers housecleaning and home maintenance services.

To select a photographic background:

1. Click **Home** in the Background list.

   TROUBLE? If the Home image is not available, choose a different JPEG image from the Background list.

2. Click the **Apply** button. See Figure 4-20.

Figure 4-20	USING A PHOTOGRAPHIC IMAGE AS THE DESKTOP BACKGROUND

current background image

This image doesn't reflect Companions, Inc.'s company image, so you return to the Background list.

3. Experiment with the other photographic backgrounds by clicking them in the Background list and then previewing them in the preview area. Click the **Apply** button to see each image on your desktop rather than only in the preview area.

As you experiment, you might notice the photographic images that include "wallpaper" in their names. Recall that you can change the position of wallpaper backgrounds.

To change the position of a wallpaper image:

1. In the Background list, click **Baseball wallpaper**. The image appears in the preview area in the Stretch position, which is the default.

   TROUBLE? If the Baseball wallpaper is not available, click a different wallpaper background or a different photographic image.

2. Click the **Position** list arrow, and then click **Center**. Instead of reducing the photograph to a single small image in the middle of the screen, the center of the image—the batter and the catcher—enlarges to fill the entire screen. In effect, this brings the center of the photograph into focus.

3. Click the **Position** list arrow, and then click **Tile**. Now the batter and only part of the catcher appear. If the Baseball wallpaper photo were smaller than the screen, part of it would repeat on the right or bottom of the screen.

Besides using an image included in the Background list, you can also use any image you can access with your computer, including graphic images stored on a disk or those you find on the Web. Whereas the Background list includes only graphics in the bitmap (BMP) and JPEG formats, you can use graphics in other types of formats, such as GIF, a popular format for Web graphics.

None of the backgrounds that come with Windows XP suits Beth's corporate image, so you ask her if she would like to use a graphic of her company logo. She is enthusiastic; it would be great if clients who come to the offices could see the company logo on the office computers.

To use a graphic image as a custom desktop background:

1. If necessary, place your Data Disk in drive A.

2. Click the **Browse** button on the Desktop property sheet. The Browse dialog box opens, showing the contents of a folder on your hard drive.

   The Companions, Inc. logo is on your Data Disk, however, so you'll display the contents of the floppy drive next.

3. Click the **Look in** list arrow, and then click **3½ Floppy (A:)**.

4. Click the file **Logo**.

   TROUBLE? If Logo appears as Logo.bmp, click Logo.bmp. Your computer is set to display file extensions.

5. Click the **Open** button.

6. Click the **Position** list arrow, and then click **Center** to center the image on the screen.

7. Click the **OK** button to close the Display Properties dialog box. See Figure 4-21. The logo for Companions, Inc. appears in the middle of the desktop.

Figure 4-21	COMPANIONS LOGO AS THE DESKTOP BACKGROUND

Beth looks over your shoulder and comments that the blue in the background and the blue of the logo coordinate well. But she wants to use a contrasting color for window title bars and buttons. She asks you to change those elements to white or silver. Also, because some staff and volunteers are senior citizens, she wants to make the text of desktop elements and the icons themselves larger so they are easier to read and recognize.

Changing the Appearance of Desktop Elements

The Appearance property sheet on the Display Properties dialog box gives you control over the appearance of all the items on the desktop, including icons, title bars, borders, menus, and scroll bars. You also use the Appearance property sheet to change the window colors and font size.

To open the Appearance property sheet:

1. Click the **Appearance and Themes** button on the taskbar to restore the Appearance and Themes window, and then click **Display** to open the Display Properties dialog box. Minimize the Appearance and Themes window.

2. Click the **Appearance** tab in the Display Properties dialog box. The Appearance property sheet appears, as shown in Figure 4-22.

Figure 4-22   **APPEARANCE PROPERTY SHEET**

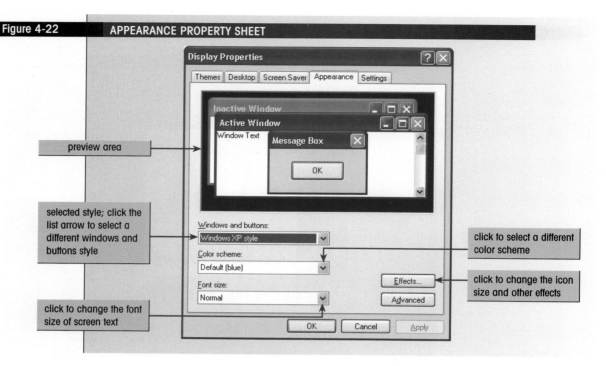

The Appearance property sheet includes several list boxes from which you select options to change the desktop's appearance. Notice the Color scheme list box. A **color scheme** is a set of colors you can apply to the elements shown in the preview area. Windows XP includes a collection of color schemes, and the default scheme for the Windows XP style is blue. However, if your computer is in a lab, your technical support person might have designed and selected a different scheme. Before you experiment with the appearance of your desktop, you should write down the current scheme so you can restore it when you are finished working through the steps in this tutorial.

The preview area on the Appearance property sheet displays many of the elements you are likely to see when working with Windows XP. After you change an appearance setting, look in the preview area to see how the new setting will affect your windows and dialog boxes.

To change the color scheme of desktop elements:

1. Make a note of the current scheme, which is displayed in the Color scheme list box.

   TROUBLE? If your Color scheme list box is empty, your technical support person might have changed scheme settings without saving the scheme. Each time you change an object's color, write down the original color so you can restore that object's color when you are finished.

2. Note the style name in the Windows and buttons text box, and then click the **Color scheme** list arrow. The list shows the color schemes you can use for the style shown in the Windows and buttons text box.

3. Click **Silver**. The preview window shows how the silver color scheme looks in the Windows XP style.

   Now you want to increase the size of the text on the desktop elements.

4. Click the **Font size** list arrow, and then click **Large Fonts**. The preview window again shows the effects of this change.

5. To increase the size of the icons, click the **Effects** button. The Effects dialog box opens, as shown in Figure 4-23.

Figure 4-23 | THE EFFECTS DIALOG BOX

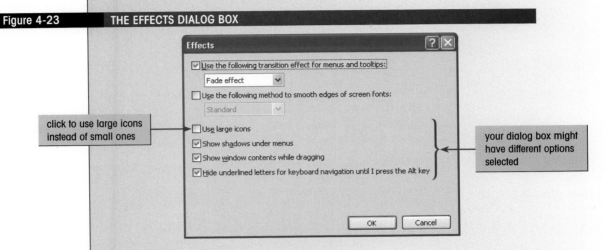

click to use large icons instead of small ones

your dialog box might have different options selected

The Effects dialog box allows you to set visual effects for windows, menus, icons, and screen fonts.

6. In the Effects dialog box, click the **Use large icons** box to insert a check, and then click the **OK** button to close the Effects dialog box.

7. Click the **OK** button in the Appearance property sheet to apply your changes to the desktop. See Figure 4-24.

Figure 4-24 | APPEARANCE OF THE MODIFIED DESKTOP

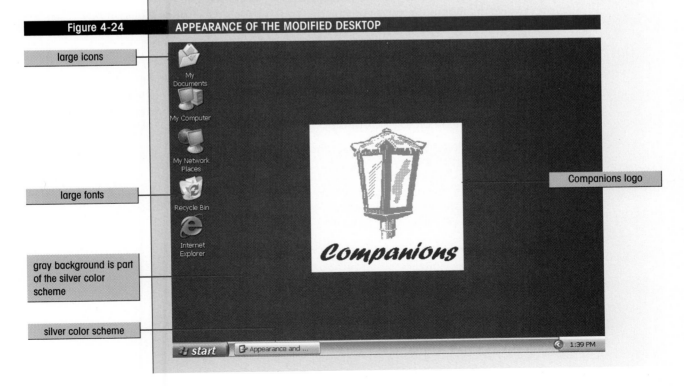

large icons

large fonts

gray background is part of the silver color scheme

silver color scheme

Companions logo

Because you applied a color scheme, Windows XP changed the color of many elements, including the taskbar, desktop icons, and icon labels. As you continue to work, you'll notice other elements have changed, including the text in shortcut menus and dialog boxes. Beth is pleased with how the desktop looks except for one thing—the background color you set earlier, the dark blue, has been replaced by a steel gray. This is because the gray desktop background is part of the silver color scheme. You can easily use the Display Properties dialog box again to change the desktop background back to blue. When you do, note the colors, fonts, and icons used on the desktop and in the dialog box.

To restore the dark blue desktop:

1. Click the **Appearance and Themes** button on the taskbar to restore the Appearance and Themes window, and then click **Change the desktop background** to open the Desktop property sheet of the Display Properties dialog box. Minimize the Appearance and Themes window.

   Note the silver color scheme applied to the title bar, tabs, and buttons in the Display Properties dialog box.

2. Click the **Color** list arrow, and then click **dark blue** (row 4, column 2) in the palette.

3. Click the **OK** button to apply the color to the desktop and close the Display Properties dialog box.

Now that you have customized the desktop, you can save the settings as a theme. Recall that a theme is a collection of customized elements, such as colors and graphics, that you apply to your desktop. If you save your current settings as a theme, you can apply all the changes—the dark blue background with the Companions logo, the silver color scheme, and large fonts—at the same time, without selecting the individual settings again. You can save the desktop settings you created for Beth as a theme called Companions.

To save the desktop settings as a theme:

1. Restore the Appearance and Themes window, and then click **Change the computer's theme** to open the Themes property sheet of the Display Properties dialog box. Minimize the Appearance and Themes window so you can see both the dialog box and portion of the desktop at the same time.

2. Click the **Theme** list arrow. See Figure 4-25.

Figure 4-25   **LIST OF THEMES**

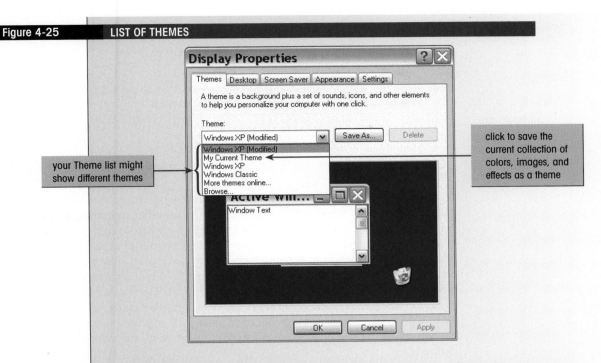

your Theme list might show different themes

click to save the current collection of colors, images, and effects as a theme

3. Click **My Current Theme**, if necessary. The My Current Theme option includes all the properties currently set in the Display Properties dialog box.

4. Click the **Save As** button.

5. In the Save As dialog box, navigate to your Data Disk. In the File name text box, type **Companions** as the name of this theme.

6. Click the **Save** button.

After you save the Companions theme on your Data Disk, restore the desktop colors and other appearance properties to their original settings.

To restore the desktop colors and appearance to their original settings:

1. Click the **Desktop** tab in the Display Properties dialog box.

2. In the Background list, locate and then click the desktop background that was in effect before you began this tutorial.

3. Click the **Appearance** tab.

4. Click the **Color scheme** list arrow, and then locate and click the color scheme you wrote down earlier, such as **Default (blue)**.

   TROUBLE? If your Color scheme list box was blank when you began working with the Appearance property sheet, skip Step 5 and instead restore each setting you changed to the original color you wrote down in the beginning of this section. Proceed to Step 6.

5. Click the **Font size** list arrow, and then click **Normal**.

6. Click the **Effects** button.

7. Click the **Use large icons** check box button to deselect it, and then click the **OK** button.

8. Click the **Apply** button. The original desktop is restored. Leave the Display Properties dialog box open.

Activating a Screen Saver

A **screen saver** blanks the screen or displays a moving design whenever you haven't worked with the computer for a specified period of time. In older monitors, a screen saver can help prevent "burn-in," or the permanent etching of an image into the screen, which occurs when the screen displays the same image for long periods of time. This is not a concern with newer monitors. However, screen savers are still handy for hiding your data from the eyes of passers-by if you step away from your computer. When a screen saver is on, you restore your desktop by moving your mouse or pressing any key on the keyboard.

You can select how long you want the computer to sit idle before the screen saver activates. Most users find settings between 3 and 10 minutes work best for them. You can change this using the options on the Screen Saver property sheet of the Display Properties dialog box.

Windows XP provides a wide variety of screen savers. Beth would like a screen saver that displays the name of the company. You decide to show her how to set up this screen saver.

To activate a screen saver:

1. Click the **Screen Saver** tab in the Display Properties dialog box. See Figure 4-26.

Figure 4-26	THE SCREEN SAVER PROPERTY SHEET

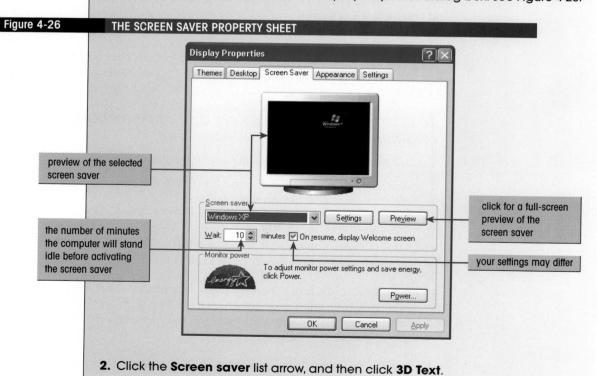

preview of the selected screen saver

click for a full-screen preview of the screen saver

the number of minutes the computer will stand idle before activating the screen saver

your settings may differ

2. Click the **Screen saver** list arrow, and then click **3D Text**.

TROUBLE? If the Screen Saver list box does not display 3D Text, you will not be able to complete these steps. Read through them to become familiar with the process.

3. Click the **Settings** button. The 3D Text Settings dialog box opens.

4. Select the text in the Custom Text box, and then type **Companions, Inc.** (including the final period). See Figure 4-27.

Figure 4-27   **THE 3D SETTINGS DIALOG BOX**

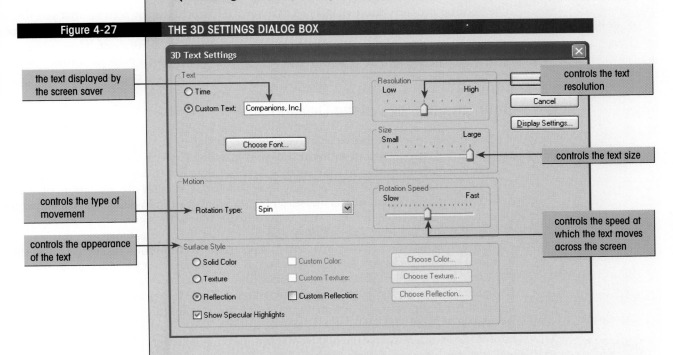

the text displayed by the screen saver

controls the text resolution

controls the text size

controls the type of movement

controls the appearance of the text

controls the speed at which the text moves across the screen

The 3D Text Settings dialog box contains several options you can set to control the screen saver. You can control the motion, the speed at which the text appears on the screen, the size of the text, the texture or color of the text, and also the way the text moves across the screen. You'll keep the defaults for all of these options.

5. Click the **OK** button.

The Preview window in the Screen Saver property sheet shows a preview of the screen saver. You can also view a full-screen preview of the screen saver.

6. Click the **Preview** button.

The screen saver fills the screen.

TROUBLE? If you move the mouse after clicking the Preview button, the screen saver will disappear, sometimes so quickly that you cannot even see it. Repeat Step 6, but make sure you don't move the mouse after you click the Preview button.

7. When you're finished previewing the screen saver move the mouse and then click the **Cancel** button to cancel your screen saver changes and close the Display Properties dialog box. If you were working on your own computer and wanted to save the changes, you would click the Apply button to save the changes or the OK button to save the changes and close the Display Properties dialog box.

Now that you have worked with the properties for the desktop background, theme, and screen saver, you are ready to explore the display properties that affect the computer monitor itself. The Settings property sheet lets you change the sharpness of the images on the desktop and the number of colors your monitor displays.

Changing Display Settings

The Settings property sheet allows you to control additional display settings that you might never need to consider. However, if you want to take full advantage of your monitor type, you should be aware of the options you have on the Settings property sheet. The settings you can change depend on your monitor type and on the **video card**, a piece of hardware inside your computer that controls visual information you see on the screen.

Changing the Size of the Desktop Area

The Settings property sheet has a Screen resolution slider bar that lets you display less or more of the desktop on your monitor. If you display less, objects will look bigger, while if you display more, objects will look smaller. You can drag the slider bar between these two extremes. When you do, you are actually increasing or decreasing the resolution, or sharpness, of the image. Resolution is measured by the number of individual dots, called **pixels**, short for "picture elements," that run across and down your monitor. The more pixels, the more you see on the screen at one time, and the smaller the objects look.

The 800 by 600 (800 pixels across and 600 pixels down) resolution shows the least information, but uses the largest text and is preferred by most users with 15-inch monitors. The 1024 by 768 resolution shows more information, but uses smaller text. Many users with 17-inch monitors prefer the 1024 by 768 resolution. The 1152 by 864 resolution shows the most information, but uses the smallest text. Most users find the 1152 by 864 resolution too small for comfortable use unless they are using a 17-inch or larger monitor. Users with limited vision might prefer the 800 by 600 setting even on larger monitors, because objects and text are bigger and easier to see. The software you use might also recommend you change the screen resolution to take advantage of special features in the software.

To change the screen resolution:

1. Open the Appearance and Themes window, and then click **Change the screen resolution** to display the Settings tab of the Display Properties dialog box. Minimize the Appearance and Themes window.

2. Make note of the original setting in the Screen resolution area so you can restore it once you finish this tutorial.

3. To select the 800 by 600 pixels resolution, if it is not already selected, drag the **Screen resolution** slider to the left. The preview monitor shows the relative size of the 800 by 600 display. See Figure 4-28.

Figure 4-28	800 BY 600 RESOLUTION

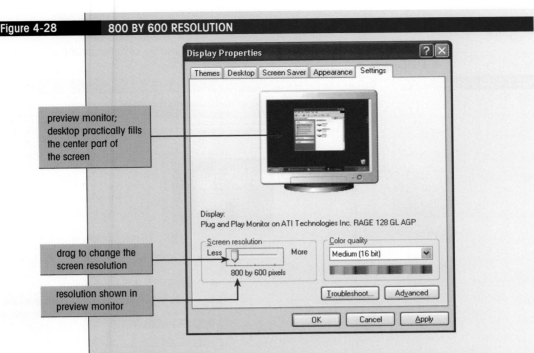

preview monitor; desktop practically fills the center part of the screen

drag to change the screen resolution

resolution shown in preview monitor

4. To select the 1024 by 768 resolution, drag the Screen area slider to the right. The preview monitor shows the relative size of the 1024 by 768 display.

5. Return the slider to the setting it was at the end of Step 2. Leave the Display Properties dialog box open.

While changing the screen resolution increases or decreases the sharpness of the images, the number of colors your monitor displays determines how realistic the images look. However, the higher the resolution and color settings, the more resources your monitor needs; the best settings for your computer balance sharpness and color quality with computer resources.

Changing the Color Settings

You can also use the Settings property sheet to change the color settings, which specify the number of colors available to your computer to create shading and other realistic effects. Beth's computers use High color, which includes up to 65,000 colors. Figure 4-29 provides additional information on common color settings. The color settings depend on your monitor, so your computer may have more or fewer settings.

Figure 4-29	COLOR SETTINGS

SETTING	DESCRIPTION
Medium (65,000 colors)	Relatively fast, requires a moderate amount of video memory, sufficient for most programs and adequate for the graphics in most games and educational programs. This is a good setting for gereral computer use.
High (16 million colors)	Requires higher-quality video card and additional video memory. This setting is useful for sophisticated painting, drawing, and graphics manipulation tasks.
Highest (over 4 billion colors)	Requires the most video memory and runs most slowly. This setting is useful for professional graphics tasks, but might not be available or might be too slow on some computer systems.

To view the color settings:

1. Click the **Color quality** list arrow to display the list of color palettes. See Figure 4-30.

Figure 4-30 | **CHANGING THE COLOR SETTINGS**

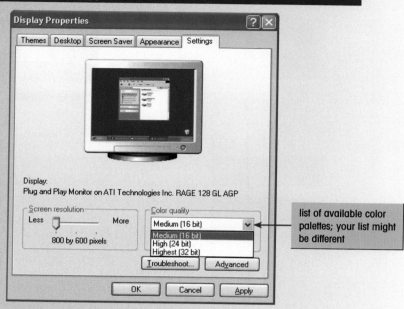

list of available color palettes; your list might be different

2. Click **High (24 bit)**. Depending on your monitor, your screen can now display up to 16 million colors, which allows realistic shading and gradation.

TROUBLE? If High (24 bit) doesn't appear in your Color quality list, skip Step 2.

3. Click the **Cancel** button to close the Display Properties dialog box without accepting any changes.

4. If you are working in a school lab, make sure you have changed all settings back to their original state before moving on to Session 4.3.

5. Close the Appearance and Themes window.

You used the Control Panel and its tools to change the properties of Beth's desktop, including the background and the appearance of desktop elements, such as windows and icons. You added a graphic to the desktop background, saved her color scheme as a theme, activated a screen saver, and experimented with the display settings. Beth can now change the desktops of other computers in her office so they all reflect the corporate image of Companions, Inc.

Session 4.2 QUICK CHECK

1. True or False: The desktop is the on-screen work area where windows, icons, menus, and dialog boxes appear.

2. What is the Control Panel used for?

3. Name three desktop properties you can change from the Display Properties dialog box.

4. If you have a recently manufactured monitor, why might you use a screen saver?

5. What does it mean to say that a monitor's resolution is 800 by 600?

6. Users with limited vision might want to use which resolution: 800 by 600, 1024 by 768, or 1152 by 864? Why?

7. What is the disadvantage of using color settings with many colors, such as Highest Color?

SESSION 4.3

In this session, you'll work with the taskbar and Start menu objects on the desktop. You'll learn how to modify the appearance and location of the taskbar, and how to add items to it. You'll work with the properties of the Start menu, and learn how to add items to the menu and how to modify the existing menu items.

Modifying the Taskbar

As you know from previous tutorials, the bar that contains the Start button and appears by default at the bottom of the desktop is the taskbar. Besides the Start button, which you can click to open the Start menu, the taskbar shows the current time and buttons for any programs or documents that you currently have open. In addition, you can display toolbars on the taskbar. These toolbars can contain buttons for the icons on your desktop, for programs you use often, and for Web pages that you want to access quickly. Including these toolbars on the taskbar makes it easy to navigate your computer and open programs, documents, and Web pages without minimizing windows or closing dialog boxes that might be open on the desktop. Figure 4-31 shows some common items that can appear on the toolbar.

Figure 4-31   SOME ITEMS THAT CAN APPEAR ON THE TASKBAR

Start button

start   My Documents   Phone log - Notepad   Desktop   1:22 PM

Quick Launch toolbar   program buttons   Desktop toolbar

Besides displaying items on the taskbar, you can change the size and position of the taskbar itself, or even hide it altogether. For example, if you are editing a long document or creating a drawing and find that the taskbar gets in your way, you can hide the taskbar or move it to the sides or top of the desktop. If the taskbar becomes crowded with toolbars and program buttons, you can resize the taskbar to show more items.

So far you've shown Beth how to work with many properties of the Windows XP desktop. Now you can show her two other parts of the Windows XP desktop: the taskbar and the Start menu. You'll start by showing her how to work with the taskbar.

Moving and Resizing the Taskbar

When you first install Windows XP, the taskbar is locked in its position at the bottom of the desktop. That way, as you learn your way around Windows, you always have access to the Start menu, which you use to start programs and shut down Windows. Before you can move or resize the taskbar, however, you must unlock it. You can do so by right-clicking the taskbar to open its shortcut menu and then clicking the Lock the Taskbar command. Because this command is listed with a check mark by default to indicate it's selected, clicking it again removes the check mark, indicating the taskbar is no longer locked.

Beth's previous computer was a Macintosh, and she's used to seeing a menu bar at the top of the desktop. She wants to know how to change the position of the taskbar to create this familiar appearance. First, you will unlock the taskbar and then move it to the top of the desktop.

REFERENCE   WINDOW   **RW**

Moving and Resizing the Taskbar

- Make sure the taskbar is unlocked. To do so, right-click any blank area on the taskbar, and then click Lock the Taskbar on the shortcut menu to remove the check mark.
- To move the taskbar, click a blank area on the taskbar, hold down the left mouse button, and drag the taskbar to a new location (the top, bottom, left, or right edge of the desktop).
- To resize the taskbar, move the mouse pointer over the taskbar border until the pointer changes to a $\updownarrow$. Then drag the border to the desired width.

To move the taskbar:

1. Right-click any blank area on the taskbar, and then, if necessary, click **Lock the Taskbar** on the shortcut menu to remove the check mark.

   TROUBLE? If the Lock the Taskbar command is already unchecked, skip Step 1.

2. Drag the taskbar to the top of the desktop. See Figure 4-32. Notice that the icons currently on the desktop moved down slightly to make room for the newly placed taskbar.

Figure 4-32	MOVING THE WINDOWS XP TASKBAR TO THE TOP OF THE DESKTOP

taskbar relocated to the top of the desktop

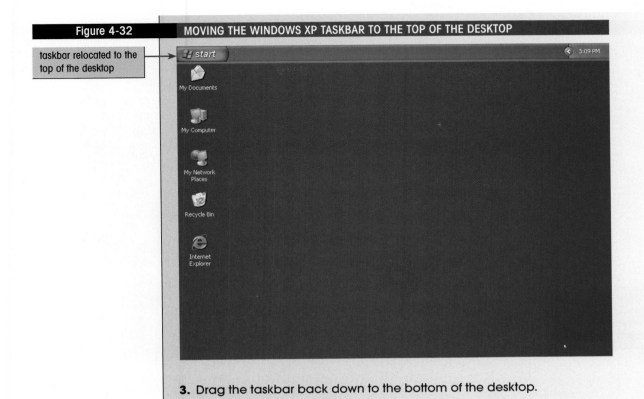

3. Drag the taskbar back down to the bottom of the desktop.

Beth has also noticed that when she has several programs running simultaneously, the icons for those programs fill the taskbar, sometimes to such an extent that the individual icons are compressed beyond recognition. You tell her that one way of dealing with that problem is to increase the size of the taskbar. This is easily accomplished by dragging the taskbar border to make the taskbar larger. Try this now.

To increase the size of the taskbar:

1. Move the mouse pointer over the top edge of the taskbar until the pointer changes to $\updownarrow$.

2. Drag the top border up, releasing the left mouse button when the taskbar has increased in height. See Figure 4-33.

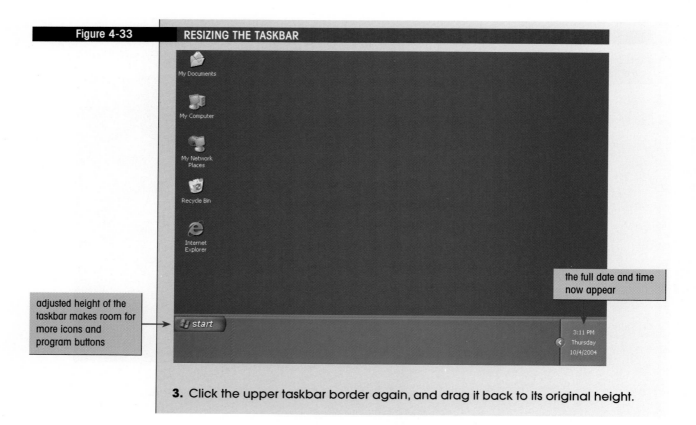

Figure 4-33 RESIZING THE TASKBAR

the full date and time now appear

adjusted height of the taskbar makes room for more icons and program buttons

3:11 PM
Thursday
10/4/2004

3. Click the upper taskbar border again, and drag it back to its original height.

Resizing the taskbar is one way to change its appearance. You also can change other taskbar properties, such as those that determine when the taskbar appears.

Setting Taskbar Appearance Properties

In addition to resizing and relocating the taskbar, you can set taskbar appearance properties using the Taskbar and Start Menu Properties dialog box. Using this dialog box, you can increase the amount of screen space available for your program windows by hiding the taskbar. In this case, the taskbar is not closed, removed, or minimized, but is hidden either under the border of the desktop or under the program windows open on the desktop. It still remains active and accessible—you can use the mouse to point to the area of your screen where the taskbar is located to redisplay the taskbar.

By default, the taskbar appears on top of windows on the desktop, but you can change this setting in the Taskbar and Start Menu Properties dialog box so that program windows and dialog boxes cover the taskbar when necessary. Other taskbar appearance properties that you can set include whether to show the Quick Launch toolbar on the taskbar. The Quick Launch toolbar contains icons you can click to open programs quickly, show the desktop, or perform other tasks. You'll have a chance to add the Quick Launch toolbar to the taskbar later in this session.

Beth wants to see how to increase the amount of desktop space by hiding the taskbar or letting windows cover it. You'll show her how to change these taskbar appearance properties.

To set taskbar appearance properties:

1. Right-click a blank area in the taskbar, and click **Properties** on the shortcut menu. The Taskbar and Start Menu Properties dialog box opens, as shown in Figure 4-34.

Figure 4-34	THE TASKBAR AND START MENU PROPERTIES DIALOG BOX

locks or unlocks the taskbar in its current position

hides the task bar unless the mouse pointer is resting on it

places the taskbar on top of all other windows

shows or hides the clock and unused icon on the right side of the taskbar

Taskbar and Start Menu Properties

Taskbar | Start Menu

Taskbar appearance

start | 2 Internet... | Folder

☐ Lock the taskbar
☐ Auto-hide the taskbar
☑ Keep the taskbar on top of other windows
☑ Group similar taskbar buttons
☐ Show Quick Launch

Notification area

« 1:23 PM

☑ Show the clock

You can keep the notification area uncluttered by hiding icons that you have not clicked recently.

☑ Hide inactive icons   Customize...

OK | Cancel | Apply

if you have more than one document open in the same program, this option groups them on one taskbar button

shows the Quick Launch toolbar on the taskbar

2. Make note of the options currently selected in this dialog box, as you will need to restore these options when you are finished with this tutorial.

3. Click the **Auto-hide the taskbar** check box to select this option, and then click the **Apply** button. The taskbar disappears from the bottom of the desktop.

   TROUBLE? If the Auto-hide the taskbar check box is already selected, skip Step 3.

4. Move the mouse pointer over the location where the taskbar previously appeared, and note that the taskbar is visible as long as the mouse pointer is over its location.

5. Deselect the **Auto-hide the taskbar** check box, and then click the **Apply** button. Now the taskbar is visible again.

6. Click to deselect the **Keep the taskbar on top of other windows** check box, and then click the **Apply** button.

   TROUBLE? If the Keep the taskbar on top of other windows check box is already deselected, skip Step 6.

7. Drag the Taskbar and Start Menu Properties dialog box so that a portion of it appears over your taskbar. Note that the dialog box now appears over the taskbar.

8. Return the options in this dialog box to the state they were in Step 2, and then click the **OK** button to close the dialog box.

The Taskbar tab in the Taskbar and Start Menu Properties dialog box also includes options relating to toolbars, and you will learn about customizing those next.

Working with Taskbar Toolbars

One of the features of the taskbar is that you can use it to display toolbars. For example, you can display the Quick Launch toolbar, which contains icons for starting Internet Explorer and your e-mail software. When you are working with programs and documents that cover your desktop, you can access your e-mail, for example, without minimizing all the windows open on the desktop. Figure 4-35 describes the toolbars you can include on the taskbar.

Figure 4-35	TASKBAR TOOLBARS
TASKBAR TOOLBAR	**DESCRIPTION**
Quick Launch	Use to access icons you can click to quickly open programs, show the desktop, or perform other tasks.
Desktop	Use to access items on your desktop, such as the Recycle Bin and My Computer, from the taskbar. Open the Desktop toolbar by clicking the double chevron (»).
Links	Use to access links to product information on the Web and add Web links by dragging them to the toolbar. Open the Links toolbar by clicking the double chevron (»).
Address bar	Use to open any Web page you specify. Open the Address bar by double-clicking it.
New	Create a new taskbar toolbar to place a shortcut to a folder on the taskbar.

Displaying a Toolbar on the Taskbar

Two taskbar toolbars are especially helpful if you have shortcut and document icons on the desktop. The Quick Launch toolbar includes a desktop icon that you can click to show the desktop—then you can add or delete shortcut icons, for example, without minimizing or closing open windows. The Desktop toolbar has an icon for each object on the desktop, including system icons, such as My Computer and the Recycle Bin, shortcut icons, and document icons.

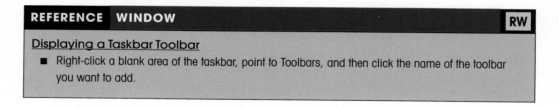

REFERENCE WINDOW   RW

Displaying a Taskbar Toolbar
- Right-click a blank area of the taskbar, point to Toolbars, and then click the name of the toolbar you want to add.

Beth often has several programs running at once, filling the screen and hiding the desktop. She has seen the benefit of placing icons on the desktop, but wants to be able to access those desktop icons without having to minimize all of her programs. You suggest that she place a Desktop toolbar on her taskbar. The Desktop toolbar includes double chevrons (>>) that you can click to display all of the icons that appear on the desktop. Beth also wants the toolbar itself to include an icon for the My Documents folder so she can quickly find the documents stored there. In addition, she occasionally wants to show the desktop itself so she can work with the shortcut and document icons. To do so, you'll show her how to add the Quick Launch toolbar to the taskbar.

To display the Quick Launch and Desktop toolbars:

1. Right-click a blank area of the taskbar.

2. On the shortcut menu, point to **Toolbars** and then click **Quick Launch**. A toolbar containing icons for your Web browser, e-mail software, and desktop appears on the left side of the taskbar. (Your Quick Launch toolbar might also contain other icons.) Now you can add the Desktop toolbar using the same shortcut menu.

> TROUBLE? If the Quick Launch command is already checked, skip Step 2, and continue with Step 3.

3. Right-click a blank area of the taskbar.

4. On the shortcut menu, point to **Toolbars** and then click **Desktop**. See Figure 4-36.

| Figure 4-36 | DISPLAYING THE QUICK LAUNCH AND DESKTOP TOOLBARS |

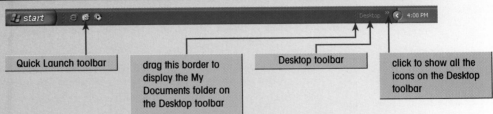

The Desktop toolbar first appears as a button with a "Desktop" label and double arrows you can click to see all the icons on the desktop. You can resize the toolbar to show more icons.

5. Point to the left border of the Desktop toolbar until the pointer changes to ◄──►. Then drag left until you see the My Documents folder.

6. To see all the icons on the desktop, click the **double chevrons (>>)** on the Desktop toolbar. See Figure 4-37.

| Figure 4-37 | MY DOCUMENTS ICON ON THE DESKTOP TOOLBAR |

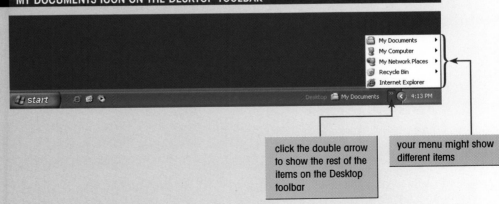

Beth likes having the icon for the My Documents folder on the Desktop toolbar, but wishes she could see more icons. She would like the toolbar to look more like the Quick Launch toolbar, with no names next to the icons and no title displayed for the toolbar. You explain that you can modify the toolbar's appearance by changing its properties.

Modifying the Appearance of a Taskbar Toolbar

You can modify the appearance of a taskbar toolbar by showing or hiding its title, and by showing or hiding the text labels for each icon. On the taskbar shortcut menu, these commands are checked by default. To hide the title and text labels, you remove the check mark from each command. You will modify the Desktop toolbar by hiding its title and text labels.

To modify the appearance of the Desktop toolbar:

1. Right-click a blank area in the Desktop toolbar.

2. On the shortcut menu, click **Show Text** to remove the check mark from this command.

   TROUBLE? If you don't see the Show Text entry on the shortcut menu, you may have right-clicked one of the buttons on the Desktop toolbar. Be sure to click a blank area on the toolbar. Also, be sure the Lock the Taskbar command is not selected on the Taskbar shortcut menu.

3. Right-click a blank area in the Desktop toolbar again, and deselect **Show Title** on the shortcut menu.

   Figure 4-38 displays the modified appearance of the toolbar. Note that each item on the desktop is matched by an item in the toolbar and that the icons are small, like those on the Quick Launch toolbar.

Figure 4-38	MODIFIED DESKTOP TASKBAR

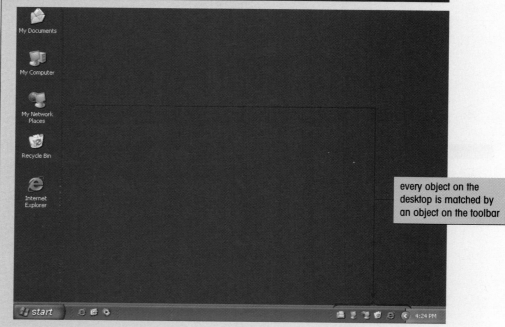

every object on the desktop is matched by an object on the toolbar

Now Beth can access all the items on her desktop without minimizing open windows.

Creating a Custom Toolbar

If the standard taskbar toolbars that Windows XP provides do not meet your needs, you can create your own taskbar toolbar. For example, if you often work with documents contained in folders in the My Documents folder, you could add each folder to a custom toolbar so you can access those documents quickly. To create a custom toolbar, you use the New Toolbar command on the taskbar shortcut menu.

REFERENCE WINDOW   RW

Creating a Custom Taskbar Toolbar

- To create a new toolbar, right-click a blank area of the taskbar, point to Toolbars, and then click New Toolbar.
- In the New Toolbar dialog box, click the folder or object you want to turn into a toolbar, and then click the OK button.

Beth is happy with the new appearance of the taskbar. However, she notices that when she clicks the My Computer icon on the Desktop toolbar it opens the My Computer window. Beth finds the My Computer window useful and wonders if you could create a taskbar toolbar displaying all of the icons in the My Computer window. This would give her even quicker access to all of the drives on her computer.

To create a toolbar for the My Computer window:

1. Right-click a blank area on the taskbar, point to **Toolbars**, and then click **New Toolbar** on the shortcut menu.

The New Toolbar dialog box opens, showing the hierarchy of objects on your computer that is familiar to you from your work with My Computer and Windows Explorer. In the New Toolbar dialog box, you select a drive, folder, or object whose contents you want to display in a toolbar on the taskbar. You want to display the contents of the My Computer window, which appears near the top of the hierarchy.

2. Click **My Computer** in the New Toolbar dialog box, and then click the **OK** button.

The My Computer toolbar appears on the taskbar. However, it makes the taskbar too crowded, so you will modify the appearance of the new toolbar by deselecting the Show Title and Show Text commands on the taskbar shortcut menu.

3. Right-click a blank area of the My Computer toolbar, and deselect **Show Text** on the shortcut menu.

4. Right-click a blank area of the My Computer toolbar again, and deselect **Show Title** on the shortcut menu.

Figure 4-39 displays the new My Computer toolbar on your taskbar.

Figure 4-39   **TOOLBARS ON THE TASKBAR**

Quick Launch toolbar   Desktop toolbar   My Computer toolbar
(your icons might be
different)

Having seen how to create and modify toolbars on the taskbar, you should now restore the taskbar to its original state, deleting the Quick Launch, Desktop, and My Computer toolbars. Note that this will not affect the desktop or the My Computer window. These toolbars contain shortcuts to those objects, not the objects themselves.

To remove a toolbar from the taskbar:

1. Right-click a blank area of the taskbar, and then point to **Toolbars** on the short-cut menu.

2. Click **Quick Launch** on the Toolbars submenu to deselect it.

   The menu closes and the Quick Launch toolbar is removed.

3. Use the same technique to remove the Desktop and My Computer toolbars from the taskbar.

Now the taskbar appears as it did when you started this tutorial.

Editing the Start Menu

The final component on your Windows XP desktop that you can customize is the Start menu. The Start menu lists the programs, tools, and windows you want to access quickly. For example, you can click an item on the Start menu to open the My Documents folder or the Help and Support Center window. You can also point to My Recent Documents to display a list of recently opened documents. To quickly access one of the documents in the My Recent Documents list, click a document name, and Windows XP locates and starts the program that created the document, and then opens the document. Most of the items on the Start menu are created for you by Windows XP or by the various programs you install. However, you also can determine the content and appearance of your Start menu, removing items you don't use and adding those you do. In addition, the left pane of the Windows XP Start menu automatically shows the programs you use most frequently. See Figure 4-40.

Figure 4-40   CUSTOMIZING THE START MENU

you can add other desktop items to this pane

this item appears as a submenu—you point to the item to see a list of its contents

these items appear as links you click to open a window

the programs you've used recently will be listed here

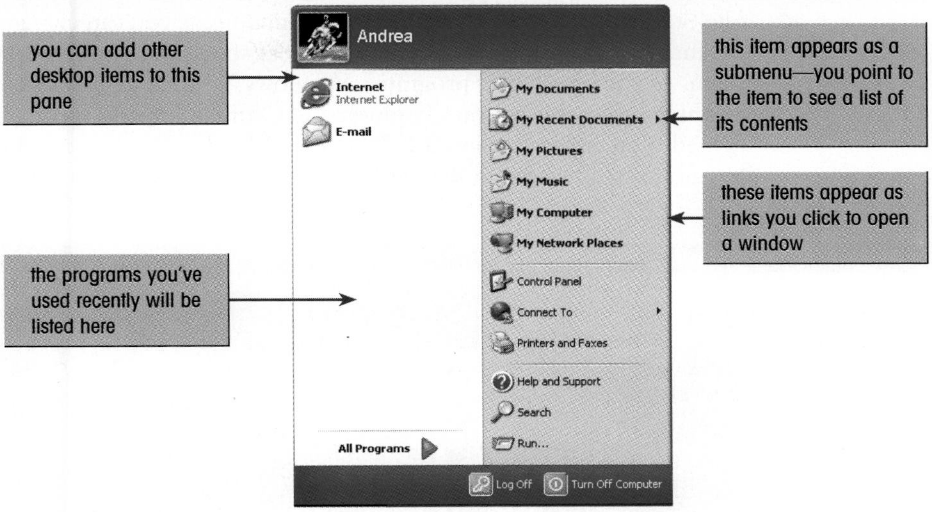

Controlling the Appearance of the Start Menu

One feature of the Start menu you can control is whether the menu displays small or large icons. The default is to use large icons, but you can save screen space by changing this to the smaller icon style.

Because the Start button is considered part of the taskbar, you change settings for the Start menu using the same dialog box you used earlier to control the appearance of the taskbar. This time, however, you can open the Taskbar and Start Menu Properties dialog box using the Control Panel.

To change the size of the icons on the Start menu:

1. Open the Control Panel, click **Appearance and Themes**, and then click **Taskbar and Start Menu**. Minimize the Appearance and Themes window.

   The commands for customizing the Start menu are available on the Start Menu tab of this dialog box.

2. In the Taskbar and Start Menu Properties dialog box, click the **Start Menu** tab.

3. Click the **Customize** button.

4. On the General tab of the Customize Start Menu dialog box, click the **Small icons** option button.

5. Click the **OK** button. The Taskbar and Start Menu Properties dialog box stays open. Next, you'll open the Start menu to view the small icons.

6. Click the **Start** button ⟨ *start* ⟩ on the taskbar. The Start menu shows small icons.

7. Click outside of the Start menu to close it.

Now that you have plenty of room on the Start menu, you can learn how to add items to it.

Adding an Item to the Start Menu

The Start menu lists shortcuts on the left and items you can change on the right. By default, the Internet Explorer and Outlook Express shortcuts appear at the upper-left of the Start menu. As you open other programs, Windows XP adds their shortcuts to the Start menu, listing them below the Internet Explorer and Outlook Express shortcuts. For example, after you opened Notepad in Session 4.1, Windows XP added a Notepad shortcut to the Start menu. The items on the right of the Start menu open dialog boxes or submenus. See Figure 4-41.

Figure 4-41	A TYPICAL START MENU

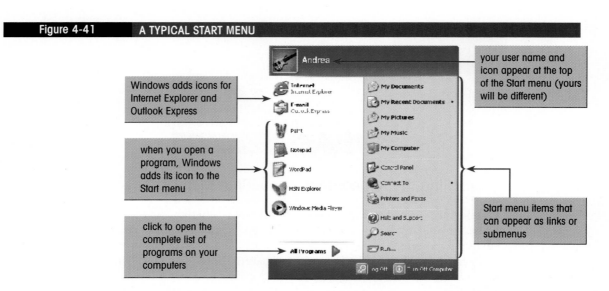

Most of the work you'll do to modify the Start menu will be to add, delete, and change the items on the right. For example, you can remove an item if you rarely use it, or change an item that displays a submenu to open a window instead. You can also add an item to access a feature not currently listed on the Start menu.

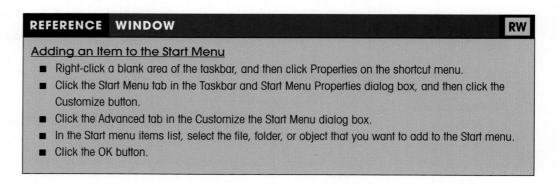

REFERENCE WINDOW   RW

Adding an Item to the Start Menu
- Right-click a blank area of the taskbar, and then click Properties on the shortcut menu.
- Click the Start Menu tab in the Taskbar and Start Menu Properties dialog box, and then click the Customize button.
- Click the Advanced tab in the Customize the Start Menu dialog box.
- In the Start menu items list, select the file, folder, or object that you want to add to the Start menu.
- Click the OK button.

Beth wants to see how she could use the Start menu to access the Favorites folder, which includes the same items that appear in the Favorites pane of Windows Explorer—folders, files, and Web pages to which you want quick access. You will add the Favorites item to the Start menu.

To add the Favorites item to the Start menu:

1. Make sure the Taskbar and Start Menu Properties dialog box is open to the Start menu tab.

   TROUBLE? If the Taskbar and Start Menu Properties dialog box is not open, right-click a blank area of the taskbar, click Properties, and then click the Start Menu tab.

2. Click the **Customize** button.

3. Click the **Advanced** tab in the Customize Start Menu dialog box.

4. Scroll the Start menu items, and then click the **Favorites menu** check box to select this option.

5. Click the **OK** button and then click the **Apply** button.

The Taskbar and Start Menu Properties dialog box remains open. Now view the modified Start menu to verify it contains a Favorites item.

To test the new Start menu item:

1. Drag the Taskbar and Start Menu Properties dialog box to the right, if necessary, so it will not be obstructed by the open Start menu.

2. Click the **Start** button  on the taskbar. See Figure 4-42.

Figure 4-42	NEW ITEM ON THE START MENU

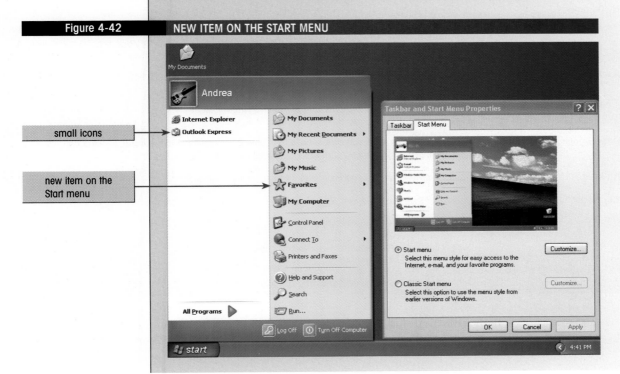

small icons

new item on the Start menu

Note that the Start menu now includes a Favorites item.

Selecting Start Menu Settings

When you worked with the Advanced tab in the Customize Start Menu dialog box, you might have noticed that the Start menu items list includes settings for your Start menu. As you saw in the last section, you select check boxes to add items to the Start menu. Other settings let you display an item on the Start menu as a link or as a submenu. If you display an item as a link, you click it to open the appropriate dialog box or window. For example, the My Computer item appears on the Start menu as a link by default—you click My Computer to open its window. If you display an item as a submenu, you point to the item until a submenu appears, and then you click a command on the submenu. For example, you can also display the My Computer item as a submenu. When you point to My Computer, a submenu appears listing the contents of the My Computer window, including 3½ Floppy (A:) and your local hard disk. Figure 4-43 describes the settings you can select for your Start menu.

Figure 4-43	START MENU OPTIONS
START MENU	**DESCRIPTION**
Control Panel	Display this item as a link you click to open the Control Panel, as a submenu that lists individual tools or categories in the Control Panel, or don't display this item
Enable dragging and dropping	Drag and drop to change position or add to the Start menu
Favorites menu	Display this item to list your favorite Web sites, files, and folders
Help and Support	Display this item as a link to the Help and Support window
My Computer	Display this item as a link you click to open the My Computer folder, as a submenu that lists the contents of My Computer, or don't display this item
My Documents	Display this item as a link you click to open the My Documents folder, as a submenu that lists the contents of My Documents, or don't display this item
My Music	Display this item as a link you click to open the My Music folder window, as a submenu that lists the contents of My Music, or don't display this item
My Network Places	Display this item as a link you can click to open the My Network Places folder window, as a submenu that list the contents of My Network Places, or don't display this item
My Pictures	Display this item as a link you click to open the My Pictures folder window, as a submenu that lists the contents of My Pictures, or don't display this item
Network Connections	Display this item as a link you click to open the Network Connections folder window, as the "Connect to" submenu that lists the contents of Network Connections, or don't display this item
Printers and Faxes	Display individual printers and fax boards attached to your computer
Run command	Display the Run command as a link you click to open the Run dialog box
Scroll Programs	When you point to All Programs, display the programs as a list you can scroll
Search	Display the Search command as a link you click to open the Search window
System Administrative Tools	Display this item as a link you click to open the System Administrative Tools window, as a submenu that lists the contents of the window, or don't display this item

Beth wants to display the My Computer item as a submenu on the Start menu so she can easily access her floppy drive. The My Computer submenu will contain the 3½ Floppy (A:) shortcut icon that she can click to open her floppy drive quickly. You'll show her how to do this.

To change the My Computer command on the Start Menu to display a submenu:

1. In the Taskbar and Start Menu Properties dialog box, click the **Customize** button, and then click the **Advanced** tab on the Customize Start Menu dialog box.

2. Scroll the Start menu items list to locate My Computer, and then click the **Display as a menu** option button under the My Computer icon.

3. Click the **OK** button and then click the **Apply** button. Leave the Taskbar and Start Menu Properties dialog box open on the right side of your desktop.

Now verify that you can point to My Computer on the Start menu, and then click a command on the submenu to show the contents of the floppy drive.

To test the My Computer submenu on the Start menu:

1. Click the **Start** button 🛝 start and then point to **My Computer**. See Figure 4-44.

| Figure 4-44 | NEW SUBMENU ON THE START MENU |

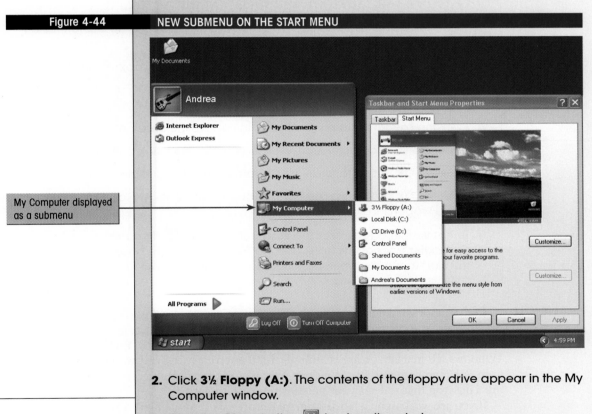

My Computer displayed as a submenu

2. Click **3½ Floppy (A:)**. The contents of the floppy drive appear in the My Computer window.

3. Click the **Close** button ☒ to close the window.

Beth feels the changes you made to the Start menu reflect the way she likes to work.

Removing an Item from the Start Menu

Now that you've seen how to add an item to the Start menu and change another, you should restore the Start menu to its default state by removing the Favorites icon and changing the My Computer item from a submenu back to a link. To remove an item, you use the same dialog box you opened to add and modify an item.

REFERENCE WINDOW   **RW**

Removing a Start Menu Item
- Right-click a blank area of the taskbar, and then click Properties on the shortcut menu.
- Click the Start menu tab on the Taskbar and Start Menu Properties dialog box.
- Click the Customize button to open the Customize Start Menu dialog box.
- In the Start menu items list, deselect the item that you want to remove, and then click the OK button.

To restore the Start menu to its original state:

1. In the Taskbar and Start Menu Properties dialog box, click the **Customize** button on the Start menu tab.

2. On the General tab of the Customize Start Menu dialog box, click the **Large icons** option button.

3. Click the **Advanced** tab.

4. Click the **Favorites menu** check box to remove the check mark.

5. Under the My Computer icon, click the **Display as a link** option button.

6. Click the **OK** button to close the Customize Start Menu dialog box.

7. Click the **OK** button to apply your changes and close the Taskbar and Start Menu Properties dialog box.

8. To test your changes, click the **Start** button _start_ to confirm that My Computer appears as a link and the Favorites item has been removed from the Start menu, and then click outside the menu to close it.

Beth is impressed with how much she can personalize Windows XP to suit her needs and preferences. She customized the taskbar by adding taskbar toolbars and changing its appearance, and modified the Start menu to reflect her working style. Your ability to customize Windows XP in a lab setting is limited, and the settings are likely to be changed by the next user. But if you are running Windows XP on your own computer, you will find that designing a desktop that reflects your needs is time well spent.

If you are working in a lab setting, make sure you return all settings to their original state before leaving the lab.

Session 4.3 Quick Check

1. How do you move the taskbar to the top of your computer screen?

2. To hide the taskbar, select _____ from the Taskbar and Start Menu Properties dialog box.

3. Why might you want to include the Desktop toolbar on the taskbar?

4. True or False: You can customize the Start menu by displaying the Control Panel item as having a submenu.

5. To modify the collection of objects and properties on your computer, you can open the _____.

REVIEW ASSIGNMENTS

1. *Creating Shortcuts* Practice placing a document on the desktop and printing it, using a printer shortcut icon.

   a. Create a shortcut on the desktop to the printer you use regularly.
   b. Open Notepad and create a new text document on your desktop, typing your name and the list of classes you currently are taking. Name this document **Classes**. Close Notepad.
   c. Drag the Classes document icon to the printer shortcut. Your document prints.
   d. Now use the techniques you learned in Tutorial 3 to print an image of your desktop. (Use the Print Screen key to save an image of the desktop, open WordPad, type your name and the date at the top of the document, paste the image into WordPad, and then print the image from WordPad.)
   e. When you are finished, delete both icons from your desktop.

2. *Create a Shortcut to a Folder* Beth recently assigned Sally Hanson, an undergraduate at one of the local colleges, to provide housekeeping for three clients. Sally plans to be out of the area over spring break, so Beth needs to write a memo to each client, asking if they need replacement help. Beth would like to be able to access the correspondence concerning Sally Hanson more easily.

   a. Start Windows Explorer and then create a new folder called Sally on your Data Disk.
   b. Start Notepad and then compose the three memos, typing your own text. Save the memos in the Sally folder on your Data Disk with the names **Smith**, **Arruga**, and **Kosta** (the names of the three clients). Close Notepad when you are finished.
   c. Drag the Sally folder from Windows Explorer to the desktop, using the left mouse button, to create a shortcut to the folder.
   d. Name the shortcut icon Sally.
   e. Test the shortcut icon by opening the Sally folder, and then open one of the memos. Use two different methods to open these two objects, and write down which methods you used.
   f. Arrange your desktop so you can see the open memo in Notepad, the open folder window, and the shortcut icon. You might need to resize the windows to make them smaller. Then print an image of the desktop. (See Step 1d.)
   g. Remove the desktop shortcut to the folder when you are done.

3. *Create a Bitmap on the Desktop* In this tutorial, you created a new text document directly on the desktop. In this review assignment, you'll create a new bitmap image document on your Data Disk. You'll use the mouse to write your signature. Then you'll use this bitmap image as your desktop background.

    a. Use My Computer to open drive A and display the contents of your Data Disk.

    b. Right-click an empty area of the drive A window, point to New, and then click Bitmap Image.

    c. Name the new file **My Signature**.

    d. Start Paint, and then open **My Signature**.

    e. Drag the mouse over the empty canvas to write your signature. (This will be awkward, even for experienced mouse users.)

    f. Exit the program and save your changes. Close the drive A window.

    g. Click Start, click Control Panel, click Appearance and Themes, and then click Change the desktop background to open the Desktop property sheet of the Display Properties dialog box.

    h. Click the Browse button and then use the Look in list arrow at the top of the dialog box to select the 3½ Floppy drive. Select the **My Signature** bitmap image on your Data Disk, and then click the Open button. Your signature appears as the wallpaper in the preview monitor.

    i. Print an image of the screen. (See Step 1d.)

    j. Click the Cancel button to preserve the desktop's original appearance.

4. *Explore Your Computer's Desktop Properties* Answer each of the following questions about the desktop properties on your lab computers.

    a. Open the Display Properties dialog box. What resolution is your monitor using? What other resolution settings are available for your monitor? Drag the slider to find out. If it's an older monitor, it might not have higher resolutions available.

    b. What color quality are you using?

    c. Is Windows XP using a screen saver on your machine? Which one? After how many minutes of idle time does it engage?

    d. What is your desktop's default color scheme?

    e. Does your computer use a desktop theme? If so, which one?

    f. Does your desktop display a special background? Which one?

Explore   g. On the Screen Saver tab, click the Power button to open the Power Options Properties dialog box. What power scheme is your computer using, if any? What settings are in effect for that power scheme?

Explore   h. In the Power Options Properties dialog box, click the Advanced tab. Turn on the option to show the power icon on the taskbar. A power icon, like a plug, appears on the taskbar. Point at the power icon. What ScreenTip appears? Go back to the Power Options Properties dialog box, turn this option off, and then close the Power Options Properties dialog box.

    i. Close the Display Properties dialog box and the Appearance and Themes window, if necessary.

5. *Customizing Your Desktop* The ability to place icons directly on the desktop gives you the opportunity to create a truly docucentric desktop. Figure 4-45 shows Beth's desktop after she's had a chance to create all the shortcuts you recommended and to add additional shortcuts for programs, folders, files, and other resources she uses regularly.

Figure 4-45

Notice that this desktop has shortcuts not just for drives and documents, but also for programs, tools, and other Windows XP objects. Also notice that some icons are document icons, not shortcuts. All the icons are arranged logically so they are easy to find. If you have your own computer, create a desktop that meets your needs.

Use the following strategy:

Explore

a. Right-click the desktop, point to Arrange Icons By, and make sure Auto Arrange is not checked. If it is, click Auto Arrange to remove the check mark from this command.

b. Use My Computer to locate the drives on your computer, and then create a shortcut on the desktop to each of the local or network drives you use regularly.

c. If you haven't done so already, use My Computer to create folders for the work you usually do on your computer. You might want a folder for each class you're taking, letters you write, projects, or hobbies. Then create a shortcut on the desktop to each folder you use regularly. Use any method you learned in this tutorial to create the shortcuts.

d. Create shortcuts for each document you use repeatedly. Avoid overcrowding your desktop.

e. If you know how to locate program files, create shortcuts on the desktop to the programs you use most often.

f. Group the icons on your desktop so that similar objects are in the same location.

g. Print a copy of your desktop in its final form. (See Step 1d.)

6. *Customizing Your Start Menu* A simple way of adding items to your Start menu is to drag icons from the desktop or My Computer window to the Start menu. For example, you can click a file icon and drag it onto the Start menu, and Windows XP will automatically add that item to the Start menu. Similarly, you can remove any item from the Start menu by clicking the item and dragging it off the Start menu. For example, if you drag a Start menu item onto the desktop, it appears as a shortcut on the desktop. Dragging the same item off the Start menu and onto the Recycle Bin deletes the item.

Figure 4-46 shows a Start menu with a Recycle Bin item. While most Start menu items can be created using either the drag-and-drop technique or the Add method in the Taskbar and Start Menu Properties dialog box, you can only add a Recycle Bin item by dragging. Try this technique by performing Steps a through d below.

Figure 4-46

Explore

a. Drag the Recycle Bin icon to the Start button (you will have to point to the Start button for a few seconds to allow it to open), and drop the icon at the top of the left pane. An insert bar (a thick, dark horizontal line) appears to guide you.

b. Print a copy of the Start menu you created, showing the two new entries. (See Step 1d.)

c. When you click the Recycle Bin item on the Start menu, what do you see? What are the advantages and disadvantages of using the Start menu and Recycle Bin this way?

Explore

d. Remove the Recycle Bin item from the Start menu by right-clicking it and then clicking Remove From This List.

7. *Customizing a Taskbar Toolbar* You can also use the drag-and-drop technique to customize a taskbar toolbar. By dragging an icon from a folder or the desktop onto one of the toolbars on the taskbar, you can create additional buttons for quick one-click access to your favorite files and programs.

Figure 4-47 shows a modified Quick Launch toolbar with icons for Notepad, WordPad, and Windows Explorer added.

Figure 4-47

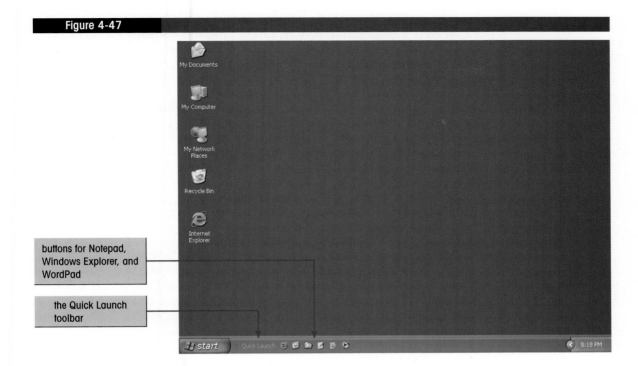

buttons for Notepad, Windows Explorer, and WordPad

the Quick Launch toolbar

Make similar changes to your Quick Launch toolbar by performing Steps a through h below.

a. Add the Quick Launch toolbar to the taskbar. Make sure the taskbar is not locked, and then widen the Quick Launch toolbar so you can see most of its icons.

Explore

b. Open the Start menu so you can see the Accessories submenu, hold down the Ctrl key, and drag icons for Notepad, WordPad, and Windows Explorer from the Accessories submenu on your Start menu to the Quick Launch toolbar on your taskbar. Be sure to hold down the Ctrl key while dragging and dropping these icons, or you'll move the icons off the Start menu.

c. Modify the properties of the Quick Launch toolbar so that it shows the toolbar's title. Widen the Quick Launch toolbar again.

d. Print a copy of your screen showing the revised Quick Launch toolbar. (See Step 1d.)

e. Test each new button on the toolbar to verify that it opens the appropriate program.

f. Summarize what you've done and discuss the advantages of using the Quick Launch toolbar to launch your favorite programs. Which is easier, the Quick Launch toolbar or the Start menu, and why? What is the most effective use of the Quick Launch toolbar? Would you place all of your programs on the toolbar? Why or why not?

g. Delete the Notepad, WordPad, and Windows Explorer buttons from the Quick Launch toolbar by dragging them to your Recycle Bin.

h. Remove the title from the Quick Launch toolbar.

PROJECTS

1. Knowing that you have two years left in your college degree program, your parents decide to splurge and give you a computer, complete with Windows XP, for your birthday. Your parents spent hours getting everything loaded and configured for you, so when you pick it up this weekend you can get right to work on a major project due on Monday. You have about half an hour before your roommate returns with your car, so

take out an 8½ by 11-inch piece of paper, and draw the desktop that will give you the quickest access to all documents, devices, and/or programs needed to carry out the tasks listed below. Indicate shortcut icons with an arrow. Also draw a window showing your 3½-inch disk contents, using the information provided in the "To Do List."

To Do List

a. Finish typing paper for American History project, using WordPad.
   ____currently saved on disk
   ____will need to print
b. Finish lab report for Organic Chemistry, using WordPad.
   ____currently saved on disk
   ____will need to print
c. Insert bitmap image saved on disk into Organic Chemistry lab report.
d. Review outline for Office Procedures class test, created in WordPad.
   ____currently saved on disk
   ____will need to print

2. You provide computer support at Highland Yearbooks, a company that publishes high school and college yearbooks. Highland has just upgraded to Windows XP, and you'd like to get right to work customizing the desktops of Highland employees for optimal performance. You start with the computer belonging to John McPhee, one of the sales representatives. Create a desktop for John that takes the following circumstances into account. When you are done, print an image of the desktop. (See Step 1d in the Review Assignments.) Then make sure you remove any shortcuts you created, and restore the desktop to its original settings. On the back of your printout, write which options you changed to meet John's needs.

   a. John keeps a Notepad file with a time-date stamp of long-distance phone calls stored on the desktop with a shortcut to that file on his Start menu.
   b. John wants to be able to print the phone log file quickly, without having to open it first.
   c. The company colors at Highland Yearbooks are blue and gold. John would like a blue desktop with gold title bars.

Explore ▶

3. In this tutorial you learned how to use the Control Panel to customize display properties, such as the desktop background and theme. You can also use the Control Panel to customize other parts of your computer, such as the mouse and system sounds. Open the Control Panel, explore its contents to explain how to use the Control Panel to complete the following tasks, and then answer the questions below. (*Hint*: Use the Windows XP online Help, if necessary.)

   a. What is a sound scheme? How can you change the sound scheme?
   b. How can you find basic system information such as the version of your operating system and the speed of your computer?
   c. How do you change the date and time? How can you have Windows XP automatically adjust the time during Daylight Savings Time?
   d. What does "contrast" on your screen mean? How can you adjust the contrast to improve readability?

4. Your cousin, Joey, has Windows XP on his new computer but has not taken much time to learn about all of the customizable and timesaving features it offers him. In WordPad, type a letter to Joey, explaining three main features covered in this tutorial. Because you know that he is more likely to try to use these features if he has directions in front of him, include basic instructions on how to access them.

5. You just printed your letter to Joey in Project 4 and then remembered the concept of docucentric desktops you learned in this tutorial. You think that if Joey can conceptualize this, it will really expand his Windows XP horizons. You decide to add a note explaining the difference between the docucentric and program-centric desktop. Write a paragraph about this difference.

Explore   6. You are trying to save money on your electric bill and are wondering if you can take advantage of the Windows XP power management features. Open the Power Options Properties dialog box in the Control Panel, and print the screen you see, using the techniques you learned earlier in this book. On the printout, write a paragraph describing the power management features available specifically to your computer and how they can help save money.

Explore   7. You want to personalize your computer so that it reflects your interests or hobbies. One way to do this is to apply a desktop theme. Use the Display Properties dialog box to explore the themes you can use, and then select and apply one that seems best for you. Save the theme on your Data Disk as **Personal Theme**. Then open a dialog box, and print an image of the desktop. (See Step 1d in the Review Assignments.)

8. You have been asked to give a presentation at a *Computer Users with Special Needs* seminar on campus. You have a half hour to present participants with information on Windows XP Accessibility Options in the Control Panel. Using the online Help as a guide, write a handout describing the ways one can configure Windows XP for computer users with special needs. Include in your handout instructions for turning these features on and off.

Explore   9. You are having problems with your monitor—the display flickers and images are occasionally garbled. In addition, when you move the mouse or resize windows, the screen does not redraw to reflect your changes. Use a troubleshooter in the Control Panel to find the solution to your problems. When you find a solution, print the page in the troubleshooter that addresses your problems.

QUICK | CHECK ANSWERS

Session 4.1

1. False

2. False

3. You delete not only the icon but also the document.

4. You delete only the icon but not the document.

5. 1) Use the left mouse button to drag the floppy drive icon from the My Computer or Windows Explorer window to the desktop; 2) use the right mouse button to drag the floppy drive icon from the My Computer or Windows Explorer window to the desktop, and then click Create Shortcuts here; 3) click the floppy drive icon in the My Computer or Windows Explorer window, click File on the menu bar, click Create Shortcut, and then click Yes.

Session 4.2

1. True

2. You can use the Control Panel to change the way Windows looks and behaves.

3. Here are five: Themes, Background, Screen Saver, Appearance, Settings. You could also mention the properties on each of these sheets, such as color palette, resolution, and so on.

4. To display a moving image after a specified period so that you can keep your work private

5. There are 800 pixels across and 600 down.

6. 800 by 600, because it displays the largest objects

7. It requires extra video memory and runs more slowly.

QUICK | CHECK ANSWERS

Session 4.3

1. Right-click the taskbar, click Lock the Taskbar to remove the check mark, if necessary, click a blank area on the taskbar, and then drag it to the top of the desktop.

2. Auto-hide the taskbar

3. For quick access to desktop icons without minimizing windows

4. True

5. Control Panel

OBJECTIVES

In this tutorial you will:

- Explore the structure of the Internet and the World Wide Web

- Open, view, navigate, and print Web pages in Internet Explorer

- Download a file from the World Wide Web

- Enable Active Desktop in order to add, move, resize, close, and remove Active Desktop items

- Schedule the automatic retrieval of data from the Web

- Use an HTML file as a desktop background

- Send and receive e-mail using Outlook Express

LABS

The Internet: World Wide Web

Web Pages & HTML

BRINGING THE WORLD WIDE WEB TO THE DESKTOP

Using Active Desktop at Highland Travel

CASE

Highland Travel

Highland Travel, a company that offers guided tour packages to Scotland, recently hired you as an advertising manager. During your first day at work, you meet with the company's technical support person, Scott Campbell. After describing the training you'll receive, Scott explains that Highland Travel uses the Internet and the World Wide Web to promote the company, to provide services to clients, and to improve communication among employees. The company recently upgraded its computers to Windows XP, and management wants all employees to be able to use its features to the fullest.

You tell Scott you've heard that one popular feature of Windows XP is its integration of the operating system with the Web. Scott reminds you that the Web is a set of linked documents residing on computers all around the world. He tells you that during your first week on the job, you'll go through a training program to familiarize yourself with Windows XP and particularly with its Web features. He explains that Windows XP brings the richness of the Web to your desktop with Active Desktop. **Active Desktop** is technology that transforms the Windows desktop into your own personal "communications central"—not only for launching programs and accessing files, but also for obtaining and displaying information you can find on the Web. The Windows XP desktop is called "active" because it allows you to access the Internet, particularly Web sites that provide frequently changing information, such as sports scores, stock prices, and weather maps.

Scott assures you that the training program will familiarize you with these and more features—and will introduce you to Highland Travel's Web site.

SESSION 5.1

In this session, you will learn how to use Windows XP to bring the Internet and the World Wide Web to your desktop. You will learn to use Internet Explorer to view Web sites. You will activate a link, navigate a Web page with frames, print a Web page, and download a file. Finally you'll learn how to access your favorite Web pages quickly using the History pane and the Favorites folder. For this session you will need a blank 3½-inch disk.

The Internet

When two or more computers are connected together for the purpose of exchanging information and resources, they create a structure known as a **network**. Networks facilitate the sharing of data and resources among multiple users. Networks can also be connected to each other to allow computers on different networks to share information; when two or more networks are connected, they create an **internetwork**, or **internet**. "The Internet" (uppercase "I") has come to refer to the "network of networks" that is made up of millions of computers linked to networks all over the world. Computers and networks on the Internet are connected by fiber-optic cables, satellites, phone lines, and other communications systems, as shown in Figure 5-1. Data travels across these communication systems using whatever route is most efficient.

Figure 5-1   STRUCTURE OF THE INTERNET

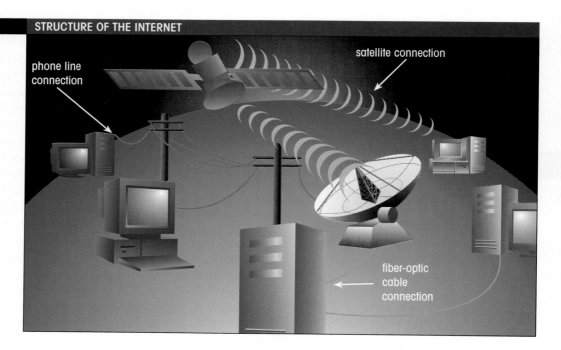

The Internet, by design, is a decentralized structure. There is no Internet "company." Instead, the Internet is a collection of different organizations, such as universities and businesses, each organizing its own information. There are no rules about where information is stored, and no one regulates the quality of information available on the Internet. Even though the lack of central control can make it hard for beginners to find their way through the resources on the Internet, decentralization has some advantages. The Internet is open to innovation and rapid growth, because different organizations and individuals have the freedom to test new products and services and make them quickly available to a global audience. One such service is the World Wide Web.

The **World Wide Web** makes it easy to share and access data stored on computers around the world with minimal training and support, and for this reason, Microsoft designed Windows XP to offer easy Web access. The Web is a system of **hypertext documents**—electronic files that contain elements known as **hyperlinks** or just **links**, which target other parts of a document or other documents altogether. A link can be a word or a phrase or a graphic image. Figure 5-2 shows a Colorado touring company hypertext document with several links. Each link targets a separate document that offers more information about the company. You can also connect to other file types, including scanned photographs, graphic images, film clips, sounds, online discussion groups, and computer programs.

| Figure 5-2 | WEB PAGE WITH LINKS TO WEB PAGES CONTAINING ADDITIONAL INFORMATION |

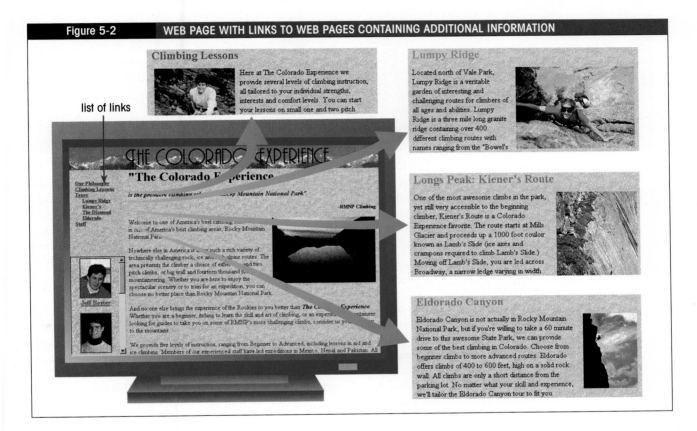

Each hypertext document on the Web is called a **Web page** and is stored on a computer on the Internet called a **Web server**. A Web page can contain links to other Web pages located anywhere on the Internet—on the same computer as the original Web page or on an entirely different computer halfway across the world. The ability to cross-reference other Web pages with links is one of the most important features of the Web.

Navigating Web pages using hypertext is an efficient way to access information. When you read a book, you follow a linear progression, reading one page after another. With hypertext, you progress through the pages in whatever order you want. Hypertext allows you to skip from one topic to another, following the information path that interests you, as shown in Figure 5-3.

Figure 5-3   **FOLLOWING HYPERTEXT LINKS**

3. Finally, from Canada you jump to the Natural History Museum in the U.K.

2. A quick jump from Hawaii and you are at the Royal Tyrrell Museum of Paleontology in Alberta, Canada, where additional Web pages on dinosaurs are stored.

1. Honolulu Community College maintains a Dinosaur exhibit. From this page you can jump to a page in Alberta, Canada.

Microsoft has taken advantage of this fact by designing its Windows XP operating system to incorporate your experience on the Internet. The techniques you'll learn in this tutorial to navigate Web pages are identical to those you learned in previous tutorials to navigate the objects on your computer. Microsoft's goal with Windows XP is to make the user's experience with local files, network files, and files on computers around the world as uniform as possible.

Browsers

To access documents on the Web, you need a **browser**—a program that locates, retrieves, displays, and organizes documents stored on Web servers. Your browser allows you to visit Web sites around the world; view multimedia documents; transfer files, images, and sounds to your computer; conduct searches for specific topics; and run programs on other computers. In Figure 5-3, the dinosaur Web documents that you see appear in a browser window. Windows XP includes a set of communications software tools called **Internet Explorer**, which includes the Internet Explorer browser, as well as tools for other Internet functions such as electronic mail, or **e-mail**, electronic messages sent between users over the Internet. Another popular communications software package is **Netscape Communicator**, which includes the Netscape Navigator browser. This tutorial assumes that you'll do your browsing with Internet Explorer. If you're using Netscape Communicator or another browser, talk to your instructor to resolve any difficulties in completing the steps in this tutorial.

Microsoft integrated the Internet Explorer browser into the Windows XP operating system to make its functions available to many Windows XP components. For example, the Windows Explorer utility that you used in Tutorial 3 to navigate files on your Data Disk uses Internet Explorer features so that it can function as a browser. The My Computer window works similarly. For example, when you are connected to the Internet, you can open the My Music folder in My Computer, and then click a link to shop for music online. The Internet Explorer window will open, showing a Web page where you can buy music CDs online. Using Windows Explorer, you can open the Favorites pane, for example, and click a link to MSN to open the MSN Web page, which contains links to news and general interest articles and to other Web pages.

In fact, Internet Explorer, Windows Explorer, and My Computer share many similarities. They have a common look and feel, with similar menu commands, toolbars, panes, and Address bar. For example, you can open the Favorites pane in Windows Explorer, My Computer, or Internet Explorer to access the same list of files, folders, and Web pages, no matter which window you have open. As you work through this tutorial, you'll learn more ways these three tools are integrated, making it easy to find information anywhere, whether on your computer, a network, or the Internet.

There are many advantages to using the same tools to access information regardless of its location. Computer users in the past had to use one tool to access local files, another to access network files, and many additional products such as e-mail, files, and other computers to access information on the Internet. The Windows XP operating system allows you to view information anywhere with a single set of techniques.

When you attempt to view a Web page, your browser locates and retrieves the document from the Web server and displays its contents on your computer. As shown in Figure 5-4, the server stores the Web page in one location, and browsers anywhere in the world can view it.

Figure 5-4	USING A BROWSER TO VIEW A WEB DOCUMENT ON A SERVER

For your browser to connect to the World Wide Web, you must have an Internet connection. In a university setting, your connection might come from your campus network. If you are working on a home computer and gaining Internet access from your modem over a phone line, your connection is called a **dial-up connection** and is maintained via an account with an **Internet service provider (ISP)**, a company that sells Internet access. See Appendix A, "Connecting Computers over a Phone Line," for more information. With a dial-up connection, you are connected to the Internet only as long as your modem "stays on the line," whereas on most institutional networks, you are always connected to the Internet because the network is actually a part of the Internet. If you are using a dial-up connection to connect to your institution's network, you have probably received instructions that help you establish this connection. Use these instructions any time you need to be connected to the Internet during this tutorial. If you are working from home, connect to the Internet using the instructions provided by your ISP.

Starting **Internet Explorer**

Scott suggests that you use Internet Explorer, the browser that comes with Windows XP, to start exploring the Web by connecting to the Highland Travel page. When you connect to the Internet without specifying a particular Web page, Windows XP automatically loads your **home page**—the Web page designated by the operating system as your starting point. Windows XP designates the Microsoft Network (MSN) pages as the default home page, but you can easily designate a different home page. If you are at an institution such as a university, a home page has probably already been designated for you. Note that "home page" can also refer to a personal Web page or to the Web page that an organization or business has created to give information about itself.

You'll notice a lot of similarities between Internet Explorer (designed to locate information on the Internet) and Windows Explorer (designed to locate information on your computer or network).

REFERENCE WINDOW	**RW**

Starting Internet Explorer
- Click the Start button on the taskbar.
- Point to All Programs and then click Internet Explorer.

To start Internet Explorer:

1. Click the **Start** button ![start], point to **All Programs**, and then click **Internet Explorer**. Note that the Internet Explorer icon might also appear in the upper-right section of the Start menu—you can also click that icon to start Internet Explorer.

   If you are in a university setting, you are probably already connected to the Internet, and your home page will appear immediately.

   TROUBLE? If you are working from a computer with a dial-up connection already set up and are not currently connected to the Internet, Windows XP will attempt to connect you. Wait and follow the prompts that appear. If you can't establish a connection, check with your technical support person in the lab, or if you are using your own computer, use Network Connections as instructed by your ISP, or call your ISP's technical support line for assistance. If an error message appears, it's possible that the server on which your home page is stored is temporarily busy or unavailable.

2. If necessary, click the **Maximize** button ![] to maximize the Internet Explorer window. Figure 5-5 shows the MSN home page in the Internet Explorer window.

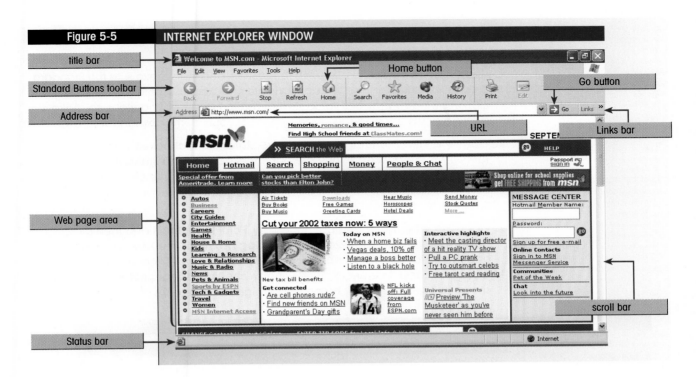

Figure 5-5   INTERNET EXPLORER WINDOW

Figure 5-6 describes the elements of the Internet Explorer window.

Figure 5-6	**ELEMENTS OF THE INTERNET EXPLORER WINDOW**
FOLDER	**DESCRIPTION**
Title bar	Shows the name of the open Web page and includes the resizing buttons
Standard Buttons toolbar	Contains buttons you can click to perform common tasks, such as moving to the next or previous page and printing a Web page
Address bar	Shows the address of the current Web page; you can also type an address here
Web page area	Shows the current Web page
Status bar	Shows information about the browser's actions; for example, indicates that a page is loading or is done loading
Scroll bars	If a Web page is wider or longer than the browser window, use the scroll bars to move up and down or right and left
Home button	Click to open the Web page specified as the home page for your browser
Go button	After you type an address in the Address bar, you can click the Go button or press the Enter key to have the browser find the page at that address
Links bar	Contains links to Web pages you visit often
URL	Uniform Resource Locator; the address of the Web page you want to visit

    The instructions in this tutorial will be easier to follow if your window matches those in the figures. The following steps help you set up the Internet Explorer window so it matches the one in the figures.

To set up the Internet Explorer window to match the figures in this tutorial:

1. Click **View** on the menu bar, point to **Toolbars**, and then make sure the **Standard Buttons, Address Bar**, and **Links** options are checked. The status bar in the Internet Explorer window provides valuable information about your actions, so make sure the status bar appears at the bottom of your Internet Explorer window.

2. Open the **View** menu again. Make sure **Status Bar** is checked and Lock the Toolbars is unchecked. If they are not checked, click the **Status Bar** command to check it and click the **Lock the Toolbars** command to uncheck it. Next, you can show text labels for each button on the Standard Buttons toolbar so that the toolbar is easier to use.

3. Open the **View** menu again, if necessary. Point to **Toolbars** and then click **Customize**. In the Customize Toolbar dialog box, click the **Text options** list arrow, and then click **Show text labels**, if necessary. Click the **Close** button to close the dialog box. Your Internet Explorer window should appear similar in form to that shown in Figure 5-7. (Your home page might be different.)

Figure 5-7	HOME PAGE DISPLAYED IN INTERNET EXPLORER

Address bar indicates Web page address

Web page set up as home page

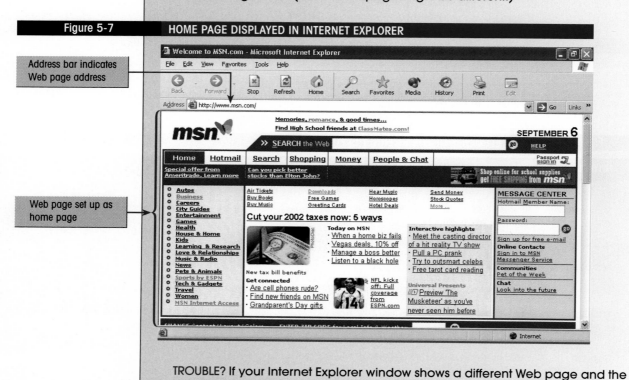

TROUBLE? If your Internet Explorer window shows a different Web page and the Address bar shows a different address, your home page is different from the one in Figure 5-7.

Now you can use Internet Explorer to open and view a Web page.

Opening a Page on the Web

Each page on the Web is uniquely identified by an address called a **URL**, or **Uniform Resource Locator**. A company may advertise its Web page by publishing the page's URL, such as "http://www.microsoft.com" in brochures, advertising pieces, and employees' business cards. A URL consists of three things: a protocol type, a server address, and a file pathname. Let's examine each of these items more closely.

A **protocol** is a standardized procedure used by computers to exchange information. Web documents travel between sites using **HyperText Transfer Protocol**, or **HTTP**. A Web page whose URL begins with the letters "http://" tells the Web browser to use the HTTP protocol when retrieving the page.

The **server address** gives the name of the Web server that is storing the Web page. You can usually learn a great deal about the Web server by examining the server address. For example, in the server address "www.northern.edu" the "www" indicates that the server is on the World Wide Web, "northern" indicates the name of the organization that owns the server (Northern University), and "edu" indicates that it's an educational site. Other common site types include "com" for commercial sites, "gov" for government agencies, and "org" for nonprofit organizations.

Finally, each file stored on a network server must have a unique pathname, just as files on a disk do. The **pathname** includes the folder or folders the file is stored in, plus the filename and its extension. The filename extension for Web pages is usually html, or just htm.

Try deciphering the following URL:

http://www.northern.edu/education/programs.html

The protocol is HTTP, the server address is www.northern.edu, the pathname is education/programs.html, and programs.html is the filename. So the Web browser knows it must retrieve the programs.html file from the /education folder located on the Web server at www.northern.edu, using the HTTP protocol.

Scott has given you the URL for the Highland Travel Web page, which is:

http://www.course.com/downloads/newperspectives/windowsxp/highland

You will access this Web page next using the URL that Scott has provided.

REFERENCE   WINDOW   **RW**

Opening a Page Using a URL
- Select the contents of the Address box.
- Type the URL in the Address box, and then press the Enter key.

To open a page on the Web with a URL:

1. Click the **Address** box on the Address bar. The contents of the Address box, which should be the URL for your home page, are selected. Anything you type will replace the selected URL.

   TROUBLE? If the contents of the Address box are not selected, select the address manually by dragging the mouse from the far left to the far right of the URL. Be sure to select the entire URL.

2. Type **http://www.course.com/downloads/newperspectives/windowsxp/highland** in the Address box. Make sure you type the URL exactly as shown.

3. Press the **Enter** key. Highland Travel's Welcome page opens in the Internet Explorer window. See Figure 5-8.

Figure 5-8   CONNECTING TO HIGHLAND TRAVEL SITE

URL

Highland Travel page; you might see a different graphic

graphic links

text links

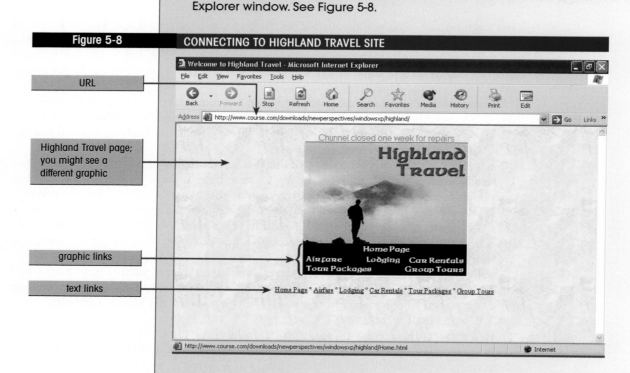

TROUBLE? If you receive a Not Found error message, the URL might not be typed correctly. Repeat Steps 1 through 3, making sure that the URL in the Address box matches the URL in Step 2. If you still receive an error message, ask your instructor or technical support person for help. If you see a different Web page from the one shown in Figure 5-8, click View on the menu bar and then click Refresh.

You can access information about the Highland Travel company by navigating through its Web pages. Spend some time doing that now.

Navigating the Web by Activating Links

Web Pages & HTML

A hypertext link on the Web, like a link in a chain, is a connector between two points. Links can appear in two ways: as text that you click or as a graphic that you click. A **text link** is a word or phrase that is usually underlined and often boldfaced or colored differently from the words around it. A **graphic link** is a graphic image that you click to jump to—or connect to—another location (note that graphic images can be or include text). When you aren't sure whether a graphic image is a link, point to it with the mouse pointer. When you move the mouse pointer over a link—text or graphic—the pointer changes shape from ↖ to 🖑. The 🖑 pointer indicates that when you click, you will activate that link and jump to the new location. The destination of the link appears in the status bar, and, for some graphic links, a small ScreenTip appears next to your pointer.

The Highland Travel page contains both text and graphic links. The text links are at the bottom of the page, underlined, and in color. The graphic links are the words in a fancy font at the bottom of the Highland Travel photo, although graphic links are often images or photos. The links give your browser the information it needs to locate the page. When you activate a link, you jump to a new location. The target of the link can be another location on the current page (for example, you can jump from the bottom of the page to the top), a different page on the current Web server, or a different page located on an entirely different Web server. When you activate a link, there are three possible outcomes:

- You successfully reach the target of the link. The browser contacts the site you want, connects to the site, transfers the data from the site to your computer, and displays the data in your browser window.

- The link's target is busy, perhaps because the server storing the link's target is overwhelmed with too many requests. You can click the Stop button 🔘 to prevent your browser from further attempting to make the connection. You'll have to try this link later or try a different link.

- The link points to a target that doesn't exist. Documents are often removed from Web servers as they become obsolete, or moved to new locations, and links that point to those documents are not always updated. If you click an obsolete link, a message box appears. If an error message box appears, click the OK button and try a different link. Otherwise click the Back button 🔙 to return to the page you were previously viewing.

The amount of time it takes to complete a link, called the **response time**, can vary, depending upon the number of people trying to connect to the same site, the number of people on the Internet at that time, the site design, and the speed of your Internet connection. In fact, one of the differences you might notice between clicking links on your desktop (which target local objects, such as My Computer or a desktop document) and clicking those that target Web pages on the Internet is the difference in response time. Linking to local objects is usually instantaneous, whereas linking to pages on the Web can take many seconds, because of the time required for the data to be transferred over your Internet connection.

As you can see in Figure 5-9, activating a link starts a multistep process. When you point to a link, the status bar displays a message that the browser is connecting to the address of the link's target, its URL. When you click the link, the activity indicator animates. The status bar displays a series of messages indicating that your browser is connecting to the site, is waiting for a reply, is transferring data, and finally, is done.

Figure 5-9   **ACTIVATING A LINK**

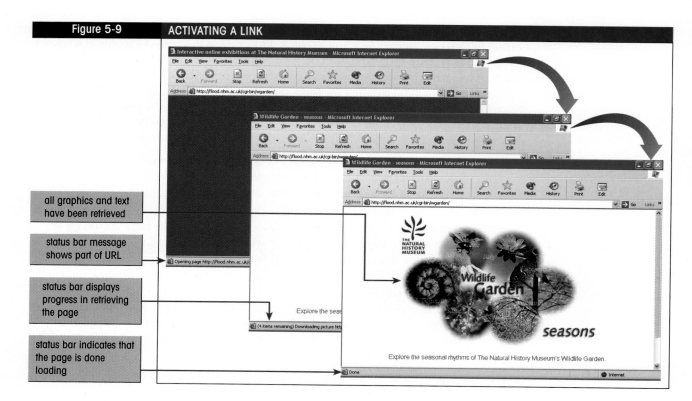

all graphics and text have been retrieved

status bar message shows part of URL

status bar displays progress in retrieving the page

status bar indicates that the page is done loading

You can see the Web page build as your browser transfers information to the screen in multiple passes. The first wave brings a few elements to the page, and with each subsequent pass, the browser fills in more detail, until the material is complete. Try activating one of the Highland Travel links to access the company's home page.

To activate a link:

1. Point to the text link **Home Page**—the one at the bottom of the page. (You could also point to the graphic link, the one with the fancy font; both links target the same page.) Notice that the pointer changes shape from ☇ to ☝, indicating that you are pointing to a hypertext link. The status bar shows the URL for that link. See Figure 5-10.

Figure 5-10	CLICKING A TEXT LINK

graphics links

text links

link's target appears in the status bar

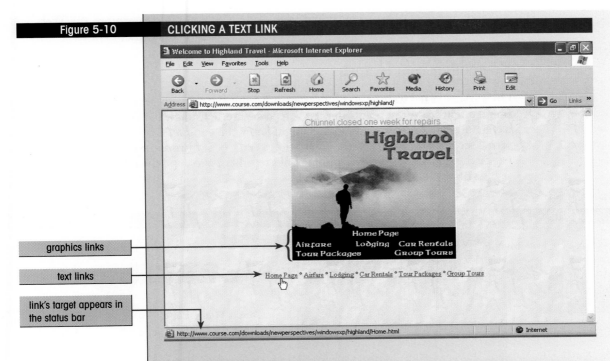

2. Click the **Home Page** text link to activate the link. The status bar notes the progress of the link. When the status bar displays "Done," the link is complete, and the Web page that is the target of the link appears. See Figure 5-11.

Figure 5-11	COMPLETED LINK

You've opened the Highland Travel home page. Now you can explore the contents of this page.

Scott mentions that if you spend time using Windows XP to explore the Web, you'll probably encounter Web pages with frames. You will learn about frames next.

Navigating with Frames

On a Web page, **frames** logically separate information into sections. For example, one frame might list the contents of the Web page, another might include links you can click to navigate related pages, and another might show the content. Each frame can have its own set of scroll bars, as shown in Figure 5-12. The NEC Products page is made up of two pages: the one on the left lists graphic links to other pages, and the one on the right displays the list of product categories.

Figure 5-12	WEB PAGE MADE UP OF FRAMES

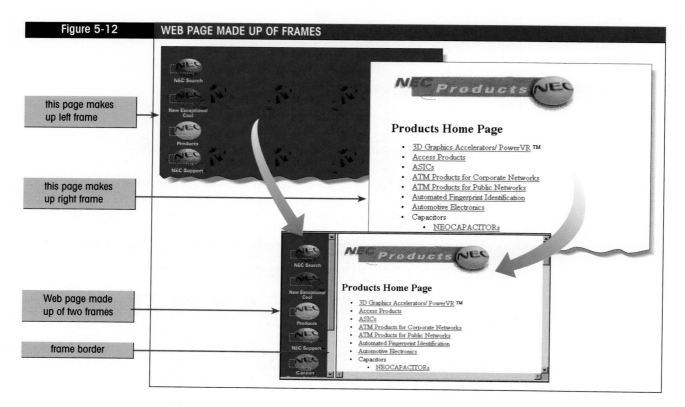

Many Web sites today use frames because they allow the user to see different areas of information simultaneously. When you scroll through the contents of one frame, you do not affect the other frames. Scott suggests you view the Tour Packages page, which uses frames, to learn about this season's Highland Travel tours.

To view a page with frames:

1. Click the **Tour Packages** text link, located in the yellow box on the left of the home page. The Tour Packages page opens. This page consists of four frames that contain (1) the Tour Packages heading at the top, (2) information on the left about the specified tour, (3) a scroll box on the right, listing the tour itinerary for each tour, and (4) graphic links to four different tours on the bottom. See Figure 5-13.

Figure 5-13	VIEWING A WEB PAGE WITH FRAMES

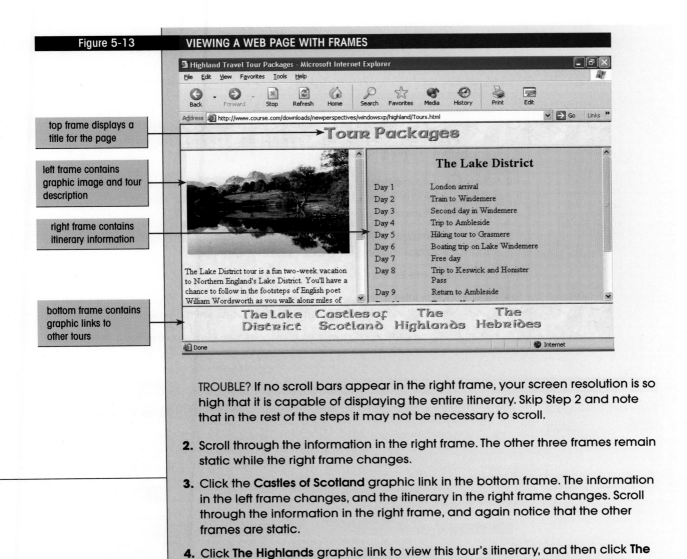

top frame displays a title for the page

left frame contains graphic image and tour description

right frame contains itinerary information

bottom frame contains graphic links to other tours

TROUBLE? If no scroll bars appear in the right frame, your screen resolution is so high that it is capable of displaying the entire itinerary. Skip Step 2 and note that in the rest of the steps it may not be necessary to scroll.

2. Scroll through the information in the right frame. The other three frames remain static while the right frame changes.

3. Click the **Castles of Scotland** graphic link in the bottom frame. The information in the left frame changes, and the itinerary in the right frame changes. Scroll through the information in the right frame, and again notice that the other frames are static.

4. Click **The Highlands** graphic link to view this tour's itinerary, and then click **The Hebrides** graphic link. You have now viewed information on all four tours.

By using frames, the designer of this Web page made it possible for you to view only the information you choose to view.

Returning to a Previously Viewed Page

You've already seen in earlier tutorials how Windows XP allows you to navigate the devices and folders on your local and network drives, using the Back and Forward buttons in Windows Explorer and My Computer. These buttons are also found on the Standard Buttons toolbars in most browsers. The Back button returns you to the Web page you were most recently viewing, and the Forward button reverses the effect of the Back button. Both the Back and Forward buttons contain lists of visited sites; you can return to those sites by clicking the list arrow to the right of either button and clicking the site from the drop-down list.

To return to a previously viewed Web page:

1. Click the **Back** button ⬅ repeatedly to navigate back through the tour itineraries you viewed. You return to the Highland Travel Home Page, the page you were visiting before you viewed the Tours framed page.

   TROUBLE? If you click the small down arrow (not the Forward button) to the right of the Back button, a list opens. Click the arrow again to close the list, and then repeat Step 1. This time make sure you click ⬅.

2. Click ⬅ until the Back button dims, indicating that you have reached your starting point, usually your home page. Now try moving forward again to return to the Tour Packages page.

3. Click the **Forward** button ➡ repeatedly until the Forward button dims, indicating that you are looking at the last page you visited.

4. Click the **Home** button 🏠 to return to your Home Page.

   Now you'll use the Back list to see how you can return to a page you've visited without having to navigate through all the pages you've seen in a given session.

5. Click the **Back button** list arrow (the small down arrow to the right of the Back button). The Back list opens. See Figure 5-14.

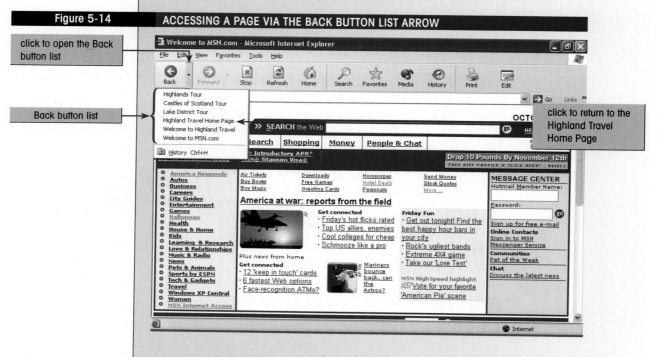

Figure 5-14 **ACCESSING A PAGE VIA THE BACK BUTTON LIST ARROW**

click to open the Back button list

Back button list

click to return to the Highland Travel Home Page

6. Click **Highland Travel Home Page** to return to the Highland Travel Home Page.

Scott explains that one limitation of the Back and Forward buttons is that they apply only to your current session in the browser. If you exit Internet Explorer and restart it, the Back list starts afresh. However, you can always use the History pane to access those pages quickly. Scott wants you to try this technique now.

Navigating with the History Pane

As mentioned earlier, Internet Explorer has a lot in common with Windows Explorer. Many of the menu commands and buttons are the same. In addition, Internet Explorer has the same Explorer bar that Windows Explorer has, allowing you to divide the Internet Explorer window into two panes. All of the tools you used in Tutorial 3 with the left pane in Windows Explorer apply to the left pane in Internet Explorer. For example, in Internet Explorer you can display the History pane, which lists the files, folders, and pages you've visited recently. This is the same History pane you opened in Windows Explorer, showing the same list of items. The History pane is particularly helpful in Internet Explorer because if you visit many sites on a certain day, you can quickly find one of those sites later in the History pane and revisit it.

You can change the setup in the History pane to view pages by date, by site, by the number of times visited, and in the order visited on the current day. You can also search the pages in the History pane to locate a specific Web site you've recently visited.

To use the History pane:

1. Click the **History** button 🕒 on the Standard Buttons toolbar to open the History pane. (Note that you could also click View, point to the Explorer bar, and then click History to open the History pane.) See Figure 5-15.

| Figure 5-15 | DISPLAYING THE HISTORY PANE |

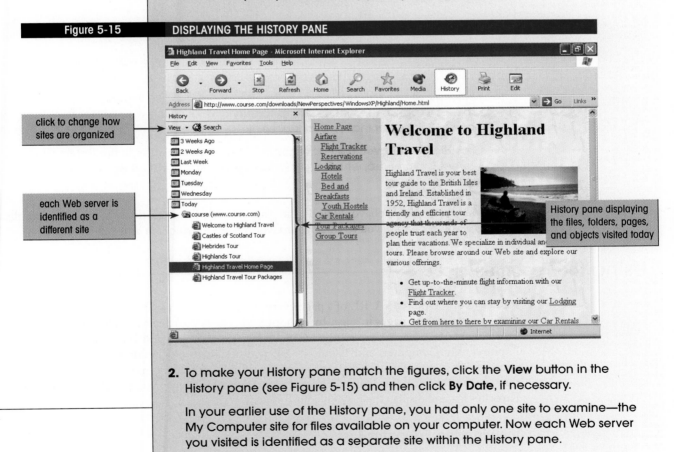

click to change how sites are organized

each Web server is identified as a different site

History pane displaying the files, folders, pages, and objects visited today

2. To make your History pane match the figures, click the **View** button in the History pane (see Figure 5-15) and then click **By Date**, if necessary.

In your earlier use of the History pane, you had only one site to examine—the My Computer site for files available on your computer. Now each Web server you visited is identified as a separate site within the History pane.

3. Click the **course (www.course.com)** icon in the History pane. Internet Explorer collapses the Course list so that only the course (www.course.com) heading appears. See Figure 5-16.

Figure 5-16 | **WEB SERVERS VISITED**

Web pages accessed today at the Course site →

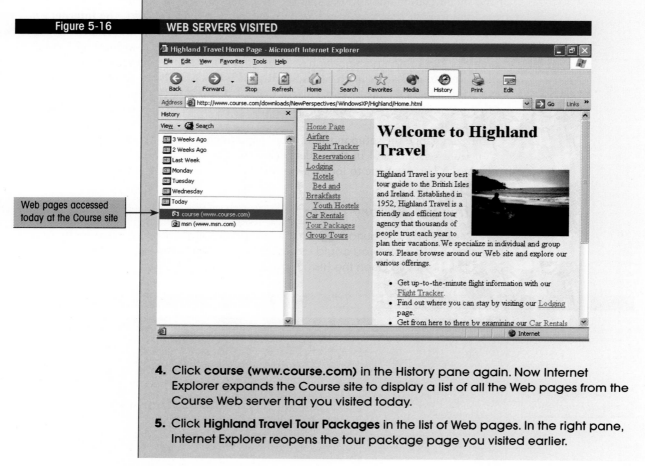

4. Click **course (www.course.com)** in the History pane again. Now Internet Explorer expands the Course site to display a list of all the Web pages from the Course Web server that you visited today.

5. Click **Highland Travel Tour Packages** in the list of Web pages. In the right pane, Internet Explorer reopens the tour package page you visited earlier.

As you explore the Web, you'll find pages that are your favorites, those you visit frequently. Internet Explorer allows you to track your favorite sites for frequent and easy access.

Using the Favorites List

Rather than retyping the URL of a page every time you want to visit it, you can save the location of your favorite pages in a list. In Windows XP, this is your **Favorites list**, and it contains shortcuts to the files, folders, objects, and Web pages that you visit most often. In Internet Explorer, My Computer, and Windows XP, you designate files, folders, and Web pages as your favorites—those which you want to organize for quick access—and Windows XP includes them in the Favorites list. When you want to retrieve a Web page, you can click an icon in the Favorites list and display the page in your browser.

Viewing the Favorites List

You can display your Favorites list in a variety of ways. You can use the Favorites menu available on the Internet Explorer menu bar or the Favorites button on the Standard Buttons toolbar. You can also display the contents of your Favorites list in the Explorer Bar for Internet

Explorer, Windows Explorer, and My Computer. You can even display the Favorites list on your Start menu. The method you use to access your favorites depends on your personal preference. In any case, the Favorites list includes any file, folder, or Web page you've added to it. If you use Internet Explorer to add the Web page of your favorite online travel site to the Favorites list, for example, the Web page also appears in the My Computer Favorites list.

Steve suggests you add the Highland Travel Web page to your Favorites list. First, you must open the Favorites list. You decide to display the Favorites pane in the Explorer bar.

To display the Favorites list:

1. Click the **Favorites** button ☆ on the Standard Buttons toolbar to open the Favorites list. (Note that you can also click View, point to the Explorer bar, and then click Favorites to open the Favorites list.) Internet Explorer displays the Favorites list in the Favorites pane, as shown in Figure 5-17.

| Figure 5-17 | DISPLAYING THE FAVORITES LIST |

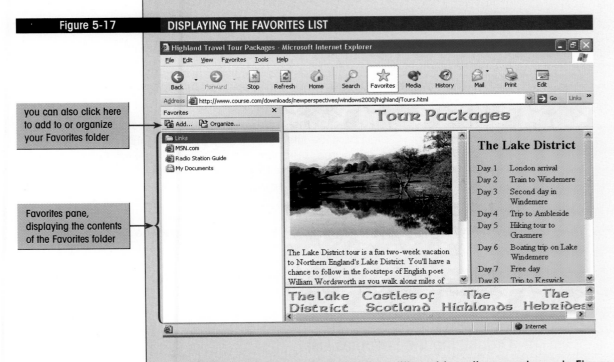

you can also click here to add to or organize your Favorites folder

Favorites pane, displaying the contents of the Favorites folder

TROUBLE? Your Favorites list might be different from the one shown in Figure 5-17.

The Favorites list shown in Figure 5-17 contains shortcuts to a Web page containing a radio station guide and a page for the Microsoft Network (MSN). Now you can add the home page for Highland Travel to your Favorites list.

Adding an Item to the Favorites List

To add a Web page, you must first access the page in Internet Explorer, and then you can use the Add to Favorites command. Windows XP adds the new page to the top of the Favorites list. You can add the page using the title of the Web page as its name, or you can change the name to something more meaningful to you.

If you are working on a network, you might not be able to change the content of the Favorites list. If that's the case, you will not be able to complete these steps or the ones that follow. Instead read through this material—if you've completed Tutorial 3, this information will be familiar to you.

REFERENCE WINDOW   **RW**

Adding a Web Page to the Favorites Folder
- Open the Web page in Internet Explorer.
- Click Favorites on the Internet Explorer menu bar, and then click Add to Favorites.
- Click the OK button.

To add the Highland Travel Home Page to the Favorites list:

1. Click the **Back** button ⬅ to return to the Highland Travel Home Page. This is the page you want to add to the Favorites list.

2. Click **Favorites** on the menu bar, and then click **Add to Favorites**. The Add Favorite dialog box opens.

   Note that you can also click the Add button in the Favorites pane to open the Add Favorite dialog box. The title of the Web page appears in the Name text box—in this case, the name is Highland Travel Home Page. To change this, you could enter a different name in the Name text box. Highland Travel Home Page is appropriate for this Web page, so you won't change it.

3. Click the **OK** button.

   An icon for the Highland Travel Home Page is added to the Favorites folder.

If you have many favorites in your Favorites list, you will want to organize them in a logical manner. Creating and using subfolders is one way of effectively organizing a long Favorites list.

Organizing the Favorites List

As you add more items to the Favorites list, you will find that you need to organize its contents: deleting some items and moving others to new folders. Using folders is an excellent way to organize your favorite files and pages.

REFERENCE WINDOW   **RW**

Organizing the Favorites List
- Click Favorites on the Internet Explorer menu bar, and then click Organize Favorites to open the Organize Favorites dialog box.
- To create a new folder, click the Create Folder button.
- To move an item into the Favorites folder, select the item, click the Move to Folder button, select the new folder for the item, and then click the OK button.
- To remove an item from the Favorites folder, select the item and then click the Delete button.

You decide to create a folder for the Highland Travel Web pages.

To organize your Favorites list:

1. Click **Favorites** on the Internet Explorer menu bar, and then click **Organize Favorites**. The Organize Favorites dialog box opens. You can also click the Organize button in the Favorites pane to open this dialog box.

2. Click the **Create Folder** button, type **Highland Travel** for the new folder name, and then press the **Enter** key. Now you'll move the Highland Travel Home Page into the new folder you created.

3. In the Organize Favorites dialog box, click the **Highland Travel Home Page** icon in the list box to select it.

4. Click the **Move to Folder** button. The Browse for Folder dialog box opens. You use this dialog box to find the folder in which you want to store the selected Web page.

5. Click the **Highland Travel** folder, and then click the **OK** button.

6. Click the **Close** button to close the Organize Favorites dialog box. A folder for Highland Travel now appears in the Favorites pane.

7. Click the **Highland Travel** folder in the Favorites pane. The contents of the folder appear as shown in Figure 5-18.

Figure 5-18	THE HIGHLAND TRAVEL FOLDER IN THE FAVORITES LIST

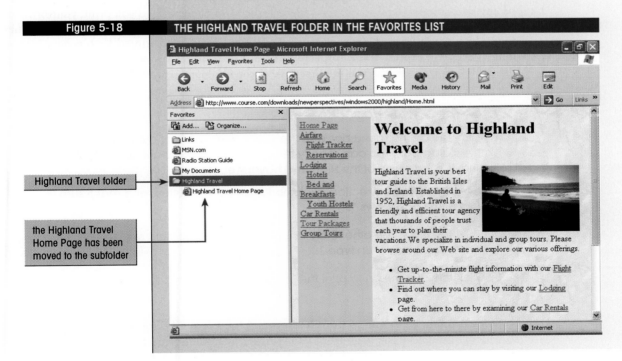

Highland Travel folder

the Highland Travel Home Page has been moved to the subfolder

Before completing your work with the Favorites list, you should remove the folder you created, and then close the Favorites pane.

To delete an item from the Favorites list:

1. Click the **Organize** button in the Favorites pane. The Organize Favorites dialog box opens.

2. Click the **Highland Travel** folder in the Organize Favorites dialog box. This is the folder you want to remove from the Favorites list.

3. Click the **Delete** button. A message box appears asking you to confirm you want to delete the folder and its contents.

4. Click the **Yes** button.

5. Click the **Close** button to close the Organize Favorites dialog box.

6. Click the **Close** button ⊠ in the Favorites pane to close the Favorites list.

Although reducing paper consumption is an advantage of browsing information online, sometimes you'll find it useful to print a Web page.

Printing a Web Page

You might want to refer to the information you find on the Web later when you don't have computer access. This is when printing a Web page becomes useful. Although Web pages can be any size, printers tend to use 8½ × 11-inch sheets of paper. When you print, your browser automatically reformats the text of the Web page to fit the paper dimensions. Because lines might break at different places or text size might be altered, the printed Web page might be longer than you expect. You can specify the number of pages you want to print in the Print dialog box. You decide to print the first page of the Highland Travel Web page.

To print a Web page:

1. Click **File** on the menu bar, and then click **Print**. The Print dialog box opens. In this dialog box, you can specify the print options you want. You only want to print the first page of the Highland Travel Web page.

2. In the Page Range section, click the **Pages** option button, and make sure the Pages text box shows 1.

   TROUBLE? If a value other than 1 appears in the Pages text box, select the text in the text box, and then type 1.

3. Click the **Print** button to print the first page of the Highland Travel Home Page.

Some printers are set up to print headers and footers in addition to the Web page itself, so when you retrieve the page from your printer, you might find the page's title, its URL, the date, and other similar information at the top and bottom of the page.

Downloading a File

Scott explains that Windows XP also makes it easy to transfer files stored on the Internet to your computer. Although a Web page appears in your browser window and you can add the page to your Favorites list or find it in your History list, the page itself is still stored on a remote computer (a computer located elsewhere on the Internet.) To store the Web page on your computer, you must download it from the remote computer. **Downloading** is the process of saving a copy of a file located on a remote computer to your own computer. The method you use to download information you find on the Web depends on how the file appears on the Web page. If you want to save the Web page itself, you use the Save As command on the File menu. If you want to save a graphic image located directly on the Web page, you save it by right-clicking the object you want and then using the Save Picture As command that appears on the shortcut menu.

You liked the Lake District graphic on the Tours page, so you decide to download and use it as a background image on your desktop.

To download a file:

1. Click the **Forward** button ➡ to return to the Lake District tour page.

2. Write "Windows XP Tutorial 5 Lake District graphic" on the label of a blank, formatted 3½-inch disk. Insert the disk into drive A.

3. Right-click the **Lake District** graphic to open its shortcut menu. See Figure 5-19.

Figure 5-19	SAVING A WEB GRAPHIC

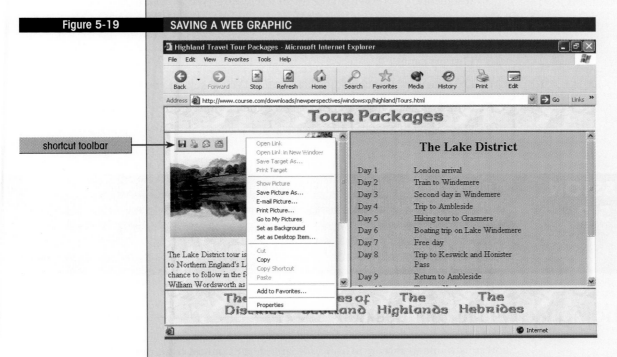

4. Click **Save Picture As** on the shortcut menu. Note that you could also click the Save as button on the shortcut toolbar. The Save Picture dialog box opens.

5. Click the **Save in** list arrow, and then click 3½ **Floppy (A:)**. Make sure the name "lake" appears in the File name box and the type is JPEG, a common graphic image type used in Web pages.

> **TROUBLE?** If a name other than "lake" appears in the File name box, replace it with the name "lake." If a type other than JPEG appears in the Save as type text box, click the Save as type list arrow and then click JPEG (*.jpg).
>
> **6.** Click the **Save** button. Windows XP transfers the file over the Internet from the Tour Packages Web page to your disk.
>
> **7.** Close Internet Explorer.

The file is stored on your disk, and you could open it in a graphics program (such as Paint) and work with it there. Note that content appearing on Web pages is often copyrighted, and you should always make sure you have permission to use it before doing so. Since Highland Travel owns this graphic, Scott tells you that you can use it.

You have now used Internet Explorer to view information on the Web, navigate links, and print and save information from the Web.

Session 5.1 QUICK CHECK

1. What is a home page?

2. The address of a Web page is called a(n) _____.

3. If someone gives you the URL of an interesting Web page, how can you view the page?

4. What does a URL with "edu" in it tell you about that site's Web server?

5. Each Web server you visit appears as a different _____ in the History pane.

6. Describe how you could quickly locate a Web page that you viewed a few days earlier.

7. True or False: Only Web pages and folders can be stored in the Favorites folder.

8. How can you download a graphic image that you find on the Web?

SESSION 5.2

In this session, you will learn how to set up your computer so that it automatically delivers Web page content to your desktop. You'll add an Active Desktop item to your Windows XP desktop. You'll update the Active Desktop item using the Synchronize command, and you'll set up a schedule for automatic updates. Finally, you'll use a Web page as a background for your Windows XP desktop. For this session you need the Data Disk for Windows XP Tutorial 5.

Bringing the Web to Your Desktop

Scott now wants to show you how you can receive content from the Web without having to go look for it. When you connected to the Highland Travel Web page in Session 5.1, you had to go looking for it. You were told where to find the information (that is, you were given a URL), and then you went to that location and "pulled" information from the Web server onto your own computer.

Another way of retrieving data, called **push technology**, brings information to your computer without your having to go get it. True push technology occurs when the author of a Web site modifies the site so that it automatically sends information to users, without requiring the user to manually access the site and retrieve the data. Once the data has been retrieved, the user can view it without being connected to the Internet or any network. This is a technique known as **offline viewing** because the user is not "online" with the Web server.

Scott explains that you're going to begin your exploration of push technology and offline viewing by adding to the desktop content that changes frequently—Active Desktop items. An **Active Desktop** item is an object that you place on your desktop that receives updates from a Web page that pushes the updates to users on a set schedule. For example, you could place a selection of Active Desktop items on your desktop, as in Figure 5-20.

| Figure 5-20 | WINDOWS XP DESKTOP WITH ACTIVE DESKTOP ITEMS |

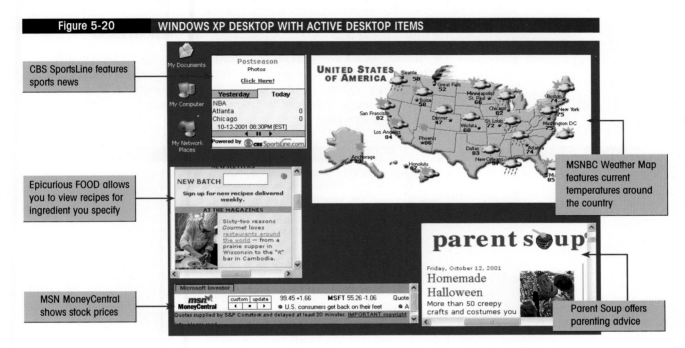

You can set Active Desktop items to be updated each day, each hour, or on any schedule you choose. Every morning when the user of the computer shown in Figure 5-20 checks her desktop, for example, each active desktop item will have been automatically updated. The weather map will show the morning's weather instead of weather from the night before, the news service will display the most recent news, and other Active Desktop items are updated in a similar fashion. This user has created her own "mini-newspaper," made up of only the information that interests her.

Some Active Desktop items are interactive, allowing you to enter information and receive a response. The Epicurious FOOD Active Desktop item, for example, allows you to enter ingredients, such as beans and rice, and when you click the Get Recipes button, Internet Explorer starts (and connects to the Internet if you're not already connected) and displays recipes from the Epicurious site containing those ingredients. Microsoft maintains a collection of Active Desktop items at its Active Desktop Gallery Web site, which you'll access next.

Adding an Active Desktop Gallery Item to the Desktop

When you're connected to the Internet, you can add, update, and use Active Desktop items. If you specify that you want Active Desktop items to be available for offline viewing, you can view the items and their contents when you're not connected to the Internet, but you cannot update the items or add others.

Now you'll use the Customize Desktop button in the Display Properties dialog box to add Web content to your desktop. Although you can add any Web page to your desktop, you'll start by opening the Desktop Gallery on the Microsoft Web site. The Desktop Gallery contains popular Active Desktop items, including a weather map and sports scores.

To add a weather map from the Active Desktop Gallery to your desktop:

1. Right-click a blank area of the desktop, and then click **Properties** on the shortcut menu. The Display Properties dialog box opens.

2. Click the **Desktop** tab and then click the **Customize Desktop** button.

3. Click the **Web** tab in the Desktop Items dialog box. See Figure 5-21. In this dialog box, the Web pages box lists the Web pages you want to view on your desktop. To add a page to this list, you click the New button, and then enter the URL of the Web page you want, or open the Microsoft Desktop Gallery to select an Active Desktop item.

| Figure 5-21 | THE WEB TAB IN THE CUSTOMIZE ITEMS DIALOG BOX |

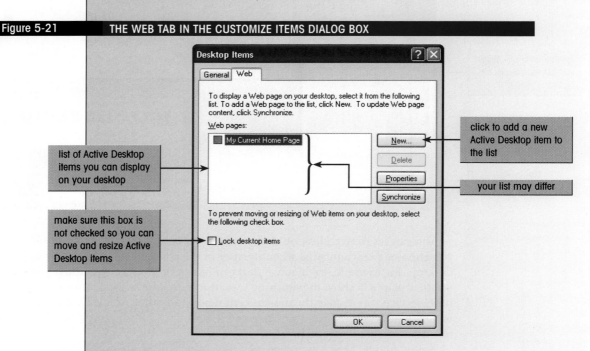

list of Active Desktop items you can display on your desktop

make sure this box is not checked so you can move and resize Active Desktop items

click to add a new Active Desktop item to the list

your list may differ

4. Click the **New** button.

5. In the New Desktop Item dialog box, click the **Visit Gallery** button. Windows XP opens the Active Desktop Gallery Web page in Internet Explorer.

   TROUBLE? If you are prompted to download a Stock Ticker from Microsoft, talk to your network manager or instructor to decide whether this program can be retrieved and loaded onto your computer.

6. Scroll the Desktop Gallery list to locate the MSNBC Weather Map, shown in Figure 5-22.

Figure 5-22	SELECTING THE MSNBC WEATHER MAP

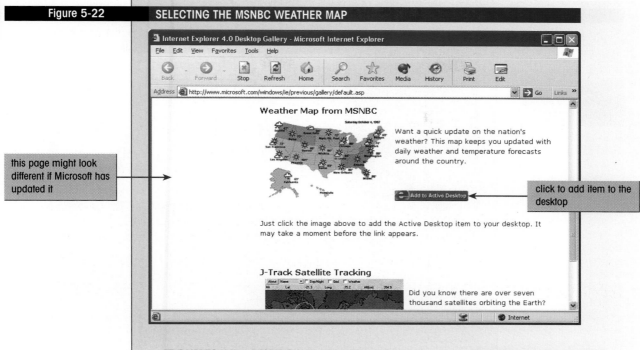

this page might look different if Microsoft has updated it

click to add item to the desktop

TROUBLE? If the MSNBC Weather Map doesn't appear in the list, select a different Active Desktop item.

7. Click the **Add to Active Desktop** button below the MSNBC Weather Map. Click the **Yes** button if an Internet Explorer message box appears asking if you want to add this item to your Active Desktop. A second message box appears that asks you to confirm the procedure.

8. Click the **OK** button to add the item to your desktop. The download process might take one or several minutes, depending on the speed of your Internet connection. If the Synchronization dialog box opens, wait until it closes before continuing.

9. Once the download is complete, close your browser. The item you added appears on your desktop. See Figure 5-23.

Figure 5-23	ADDING AN ACTIVE DESKTOP ITEM

weather map on your desktop (your desktop might look different)

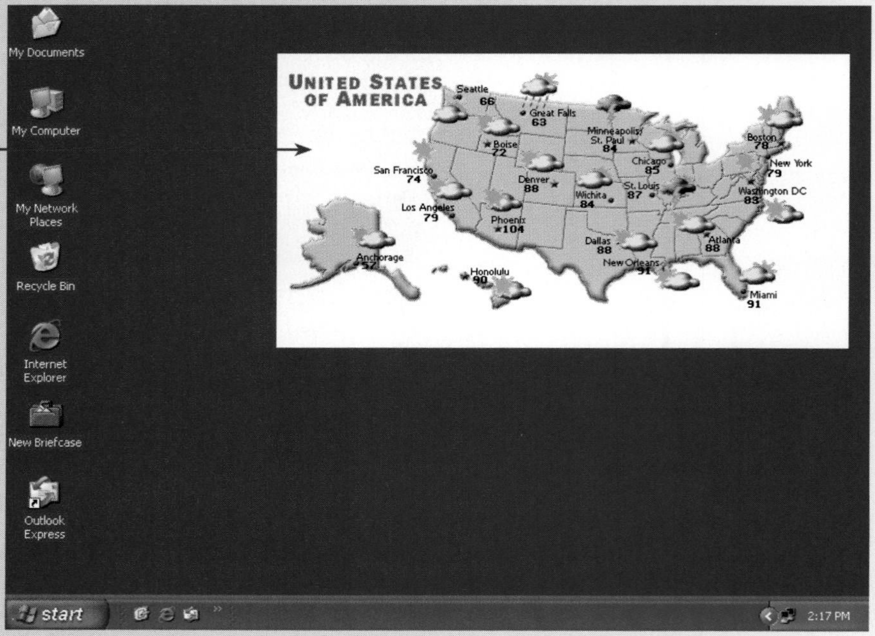

TROUBLE? If the Active Desktop item appears but doesn't look like a weather map, the MSNBC site might be busy. A desktop item will still appear, but it won't include the map. Continue with the steps, using the Active Desktop item.

TROUBLE? If scroll bars appear around your Active Desktop item or the item is off-center, you can move and resize the item; you'll learn how to do so in the next section.

When an Active Desktop item is on your desktop, it occupies a rectangular block that appears as part of the background. However, you can resize and move the Active Desktop item to suit your needs.

Resizing and Moving Active Desktop Items

To move or resize an Active Desktop item, you must first point to it to select it. When an Active Desktop item is selected, a title bar and border appear, which you can manipulate to move and resize the item just as you would any other Windows XP window (such as the My Computer window). You can move the Active Desktop item by dragging it. You can also resize the item using one of three techniques. You can use the sizing buttons on the item's title bar, you can use the sizing commands available from a menu by clicking the item's list arrow on its title bar, or you can drag the item's borders.

Practice moving Active Desktop items by moving the weather map.

To move the weather map:

1. Point to the top of the weather map. A border appears around the entire Active Desktop item, and a bar, similar to a window's title bar, appears at the top. This bar includes a Close Pane button ✕, sizing buttons, and a list arrow on the left that opens a menu for that item. See Figure 5-24.

Figure 5-24	SELECTING AN ACTIVE DESKTOP ITEM

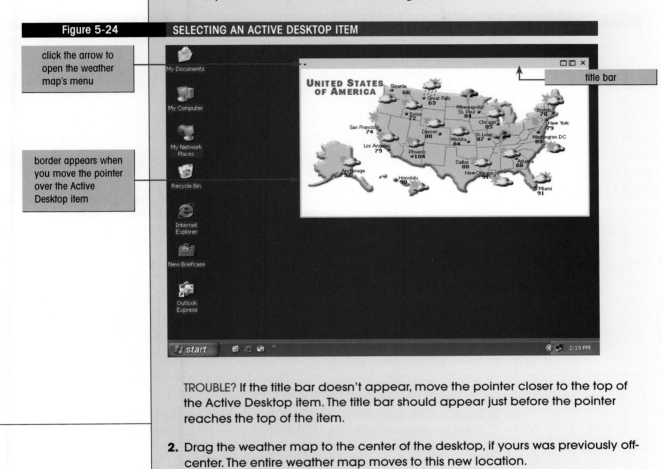

click the arrow to open the weather map's menu

title bar

border appears when you move the pointer over the Active Desktop item

TROUBLE? If the title bar doesn't appear, move the pointer closer to the top of the Active Desktop item. The title bar should appear just before the pointer reaches the top of the item.

2. Drag the weather map to the center of the desktop, if yours was previously off-center. The entire weather map moves to this new location.

You can also use the border around the weather map to resize it. For example, you drag the left and right borders to widen the item or make it narrower, you drag the top and bottom borders to lengthen or shorten the item, and you drag any corner out to enlarge or reduce both dimensions proportionally.

To resize the weather map:

1. Point to the lower-right corner of the weather map. The gray border appears and the mouse pointer changes from ⇖ to ⬊.

2. Drag the corner border to the lower right. The Active Desktop item expands in size. If your map has scroll bars, drag down and to the right until the scroll bars disappear.

You can also change the size of a desktop item by clicking one of the buttons on the upper-right corner of the item border. Figure 5-25 describes the four buttons available on the border and how to use them to modify the desktop item. These sizing commands are also available on the window's menu, which you open by clicking the down arrow button in the left corner of the titlebar.

Figure 5-25	RESIZE BUTTONS FOR THE ACTIVE DESKTOP ITEM	
NAME		**DESCRIPTION**
	Cover Desktop	Extend the item across the entire desktop
	Split Desktop with Icons	Move all desktop icons to the far left and fill the remaining desktop with the item
	Reset to Original Size	Reset the item to a window on the desktop
✕	Close Pane	Close the item

To see how these buttons work, you'll try resizing the image: first to fill the whole desktop, then to split the desktop between the icons and the item, and finally to restore the item to its original size and position. Note that you see only three of these buttons at a time. The middle button changes depending on the item's current size.

To use the sizing buttons:

1. Move your mouse pointer over the top border of the image to redisplay the title bar (if necessary), and click the **Cover Desktop** button ☐. The weather map fills the entire desktop.

2. Move the mouse pointer to the top of the weather map, and then click the **Split Desktop with Icons** button ☐☐. The weather map is reduced in size, moving to the right of the icons on the desktop.

3. Move the mouse pointer to the top of the weather map again, and click the **Reset to Original Size** button ☐. The weather map is restored to its original size on the desktop.

Figure 5-26 shows the weather map in each of the three sizes.

Figure 5-26	THE WEATHER MAP IN THREE SIZES

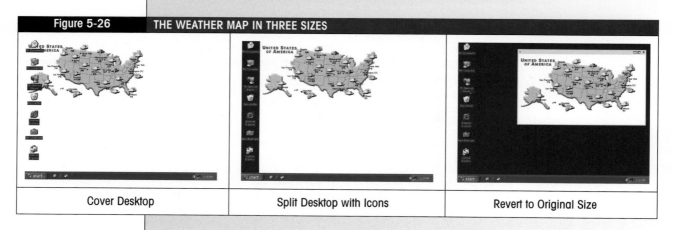

Cover Desktop	Split Desktop with Icons	Revert to Original Size

You might be wondering how you update the weather map to reflect current conditions. You will learn how to do that next.

Updating **Active Desktop Items**

The process of retrieving current information is called **synchronization**. When you synchronize an Active Desktop item, you refresh and update its content. For example, the weather map shows the weather that was current when you added the MSNBC Weather Map item to the desktop. To see how the weather has changed since you added that item, you must synchronize that Active Desktop item.

Windows XP allows you to synchronize not just Web content, but any information available over your network. For example, if you are working on a corporate network and are leaving on a trip, you can retrieve a file for offline viewing on your laptop. Windows XP will make a copy of that file available to you, but it might not be current with the network file when you return. You can change this by synchronizing your copy with the network version. Similarly, you can synchronize the weather map on your desktop with the map available on the Web server.

REFERENCE WINDOW   **RW**

Synchronizing an Active Desktop Item
- Move the mouse pointer over the upper border of the Active Desktop item to display the title bar.
- Click the down arrow on the left edge of the title bar to display the menu.
- Click Synchronize.

Now you can synchronize the weather map to show current weather conditions.

Synchronizing Active Desktop Items Manually

Files and Web pages can be synchronized on a fixed schedule or manually. When you manually synchronize, you use the Synchronize command on the Active Desktop item to connect to the original Web page and then transfer current information from that Web page to your desktop. After you synchronize, the Active Desktop item shows updated information.

To synchronize the weather map:

1. Move the mouse pointer over the upper border of the weather map to display the title bar.

2. Click the down arrow located on the left edge of the title bar, and then click **Synchronize** on the menu. See Figure 5-27.

Figure 5-27	SYNCHRONIZING THE WEATHER MAP

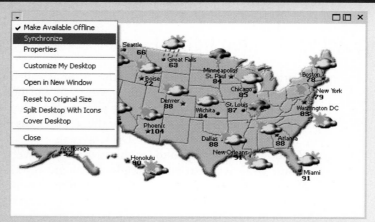

3. Windows XP connects to the Web server and updates the weather map with the latest weather information.

If you always had to update the weather map manually, having it on your desktop would not be much of an improvement over simply visiting the page on the Web. Windows XP allows you to schedule automatic updates.

Viewing an Update Schedule

The advantage of synchronization is the ability of Windows XP to access the page for you on a schedule. For example, you could have an Active Desktop item that downloads the latest stock market information every five minutes. By glancing at your desktop, you can view data that is no more than five minutes old.

Most Active Desktop items retrieved from the Active Desktop gallery have a schedule already set. The schedule is one of the properties of the Active Desktop item.

To view the schedule for the weather map:

1. Redisplay the title bar for the weather map, click the down arrow, and then click **Properties** on the menu. The MSNBC Weather Properties dialog box opens.

2. Click the **Schedule** tab. As shown in Figure 5-28, the weather map uses the MSNBC Weather Recommended Schedule.

Figure 5-28	THE MSNBC WEATHER PROPERTIES DIALOG BOX

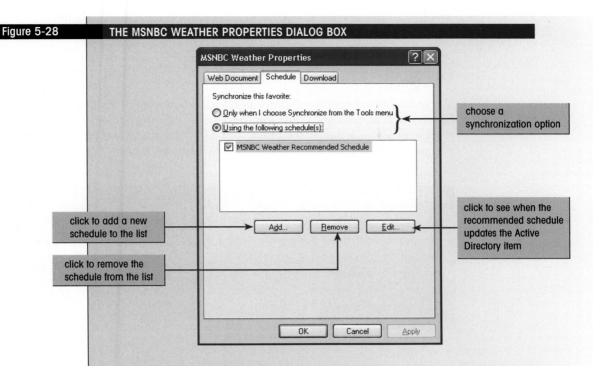

click to add a new
schedule to the list

click to remove the
schedule from the list

choose a
synchronization option

click to see when the
recommended schedule
updates the Active
Directory item

3. To see when the MSNBC Weather recommended schedule downloads updated weather maps, click the **Edit** button. As shown in Figure 5-29, under the recommended schedule the map is updated every night at 12:00 AM.

Figure 5-29	THE MSNBC WEATHER RECOMMENDED SCHEDULE

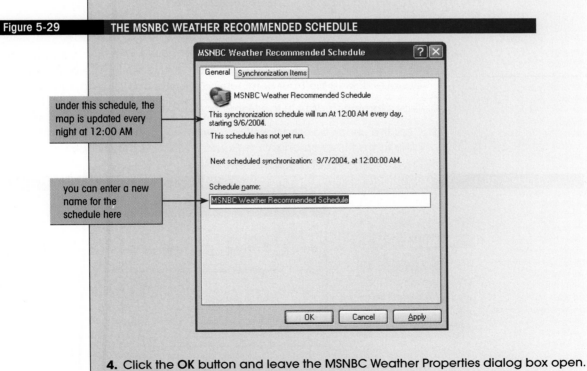

under this schedule, the
map is updated every
night at 12:00 AM

you can enter a new
name for the
schedule here

4. Click the **OK** button and leave the MSNBC Weather Properties dialog box open.

The recommended schedule may not be ideal for you. Fortunately, you can change it to suit your individual needs.

Editing an Update Schedule

You realize as you examine the current schedule that most of the time your computer will not be turned on at midnight to run the synchronization. A much better time would be 9:00 AM, shortly after you arrive at the office, and 3:00 PM, shortly before you leave. To make this change, you have to create two schedules: one for the morning and one for the afternoon.

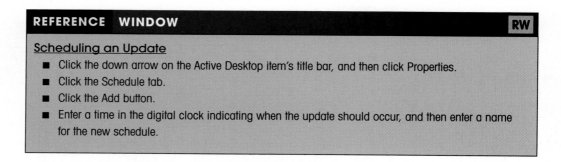

REFERENCE WINDOW   RW

Scheduling an Update
- Click the down arrow on the Active Desktop item's title bar, and then click Properties.
- Click the Schedule tab.
- Click the Add button.
- Enter a time in the digital clock indicating when the update should occur, and then enter a name for the new schedule.

Now you can create an update schedule to synchronize the weather map once in the morning and once in the afternoon.

To create an update schedule:

1. Click the **Add** button in the MSNBC Weather Properties dialog box.

2. In the New Schedule dialog box, set the time value to **9:00 AM**. (You can set the time value by clicking the up and down arrows next to the digital clock or by double-clicking the hour or minutes digits, and then typing new values.)

3. Type **Morning Update** in the Name box.

4. Click the check box to allow Windows XP to connect to the Internet automatically to begin synchronization. Figure 5-30 shows the completed dialog box.

Figure 5-30   SCHEDULING THE MORNING UPDATE

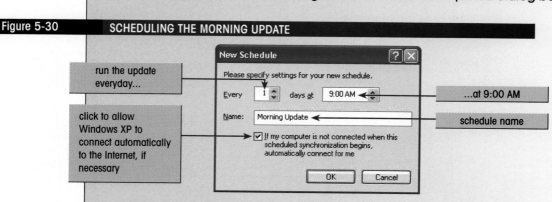

5. Click the **OK** button. The Morning Update schedule is added to the list of schedules. Now Windows XP will synchronize the weather map Active Desktop item every morning at 9:00 AM.

6. Click the **Add** button again, and then add a new schedule named "Afternoon Update," which will update the map at 3:00 PM every day (automatically connecting to the Internet if needed).

7. Click the **OK** button to close the New Schedule dialog box. Figure 5-31 shows the new list of scheduled updates in the MSNBC Weather Properties dialog box.

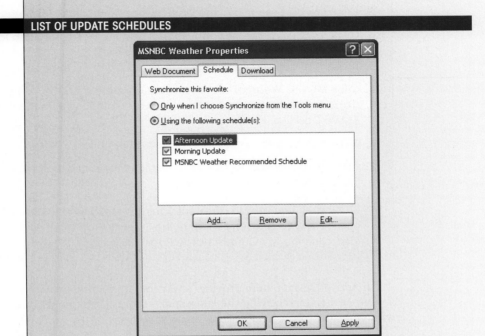

Now that you've seen how to work with Active Desktop items and update schedules, you should remove the weather map from your desktop.

Removing an Active Desktop Item

When you remove an Active Desktop item, you can either close the item (by clicking the down arrow button on the title bar) or delete it. Closing the item keeps the information about the item and its update schedule available for future use. You can restore the item later by opening the Display Properties dialog box and selecting the item on the Web property sheet. Deleting the item removes the file and all information about it from your computer. If you wanted to access the deleted Active Desktop item again, you would have to go back to the Web site and download the item again to reinstall it.

To delete the update schedules and weather map:

1. In the MSNBC Weather Properties dialog box, click **Morning Update** and then click the **Remove** button. When a message box appears, click the **Yes** button to confirm the deletion.

2. Remove the Afternoon Update schedule using the technique used in Step 1.

3. Click the **OK** button to close the MSNBC Weather Properties dialog box. Next you can remove the weather map Active Desktop item from the desktop and from the list of Web pages you can add to the desktop.

4. Right-click an empty area on the desktop, and then click **Properties** on the shortcut menu.

5. Click the **Desktop** tab in the Display Properties dialog box.

6. Click the **Customize Desktop** button, and then click the **Web** tab. The Web property sheet shows a list of all available Active Desktop objects for your desktop. Those that currently appear on the desktop have their check boxes selected.

7. Click **MSNBC Weather** and then click the **Delete** button. A message box appears asking you to confirm that you want to delete the item from your Active Desktop.

8. Click the **Yes** button and then click the **OK** button.

9. Click the **OK** button to close the Display Properties dialog box. You've restored the desktop to its original state.

TROUBLE? If you had to deselect your home page from the desktop earlier, open the Web property sheet in the Display Properties dialog box again, and then click the My Current Home Page check box.

An Active Desktop item provides a way for you to interact with your desktop by updating a weather map or receiving the latest sports scores. You can also use a Web page to interact with your desktop, as you'll see in the next section.

Using an HTML File as a Background

In Tutorial 4, you worked with the Display Properties dialog box to change your desktop's color and background, and then to display a graphic image on your desktop. Active Desktop technology extends your control over your desktop's background by allowing you to use Web pages as backgrounds. Like an Active Desktop item, you can also interact with a Web page you use as a desktop background. You can click any links the Web page contains, and Internet Explorer will start and open the corresponding Web page. However, unlike an Active Desktop item, after you select a Web page for the desktop background, you cannot update its contents by synchronizing. To use the new version of the Web page as the desktop background, you'd have to save and retrieve the new Web page as a new background. For this reason, if you want to include a frequently updated Web page on your desktop, add it as an Active Desktop item, not as a Web page background.

To create Web pages, you use a language called HTML, which stands for Hypertext Markup Language. HTML uses special codes to describe how the page should appear on the screen. Figure 5-32 shows a Web page as it appears on your computer screen and behind it, the underlying HTML code. It is this code that the browser interprets when a Web page is viewed.

Figure 5-32	WEB PAGE AND THE HTML CODE IT EMPLOYS

HTML code

Web page

A document created using the HTML language is called an HTML file and is saved with the .htm or .html extension. Most Web pages are HTML files.

Because Windows XP enables you to use an HTML file as your desktop background, your Windows XP desktop background can feature text, clip art, photos, animated graphics, links, and multimedia objects such as sound and video. Your desktop can also include **applets**, programs attached to a Web page that extend its capabilities. Some applets add movement and interesting visual effects to your page, whereas others are capable of asking you questions, responding to your questions, checking your computer settings, and calculating data. There are even applets that allow you to play interactive games against the computer or against another person logged on to the Web.

You can use a word-processing program such as Microsoft Word to save a document as an HTML file, or you can create a new one using FrontPage Express, the Web page editor included with Windows XP. If you learn the HTML language, you can use a simple text editor (such as Notepad) to create a more complex and sophisticated HTML file. Alternately, you can use the Internet Explorer browser to save an existing Web page as an HTML file that you can then use as your wallpaper.

The added control Windows XP gives you over background wallpaper makes it possible to make the desktop a launchpad for your most important projects. A corporation, for example, might create an HTML file that contains important company information, an updatable company calendar, links to company documents, a company directory, and so on. Scott wants to show you a Web page he's designing to be used as a background for all Highland Travel computers. He has created an HTML file in his Web page editor and has placed it on a disk for you to examine. The Highland Travel desktop background Web page is on your Data Disk.

To use a Web page as a background:

1. If necessary, insert your Data Disk into the floppy drive.

2. Right-click a blank area of the desktop, and then click **Properties** on the shortcut menu.

3. In the Display Properties dialog box, click the **Desktop** tab and note the current Desktop background. You'll restore this background to your desktop after you learn how to use a Web page as the desktop background. The Highland Travel HTML file is on your Data Disk, so you need to navigate to drive A next.

4. Click the **Browse** button, click the **Look in** list arrow, click 3½ **Floppy (A:)**, and then click the **Highland** file.

5. Click the **Open** button. The filename appears in the Background list, and a pre-view appears in the preview monitor.

6. Click the **OK** button. The HTML file appears on your desktop as a background. Figure 5-33 points out some of the features an HTML file allows you to employ on a desktop background.

| Figure 5-33 | PLACING AN HTML FILE ON THE DESKTOP |

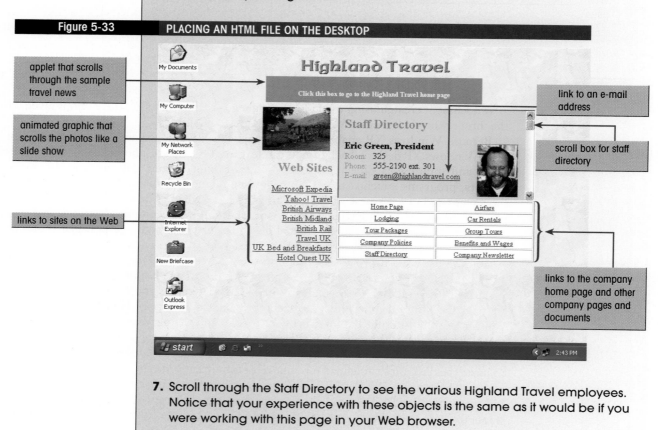

7. Scroll through the Staff Directory to see the various Highland Travel employees. Notice that your experience with these objects is the same as it would be if you were working with this page in your Web browser.

The difference between using an HTML file as your desktop background and using a graphic file, as you did in Tutorial 4, is that a graphic is simply a picture that adds interest to your desktop background, whereas an HTML file allows you to interact with the information in your background. If the HTML file contains links, you can click those links to connect to the sites they target. Try clicking one of the links on the page.

To activate a desktop link:

1. Click the **Home Page** link in the first row of the table below the Staff Directory. Your browser starts and after a moment the link's target appears in the browser window—the familiar Highland Travel page.

2. Close your browser. You return to the desktop.

Scott explains that once he finishes developing his page, the company will place it on all company desktops as a background, so all employees have access to the information it contains. Because it isn't finished, he recommends that you remove it from your desktop.

To restore the desktop to its original appearance:

1. Right-click a blank area of the desktop, and then click **Properties** on the short-cut menu.

   TROUBLE? If you right-click an area of the Web page that has Web content, properties for that object appear, instead of desktop properties. Make sure the dialog box that opens is the Display Properties dialog box. If it isn't, try right-clicking a different area, and make sure it is blank.

2. Click the **Desktop** tab.

3. Scroll the Background list and then click the name of the original background, the one you noted in the previous steps.

4. Click the **OK** button.

You've completed your work with bringing Web content directly to your desktop. As you've seen, Windows XP provides a rich variety of tools to connect your computer with the Internet.

Session 5.2   QUICK CHECK

1. What is offline viewing?

2. What is push technology?

3. An object on the desktop that receives pushed content is called a(n) _____ .

4. What is synchronization?

5. How would you schedule an object to be synchronized 24 times a day, once each hour?

6. What is HTML?

7. What are some advantages of using an HTML file for your desktop background?

SESSION 5.3

In this session, you'll learn about e-mail. You will learn how to start Outlook Express—the Windows XP e-mail program. You'll see how to customize Outlook Express, and you'll examine the properties of your mail account. You'll send and receive e-mail messages and reply to an e-mail message.

Getting Started with Outlook Express

Outlook Express, one of the tools that comes with Windows XP, allows you to send, receive, and manage **electronic mail** or **e-mail**—electronic messages transferred between users on a network. As more people connect to the Internet, communicating by e-mail is becoming more common. When you need to send information to someone else, an e-mail message saves time and money, because you don't need to wait for postal delivery nor make expensive long-distance phone calls. You can send e-mail to and receive e-mail from anyone in the world who has an e-mail address, regardless of the operating system or type of computer the person is using.

Just as you need an Internet account to browse the World Wide Web, you likewise need an account on a **mail server**, a computer that handles the storage and delivery of e-mail. Most Internet service providers also provide access to mail servers.

Scott informs you that the company's systems administrator has just established a mail server on the company network to handle all e-mail messages. He hands you a slip of paper with your account information, including your user ID, password, and e-mail address. A **user ID**, also called a **user name**, is the name that identifies you on the mail server. A **password** is a personal code that verifies that you have the right to read incoming mail and send mail. An **e-mail address** consists of the user ID, the @ symbol, and a host name. For example, Scott's e-mail address is:

scampbell@highlandtravel.com

Thus Scott's user name is scampbell, and the address of the company's mail server is highlandtravel.com. Like URLs, every e-mail address is unique. Many people might use the same host, but user IDs distinguish one e-mail address from another.

Customizing the Outlook Express Window

You use Outlook Express to compose, send, and receive e-mail messages. The Outlook Express window is divided into sections so that you can differentiate the messages you've received from those you've sent or are ready to send. To make Outlook Express suit your needs, you can customize the window by choosing to display or hide these sections and other elements. Now you can start Outlook Express and then explore the features you can customize. You start Outlook Express by clicking the Outlook Express button 🗐 on the Quick Launch toolbar, clicking the Outlook Express icon on the desktop, or using the Start menu.

To start Outlook Express:

1. Click the **Start** button [🏁 start] on the taskbar, point to **All Programs**, and then click **Outlook Express**. Note that the Outlook Express icon might also appear in the upper-right section of the Start menu.

   TROUBLE? If more than one e-mail program is installed on your computer, and Outlook Express is not your current default mail program, a dialog box appears asking if you want Outlook Express to be your default mail program. If you are using your own computer and want to use Outlook Express as your mail program, click the Yes button. If you are using a school or institutional computer, click the No button or ask your technical support person for assistance.

   TROUBLE? If the Identity Logon dialog box opens, you are using a version of Outlook Express that is configured for multiple users. If your name appears, click it and then enter the password as requested. Otherwise, ask your technical support person for assistance.

   TROUBLE? If a connection dialog box appears, you are probably not connected to the Internet. Click the Connect button and follow the directions that appear on your screen. If you are prompted to enter your username and password and you do not know them, consult your technical support person.

   TROUBLE? If the Internet Connection Wizard starts, click the Cancel button and the Yes button twice to exit the wizard. Contact your instructor or technical support person about setting up an Internet account on your computer.

2. If necessary, click the **Maximize** button [🔲]. Figure 5-34 shows the maximized Outlook Express window.

Figure 5-34	OUTLOOOK EXPRESS WINDOW

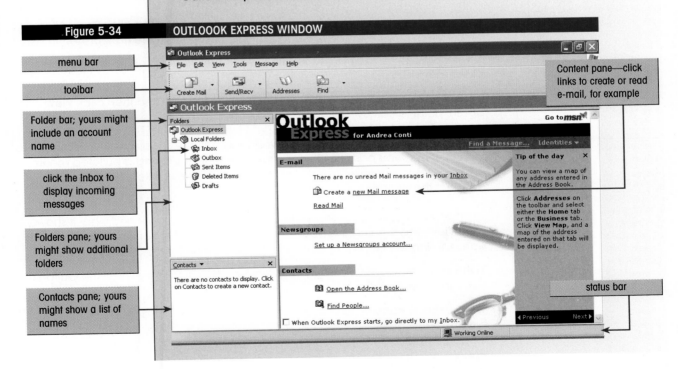

Figure 5-35 lists the components you can customize in the Outlook Express window.

Figure 5-35	COMPONENTS TO CUSTOMIZE IN THE OUTLOOK EXPRESS WINDOW
COMPONENT	**DESCRIPTION**
Contacts pane	Lists people whose e-mail addresses or other contact information you have saved
Folder bar	Identifies the current mail folder
Folders pane	Displays the hierarchy of mail folders that you can use to store and organize messages
Outlook bar	Contains icons for the folders in the Folders list (because this repeats the information in the Folders list, you don't need to view it unless you find it easier to use than the Folders list)
Status bar	Displays messages about the current folder
Toolbar	Displays the toolbar buttons used to accomplish most tasks
Info pane	An informational window at the bottom of the Outlook Express window, which may not be an available option for you, depending on how Outlook Express is installed on your computer
Content pane	Shows links you can click to perform typical Outlook Express tasks; can also show a list of messages you have sent or received

Before you start using Outlook Express, first ensure that your Outlook Express window matches the one shown in the figures.

To set up the Outlook Express window:

1. Click the **Inbox** icon in the Folders list.

   TROUBLE? If you see more than one Inbox on the Folders list, you might have more than one mail account. Click Inbox under Local Folders.

2. Click **View** on the menu bar, point to **Current View**, and then click **Show All Messages**, if necessary, so you can view all messages in the right pane.

   You want to sort your messages in the order they were received, in ascending order (newest first).

3. If necessary, click **View**, point to **Sort By**, click **Received**, and then click **View** again, point to **Sort By**, and click **Sort Ascending**.

   TROUBLE? If the Received and Sort Ascending options are already bulleted in the Sort By list, you can skip Steps 2 and 3. Note that clicking a bulleted menu option does not deselect it. Clicking a checked menu option, however, does deselect the option.

4. To change the arrangement of the Outlook Express window and what it shows, click **View** and then click **Layout**. The Window Layout Properties dialog box opens, listing the items you can hide or show in the Outlook Express window.

5. In the Basic area, make sure all check boxes are checked *except* the Outlook Bar and Views Bar.

6. In the Preview Pane area of the Window Layout Properties dialog box, make sure the **Show preview pane** and **Show preview pane header** check boxes are both selected and that the **Below messages** option button is selected. See Figure 5-36.

Figure 5-36   CHECKING OUTLOOK EXPRESS LAYOUT

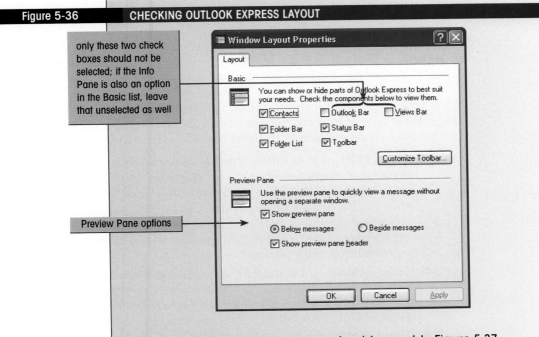

only these two check boxes should not be selected; if the Info Pane is also an option in the Basic list, leave that unselected as well

Preview Pane options

7. Click the **OK** button. Your screen should resemble Figure 5-37.

Figure 5-37   DEFAULT OUTLOOK EXPRESS WINDOW

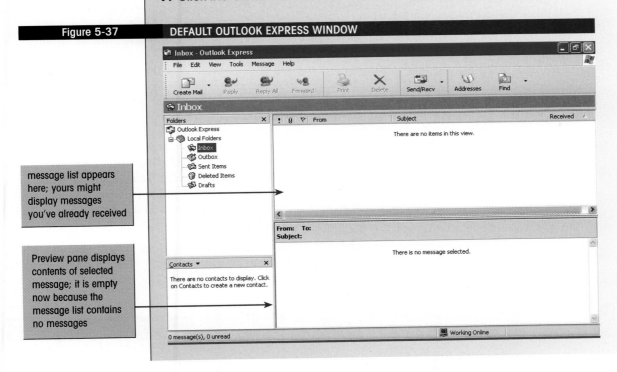

message list appears here; yours might display messages you've already received

Preview pane displays contents of selected message; it is empty now because the message list contains no messages

Now that you have ensured that your window matches the one shown in the figures, you are ready to check the status of your e-mail account using Outlook Express.

Setting Up an Outlook Express Account

Once you have an account with a mail service provider (usually this is your ISP), you add your account to Outlook Express. If you are in a university or other institution, this has probably been done for you, but if you are using your own computer, you will probably have to add it yourself.

Most Internet service providers include mail service as part of their Internet services package. What type of mail account you choose depends on how you plan to access your mail. Outlook Express supports POP, IMAP, and HTTP account types.

- With a **POP**, or **Post Office Protocol** account, your mail server receives incoming mail and delivers it to your computer. Once messages are delivered, they are usually deleted from the mail server. POP accounts work best when you have only a single computer, since POP is designed for offline mail access. To receive POP mail if you are away from your computer, you must be able to set up a POP mail account on a different computer—an impossibility in many places.

- With an **IMAP**, or **Internet Message Access Protocol** account, mail is stored on a mail server, not on your computer. Thus you can access your mail from any computer on which you have an account, without having to transfer files back and forth between computers.

- With an **HTTP** account, known as **Web-based e-mail**, you use the same HTTP protocol used on the Web. You set up an account with a Web-based e-mail provider, and your mail is stored on that provider's mail server. You can access your messages from any Web browser. Libraries, hotels, airports, and banks are increasingly making computers with Web access available to the public, so you don't need to own a computer to use Web-based e-mail. Moreover, Web-based e-mail accounts are often free. However, because messages are stored on a server and not on your local computer, mail retrieval is limited by the speed of your Internet connection. Web-based accounts currently don't offer the same breadth of features you find with a traditional e-mail program. The largest provider of free Web-based e-mail is **Hotmail**, a Microsoft service that is made available from Internet Explorer via the Links toolbar or from Outlook Express when you set up a new mail account. Outlook Express allows you to add a Hotmail account to your Folders list, and it treats incoming mail just as it would in a POP account. Hotmail also allows you to check POP mail.

Before you can send and receive e-mail messages, you need an e-mail account with an ISP or other provider, and then you need to provide Outlook with the appropriate information to access this account.

REFERENCE WINDOW   **RW**

Setting Up an E-Mail Account
- In the Outlook Express window, click Tools and then click Accounts.
- Click the Add button.
- Click Mail. Follow the steps in the Internet Connection Wizard.

The following steps will help you determine whether or not you already have a mail account. If you don't, you will need to set one up before you can continue with this tutorial. Outlook Express can help you with this task. You can set up a Hotmail account almost instantaneously, but to set up a POP or IMAP account, you will need to provide the account information, such as your incoming and outgoing mail server address and type, your username and password, and your e-mail address.

To examine your mail account:

1. Click **Tools** on the menu bar, and then click **Accounts** to open the Internet Accounts dialog box.

2. Click the **Mail** tab, if necessary. See Figure 5-38, which shows one mail account already set up.

| Figure 5-38 | MAIL ACCOUNTS |

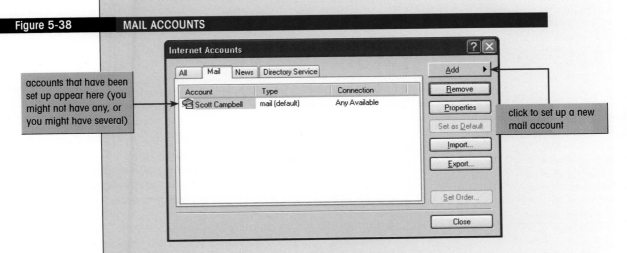

accounts that have been set up appear here (you might not have any, or you might have several)

click to set up a new mail account

3. Click the account you want to use.

   TROUBLE? If no account with your name is listed, no account has been set up for you. You can set up an account yourself by clicking the Add button and then clicking Mail to start the Internet Connection Wizard. This Wizard walks you through the steps of setting up a mail account. If you do not know the answers to all the questions the Wizard asks, you will need to get further assistance from your technical support person or your Internet service provider.

4. Click the **Properties** button. Your name and e-mail address should appear in the account Properties dialog box; Outlook Express uses this information when you send and receive e-mail. See Figure 5-39.

Figure 5-39   **CONFIGURING E-MAIL PROPERTIES**

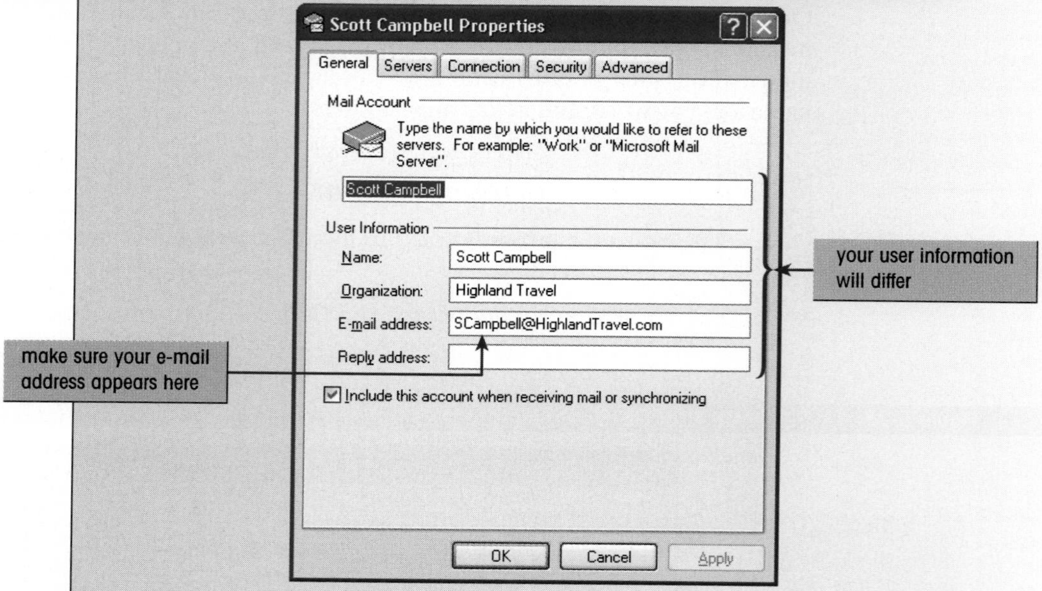

make sure your e-mail
address appears here

your user information
will differ

TROUBLE? If your new mail account doesn't appear in the list of accounts, click
the Close button in the Internet Accounts dialog box, click No to answer the
question about downloading services and then repeat Steps 1 through 4. Your
account should appear. If the name and e-mail address boxes are blank, ask
your instructor or technical support person what to enter in them.

5. Click the **Servers** tab (your tab may be labeled "server") to check your mail
server information. Your account name (userID) and password should appear,
along with information about your mail server. (Your password will appear as
a series of bullets for security.) For an HTTP account such as Hotmail, you would
see the URL of the mail provider's Web page, but Highland Travel uses POP
accounts, so each account must identify the incoming and outgoing mail
server address, as shown in Figure 5-40.

Figure 5-40	CHECKING MAIL SERVER INFORMATION

if you have a different mail sever type, such as HTTP, your server options will differ

Scott Campbell Properties

General | Servers | Connection | Security | Advanced

Server Information

My incoming mail server is a [POP3] server.

Incoming mail (POP3): mail.HighlandTravel.com

Outgoing mail (SMTP): mail.HighlandTravel.com

your mail server addresses will differ

Incoming Mail Server

Account name: SCampbell

Password: ●●●●●●●

user ID and password; yours will differ

☑ Remember password

☐ Log on using Secure Password Authentication

Outgoing Mail Server

☐ My server requires authentication   Settings...

OK   Cancel   Apply

TROUBLE? If any of these boxes is blank, ask your instructor or technical support person what to enter in them.

6. Click the **OK** button to close the account Properties dialog box, and then click the **Close** button in the Internet Accounts dialog box.

Now that you have ensured that Outlook Express can handle your e-mail, you're ready to send e-mail messages.

Sending E-Mail

An e-mail message uses the same format as a standard memo: it typically includes From, Date, To, and Subject lines, followed by the content of the message. The **To line** indicates who will receive the message. Outlook Express automatically supplies your name or e-mail address in the **From line** and the date you send the message in the Date line (as set in your computer's clock). The **Subject line**, although optional, alerts the recipient to the topic of the message. Finally, the **message area** contains the content of your message. You can also include additional information, such as a **Cc line**, which indicates who will receive a copy of the message, or a Priority setting, which indicates the importance of the message.

When you prepare an e-mail message, you should remember some common-sense guidelines:

- Think before you type; read before you send. Your name and your institution's name are attached to everything you send.
- Type both uppercase and lowercase letters. Using all uppercase letters in e-mail messages is considered shouting, and messages in all lowercase letters are difficult to read and decipher.

■ Edit your message. Keep your message concise so the reader can understand your meaning quickly and clearly.

■ Send appropriate amounts of useful information. Like junk mail, e-mail messages can pile up quickly. If you must send a longer message, attach it as a file.

■ Find out if personal e-mail messages are allowed on a work account. E-mail is not free. (Businesses pay to subscribe to a server.)

■ E-mail at your workplace or school is not necessarily confidential. Your employer, for example, might be able to access your e-mail.

To send an e-mail message, you first compose the message and then click the Send button in the message window. Because it's inefficient to send the message immediately, Outlook Express stores the message in the Outbox folder until you click the Send/Recv button on the Standard Buttons toolbar or until a specified period of time has passed. Then Outlook Express sends the message from your computer to the network, which routes it to the recipient. Outlook Express lists the messages it sent in the Sent folder.

Before you send your first e-mail message in this tutorial, you'll explore the folders in Outlook Express.

Viewing Outlook Express Folders

Outlook Express organizes all the messages it handles, outgoing and incoming, into folders that allow you to sort your messages, located in the Folders list in the Outlook Express window. Figure 5-41 describes the Outlook Express folders that you can use to store mail.

Figure 5-41	OUTLOOK EXPRESS FOLDERS
FOLDER	**DESCRIPTION**
Inbox	Stores messages that have just been delivered and messages that you've read but haven't discarded or filed
Outbox	Stores messages that you've finished composing and plan to send as soon as you connect to your mail server
Sent Items	Stores a copy of every message you've sent until you discard or file them
Deleted Items	Stores the messages you've discarded; they remain in this folder until you delete them from here, and then they are irretrievable
Drafts	Stores messages that you have written but not finished

When a folder contains one or more messages that you have not sent or read, the folder name appears in boldface and Outlook Express places the number of new or pending messages in that folder within parentheses.

The name of any folder that contains subfolders is preceded by a plus box ⊞ or minus box ⊟ in the Folders list. When ⊞ appears in front of a folder's name, its subfolders are hidden. When ⊟ appears, its subfolders are visible. Outlook Express automatically starts with Local Folders open. To see the contents of a folder, you click its name in the Folders list.

To work with Outlook Express folders:

1. Click **Outbox** in the Folders pane. It will probably be empty, unless you have other outgoing mail. See Figure 5-42.

| Figure 5-42 | VIEWING THE OUTBOX FOLDER |

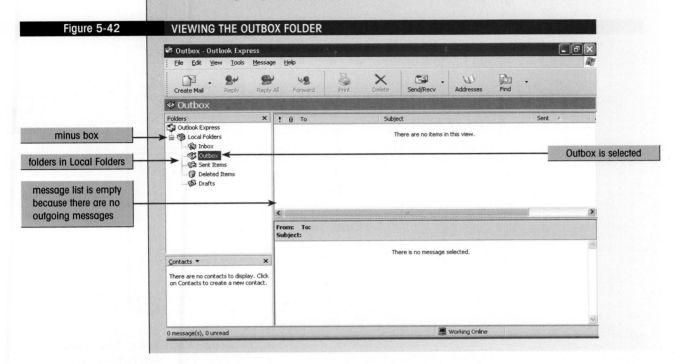

minus box

folders in Local Folders

Outbox is selected

message list is empty because there are no outgoing messages

Now you're ready to compose and send your first message.

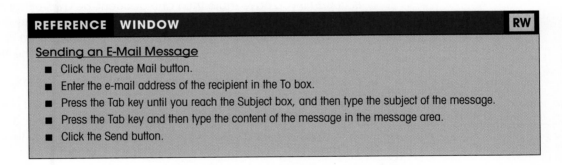

REFERENCE WINDOW   RW

Sending an E-Mail Message
- Click the Create Mail button.
- Enter the e-mail address of the recipient in the To box.
- Press the Tab key until you reach the Subject box, and then type the subject of the message.
- Press the Tab key and then type the content of the message in the message area.
- Click the Send button.

After you compose a message and click the Send button, Outlook Express places the message in the Outbox and then sends it immediately if you're connected to your mail server and if you haven't changed Outlook's default settings. Because you've opened the Outbox, you'll be able to watch this happen. Remembering that Scott wanted you to contact Katie Herrera about a Highland Travel golf tour as soon as you got settled, you decide to compose your first message to her. Her e-mail address is kherrera@highlandtravel.com.

To send an e-mail message:

1. Click the **Create Mail** button. The New Message window opens, which allows you to compose a new message. See Figure 5-43.

Figure 5-43   THE NEW MESSAGE WINDOW

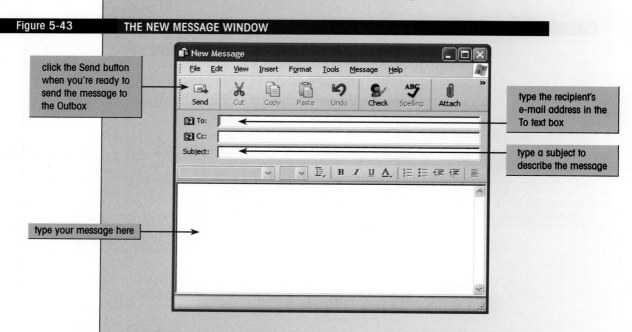

click the Send button when you're ready to send the message to the Outbox

type the recipient's e-mail address in the To text box

type a subject to describe the message

type your message here

TROUBLE? If you receive an error message at any point during these steps, check your mail server properties using the procedure you learned in the previous section. Write down your settings and then ask your instructor or technical support person for help.

TROUBLE? If you have more than one account, be aware that in the outgoing message, Outlook Express identifies the sender for the currently selected account. If, for example, you want to send a message from your Hotmail account, click Hotmail in the Folders list before you click the New Mail button.

2. Type **kherrera@highlandtravel.com** in the To text box, and then press the **Tab** key.

3. Type your own e-mail address in the Cc text box, and then press the **Tab** key. Note that normally you would not copy yourself on an e-mail sent to another person. You are sending a copy to yourself only to ensure that you will receive mail later for practice in other sections of this tutorial.

4. Type **Golf Tour** in the Subject text box, and then press the **Tab** key.

5. Type the following message in the content area:

Scott Campbell suggested I contact you regarding the new St. Andrews Golf Tour we're starting next summer.

Thank you,

(your name)

As you send the message, make sure you are watching the Outbox. Read all of Step 6 before you perform it, so you know what to watch for.

6. Click the **Send** button. Outlook Express moves your message into the Outbox; the Outbox is briefly boldfaced and followed by a (1) in the Local Folders list, indicating there is one outgoing message. See Figure 5-44.

Figure 5-44	SENDING A MESSAGE

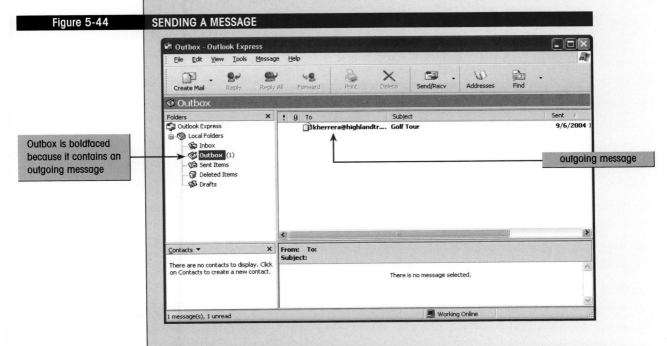

Outbox is boldfaced because it contains an outgoing message

outgoing message

Outlook Express sends the message. The message and the (1) disappear, the Outbox is empty, and the Outbox is no longer boldfaced in the list.

TROUBLE? If Outlook Express does not send the message immediately and the (1) does not disappear, Outlook Express might be configured only to send messages when you click the Send/Recv button. Click, and watch Outlook Express send the message. Note that you may also receive new messages at this point. You'll learn how to access and read new messages shortly. If you want to change this setting, click Tools, click Options, click the Send tab, click the Send messages immediately check box, and then click OK to indicate that you want outgoing mail sent immediately.

TROUBLE? If Outlook Express requests a password, you might need to enter a password before you can send and receive your mail messages.

The time it takes to send an e-mail message depends on the size of the message, the speed of your Internet connection, and the quantity of Internet traffic at that time. When you send an e-mail, your outgoing mail server examines the host name in the e-mail address, locates the host, and delivers the message to that host. Because your mail server is not connected to every other host, e-mail is rarely sent along a direct path to the recipient. Instead, the message is handed from one host to another until the e-mail reaches its destination. Figure 5-45 shows how the Internet routes a message from a student at the University of Alaska to a student at the University of the Virgin Islands.

Figure 5-45 | INTERNET E-MAIL ROUTES

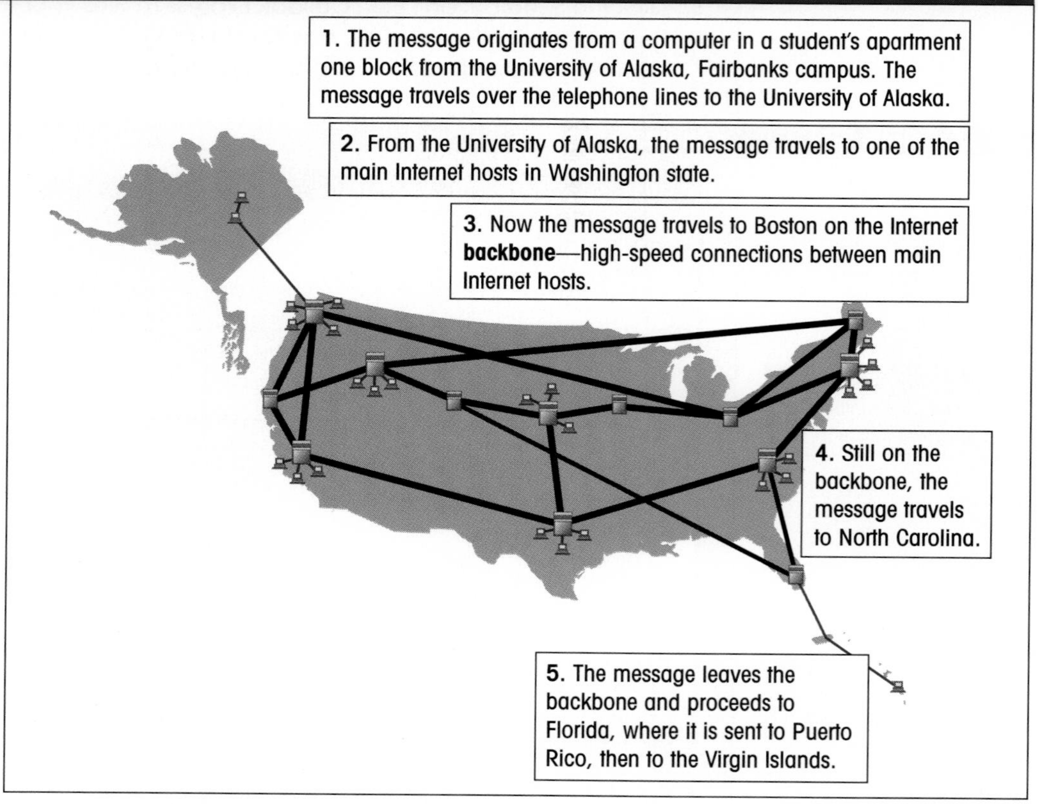

1. The message originates from a computer in a student's apartment one block from the University of Alaska, Fairbanks campus. The message travels over the telephone lines to the University of Alaska.

2. From the University of Alaska, the message travels to one of the main Internet hosts in Washington state.

3. Now the message travels to Boston on the Internet **backbone**—high-speed connections between main Internet hosts.

4. Still on the backbone, the message travels to North Carolina.

5. The message leaves the backbone and proceeds to Florida, where it is sent to Puerto Rico, then to the Virgin Islands.

Receiving E-Mail

How you receive e-mail depends on your account. For example, if you are using a Web-based account, you connect to your provider's Web page and view your messages there. If you are using a POP account, your mail server collects your mail and holds it until your mail program contacts the mail server and requests any mail addressed to your user ID. Your mail program then downloads any waiting messages to your computer. (Remember that the Outlook Express mail program allows you to set up a Hotmail account so that it too can receive local mail delivery.)

You can check your e-mail at any time by clicking the Send/Recv button 🖳 in Outlook Express. Your mail server delivers any e-mail messages that have arrived since you last checked and sends any messages currently in the Outbox. Some people check for new e-mail messages sporadically during the day, while others check at regular intervals, such as every hour or every morning and evening. If you are always connected to the Internet, Outlook Express automatically checks for messages at a specified interval. You can set this interval on the General tab of the Options dialog box. You access the Options dialog box from the Tools menu.

Remember that you sent a copy of your e-mail to yourself for the purpose of completing this tutorial. You'll now check to see whether the copy arrived.

To check for incoming mail:

1. Click the **Send/Recv** button. If a dialog box opens requesting your password, enter your password and follow the instructions in the dialog box.

2. Click **Inbox** in the Folders list. New messages appear in the message list, and a number in parentheses appears, indicating the number of new messages you've received. See Figure 5-46. Your Inbox folder might contain additional e-mail messages from other people.

| Figure 5-46 | RECEIVING MESSAGES |

unread messages appear in boldface, preceded by the unread mail icon

new messages are stored in the Inbox folder

the message list identifies the sender, some or all of the subject, and date received; your window might list additional columns

click a column button to sort columns by that button

change the width of the panes or the columns in the messages list by dragging the border

you might receive additional messages

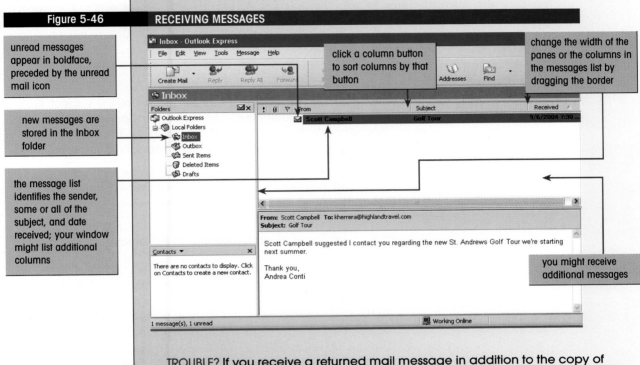

TROUBLE? If you receive a returned mail message in addition to the copy of your message to Katie, don't worry. This happens because the e-mail address you are using for Katie Herrera is fictional. You'll learn more about returned mail shortly.

TROUBLE? If enough time has elapsed since you sent the message, Outlook Express might have checked for incoming mail already. If that's the case, the copy should already appear. If no messages appear, your mail server might not have received or sent the messages yet. Occasionally, some mail servers cause mail to be delayed. Check later to see if your mail has arrived, or consult your technical support person.

Unread messages appear in boldface, preceded by the unread mail icon. The message list displays a message header for each message, which identifies the sender, subject (truncated if it's too long), and date received. Your window might list additional columns. You can change the width of the columns in the message list by dragging the column header border in the appropriate direction. You can also click a column button to sort columns by that button. For example, if you click the From button, Outlook Express sorts messages in the current folder alphabetically by name. The default sort order is by date and time received, with newest messages at the top. Note that the sender shown in Figure 5-46 is Scott Campbell. The sender on your computer will differ.

The message list displays a variety of icons that help you determine the status of the message. For example, 📭 tells you the message has been read; 📧 tells you the message has not been read; 📝 tells you the message is in progress in the Drafts folder.

You can view a message in its own window or in the preview pane. If you click to select an e-mail message from the message list, the contents of that message appear in the preview pane. If you double-click a message from the message list, a separate message window opens. Either way, after a predetermined number of seconds, the message header no longer appears in boldface, indicating that you've opened, or displayed, the message. You already saw how you can hide the preview pane if you want to view only the message list. You can also resize the preview pane by dragging its upper border up or down. For example, to enlarge the preview so you can see more of a message, drag the top border of the pane up.

Your Inbox should contain the copy of the message you sent yourself. Read it now.

To read an e-mail message:

1. If necessary, click the message you sent yourself, which has the subject "Golf Tour" in the message list. The contents of that message appear in the preview pane. After a few seconds (five seconds is the default), the Unread icon 📧 changes to Read 📭, and the message no longer appears in boldface.

2. Now try adjusting the column widths. You can use the same technique you used when you resized the panes in the Windows Explorer window. Point to the vertical line that forms one of the column borders until your pointer changes to ◄━━►.

3. Drag the pointer slightly to the right to see more of the column, or to the left to see less.

   TROUBLE? Your window may show additional columns. You can determine what information to display by clicking View, clicking Columns, and then removing the check from the box of the column display you wish to suppress.

By successfully viewing the copy of the message you sent to yourself, you've verified that Outlook Express is configured properly on your computer.

Handling Undelivered Messages

Sometimes you send an e-mail message to an Internet address that is no longer active, for example, when a person switches to a different ISP. When an outgoing mail server cannot locate a recipient's address, it sends an undeliverable mail message to the sender. This is similar to the postal service returning a letter because the street address is incorrect.

Because Katie's e-mail address is fictional, you will probably receive a returned mail message from the mail delivery subsystem of your outgoing mail server, telling you that the host was not found. Check for this message now.

To read a returned mail message:

1. Click the **Send/Recv** button 📨.

2. Click a message with "Returned mail" or something similar in the Subject column.

> **TROUBLE?** If no such message appears now, check again later. It might take a few minutes for the message to be routed to you.
>
> **3.** Read the message. It should inform you that the e-mail address had an unknown host.

If e-mail messages you send are returned undelivered, you should verify the e-mail addresses that you used. Make sure that everything is typed correctly and that the person is still using that e-mail address.

Replying to a Message

Often, you'll want to respond to an e-mail message. Although you could create and send a new message, it's easier to use the Reply feature, which automatically inserts the e-mail address of the sender and the subject into the proper lines in the message window. The Reply feature also "quotes" the sender's text to remind the sender of the message to which you are responding. When you reply to an e-mail message, you can respond to the original sender of the message, or to the sender and everyone else who received the message.

You're first going to view the message you sent yourself, this time in its own window, and then you're going to practice replying to it. To open a message in its own window, double-click the message in the message list. This allows you to display more of the message at once.

Note that this is a practice reply. Normally, you would not reply to yourself! Rather, you would reply to someone who sent you a real message.

To open a message in its own window and then reply to it:

1. Double-click the **Golf Tour** message in the Sent Items list. The message opens in its own window. Maximize this window if necessary.

2. Click the **Reply** button 👤↩. The message window opens, with your name in the To box (because you're replying to your own message) and the original message's subject in the Subject box, preceded by "Re:", which means "regarding." The message quotes your original message.

3. Type the following reply in the message area. (The insertion point automatically blinks at the beginning of a blank line.)

Thanks for the information.

(your name)

4. If necessary, scroll down to see how the original text of the message is quoted after the reply you just typed. See Figure 5-47.

Figure 5-47   REPLYING TO A MESSAGE

recipient's user ID
automatically appears

your e-mail address
appears here

subject automatically
appears, preceded
by Re:

new message

original message is
quoted, indicated by
vertical line or other
symbol

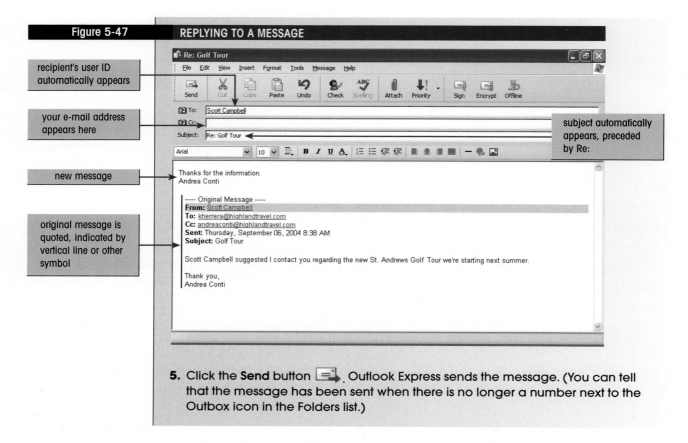

5. Click the **Send** button. Outlook Express sends the message. (You can tell that the message has been sent when there is no longer a number next to the Outbox icon in the Folders list.)

Deciding whether to quote the sender's original message when you reply to a message depends on several factors. If the recipient might need to be reminded of the message content, it's appropriate to quote. However, long messages take longer to download, so whenever possible you should delete quoted material from your messages.

Printing a Message

You can print an e-mail message using the File menu's Print command. You decide to print the message you received from yourself.

To print an e-mail message:

1. Make sure the message you received is either open in its own window or selected in the message list.

2. Click **File** on the menu bar, and then click **Print**.

3. Check the print settings in the Print dialog box, and then click the **Print** button. The message prints on the printer specified in the Print dialog box.

4. If necessary, click the **Close** button ✕ to close the message.

5. Close Outlook Express.

By default, Outlook Express formats messages using HTML. When you print a message formatted in HTML, it includes lines and boldface headings. However, if the message you are printing uses plain text instead of HTML, the printout will not contain formatting, and some of the lines might be uneven. You can change this setting by clicking Tools, clicking Options, and then specifying HTML on the Send tab. Your messages will then be sent formatted. If you need a high-quality printout of a plain text message, you can save the message as a text file, open it in a word processor, and edit it there so that it looks professional.

Scott has now finished your training on e-mail. As you continue to work with Outlook Express, you'll see other ways in which e-mail can be integrated with the workings of Windows XP and the Web.

Session 5.3 QUICK | CHECK

1. What is a mail server?

2. Identify the user ID portion and the host name portion of the following e-mail address: pcsmith@icom.net.

3. How can you view your mail account properties in Outlook Express?

4. Where can you find a copy of a message you sent?

5. Why shouldn't you type your messages in all uppercase letters?

6. Name two advantages the Reply feature has over the New Mail feature when you are responding to an e-mail.

REVIEW ASSIGNMENTS

1. *History of the Internet and the World Wide Web* Computers have been around for several decades now, but how did the Internet and the World Wide Web get started? Microsoft considered the Internet an important enough development to incorporate many of its features into the Windows XP operating system. Go to the library or use the Internet itself to locate books or articles on the Internet, and write a single-page essay on the history of the Internet. Answer questions such as:
   a. What role did the ARPANET play in the development of the Internet?
   b. What role did CERN play in the development of the World Wide Web?
   c. Over what period of time did the Internet grow? What about the World Wide Web?
   d. When did browsers first become available?

2. *Connecting to the Internet over a Modem* This tutorial mentioned that home computer users can connect to the Internet using a dial-up connection via an account with an ISP. Assume you have your own computer, and you want to connect to the Internet from home. Contact at least three ISPs in your area, ask for their rates and services, and then write a single-page essay describing your findings. Which ISP would you choose, and why?

3. *Exploring Your Home Page* In this tutorial, the figures showed the MSN home page as the home page. Your home page might be different—take some time to explore.
   a. Start the Internet Explorer browser, and print your home page.
   b. Click one of the links on your home page, and continue to click any interesting links that you encounter. Clicking whatever links interest you is often called "surfing." On your printout, circle the link you followed. Write in the margin where it took you.

c. Use the Home button to return to your home page, click another link, and then go where it leads you. Again, circle the link on your printout, indicate where you ended up, and write what you saw along the way.

4. *Connecting to Specific Web Sites*   You learned in this tutorial that you can enter a URL in the Address box of your browser to connect to a specific Web site. Using the Internet Explorer browser, enter the following URLs and print the first page of each URL.

    a. http://www.usps.gov

    b. http://www.nps.gov

    c. http://www.cnn.com

    d. Using any one of these pages as a starting point, follow links until you locate a page with frames. Record the URL of the page you found.

5. *Web Page Desktop Background*   Because he will be placing the Highland Web page on your desktop soon, Scott wants you to practice using a Web page as a desktop background.

    a. Apply the Highland Web page (not the folder), located in the root directory of your Data Disk, as your desktop background.

    b. Observe the background carefully and work with the objects that are incorporated into this Web page.

    c. Connect to the Active Desktop Gallery, and add a desktop item that would add to the usefulness of this desktop.

    d. Using the Highland desktop you just created as an example, write two paragraphs describing what a Web page background offers that a graphic image file, such as you used in Tutorial 4, does not. Give detailed information about the purpose of each element on the desktop.

    e. Restore your computer's background to its original state.

Explore   6. *E-Mailing a Web Page and a Link*   Scott wants you to share the Highland Travel Home Page with some potential clients. Internet Explorer provides tools to easily e-mail either the entire Web page or a link to the page.

    a. Connect to the Internet and open the Highland Travel Home Page in Internet Explorer.

    b. Click the Mail button ✉ on the Standard Buttons toolbar, and click Send a Link to send a link to the home page to your instructor.

    c. Click the Mail button ✉, and send the entire Web page to your instructor.

    d. What problems might there be in sending a Web page to a user? What should you know about the user's e-mail program before attempting to send the page?

Explore   7. *Editing the Links Toolbar*   Scott tells you that the Links toolbar is another place, besides the Favorites folder, where you can place shortcuts to your favorite Web sites. The Links toolbar is one of the Internet Explorer toolbars that displays icons for specific Web sites. Scott wants you to learn how to use it.

    a. Start Internet Explorer and display the Links toolbar in the Web browser. (Click View on the menu bar, click Toolbars, and then click—if necessary—to place a check mark next to Links.)

    b. Click the double arrow on the right side of the Links toolbar, and then click the Customize Links icon.

    c. Print the Web page.

    d. Using the information on this Web page, add a link to the Highland Travel Home Page to the Links toolbar.

    e. Display the Links toolbar on the Windows XP taskbar, making sure that the icon for the Highland Travel home page is visible.

    f. Using the techniques from Tutorial 2, print a copy of your screen with the revised Links toolbar.

    g. Remove the icon for the Highland Travel home page from the Links toolbar.

Explore   8. *Using Rich Text Formatting in E-Mail* Scott tells you that with Outlook Express you can use special fonts and formats to liven up your e-mail messages. You decide to test this by sending an e-mail message to Katie Herrera, telling her of your interest in working on the St. Andrews project.

   a. Start Outlook Express and compose an e-mail message to your instructor with the subject line "St. Andrews Project".
   b. In the message area, enter (in your own words) your interest in the project and willingness to participate.
   c. Turn on formatting for the message by clicking Format on the menu bar of the mail message window and then clicking Rich Text (HTML). In the message area, boldface at least one word and italicize at least one word. To boldface a word, you select it and then click the Bold button **B** . To italicize it, you select it and then click the Italic button *I* .
   d. Now color one word red: select the word, click the Font Color button **A**, and then click the color red.
   e. Send the message to your instructor.

PROJECTS

1. Internet Explorer and Windows Explorer share many of the same menus, commands, and toolbars. In fact, you can modify Windows Explorer to look and operate exactly like Internet Explorer.

   a. Open Windows Explorer.
   b. In the Address bar, enter the URL of your Home page (or use www.msn.com if you don't know the URL of your home page), and then press the Enter key. Connect to the Internet if you are not already connected.
   c. Modify the Explorer Bar so that it displays the Favorites pane.
   d. Using techniques shown in Tutorial 2, print a copy of your screen.
   e. Open the same Web page in Internet Explorer, and display the Favorites pane in that program. Compare the displays of Internet Explorer and Windows Explorer. Can you see any difference between the two?
   f. Microsoft's goal with Windows XP was to create a "single Explorer." Why do you think Microsoft set this goal? What advantages or disadvantages does the single Explorer have?

Explore   2. You have a friend who has used Windows Explorer extensively for managing his own files and folders, and you mention to him that he can also use Windows Explorer as a browser. Test this yourself first by starting Windows Explorer, opening the Favorites pane, and then clicking a link to a Web page. Observe what happens. Write a note to your friend, which you'll e-mail to him, that describes how to use Windows Explorer as a browser. Make sure you describe what happens to elements such as the left and right panes, the Address bar, the activity indicator, and the status bar.

3. In this tutorial, you learned how to access information on the Web when you either knew the URL or used a link to jump there. Internet Explorer also includes the Search Companion pane (like Windows Explorer), which helps you find the Web pages you need. Use Internet Explorer's online Help to learn about the Search Companion pane and about the general topic of searching the Web.

   a. How would you search for information on a given topic?
   b. Once the Search feature displays a list of search results, what should you do to display the Web page containing the information?
   c. Follow the directions you studied in the Help file to search for information on one of your hobbies, such as snowboarding. While you are using the Search Explorer bar, write down the exact steps you take. Was your search successful? Write down the URL of the page you connected to.

4. Internet Explorer also includes the Media pane (like Windows Explorer), which helps you find music, videos, and other multimedia files. Use Internet Explorer online Help to learn about the Media pane and about the general topic of multimedia on your PC.

   a. What kind of information can you find on the Media pane?

   b. What are multimedia files? How can you use them?

   c. Follow the directions you studied in the Help file to find one of your favorite music files. While you are using the Media Explorer bar, write down the exact steps you take. Did you successfully find the music you wanted? Write down the URL of the page you connected to.

5. You just went to California for a three-week vacation with some friends. On returning, you decide to "capture the moment" by downloading a graphic image that will remind you of your vacation activities.

   a. Use what you learned in Project 3 to locate a graphic image of surfing, rock climbing, wine tasting, or some other vacation activity, and download it to your Data Disk. (If you skipped Project 3, connect to the Highland site or your home page, and download a graphic from there.)

   b. Send an e-mail to your instructor containing the image. (You can paste the image into the e-mail document by clicking Insert on the New Message window's title bar.) Then click Picture, click Browse, locate and click the file, and then click OK.

6. Because most labs cannot accommodate subscriptions, you probably will need your own computer to complete this project. Your dream is to plan your investments so you can retire by age 55. To keep yourself posted on the stock market:

   a. Locate a Web site that contains stock market information. You could try http://www.nasdaq.com or http://www.djia.com.

   b. Place this Web page on your desktop as an Active Desktop item. (You can add the Web dialog sheet of the Display Properties dialog box.)

   c. Set up a synchronization schedule for the Web page so that it is automatically updated every morning at 8 AM.

   d. Create a log in Notepad (perhaps using the LOG feature you learned about in Tutorial 4) to record information such as the closing value of an index such as NASDAQ or the Dow on a given day.

   e. When you have recorded three days' worth of information in the log, open the log window and your synchronization schedule, and print your screen so your instructor can see which Web page you subscribed to and what information you gained. Make sure you unsubscribe from the Web page after the three days.

LAB ASSIGNMENTS

The Internet: World Wide Web

One of the most popular services on the Internet is the World Wide Web. This lab is a Web simulator that teaches you how to use Web browser software to find information. You can use this lab whether or not your school provides you with Internet access. See the Read This Before You Begin page for information on starting the lab.

1. Click the Steps button to learn how to use Web browser software. As you proceed through the steps, answer all of the Quick Check questions that appear. After you complete the steps, you will see a Quick Check Summary Report. Follow the instructions on the screen to print this report.

2. Click the Explore button on the Welcome screen. Use the Web browser to locate a weather map of the Caribbean Virgin Islands. What is its URL?

3. A scuba diver named Wadson Lachouffe has been searching for the fabled treasure of Greybeard the pirate. A link from the Adventure Travel Web site www.atour.com leads to Wadson's Web page called "Hidden Treasure." In Explore, locate the Hidden Treasure page, and answer the following questions:

   a. What was the name of Greybeard's ship?
   b. What was Greybeard's favorite food?
   c. What does Wadson think happened to Greybeard's ship?

4. In the steps, you found a graphic of Jupiter from the photo archives of the Jet Propulsion Laboratory. In the Explore section of the lab, you can also find a graphic of Saturn. Suppose one of your friends wanted a picture of Saturn for an astronomy report. Make a list of the blue, underlined links your friend must click, in the correct order, to find the Saturn graphic. Assume that your friend will begin at the Web Trainer home page.

5. Enter the URL http://www.atour.com to jump to the Adventure Travel Web site. Write a one-page description of this site. In your paper, include a description of the information at the site, the number of pages the site contains, and a diagram of the links it contains.

6. Chris Thomson is a student at UVI and has his own Web pages. In Explore, look at the information Chris has included on his pages. Suppose you could create your own Web page. What would you include? Use word-processing software to design your own Web page. Make sure you indicate the graphics and links you would use.

Web Pages & HTML

Web Pages & HTML

It's easy to create your own Web pages. There are many software tools to help you become a Web author. In this lab, you'll experiment with a Web-authoring Wizard that automates the process of creating a Web page. You'll also try your hand at working directly with HTML code. See the Read This Before You Begin page for information on starting the lab.

1. Click the Steps button to activate the Web-authoring Wizard and learn how to create a basic Web page. As you proceed through the steps, answer all of the Quick Check questions. After you complete the steps, you will see a Quick Check Summary Report. Follow the instructions on the screen to print this report.

2. In Explore, click the File menu, then click New to start working on a new Web page. Use the Wizard to create a home page for a veterinarian who offers dog day-care and boarding services. After you create the page, save it on drive A or C, and print the HTML code. Your site must have the following characteristics:

   a. Title: Dr. Dave's Dog Domain
   b. Background color: Gold
   c. Graphic: Dog.jpg
   d. Body text: Your dog will have the best care day and night at Dr. Dave's Dog Domain. Fine accommodations, good food, playtime, and snacks are all provided. You can board your pet by the day or week. Grooming services also available.
   e. Text link: "Reasonable rates" links to www.cciw.com/np3/rates.htm
   f. E-mail link: "For more information:" links to daveassist@drdave.com

3. In Explore, use the File menu to open the HTML document called Politics.htm. After you use the HTML window (not the Wizard) to make the following changes, save the revised page on drive A or C, and print the HTML code. Refer to Figure 5-48 for a list of HTML tags you can use:

Figure 5-48

HTML TAGS	MEANING AND LOCATION
`<HTML></HTML>`	States that the file is an HTML document; opening tag begins the page; closing tag ends the page (required)
`<HEAD></HEAD>`	States that the enclosed text is the header of the page; appears immediately after the opening HTML tag (required)
`<TITLE></TITLE>`	States that the enclosed text is the title of the page; must appear within the opening and closing HEAD tags (required)
`<BODY></BODY>`	States that the enclosed material (all the text, images, and tags in the rest of the document) is the body of the document (required)
`<H1></H1>`	States that the enclosed text is a heading
` `	Inserts a line break; can be used to control line spacing and breaks in lines
`<UL></UL>` `<OL></OL>`	Indicates an unordered list (list items are preceded by bullets) or an ordered list (list items are preceded by numbers or letters)
`<LI>`	Indicates a list item; precedes all items in unordered or ordered lists
`<CENTER></CENTER>`	Indicates that the enclosed text should be centered on the width of the page
`<B></B>`	Indicates that the enclosed text should appear in boldface
`<I></I>`	Indicates that the enclosed text should appear in italics
`<A HREF="URL"></A>`	Indicates that the enclosed text is a hypertext link; the URL of the linked material must appear within the quotation marks after the equal sign
`<IMG SRC="filename">`	Inserts an inline image into the document where *filename* is the name of the image
`<HR>`	Inserts a horizontal rule

a. Change the title to Politics 2000.
b. Center the page heading.
c. Change the background color to FFE7C6 and the text color to 000000.
d. Add a line break before the sentence, "What's next?"
e. Add a bold tag to "Additional links on this topic:"
f. Add one more link to the "Additional links" list. The link should go to the site http://www.elections.ca, and the clickable link should read "Elections Canada".
g. Change the last graphic to display the image "next.gif".

4. In Explore, use the Web-authoring Wizard and the HTML window to create a home page about yourself. You should include at least a screenful of text, a graphic, an external link, and an e-mail link. Save the page on drive A, then print the HTML code. Turn in your disk and printout.

QUICK | CHECK ANSWERS

Session 5.1

1. A home page is the Web page designated by the browser as your starting point, the Web page that an organization or business has created to give information about itself, or a personal Web page with information about an individual.

2. URL

3. Type the URL in the Address box, then press Enter.

4. It is an educational site.

5. site

6. Open the History pane in Internet Explorer. You can then try to locate the page by viewing the list of pages you accessed on a particular day, or you can search the contents of the History pane to locate it.

7. False

8. Right-click the image, click Save Picture As, enter a filename and destination folder, and then click Save. Or click the Save as button on the shortcut toolbar, enter a filename and destination folder, and then click Save.

Session 5.2

1. With offline viewing, your computer can access a Web page or file from a network so that you can view it later without being connected to the network.

2. Push technology allows both Web site authors and subscribers to gain more control over content delivery and schedule.

3. Active Desktop item

4. Synchronization is a process by which an offline file is updated with the most recent version of the network file.

5. Right-click the object and open its Properties dialog box. On the Schedule dialog sheet, add 24 new schedules, one for each hour of the day.

6. Hypertext Markup Language, the underlying language of Web documents

7. You can add special items such as animated graphics, links to files and Web pages, and applets to run programs for you from the desktop.

Session 5.3

1. A mail server is a computer on a network that manages the storage and delivery of electronic mail.

2. User ID: pcsmith; host name: icom.net

3. Click Tools, click Accounts, click the Mail tab, click the account with your name, and then click the Properties button.

4. the Sent Items folder

5. The recipient might interpret the uppercase letters as shouting—considered rude in most e-mail exchanges.

6. The recipient's e-mail address is automatically inserted, the subject is automatically inserted, and the original message is automatically quoted.

OBJECTIVES

In this tutorial you will:

- Find files by name, contents, and location using several methods, including wildcards

- Open and work with files from the Search Results window

- Limit a search to a specific folder

- Locate files by date, type, and size

- Search for information on the Internet

- Search for people and maps on the Internet

- Change search preferences

SEARCHING
FOR INFORMATION

Using the Search Feature to Locate Files for a Speechwriter

CASE

Speechwriter's Aide

Like thousands of other college students who are graduating soon, you've been visiting the campus job center regularly. Today, you notice that Senator Susannah Bernstein's speechwriter has posted an advertisement for an aide. When you call to inquire, Carolyn King, the senator's speechwriter, asks you to come by the next morning. Your interview goes very well. You learn that the job primarily involves locating information that Carolyn could use in writing the senator's speeches. Carolyn explains that her previous aide collected and organized information in a filing cabinet. In addition to the paper archive, the previous aide started an electronic quotations archive that includes over 100 files on a 3½-inch disk. These files contain anecdotes, jokes, and commentaries on a variety of subjects.

You explain to Carolyn that you could retrieve information efficiently if you had a computer running Windows XP with an Internet connection. Windows XP includes a powerful search tool called **Search** that helps you find files on local or network drives and helps you search for information on the Internet. The Internet contains a vast number of computers and networks that store information, which you can find and retrieve using the Search tool. With Windows XP and an Internet connection, you can use your office computer to access information from around the world. Carolyn is intrigued and by the end of the interview, she offers you the job.

After a week of training and orientation, Carolyn assigns you office space that includes a computer running Windows XP and an Internet connection. She promises that your first assignment will come soon and in the meantime, asks you to become familiar with the information on the quotations archive disk. You will use the Windows XP Search tool to do this.

SESSION 6.1

In this session, you will learn techniques for searching for files by their filenames, by the text they contain, and by file date, type, and size.

Search Strategies

As you install programs and store data on your computer, the number of files and folders you have increases. You have already learned to use My Computer and Windows Explorer to organize your files and folders. Windows XP offers another tool to help you find files so you can access the information they contain. Use the **Search tool** to find any kind of file, whether you know its complete name, partial name, or other facts, such as text the file contains, the file type (for example, a WordPad document or a Paint graphic), or the date the file was created or modified.

The Search tool provides many options that help you define and narrow your search so you can quickly find one or more files. Before you use Search, you should develop a strategy for finding the files you want. Determine what you already know about the files, and then choose the appropriate Search option. Figure 6-1 lists the search methods you can use to find files, and guidelines for when to choose a particular method.

Figure 6-1	SEARCH STRATEGIES	
SEARCH BY	**DESCRIPTION**	**WHEN TO USE**
Filename	Provide all or part of the filename	You know some or all of the filename Example: You want to find all the files related to the Hawthorne Company and know that the filenames include "Hawthorne," but don't know where the files are stored
Keyword	Provide text that appears in the file's contents	You know text that the files contain Example: You want to find a file that contains quotations by Albert Einstein but don't remember the name of the file
Location	Identify the drive or folder containing the file	You know where you stored the files you want Example: You want to find all the budget files in the budget 2004 folder but don't want to navigate your computer's file system
Date	Specify a date or range of dates when files were created, modified or accessed	You know when the files were created, modified, or accessed Example: You want to find a file you created last week but can't remember its name or location
Size	Specify the size of the files	You know the approximate or exact size of the files Example: You want to find files that are larger than 1 MB but don't know where they are stored
Type	Identify the file type, such as .doc or .bmp	You know the file type Example: You want to find an Excel (.xls) file but don't remember its filename

Note that you also can use the search strategies in combination. For example, if you are looking for a file you modified last month in a folder called "Budgets," you can speed the search by providing both a date and a location.

You can access the Windows XP Search tool when you're working in the My Computer or Windows Explorer window. When you do, the **Search Companion** pane opens in the Explorer bar. The Search Companion guides you through your search, offering options that change depending on your search strategy. For example, when you are searching for files, the Search Companion asks you questions about the file's name, contents, type, location, and date. Your responses help the Search Companion find the files you want. You can also access the Search tool from the Start menu. In this case, the Search Results window opens, displaying the Search Companion in the left pane. The Search Results window will be familiar to you because it includes the same features as the My Computer window, such as the Standard Buttons toolbar and similar menus on the menu bar.

Before you prepare to show Carolyn the Search tool, you browse through the quotations archive disk to learn more about its content and organization. You discover that the data on the disk is organized into several folders. You open a few files and find quotes from a wide variety of people—historical figures such as Eleanor Roosevelt and Gandhi, as well as more modern personalities such as Jay Leno and Alice Walker. As you read a file, Carolyn stops by and asks if you could look for appropriate material for a speech on successful leadership that the senator will deliver next week at Stanton College. You see that the quotations archive disk contains so many files that opening and reading all of them would be time-consuming, so you decide to use the Search tool to locate quotations on the topic of leadership.

Starting the Windows XP Search Tool

To start using the Search tool from My Computer or Windows Explorer, you can click the Search button 🔎 on the Standard Buttons toolbar in either of these windows, or you can right-click the folder or device you want to search and then click Search on the shortcut menu. You also can start the Search tool by clicking the Search command on the Start menu.

You didn't create the quotations files, and you know very little about them, so Search is just the tool to help you locate quotations for Senator Bernstein's speech. You'll start Search from the Start menu.

To start Search and specify that you want to search for files or folders:

1. Make sure your Data Disk is in drive A, click the **Start** button ⊞ start on the taskbar, and then click **Search**. The Search Results window opens, as shown in Figure 6-2. Resize the Search Results window if necessary, so your screen matches the figure.

| Figure 6-2 | THE SEARCH COMPANION PANE IN THE SEARCH RESULTS WINDOW |

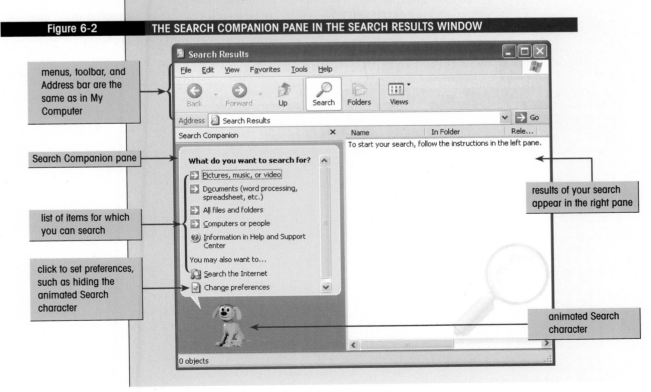

menus, toolbar, and Address bar are the same as in My Computer

Search Companion pane

list of items for which you can search

click to set preferences, such as hiding the animated Search character

results of your search appear in the right pane

animated Search character

The Search Results window is divided into two sections. In the left pane (the Explorer bar) is the Search Companion, which lists the information and objects you can find. After you conduct a search, the results appear in the right pane. You can use the same tools you use in My Computer to explore the search results. For example, you can change the view, sort the results, and open files. You can also change the Explorer bar so it displays a different pane, such as the Folders pane or History pane, if necessary.

Figure 6-3 describes the information you can find using the Search Companion.

Figure 6-3	SEARCH COMPANION OPTIONS
SEARCH OPTION	**DESCRIPTION**
Pictures, music, or video	Finds files that contain images, such as drawings, pictures, and photographs; sound, such as music or spoken word; and video, such as animation or movies
Documents (word processing, spreadsheets, etc.)	Finds files that were created in a program such as a word-processing program. If you know the type of file you are looking for, this option takes fewer steps than searching for All files or folders.
All files and folders	Finds files or folders, including system folders and program files, on local or network drives
Computers or people	Finds computers on your network, people in your Address Book, or people on the Internet
Information in Help and Support Center	Opens the Search tab in the Help and Support Center so you can find Help topics
Search the Internet	Finds information on the Internet
Change Preferences	Lets you customize the way the Search tool finds information and change the appearance of the Search Companion pane

To find information, you respond to questions in the Search Companion pane. These responses are **search criteria**, one or more conditions that information must meet to have Search find it. For example, you could provide search criteria specifying all or part of a filename and the drive containing the file. Search then locates and displays every file that matches those criteria. You can specify the criteria shown in Figure 6-4.

Figure 6-4	SEARCH CRITERIA	
OPTION	**DESCRIPTION**	**SEARCH STRATEGY**
All or part of the filename	Search for files or folders that contain the specified text	Filename
A word or phrase in the file	Search for files that include the specified words or phrases in their contents (not in the filename)	Keyword
Look in	Search a particular location, such as a computer, drive, or folder	Location
When was it modified?	Search for files that were created or last modified on a particular date or within a range of dates	Date
What size is it?	Search for files that are small, medium, large, or a specific file size	Size
More advanced options	Search for files of a particular type and select search settings, such as whether to search subfolders or perform a case-sensitive search	Type

In the next section, you'll search by filename and location to find a file.

Searching by Name and Location

To find any type of file by its name, you need to provide the Search Companion with as much of the filename as possible. In many cases, you will know the exact name of the file you want to locate but not recall where the file is stored. However, in those instances where you do not know the complete filename, you can use a word or phrase that may be part of the filename to search for the file. Any letters or words you type to define the search are called a **search string**. By default, Search Companion is not case sensitive when searching for filenames, so you can type the search string in either uppercase or lowercase letters.

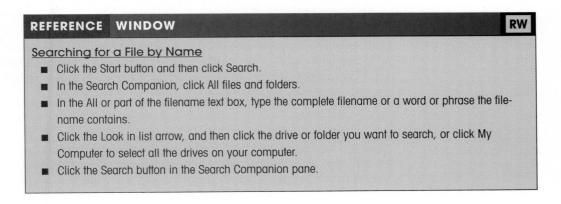

REFERENCE WINDOW   **RW**

Searching for a File by Name
- Click the Start button and then click Search.
- In the Search Companion, click All files and folders.
- In the All or part of the filename text box, type the complete filename or a word or phrase the filename contains.
- Click the Look in list arrow, and then click the drive or folder you want to search, or click My Computer to select all the drives on your computer.
- Click the Search button in the Search Companion pane.

For the most part, people name their files with names that reflect the files' contents. You assume that the previous aide would have named files related to leadership with a filename that contained the word "leadership." Therefore, you decide to conduct a search of files and folders on your disk using the search string "leadership."

To begin searching for files containing "leadership" in their filenames:

1. In the What do you want to search for? list in the Search Companion pane, click **All files and folders**. See Figure 6-5.

Figure 6-5   **SEARCHING FOR FILES BY NAME**

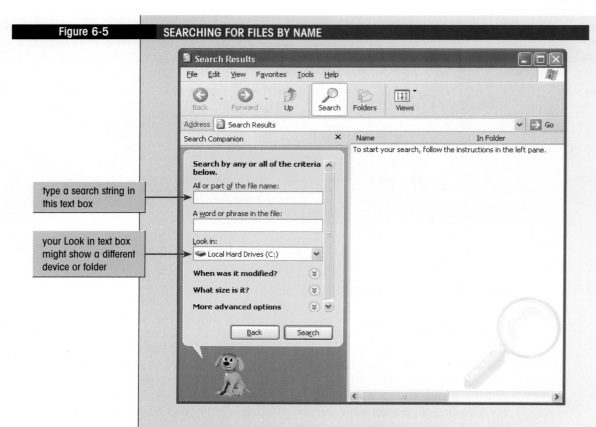

type a search string in
this text box

your Look in text box
might show a different
device or folder

If you know the full name of the file you are trying to locate, you can supply the
Search Companion with the complete filename in the All or part of the file
name text box. If you do not know the complete filename but perhaps know
only one or two words of it, the Search Companion can work with that information to locate the file. In this case, you do not know the filename but are looking for files that contain the word "leadership" in their filenames.

2. In the All or part of the file name text box, type **leadership**.

Now that you've entered a criterion for the filename, you can specify a file location. When
you start Search, a folder or drive name, such as Local Hard Drives (C:), appears in the Look in
list box, which specifies where Search will look for the file. If your computer has multiple drives
and you aren't sure which drive contains the file, you can search your entire computer by clicking My Computer in the Look in list box. However, if you know which drive contains the file,
you can speed your search by limiting the search to that drive. All the files you are looking for
are located on your Data Disk, so you can specify your floppy drive as the search location.

To search for files by location:

1. Click the **Look in** list arrow in the Search Companion pane, and then click
3½ Floppy (A:). Windows XP will now search only the files on your Data Disk.

2. Click the **Search** button in the Search Companion pane. Windows XP searches
for all files on drive A whose names contain the search string you entered. Then
it displays any matching files in the Search Results pane.

TROUBLE? If nothing appears, Windows XP might not be including subfolders in its search. Click the Back button 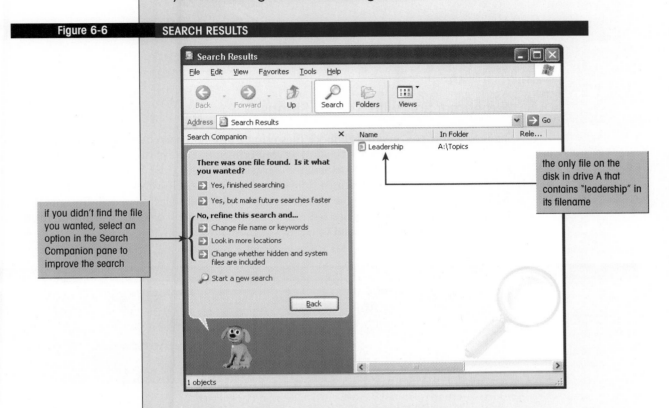, scroll the Search Companion pane, click More advanced options, and then make sure the Search Subfolders check box is selected. This ensures that Search will search all folders on the Data Disk, not just the files contained in the root directory. Click the Search button again to show the results.

3. Click **View** on the menu bar, and then click **Details** if necessary to ensure that you are viewing file details. See Figure 6-6.

Figure 6-6	SEARCH RESULTS

if you didn't find the file you wanted, select an option in the Search Companion pane to improve the search

the only file on the disk in drive A that contains "leadership" in its filename

TROUBLE? If your results show .txt extensions after the filenames, your computer is set to show file extensions. Showing or hiding file extensions does not affect the Search tool. If you want to hide file extensions, click Tools on the menu bar, click Folder Options, click the View tab, select the Hide file extensions for known file types check box, and then click the OK button.

The Search Results list shows one file, Leadership. The In Folder column shows the file location, A:\Topics. The location begins with the drive—in this case, A. If the file is in a folder, a backslash (\) separates the drive from the folder name. In this case, files in A:\Topics are in the Topics folder on drive A. If a folder contains subfolders, additional backslashes separate the folders from one another. Figure 6-7 shows how this notation works on a disk in drive A that contains two folders, Politics and Speeches, both of which have subfolders.

| Figure 6-7 | FILE LOCATIONS |

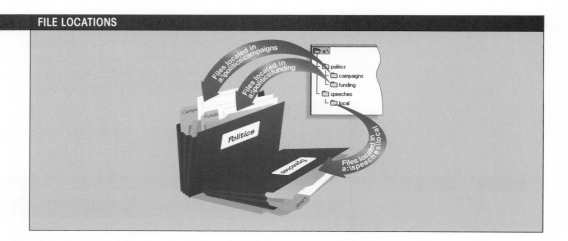

Experimenting with Search Strings

You wonder if you would find more files using a different search string. One rule of thumb is to use the root of your search word as your criterion. For example, if you decide to search for files on political topics for Senator Bernstein's speech, using "politics" as your search string would not find a file named Politician, for example. However, using the root "politic" without the added "s" as your search string would yield files named Politician, Political Quotations, or Politics. Figure 6-8 shows several examples of search strings that use the root of a word. (You don't need to try any of these now.)

| Figure 6-8 | CHOOSING EFFECTIVE SEARCH STRINGS | |

TOPIC	USE THIS SEARCH STRING:	FINDS THESE FILENAMES:
politics	politic	Politics, Politicians, Political Quotations
education	educ	Education, Educational Issues, Educators
computers	comput	Computers, Computing, Computerization

Of course, if the root of the word is very general, Search might find files you don't want. Searching for "lead" instead of "leader" would display a filename such as "Lead Corrosion." Fortunately, it's easy to adjust your search string until you find only those files you want.

Now that you know the archive disk has a file containing quotations specifically about leadership, you look for files on leaders, using "leader" as your search string. To perform a new search, you can change the existing criteria, add a new criterion, or start a new search. You want to change the search string from "leadership" to "leader" but still search only the disk in drive A. You will change only the filename instead of starting a new search.

To search for files containing the search string "leader" on drive A:

1. Click **Change file name or keywords** in the Search Companion pane. See Figure 6-9.

Figure 6-9   CHANGING SEARCH CRITERIA

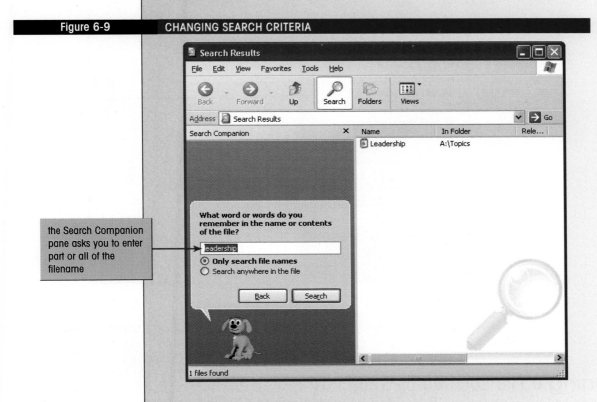

the Search Companion pane asks you to enter part or all of the filename

2. Type **leader** in the text box in the Search Companion pane.

   TROUBLE? If an entry is already selected in a text box, you can type to replace its contents. If an entry is not selected, double-click the text box to select the contents, and then type. You also can click once and then edit the text box contents.

3. Click the **Search** button in the Search Companion pane. The right pane in the Search Results window now lists three files that might contain information on leadership. See Figure 6-10.

Figure 6-10   RESULTS OF AN EXPANDED SEARCH

You decide to open the Leadership file to see if it contains any quotes the senator might find useful.

Opening a File Located by Search

Once you locate a file using the Search Companion, you can open it directly, as you would from My Computer or Windows Explorer. You can right-click the file, and then click Open on the shortcut menu, or click it and then press Enter, or you can double-click it. Windows XP locates and starts the program that created the file and then it opens the file. If Windows XP cannot open your file, you might not have the necessary program for that file type installed on your computer. In this case, Windows XP prompts you to select the program you want to use to display the file.

To open a file from the Search Results window:

1. Double-click the **Leadership** file in the right pane of the Search Results window. The file opens in Notepad.

   TROUBLE? If the text of the quotations extends beyond the right border of the Notepad window, click Format on the menu bar, and then click Word Wrap.

2. Browse through the contents of the file, and note that it contains several quotations on leadership. When you are finished, click the Notepad **Close** button ☒ to close Notepad. Click **No** if you are prompted to save your changes.

You show Carolyn the files you found for the speech at Stanton College. Carolyn is pleased that you found helpful material for her. She says that Senator Bernstein will be participating in an atomic energy symposium next month, so anything you can find on that topic would be also useful. You decide to check the quotations archive disk to see if it has any files containing quotations by Albert Einstein, but you can't remember how to spell his name. If you make a spelling error, Search won't locate the files you want.

Using Wildcards

Wildcards are characters that you can substitute for all or part of a filename in a search string. For example, you can use wildcards to approximate a filename. You can also use wildcards to locate a group of files whose names follow certain specific patterns, such as all files that begin and end with certain characters, or all files with a specified string in a specified location.

Search recognizes two wildcards: the asterisk and the question mark. The * (asterisk) wildcard stands in place of any number of consecutive characters in a filename. With the search string "m*n" for example, Search locates files with names that start with "m" and end with "n, "such as Men, Magician, or Modern, but not Male or Women. When you use the asterisk wildcard in a search string, the Search tool allows additional characters only in those places indicated by the wildcard. Search does not include filenames with characters before the "m" or after the "n." If this is not what you want, you can use additional wildcards. If you specify the search string "*m*n*" Search includes Men, Magician, Modern, Women, and Mention, but not Male. These files have the letter "m" in common, which appears somewhere in the name, followed later by "n."

You can also use the ? (question mark) as a wildcard to select files when one character in the filename varies. For example, the search string "m?n" locates Men or Man but not Mistaken or Moon. Files that match the "m?n" criteria must have the letters "m" and "n" in their filenames, separated by a single character. Unlike the asterisk wildcard, however, the question mark wildcard does not cause Search to exclude files with characters before or after the "m" or "n." So although "m*n" excludes Women and Mental, "m?n" does not, because both of these files contain "m" and "n" separated by a single character. The question mark wildcard is often used to locate files whose names include version numbers or dates, such as Sales1, Sales2, and Sales3, or Tax2001, Tax2002, and Tax2003.

You decide to search for only those files beginning with "e" and ending with "n" because you know those are the first and last letters of Einstein's name, although you aren't sure what letters are in between. To perform this search, you use "e*n" as your search string. Try this search now.

To locate files using the asterisk wildcard:

1. Click **Change file name or keywords** in the Search Companion pane.

2. In the text box, type **e*n** and then click the **Search** button in the Search Companion pane. The Search Results pane displays files on your Data Disk whose names start with "e" followed by any number of characters and then the letter "n." Two of the files found are named Einstein. See Figure 6-11.

Figure 6-11   SEARCHING WITH THE ASTERISK WILDCARD

the Search Results pane lists files whose names start with "e" and end with "n"

your search found two files named Einstein; your icons and file order may differ

You make a mental note that the files on Einstein might be appropriate for the atomic energy symposium, and plan to print them for Carolyn before your next meeting with her.

Finding Files by Keyword

You've found two files on Einstein, and you wonder if any files specifically mention atomic energy. You search for files named "atomic" or "energy" but don't find any. You know, however, that this doesn't necessarily mean there are no quotations about atomic energy in the files. Besides searching for a file based on its name, you can also use the Search Companion to search for a word or phrase in the contents of a file. To use this feature, you search for a keyword. A **keyword** is a search string—a word or a phrase—contained anywhere in a file. The Search Companion searches through the entire text of every file to find the keyword.

When you search based on a keyword, you can specify whether your search is case sensitive. For example, if you want to find a letter you wrote to Brenda Wolf, you could enter "Wolf" as your keyword and then select a case-sensitive search to locate only files containing Wolf with an initial uppercase letter. The Case sensitive option affects only keywords you enter in the A word or phrase in the file text box—not the search strings you enter to search for files by name. The Case sensitive option is an advanced option that you can select by starting a new search, selecting the advanced options, and then clicking the Case sensitive check box.

You decide to search for the keywords "atomic energy" to try to find more files containing quotations Carolyn could use in writing her speech for the atomic energy symposium.

To look for the keywords "atomic energy" within a file:

1. Click **Start a new search** in the Search Companion pane. You want to search only the files and folders on your Data Disk.

2. Click **All files and folders**.

3. If necessary, press the **Delete** key to delete the text in the All or part of the file name text box. Note that the Look in list arrow still shows the 3½ Floppy (A:) drive as the location from your last search.

4. Click the **A word or phrase in the file** text box, and then type **atomic energy**. Because you aren't sure what case the quote might be in, you want to make sure Search isn't set to perform case-sensitive searches.

5. Scroll to the bottom of the Search Companion pane if necessary, and then click the **More advanced options** double arrow button to display the advanced search options.

   TROUBLE? If the advanced search options already appear, such as the Case sensitive check box, you don't have to click the More advanced options double arrow button.

6. Make sure the **Case sensitive** check box is not checked. If it is, click it to remove the check mark. Otherwise Search might not locate the file if the search string text is not all lowercase. If necessary, change any other settings to match the ones shown in Figure 6-12.

| Figure 6-12 | PREPARING TO SEARCH BY KEYWORD |

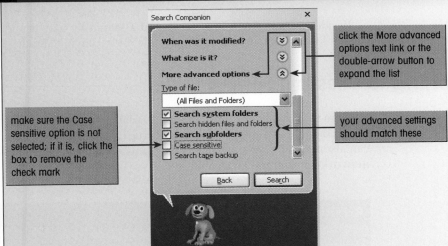

7. Click the **Search** button in the Search Companion pane. Search locates one file, Technology, located in the Topics folder. This file contains the keywords "atomic energy" in its contents.

   TROUBLE? If Search did not locate a file, check to make sure you typed the keywords "atomic energy" correctly and that drive A is selected.

Searching by keyword can be time-consuming, even on a floppy disk. To speed the search, you can index your search location.

Indexing to Speed Searches

When Windows XP searches for a file, it checks every file in the specified location to see if the file meets your search criteria. If you are searching your entire computer, for example, the search can take a long time. You can speed the search process by using the Indexing Service to **index** a disk. To index a disk, the Indexing Service reads through your files and extracts basic information, such as the name and location of your files, and organizes it in a way that makes access to that information quick and easy. After you index a disk once, Search can refer to the index to find files instead of scanning every file on your computer. The Search tool lets you enable the Indexing Service to speed your searches, which is particularly helpful if you are searching a disk containing large amounts of information or if you will search the same disk repeatedly.

You anticipate that you'll be using the Search tool often as Carolyn's aide, so you decide to use the indexing service to search more quickly.

To speed searches using the indexing service:

1. In the Search Companion pane, click **Yes, but make future searches faster** to respond to the question, "There was one file found. Is it what you wanted?"

   TROUBLE? If you do not see the "Yes, but make future searches faster" option, the Indexing Service is already enabled on your computer. You can skip Steps 1 and 2.

2. Click the **Yes, enable Indexing Service** option button, and then click the **OK** button.

Besides indexing, you also can speed a search by narrowing the search criteria so that Search looks for fewer files—for example, by specifying a folder rather than an entire drive.

Searching for Files in a Specific Folder

You can search all drives and folders available to your computer or, as you saw when you selected the drive containing your Data Disk, you can search only a single drive. You can also narrow your search by specifying a folder on your own computer or on a shared network computer.

REFERENCE WINDOW   **RW**

Searching for Files in a Specific Folder

- Start Search and then click All files and folders in the Search Companion pane.
- Click the Look in list arrow.
- Click Browse at the bottom of the list.
- In the Browse for Folder dialog box, click the plus box next to the drive containing the folder you want to search.
- If the folder is in the root directory of the drive, click the folder icon. If the folder is a subfolder, navigate to the appropriate folder.
- Click OK and then click the Search button in the Search Companion pane.

You report to Carolyn that you've found files containing quotations on atomic energy and on Albert Einstein. She's pleased you found them so quickly and asks you to find quotations by Woody Allen, one of the senator's favorite comics. You noticed a Comedy folder earlier, and you wonder whether it contains quotes by Woody Allen. You decide to use the Search Companion to search the Comedy folder for appropriate material.

To specify the Comedy folder, you navigate a folder tree similar to the one in Windows Explorer.

To search the Comedy folder on drive A for files that contain "woody allen":

1. Click **Start a new search** in the Search Companion pane, if necessary, to return to the What do you want to search for? list. Now you can specify that you want to search all the files in the Comedy folder.

2. Click **All files and folders**.

3. Click the **Look in** list arrow, and then click **Browse** at the bottom of the list. The Browse For Folder dialog box opens, displaying a list of devices, drives, and folders.

4. Click ➕ next to My Computer, and then click ➕ next to 3½ Floppy (A:). The folders on drive A appear. See Figure 6-13.

Figure 6-13	SELECTING A FOLDER

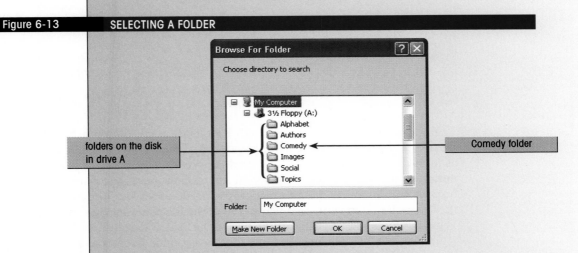

folders on the disk in drive A

Comedy folder

TROUBLE? Your list of devices, drives, and folders might look different, depending on your computer's drives and network.

5. Click the **Comedy** folder.

6. Click the **OK** button. The Look in list box in the Search Companion pane now shows Comedy. Next, specify the keyword you want to find.

7. Select the text in the **A word or phrase in the file** text box, and then type **woody allen**. This criteria tells Search to look only in the Comedy folder on drive A (and in any subfolders the Comedy folder might contain) for files whose contents include "woody allen."

8. Click the **Search** button in the Search Companion pane. Search locates two files.

You imagine that Carolyn will want you to find other quotations by author and decide to search the disk for any files or folders whose filenames contain the term "author."

Working **with Search Results**

Up until now, the file lists in the Search Results panes have been short and manageable. When your search yields many files, you can adjust the Search Results pane to display the information in a more organized format.

You noticed a folder named Author earlier and anticipate that using the search string "author" could find many files. You'll start by searching for files or folders whose filenames contain "author," and then look for ways to organize the search results.

> ### *To search for files and folders named "author" on drive A:*
>
> 1. Click the **Back** button in the Search Companion pane to enter new search criteria—you want to search for files whose names contain the word "author."
>
> 2. Type **author** in the All or part of the file name text box in the Search Companion pane. Because you are not looking for files based on keywords, you will delete the text in the next text box.
>
> 3. Delete the contents of the **A word or phrase in the file** text box.
>
> 4. Click the **Look in** list arrow, and then click **3½ Floppy (A:)** to search all folders on the disk, not just the Comedy folder.
>
> 5. Click the **Search** button in the Search Companion pane. The Search Results pane displays all files and folders that have the word "author" in their file-names. Your Data Disk has 28 such files.

You can view the files in the Search Results pane by Thumbnails, Tiles, Icons, List, or Details, and you can resize columns by dragging their borders. These options are the same as in My Computer and Windows Explorer. To change the view, you can click the Views button or the View menu. Details view, the default view, is probably the most useful view because it gives you all the information you need (name, location, size, type, and date modified of each file) to verify that you've found the file you want. Just as in My Computer and Windows Explorer, you can sort the files in the Search Results pane by any of these criteria.

You see files whose names indicate that they contain quotations from authors, labeled by last name. For example, the D-Author document contains quotations from people whose last names start with D. You decide to sort the files by name to see if the Data Disk folder contains a file for every letter of the alphabet.

> ### *To sort the files by name:*
>
> 1. Make sure the Search Results list appears in Details view. If it doesn't, click the **Views** button 🔳 ˇ on the Standard Buttons toolbar, and then click **Details**.
>
> 2. Click the **Name** button shown in Figure 6-14 until the files are arranged in ascending alphabetical order by name.

Figure 6-14   **SORTING THE SEARCH RESULTS LIST**

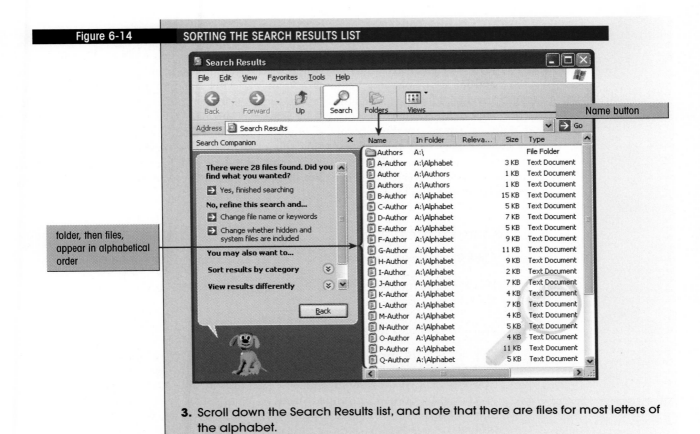

folder, then files, appear in alphabetical order

Name button

3. Scroll down the Search Results list, and note that there are files for most letters of the alphabet.

If you wanted to find quotations by a given author, you could try the file for the author's last name, located in the Alphabet folder. What else can you learn from the Search Results pane? The Type column shows that the first item on the list is a folder and that the rest of the files are text documents. You could sort by size to find that the largest file is 15 KB. You could sort the files by date modified (scroll to the right to see this option) to observe that these files were developed in the years 1994–2001.

Refining a Search

So far you've searched for files with particular filenames or keywords. You can also locate a file using criteria other than the filename or contents, including size, date, and type. With these criteria, you can answer questions such as: Are any files more than a few years old? Which files were created using a certain program? Which files are larger or smaller than a specified size? You enter the characteristic you want to study, and then Search lists all files that share that characteristic, such as all files created after 2002, all Microsoft Word files, or all files larger than 50 KB.

You can use these criteria alone or in combination with filenames and keywords.

Finding a File by Date

Searching for files by date is useful when you want a file that you were working with on a given date, but you can't remember where you stored it. You could get information about file dates quickly by opening Windows Explorer or My Computer and sorting the files in a folder by date. However, when the files are scattered among folders, Search can display files from any of those folders that meet your date criteria, whereas Windows Explorer and My Computer can display the contents of only one folder at a time.

Carolyn says that the previous aide spent the most time developing the quotations archive during the years 1994 to 1996. You decide to see whether the archive disk still has any files that were created then and note that those files might need to be updated. To do so, you'll search for files by date.

To search for files created between 1994 and 1996:

1. Click **Start a new search** in the Search Companion pane.

   TROUBLE? You might have to scroll in the Search Companion pane to see the Start a new search option.

2. Click **All files and folders**.

3. Press the **Delete** key to delete text in the All of or part of the file name text box, make sure 3½ Floppy (A:) still appears in the Look in text box, and then scroll down to click **When was it modified?** and display the options related to searching by date. You use these options to set date criteria. For example, you can find files modified in the last week, month, or year. You want to find files created within a different range of dates, so you can specify those dates.

4. Click the **Specify dates** option button. Now you can enter and select date criteria, including whether to search by modified date, created date, or accessed date (when a file was last opened, for example). You also specify the start and end dates in the from and to list boxes.

5. Click the **Specify dates** list arrow, and then click **Created Date**.

6. In the **from** text box, enter **1/1/1994** as the start date, and in the **to** text box, enter **12/31/1996** as the end date. See Figure 6-15.

Figure 6-15   **SPECIFYING START AND END DATES**

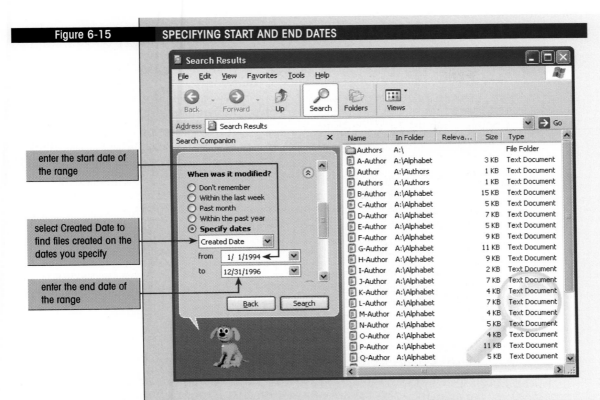

enter the start date of the range

select Created Date to find files created on the dates you specify

enter the end date of the range

7. Click the **Search** button in the Search Companion pane. The Search Results list shows 16 files in that range of dates.

You'd like to get an overview of the types of files on the quotations archive disk to see whether you have the software on your computer to open them. To do this, you can search the files on the disk by file type.

Finding a File by Type

You can use the Search Companion to look for files by their general file type or by the program that created them. The list of file types from which you can choose includes text files, sound files, bitmaps, Word documents, Web documents, and so on, depending on the resources on your computer.

You already know the archive disk has many text files, but you'd like to know how many to estimate the number of quotations it provides. Each text file has an average of 10 quotations. If the disk contains 20 text files, you can estimate that you have about 200 quotations. You decide to use file type criteria to find the number of text files on the archive disk.

To find files by type:

1. Click the **Back** button in the Search Companion pane to change your search criteria.

2. In the "When was it modified?" section, click the **Don't remember** option button to clear the dates you specified earlier. You specify file type in the advanced options section.

3. Locate and click the **More advanced options** double arrow button to display the advanced search options, if necessary. You use the Type of file text box in the More advanced options section to select the file type for which you want to search.

4. Click the **Type of file** list arrow, and then scroll down the alphabetical list to locate "Text Document."

5. Click **Text Document** and then click the **Search** button in the Search Companion pane. The Search Companion and status bar indicate that your disk has 92 text files. The disk contains about 920 quotations.

TROUBLE? If your list is much shorter, you might have forgotten to click the Don't remember option button to turn off the Date setting. Scroll up to the "When was it modified?" section, click the Don't remember option button, and then click the Search button in the Search Companion pane.

You also wonder whether the archive disk contains sound files that the senator could use in a multimedia presentation. Many spoken-word files are created in a file format called AU Format Sound. You can search for files of that type to see if the archive contains any spoken-word files.

To find one type of sound file:

1. Click the **Back** button in the Search Companion pane, and then click the **Type of file** list arrow again under More Advanced Options. Click **AU Format Sound**.

2. Click the **Search** button in the Search Companion pane. The Search Results list includes two AU Format Sound files.

Now you want to know if the archive disk contains other types of sound files besides those in the AU Format Sound format. The senator could also use music in a multimedia presentation. In addition to searching for files by type, the Search tool lets you search for files in a particular category, such as all sound files, which include MIDI and MP3 files, for example.

To find all types of sound files:

1. Click **Start a new search** in the Search Companion pane. Categories of file types appear in the Search Companion pane, including Pictures, music, or video, and Documents.

2. Click **Pictures, music, or video** in the Search Companion pane. Now the Search Companion shows the three types of files you can find—Pictures and Photos, Music, or Video. Although you can select some or all of these types, you only want to find music files.

3. Click the **Music** check box to select it. Windows XP will search the entire hard disk unless you specify where to search. To do so, you must first display the advanced search options.

4. Click **Use advanced search options**.

5. If necessary, scroll down the Search Companion pane, click the **Look in** list arrow, and then click **3½ Floppy (A:)**.

6. Click the **Search** button in the Search Companion pane. Switch to Details View, if necessary. Windows XP finds three files—the two spoken-word files you found earlier, and one MIDI Sequence file. Figure 6-16 shows the Search Results window in Details view.

| Figure 6-16 | FINDING ALL SOUND FILES |

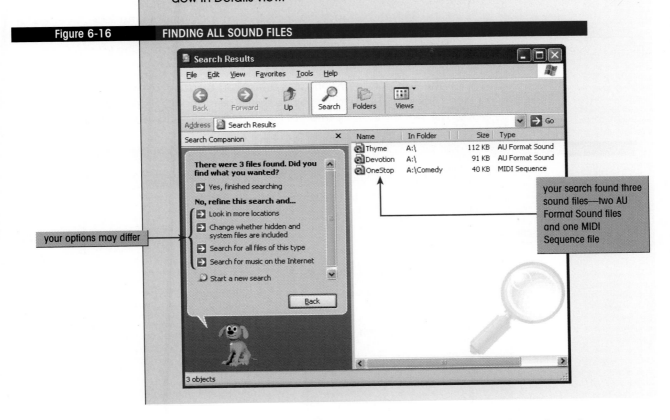

your options may differ

your search found three sound files—two AU Format Sound files and one MIDI Sequence file

Another way to find files is based on their size. You'll try that type of search next.

Finding a File by Size

You know that sound and music files are usually bigger than text files or word-processed documents. If you are short on disk space, you'll want to identify the largest files so you can move them to free up space. You can find this information by looking for a file by its size. If disk space becomes a problem on the quotations archive disk, you can find all files that are at least 25 KB and then move them to a hard disk. Try that search now.

To search for files by size:

1. Click **Start a new search** in the Search Companion pane, and then click **All files and folders**. You need to use the advanced options to search by size.

2. Click the **More advanced options** double arrow button to display the advanced search options, if necessary. Click the **Type of file** list arrow, and then click **(All Files and Folders)**, the first item in the list.

3. Click **What size is it?** to display the options related to file size.

4. Click the **Specify size (in KB)** option button, and then make sure the "at least" option is selected.

TROUBLE? If the "at least" option is not selected, click the Specify size list arrow and then click at least.

5. Enter **25** in the second text box.

6. Click the **Search** button in the Search Companion pane. The Search Results list shows the files that are 25 KB or more. You can sort these files to identify the largest more easily. You'll sort in descending order so that the largest files appear at the top of the list.

7. Click the **Size** button until the files are sorted by size in ascending order, and then click the **Size** button again to sort in descending order, with the largest files first. Not surprisingly, three of the largest files are sound files. See Figure 6-17.

| Figure 6-17 | SEARCHING FOR FILES BY SIZE |

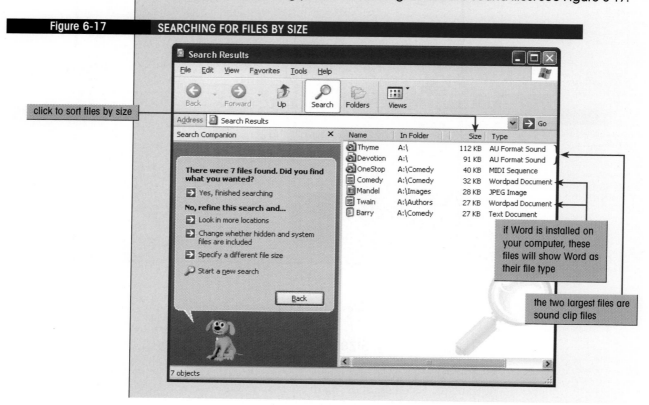

Now that you know how to find a file based on size, type, or date, you can further refine a search by using a combination of these criteria.

Finding a File Using Multiple Criteria

Carolyn is now working on the second draft of Senator Bernstein's speech at Stanton College. Carolyn informs you that because Stanton College is a women's college, Senator Bernstein is interested in having a quote on leadership by a woman. If you specify multiple criteria, such as a likely filename and keyword, you might be able to pinpoint such a quote.

You remember that some files on the archive disk have filenames containing the search string "women." You guess that a quotation about leadership probably contains the word "leader," so you could specify the root "leader" as your keyword. Search uses all the criteria you enter to perform the search.

To find a file with multiple criteria:

1. Click the **Back** button in the Search Companion pane. Try looking for files whose names contain "women."

2. Click the **All or part of the file name** text box, and then type **women**.

3. Click the **A word or phrase in the file** text box, and then type **leader**. Next, be sure to clear all the criteria you've entered before so you don't add unnecessary information to the search.

4. Scroll to the "What size is it?" section, and then click the **Don't remember** option button. The search criteria you have entered indicates that you want to find files of any size that contain "women" in their filenames and "leader" in their contents.

5. Click the **Search** button in the Search Companion pane. One file matches your criteria. See Figure 6-18.

| Figure 6-18 | USING MULTIPLE CRITERIA TO FIND A FILE |

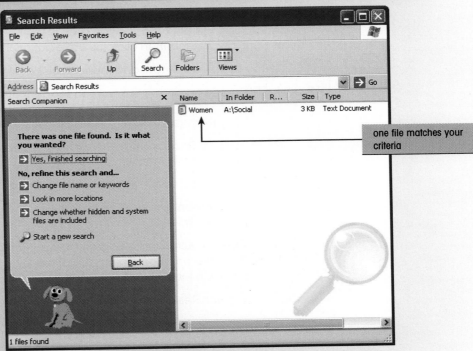

one file matches your criteria

6. Double-click the **Women** file in the right pane to open the file in Notepad. You see a quotation on leaders by Mother Teresa that the senator might want to use in her speech.

7. Close Notepad.

You've learned how to refine a file search by specifying date, type, size, or a combination. When you develop effective criteria, you can save your search settings in case you want to perform that same search again.

Saving Search Settings

After you enter criteria to find files and other information, especially if you are using multiple criteria, you might want to save your search settings. For example, if you regularly search sales documents for sales from the West region, you can create criteria to search a disk for files created in the last month containing the keyword "West." If you save your search settings, you can perform that search every month without re-creating the search criteria.

You save search settings in a file in the Saved Search format. To perform the search again, you can open the Saved Search file to start the Search tool and conduct a new search using the same criteria.

As you create other quotations disks, you might need to find other files containing quotations on women's leadership. You can save the search settings so you don't have to enter the multiple criteria again.

To save and test your search settings:

1. In the Search Results window, click **File** on the menu bar, and then click **Save Search**. The Save Search dialog box opens. This dialog box works just like the standard Save As dialog box—you specify the name and location of the file you want to save and then click the Save button.

2. Click the **Save in** list arrow, and then select **3½ Floppy (A:)**.

3. In the File name text box, type **women leaders** and then click the **Save** button. This saves the search settings in a file named "women leaders" on the root directory of your floppy disk.

4. Close the Search Results window. Next, you will open the file to make sure it performs the search correctly.

5. Open My Computer and navigate to the drive containing your Data Disk.

6. Double-click **women leaders**. The Search Results window opens and displays the saved search criteria.

7. Click the **Search** button in the Search Companion pane. This time the search finds two files—the one containing quotations by women and the saved search file called women leaders. Both meet your search criteria.

8. Close the Search Results and My Computer windows.

In this session, you used the Windows XP Search Companion to search for files by name and location, keyword, type, and size. You learned how to use wildcards and refine your search, and how to save your search settings to conduct future searches.

Session 6.1 QUICK | CHECK

1. To search for a file only on drive A, what do you do in the Search Companion pane?

2. True or False: The right pane in the Search Results window displays only the files whose names exactly match the search string you entered.

3. What is a wildcard? What is the difference between the asterisk wildcard and the question mark wildcard?

4. How do you display the files in the Search Results list in alphabetical order?

5. If you want to use the Search Companion to display only the bitmapped images on your floppy disk, what should you do?

6. If the Search Results list shows the file you were looking for, how do you open the file for editing?

7. What is a keyword?

SESSION 6.2

In this session, you will learn how to use the Search Companion to search the Internet, including searching for Web pages that contain specific kinds of information. You'll learn how to narrow your search to focus on Web pages relevant to the information you want to find. You'll also learn to search for people and maps on the Web, and how to modify your search preferences.

Searching for Information on the Internet

The Internet has vast resources, and to locate the information you want, you need to search for it. However, searching for a piece of information on a Web page can be a daunting task—the Internet provides access to millions and millions of Web pages. To simplify and speed an Internet search, you can use a **search service**, a Web site that helps you find information on the Internet. Most search services use software, called the **search engine**, that searches through Internet documents and compiles a list of Web pages. It organizes and indexes this list by topic. When you use the search service to find Web pages on a specific topic, the service's search engine checks the index and provides links to all the pages it finds on that topic. Because the Internet is changing so quickly, the indexes change regularly, too. If you don't find information one day, it might be available the next. Moreover, because each search service can use a different search engine to compile its Web page index, you might find different results for the same search when using different search services. Some search services also provide specific types of information. If you cannot find what you want with one search service, such as MSN, you can try another, such as Google. Figure 6-19 lists popular search services, and the types of information their indexes provide.

Figure 6-19	POPULAR SEARCH SERVICES
SEARCH SERVICE	**DESCRIPTION**
AltaVista	One of the largest and most comprehensive search engines available, AltaVista searches for keywords anywhere on a Web page
Ask Jeeves	A **meta search engine**, which searches the indexes of other search engines and eliminates redundant listings
Direct Hit	Designed to find the most popular Web sites
Google	One of the largest and fastest search engines, Google is also designed to find Web sites that directly relate to your search
HotBot	Sorts results by date
MSN	Focuses on general-interest Web sites
Northern Light	Sorts results into appropriate search folders related to content
Yahoo!	Provides a directory of Web pages, organized by categories

By default, the Windows XP Search Companion pane uses the MSN search service to help you narrow your search criteria to find pages related to the topic or question you have in mind. You can change the default search service if you like.

Searching for Web Pages with the Search Companion

When you enter search criteria to find a Web page and click the Search button in the Search Companion pane, the Search Companion pane lists categories of information that meet your search criteria. For example, if you enter "colleges," the Search Companion pane lists categories related to colleges, such as "Find a college's Web site," and "Find information about a college." You choose the category of information you want to search, and the Search Companion pane sends the search criteria to the MSN search engine. If possible, the Search Companion then asks for more information to refine the search. For example, if you select the "Find information about a college" category, the Search Companion pane asks, "For which college?" Then it sends the refined search criteria to the MSN search engine. As you provide progressively more detailed information in the Search Companion pane, the list of topics found by the search engine grows smaller. For example, at the beginning of the college search, MSN would probably find thousands of college Web sites. After you enter a college name, MSN would list fewer, making it easier to find the information you want.

Because Senator Bernstein often visits college campuses, you want to expand the set of quotations on the quotations archives disk to include quotations about higher education. You start by searching the Internet for Web sites that include quotation collections.

To search for Web sites using the Search Companion:

1. Make sure you are connected to the Internet.

2. Click the **Start** button ![start] on the taskbar, and then click **Search**. In the Search Companion pane, click **Search the Internet**. The Search Results window opens. See Figure 6-20.

| Figure 6-20 | SEARCHING THE INTERNET WITH THE SEARCH COMPANION |

type search criteria here...

...or click a link in the Search Companion pane

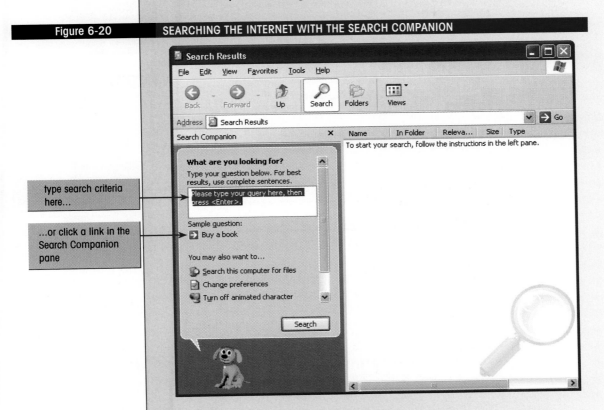

3. Maximize the Search Results window, if necessary.

TROUBLE? If America Online (AOL) is installed on your computer, your Search Companion pane may look different than the one shown in Figure 6-20. To make your Search Companion pane match the one shown in the figure, and to be able to complete the following steps, click Change preferences in the Search Companion pane, click Internet Search Behavior, and then make sure the With Search Companion option button is selected and the default search engine is MSN. Click OK in the Search Companion pane.

4. In the Search Companion pane text box, type **quotations**, and then click the **Search** button. The Search Results window changes to the Internet Explorer window—note that the title bar shows the Internet Explorer icon ![IE], the Standard Buttons toolbar includes additional buttons, such as Mail and Print, and the Address bar shows the URL of the MSN Web Search page, which opens in the right pane, listing the first 15 Web sites that feature quotations. The Search Companion stays open in the left pane. See Figure 6-21.

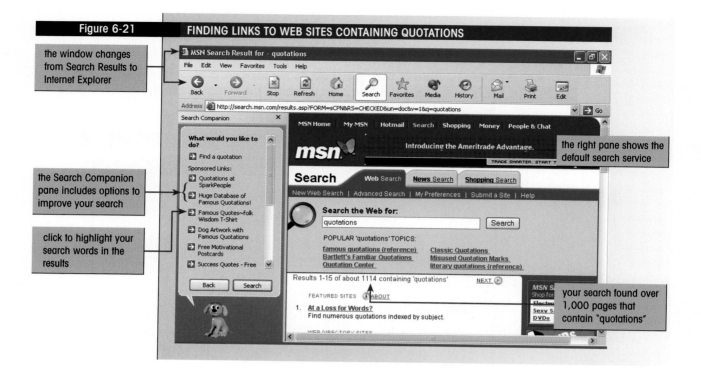

Figure 6-21   FINDING LINKS TO WEB SITES CONTAINING QUOTATIONS

the window changes from Search Results to Internet Explorer

the Search Companion pane includes options to improve your search

click to highlight your search words in the results

the right pane shows the default search service

your search found over 1,000 pages that contain "quotations"

Note that your search found over 1,000 Web pages related to quotations. To reduce this list to only pages about education quotations, you can now enter more information in the Search Companion pane to further refine the search. When you find a Web page that lists quotations about education, you can save it on your Data Disk.

To find and save a Web page containing education quotations:

1. In the Search Companion pane, click **Find a quotation**.

2. In the Who said it or what is it about? text box, type **education**.

3. Click the **Search** button in the Search Companion pane. In the right pane, a page opens containing links to quotations about education. See Figure 6-22.

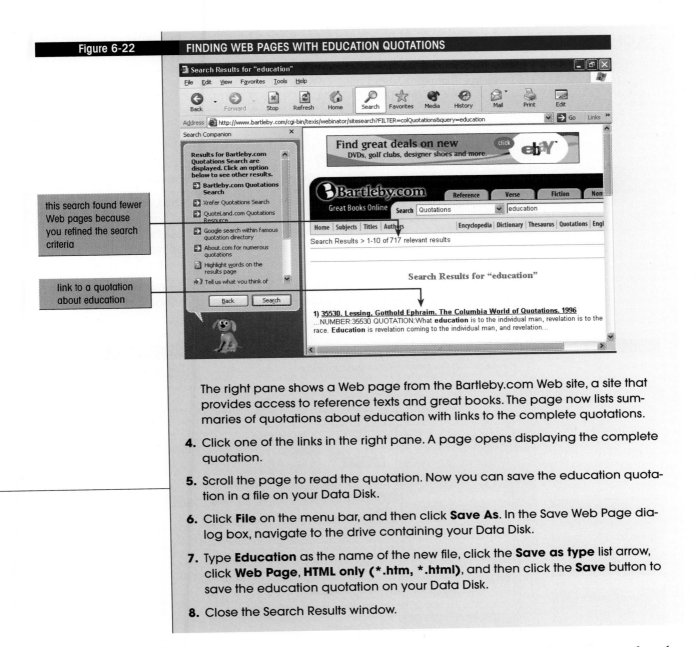

Figure 6-22   **FINDING WEB PAGES WITH EDUCATION QUOTATIONS**

this search found fewer Web pages because you refined the search criteria

link to a quotation about education

The right pane shows a Web page from the Bartleby.com Web site, a site that provides access to reference texts and great books. The page now lists summaries of quotations about education with links to the complete quotations.

4. Click one of the links in the right pane. A page opens displaying the complete quotation.

5. Scroll the page to read the quotation. Now you can save the education quotation in a file on your Data Disk.

6. Click **File** on the menu bar, and then click **Save As**. In the Save Web Page dialog box, navigate to the drive containing your Data Disk.

7. Type **Education** as the name of the new file, click the **Save as type** list arrow, click **Web Page, HTML only (*.htm, *.html)**, and then click the **Save** button to save the education quotation on your Data Disk.

8. Close the Search Results window.

Now that you've found an appropriate quotation, you can search the Internet for other types of Web pages, such as those that contain information about people.

Searching for People on the Internet

Besides finding Web pages, you also can use the Search tool to search for information on the Internet about specific people. To do so, you can use the Search Companion pane to enter a query such as "Find a person's address." The Search tool then connects to Web sites that host people search services such as Bigfoot and AnyWho. These people search services operate like electronic telephone books—you enter a name and the service looks up the mailing address, e-mail address, or telephone number. For common names the list is very long; for some names no information is available. Many people search services also let you perform reverse name searches—you enter telephone numbers, mailing addresses, or e-mail addresses to find a name.

Carolyn asks you to find contact information for sources she's using to prepare Senator Bernstein's speech. You've found some contact information by searching through journal articles written by the sources, but you also want to use the Internet as an alternate method of finding information about people. You decide to test the search service by attempting to locate information on yourself.

To use a search service to find information about a person:

1. Click the **Start** button ⏻ start on the taskbar, and then click **Search** to start a new search. Maximize the Search Results window, if necessary.

2. In the Search Companion pane, click **Search the Internet**, type **find a person's address** in the What are you looking for? text box, and then click the **Search** button. The window changes to Internet Explorer, and Windows XP uses the default search engine, MSN, to open a page containing links to people search services. The Search Companion remains open in the left pane.

3. In the Search Companion pane, click **Find contact information for a person**. The Search Companion pane displays text boxes where you can enter criteria to find a person. See Figure 6-23.

| Figure 6-23 | SEARCHING FOR PEOPLE ON THE INTERNET |

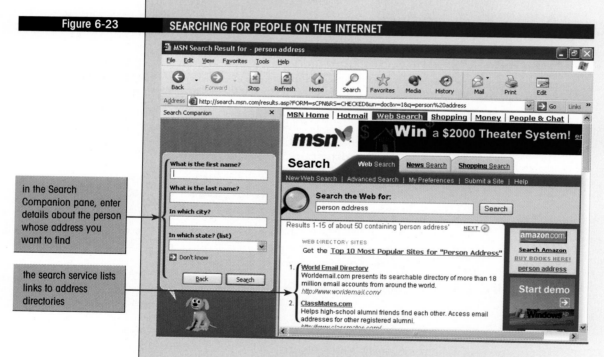

in the Search Companion pane, enter details about the person whose address you want to find

the search service lists links to address directories

4. In the What is the first name? text box, type your first name. In the What is the last name? text box, type your last name. In the In which city? text box, enter your city. Then click the **In which state?** list arrow and select your state.

5. Click the **Search** button in the Search Companion pane. If MSN has any address or phone number information on people with your name, it appears in a list.

TROUBLE? If MSN could not find the information you requested, click the Back button in the Search Companion pane, and then repeat Steps 3 through 5 using a different name, such as your instructor's name, or using a more common name and a large city. You can also click an option to view results from another search service, such as the AnyWho.com White Pages Address Finder.

Carolyn mentions that one common source of information for Senator Bernstein's speeches are speeches made by other members of Congress. She wonders if you could find a list of the current members of the U.S. Congress on the Internet. To find an organization, you can use the same techniques that you used to find a person.

To search for an organization:

1. In the Search Companion pane, click the **Back** button until you return to the "What are you looking for?" section.

2. In the Search Companion text box, type **find members of U.S. Congress**, and then click the **Search** button. See Figure 6-24.

Figure 6-24	FINDING MEMBERS OF CONGRESS

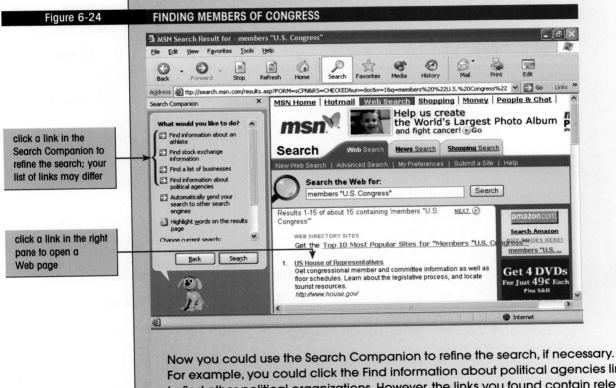

click a link in the Search Companion to refine the search; your list of links may differ

click a link in the right pane to open a Web page

Now you could use the Search Companion to refine the search, if necessary. For example, you could click the Find information about political agencies link to find other political organizations. However, the links you found contain relevant information, so you can explore those.

3. Click one or two links to locate a list of members of the U.S. Congress, and then close the Internet Explorer window.

Now that you have found information about people and organizations on the Internet, Carolyn asks you to help her search for maps on the Internet. She wants to find a map to Stanton College, which Senator Bernstein will visit next month. You can learn how to search the Internet for maps by finding one that shows your address.

Searching for a Map

In Windows XP, you find a location on an electronic map by providing addresses or other search criteria in the Search Companion pane of the Search Results window. The Search tool connects to a map service on the Internet. A **map service** provides street maps for addresses you enter into a search form. The Search tool uses the MSN map service by default, although you can send the search to other search services just as you can when you look for quotations. Once the map you want appears in the right pane of the Search Results window, you can zoom in to view more local detail or zoom out to view more of the surrounding area. To get familiar with searching for maps, try searching for your own address.

To locate a map:

1. Start the Search tool and then click **Search the Internet** in the Search Companion pane.

2. In the Search Companion, type **find a map** and then click the **Search** button. The window changes to Internet Explorer, and the MSN search service appears in the right pane, listing links to Web sites containing maps. The Search Companion remains in the left pane. MSN lists many types of maps to find, so you should refine your search.

3. In the Search Companion pane, click **Find a map of a place**.

4. Enter your address, city, and country in the appropriate text boxes.

5. Click the **Search** button in the Search Companion pane. The Expedia.com Find a Map page opens.

6. In the Best Match text box in the right pane, click an address and then click **Find a map** at the bottom of the page. (You might have to scroll the right pane to see this link.)

   The map of the place you selected appears in the right pane.

7. Scroll the right pane and then click a zoom level to see more details in the map. See Figure 6-25.

| Figure 6-25 | FINDING A MAP |

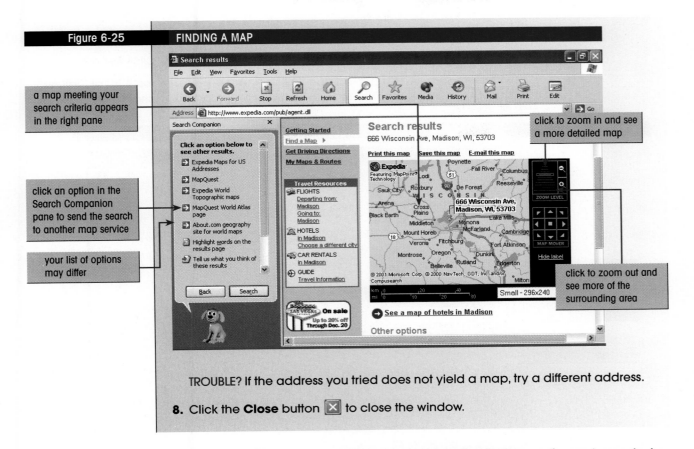

a map meeting your search criteria appears in the right pane

click an option in the Search Companion pane to send the search to another map service

your list of options may differ

click to zoom in and see a more detailed map

click to zoom out and see more of the surrounding area

TROUBLE? If the address you tried does not yield a map, try a different address.

8. Click the **Close** button ☒ to close the window.

You show Carolyn the map you found and explain that finding an electronic map is similar to finding any other kind of information on the Internet—you enter search criteria and then use a Web search service to locate the information you want. Now Carolyn wonders if you can change the default search service. She uses Google most often and is very comfortable with how it works. You can change the default search service from MSN to Google by changing search preferences.

Changing **Search Preferences**

You can customize the way the Search tool finds information and the appearance of the Search Companion pane itself. For example, as you become more experienced with creating effective search criteria, you might not want to enter additional criteria in text boxes in the Search Companion pane. You can turn off the Search Companion feature that prompts you for successively more detailed search information by choosing to use the Classic search style instead of the Search Companion. The Search Companion guides you step by step through the search process, whereas in a Classic search, you select categories and enter search queries, which use special rules to create detailed search criteria. If you are familiar with a previous version of Windows, you might prefer the Classic search style. You also probably noticed the animated character that appears at the bottom of the Search Companion pane. If that character becomes distracting, you can turn it off or change it.

Another feature you can customize is the search engine the Search tool uses to search the Internet. By default, this is MSN, but you can change this to another search engine with which you are more familiar, such as Yahoo! or InfoSeek. Carolyn wants you to change the default search service from MSN to Google.

To change search preferences:

1. Click the **Start** button on the taskbar, and then click **Search**.

2. In the Search Companion pane, click **Change preferences**. A list of features you can customize appears in the Search Companion pane. See Figure 6-26.

Figure 6-26	CHANGING SEARCH PREFERENCES

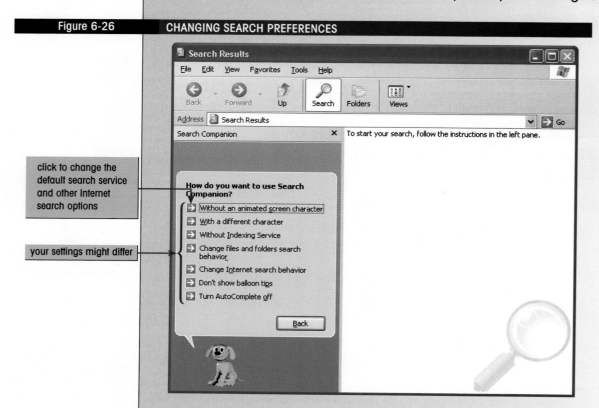

click to change the default search service and other Internet search options

your settings might differ

Figure 6-27 describes the search preference options.

Figure 6-27	SEARCH PREFERENCE OPTIONS

SEARCH PREFERENCE	DESCRIPTION
With or without an animated screen character	Show or hide the animated character at the bottom of the Screen Companion pane
With a different character	Select a different animated character to show at the bottom of the Screen Companion pane
With or without the Indexing Service	Use the Search Companion with or without using the Indexing Service to speed your searches
Change files and folders search behavior	Change how you search for files and folders, such as to manually specify search criteria
Change Internet search behavior	Change the default search service and how you search for Web sites
Show or don't show balloon tips	Show or hide ScreenTips that appear in balloons as you work in the Search Companion
Turn AutoComplete off or on	Let the Search Companion suggest entries for text you have typed before, or complete entries without suggestions

3. Click **Change Internet search behavior.** The Search Companion pane lists the Internet search behavior you can customize. Note that here you can choose to use the Classic Internet search style instead of the guided series of prompts in the Search Companion pane.

4. In the list of search engines, click **Google.** If you click the OK button now, the Search tool will now use Google as the default search service. Because you should leave the Search tool in its default state for the next person who uses your computer, you won't click the OK button now.

5. Click the **Cancel** button and then close the Search Results window.

You have searched for quotations, people, and maps, and customized the search preferences. You're confident that you can use Windows XP and its Search tool to find just about any information Carolyn needs.

Session 6.2 QUICK CHECK

1. What kind of software searches through Internet documents and compiles a list of Web pages it locates on the Internet?

2. True or False: If you don't find the information you want using Yahoo!, you probably won't find the same information using MSN.

3. If your Internet search finds thousands of Web pages, what can you do to refine the search?

4. If you are using a search service and want to find information on the movie *The Wizard of Oz*, but you don't want any pages on the book *The Wizard of Oz*, what search operators can you use?

5. How can you use Windows XP to find an e-mail address for your state's governor?

REVIEW ASSIGNMENTS

1. *Using a Search String to Find a File* The governor has asked Senator Bernstein to represent the state in meetings with representatives of Taiwan who want to set up a student exchange program. In any international exchange, language is an issue. You remember a funny story about the translation of an ad for Coca-Cola into another language. Does the quotations archive disk contain that anecdote? To find out:

   a. In the Search Companion, use the All Files and Folders option, and enter likely search strings. Make sure you select the drive containing your Data Disk. If you're having trouble locating a file, try using only part of the search string or a different search string.

   b. Once you find a file you think looks promising, open it from the Search Results window.

   c. When you've found what you want, select the text, copy it, and then paste it into a new Notepad document. Type your name in the document you just created. At the end of the document, write a few sentences listing the search string you used and the name of the file(s) you located. Print the document and then close Notepad and the Search Results window. Don't save the Notepad document.

2. **Learning More About Files** On a sheet of paper, write the answers to the following questions about the files on the Data Disk. You can answer all the questions by examining the filenames.

  a. How many files contain the text "comedy" in their filenames?
  b. How many files and folders in total are on the disk? What did you do to find the answer? (*Hint*: You can find the answer to this question with a single search.)
  c. Which letters of the alphabet are missing in the filenames of the alphabetically organized Author files?
  d. How many files are on friendship? What search string did you use to find this answer?

3. **Using Wildcards** What search strings could you use to produce the following results? Write the search strings on a piece of paper. Use a wildcard for each one. For example, a results list of Budget2000.xls, Budget2001.xls, and Budget2002.xls could come from the search string "Budget200?.xls".

  a. Comedy1.doc, Comedy2.doc, Comedy3.doc
  b. Social.txt, Society.txt, Socratic Method.txt
  c. PhotoWorks, Network, Files for Work

4. **Searching for Files by Date** You can answer the following questions about the Data Disk by using the Date option. Write the answers on a sheet of paper. Return all settings to their defaults when you are done.

  a. How many files did Carolyn's previous aide modify in 1999?
  b. How many files did the aide modify in August, 1999?
  c. Which file(s) did the aide modify on August 31, 1999?

5. **Locating Files by Size** How many files of 1 KB or less does the Data Disk contain? How many files of 15 KB or more? Return this setting to its default when you are done.

6. **Locating Files by Contents** You enjoy Dave Barry's columns. Search the contents of the files on the Data Disk to see how many of them contain the text "barry", and then record that number. Write down the name of the file that seems to contain the most Dave Barry quotations. Open the file from Search. When you are done, delete the criteria you entered.

7. **Experimenting with Search Criteria** You decide to search for appropriate quotations for Senator Bernstein's upcoming speech topics. For each speech topic, write down the criteria you used to locate a file, and then write down the file location as it appears in the In Folder column of the results list. If you find more than one file, write down the first one in the list.

  a. Senator Bernstein has been invited to give the toast at a football brunch hosted by the president of Riverside College.
  b. The family of a deceased friend has asked Senator Bernstein if she'd like to contribute any thoughts to a written memorial.
  c. Senator Bernstein is cochairing this year's Renaissance Festival downtown. The festival will feature outdoor performances of three of Shakespeare's plays, including a performance by the Young Shakespeareans Guild, a troupe of children under age 18. She's promised to give the opening remarks at the festival.

Explore

8. **Opening Files from Search** You learned how to open a text document from Search in this tutorial. You can open other types of files the same way, as long as your computer contains the program that created the file.

  a. Search for Sound Clip files on your Data Disk. Right-click one of them and then click Play. What did you hear? Click the Close button when the sound file is done playing. If you don't hear anything, your computer might not have speakers, or they might be off.
  b. Search for Video Clip files on your computer's hard drive. If you find any, right-click one of them and then click the Play button. Describe what you see. Click the Close button when the video clip is done playing.

9. *Searching and Viewing File Contents*   Find the answers to the questions below. You will probably need to search for a keyword in the file's contents. For each answer, write the name of the file you used to find the answer. (*Hint*: Once you've located and opened the file, you can scroll through it to find the answer, or open it in Notepad, click Edit on the Notepad menu bar, and then click Find. Type the keyword in the Find what box, and then click the Find Next button.)

   a. What did Elsa Einstein think about her husband Albert's theory of relativity?
   b. Do you think cartoonist Jim Borgman is an optimist or a pessimist? Why?
   c. What was Helen Keller's opinion of college?
   d. How many children did Erma Bombeck recommend that one have? (Look carefully at the filenames in the results list so you don't open more files than necessary.)
   e. What did Elbert Hubbard have to say about books? (Look carefully at the filenames in the results list so you don't open more files than necessary.)

Explore

10. *Locating Information on the Internet*   Carolyn asks that you help locate information on Taiwan for Senator Bernstein's upcoming participation in establishing a student exchange program.

   a. Use the Search Companion pane to locate information on transportation in Taiwan. Write down the search criteria you use to find specific information. Write down the URL of a page on transportation in Taiwan.
   b. Send the search to the AltaVista search engine. When you find a page of specific information, write down its URL.
   c. Locate a Web page for one of Taiwan's universities. Write down the name of the university and the URL of its Web page.

11. *Locating People on the Internet*   Use two different people search services and the Find People dialog box to locate the e-mail address of the president of your university. Were you able to find it in any of them? Did the search services have e-mail addresses for other people with the same name?

12. *Locating a Map*   Locate and then print a map of your home address.

PROJECTS

1. On which drive is your Windows folder? Start to search for files and folders. In the Search Companion pane, specify My Computer in the Look in list, and then search for "Windows." Write the answer on a piece of paper. If there are too many files in the results list, sort the files by name so that folders named "Windows" appear near the top.

2. Can you locate the e-mail address of the president of the United States? What is the e-mail address?

3. Specify the following search strings, and, searching your Data Disk, examine the results list for each search string very carefully. What generalizations about wildcards can you make from your observations?

   men
   men.*
   men.
   men*.*
   men?
   men?.*

4. You can use Search to learn about the files on your hard drive. Record how many files of each of the following types exist on your hard disk.

    a. Application. Write down the names of five application files in the Windows folder of your hard drive.

    b. Bitmap Image. Which folders on your hard drive store the most bitmapped images?

    c. Screen Saver. Write down the location of a screen saver on your hard drive.

    d. Text Document. Once the results list shows all the text documents on your hard drive, order them by Name. Are any files named README? Write down the locations of two of them. Software programs often come with a README text file that lists known software problems and answers to common questions.

5. Write down the names of 10 documents recently accessed on the hard disk.

Explore

6. You can use the Search Companion pane to locate computers on a network. If you are on a network, click "Computers or people" in the Search Companion pane. Your instructor will give you the name of a computer for which to search on your network. Enter this name in the Computer Name box, and then click the Search button. Once Search has located the computer, open it from the results list. Take a screen print of the window that opens, and then paste that in a WordPad document. Include your name and the current date in the WordPad document.

Explore

7. Search the Data Disk for pictures or photos of Abraham Lincoln. If you don't find any, search the Internet. When you locate one, try to find the size of the picture or photo file. (*Hint*: The Web page might show the size near the image. If it doesn't, try right-clicking the image and then clicking Properties.) When you find a file that is less than 300 KB, save it on your Data Disk. To do so, right-click the image, click Save Picture As, and then use Abe Lincoln.jpg as the filename.

Explore

8. Use the "Documents (word processing, spreadsheets, etc.)" option in the Search Companion pane to find only text documents (.txt) on your Data Disk. Write down the number of .txt files you find. Then use the same option to find files with a .doc extension. Write down the number of .doc files you find.

QUICK | CHECK ANSWERS

Session 6.1

1. Click the Look in list arrow, and then click 3½ Floppy (A:).

2. False

3. A wildcard is a symbol that stands in place of one or more characters. The asterisk wildcard substitutes for any number of characters; the question mark substitutes for only one.

4. Click the Name button in Details view.

5. Click All files and folders (if necessary), open the More advanced options list, click the Type list arrow, click Bitmap Image, and then click the Search button.

6. Right-click it and then click Open, double-click it, or click it and then press the Enter key.

7. A keyword is a search string—a word or a phrase—contained anywhere in a file.

Session 6.2

1. search engine

2. False

3. Refine the search by entering more detailed search criteria.

4. "Wizard of Oz" NOT book or "Wizard of Oz" -book

5. Search the Internet using the Search Companion pane to find a person's e-mail address.

CONNECTING
COMPUTERS
OVER A
PHONE LINE

Windows XP **Dial-Up Tools**

Windows XP makes communicating with computers easier than ever because it provides tools that allow you to connect your computer to other computers and to the Internet. If you are using a computer on a university or institutional network, you are probably already connected to the Internet, and you can skip this appendix. This appendix is useful for people who are not connected to the Internet but who have their own computer with a modem and access to a phone line.

Computers at universities or large companies are likely to be connected to the Internet via expensive, high-speed wiring that transmits data very quickly. Home computer owners, however, usually cannot afford to run similar cables and wires to their homes, and instead rely on phone lines that are already in place, as shown in Figure A-1.

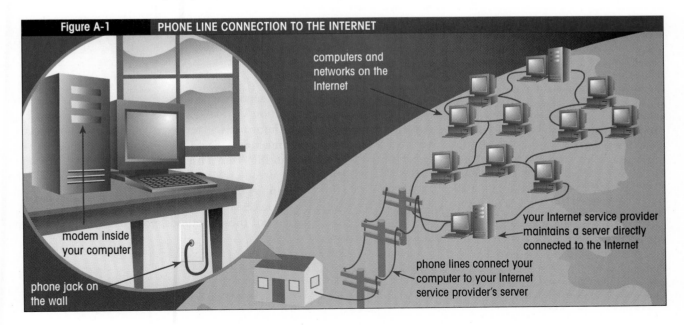

Figure A-1   PHONE LINE CONNECTION TO THE INTERNET

computers and networks on the Internet

modem inside your computer

phone jack on the wall

your Internet service provider maintains a server directly connected to the Internet

phone lines connect your computer to your Internet service provider's server

Phone lines use analog signals, which is one way to transmit voice and other data across wires, but a computer sends data as digital signals, a different way to transmit information. Phone lines cannot transmit digital signals, so when a modem uses an ordinary voice phone line, it must convert the modem's digital signals to analog, as shown in Figure A-2.

The receiving computer converts the analog signal back to digital. Data usually travels more slowly over phone wires than over the networking infrastructure of the Internet. If there are any problems with the phone connection, data can be lost. But regular phone lines are often the only practical choice for homes and small businesses. In some areas, **ISDN lines**, wires that provide a completely digital path from one computer to another, are dropping in price so that small businesses and homeowners can afford them. Whether you use a regular phone line or a faster ISDN line, Windows XP can help you establish a connection to the Internet. You will need to select an **Internet service provider (ISP)**, a company that provides Internet access. ISPs maintain servers that are directly connected to the Internet 24 hours a day. You dial into your ISP's server over your phone line to use its Internet connection. You pay a fee for this service, most often a flat monthly rate. When you use your computer's modem to connect to an ISP via your phone line, you are making a **dial-up connection**.

Once you've selected an ISP, you can use Windows XP to set up your dial-up connection. Figure A-2 shows the tools Windows XP includes for connecting to the Internet.

Figure A-2	WINDOWS XP CONNECTION TOOLS	
CONNECTION TOOL	**AVAILABLE FROM**	**DESCRIPTION**
Network Connections window	Connect To command on the Windows XP Start menu	Some computer users have one Internet account for home use and a different account for business use. The Network Connections window helps you manage multiple accounts that you use to connect to the Internet.
New Connection Wizard	In the New Connection window, click the Create a new connection command under Network Tasks in the left pane	The New Connection Wizard makes it easy to create an Internet account for the first time by prompting you for information through a series of dialog boxes.

The following sections show you how to use the New Connection Wizard to set up a new dial-up connection to your ISP so you can access the Internet and other networks.

Setting Up a Dial-Up Connection

There are three ways you can establish a connection to the Internet using your phone line. All three methods require the New Connection Wizard. The New Connection Wizard is a series of dialog boxes that prompt you for information your computer needs to connect to the Internet. Once you start the New Connection Wizard, you have three choices for setting up your connection. You can choose an ISP from a list Windows XP provides through the New Connection Wizard. If you have already selected an ISP and this ISP provided a setup CD-ROM with an installation program, you can use the CD-ROM to set up the connection. Lastly, you can manually set up the necessary dial-up connection.

To set up a dial-up connection using any of these methods, you first need to start the New Connection Wizard.

Starting the New Connection Wizard

You can use the New Connection Wizard to create a dial-up account. These steps assume you have signed up for an account with an ISP, but you have not set up the account yet. Before you perform the steps, you should gather any documentation from your ISP, such as phone number, user name or account name, and password.

To begin setting up a dial-up connection:

1. Click the **Start** button ![start] on the taskbar, point to **Connect To**, and then click **Show all connections**. The Network Connections window opens. See Figure A-3.

| Figure A-3 | THE NETWORK CONNECTIONS WINDOW |

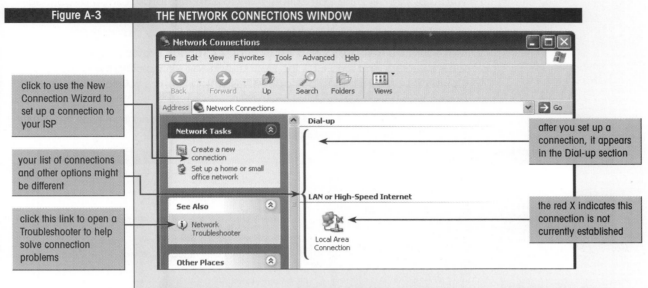

click to use the New Connection Wizard to set up a connection to your ISP

your list of connections and other options might be different

click this link to open a Troubleshooter to help solve connection problems

after you set up a connection, it appears in the Dial-up section

the red X indicates this connection is not currently established

2. Under Network Tasks, click **Create a new connection**. The Welcome to the New Connection Wizard dialog box opens, the first dialog box in the New Connection Wizard. The wizard will guide you through the steps of setting up a new connection.

   TROUBLE? If the Location Information window opens, provide the requested information and then click the OK button.

3. Click the **Next** button. The Network Connection Type dialog box opens. You can use this dialog box to connect to the Internet, connect to a business network, set up a small or home office network, or set up an advanced connection, which is usually a direct connection to another computer. These steps show you how to connect to the Internet.

4. Make sure the **Connect to the Internet** option button is selected, and then click the **Next** button. The Getting Ready dialog box opens.

At this point in the New Connection Wizard, you can choose from a list of ISPs, use the setup CD-ROM provided by an ISP, or set up a connection manually. The following section shows you how to set up an account by selecting one from the list of ISPs provided by the New Connection Wizard. After that section come sections that explain how to use a CD-ROM that an ISP provided to set up a connection and how to set up a connection manually.

Choosing from a List of ISPs

If you use a nationwide online service as your ISP, such as MSN, Earthlink, or Prodigy, you can quickly set up an automatic Internet connection by selecting an online service from a list Windows XP provides and then entering your user name and password. You can also have the Microsoft Internet Referral Service scan its list of ISPs to locate one you can access from your geographical area. If the Referral Service finds the one you want to use, you can select it and enter your user name and password to set up an automatic Internet connection.

To set up a connection by selecting an ISP from a list:

1. Make sure the New Connection Wizard is open to the Getting Ready dialog box.

   TROUBLE? If the Getting Ready dialog box is not open, start the New Connection Wizard again. Click the Start button, point to Connect To, click Show all connections, and then click Create a new connection. In the New Connection Wizard, click Next, and then click Next to open the Getting Ready dialog box.

2. Make sure the **Choose from a list of Internet Service Providers (ISPs)** option button is selected, and then click the **Next** button. The Completing the New Connection Wizard dialog box opens. This dialog box lets you set up an Internet connection using MSN Explorer or an ISP.

3. Click the **Select from a list of other ISPs** option button, and then click the **Finish** button. The Online Services window opens. See Figure A-4.

Figure A-4	THE ONLINE SERVICES WINDOW

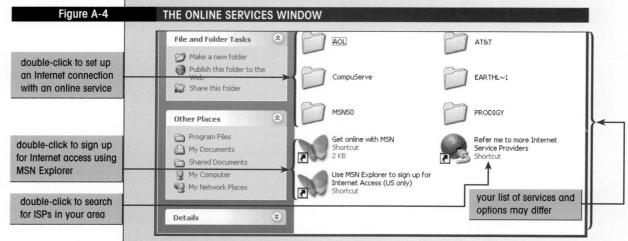

double-click to set up an Internet connection with an online service

double-click to sign up for Internet access using MSN Explorer

double-click to search for ISPs in your area

your list of services and options may differ

If you subscribe to one of these online services, double-click the appropriate folder and then double-click an HTML file to see setup instructions in Internet Explorer. For example, open the EARTHLN~1 folder and then double-click the EarthInk HTML document. You can also look for more ISPs.

4. If necessary, select a modem and then click **OK**.

5. Double-click the **Refer me to more Internet Service Providers** icon. The Internet Connection Wizard starts and dials the Microsoft Internet Referral Service.

   TROUBLE? If the computer you are using already has an Internet connection, a message might appear asking if you want to continue. Click the Yes button.

   After you connect to the Referral Service, the Internet Connection Wizard lists ISPs in your area.

6. Click the ISP you want to use, and then click the **Next** button. The Internet Account Information dialog box opens.

   TROUBLE? If the Referral Service does not find any ISPs in your area, you must use a different method to set up a connection. See "Using a Setup CD-ROM from your ISP" or "Setting Up a Connection Manually."

7. Type your user name and password, and then click the **Next** button. Your ISP documentation will provide you with a user name and password.

   TROUBLE? If you cannot find your user name in your documentation, it might be called the User ID, Member ID, Account Name, Login Name, or something similar.

8. Type a name for your connection, such as the name of your ISP, and then click the **Next** button.

9. Deselect the **Connect to the Internet Immediately** check box, and then click the **Finish** button.

10. Close the Online Services window. You return to the Network Connections window.

If you set up an Internet connection by choosing an ISP from the list of services Windows XP provided, you can now use the connection to dial up to your ISP and connect to the Internet. See "Using the Network Connections Window" for details. If you did not set up an Internet connection in the previous steps, you'll see how to do so in the following section by using a CD-ROM your ISP provided.

Using a Setup CD-ROM from Your ISP

Some ISPs create Setup CD-ROMs that include all the information you need to set up a dial-up connection to the ISP. In this case, you start the New Connection Wizard, indicate that you want to use a CD-ROM your ISP provided, and then typically step through a Setup Wizard that your ISP provided on the CD-ROM.

To set up a connection using a CD-ROM from your ISP:

1. Start the New Connection Wizard.

   TROUBLE? To start the New Connection Wizard, click the Start button, point to Connect To, click Show all connections, and then click Create a new connection.

2. In the Welcome to the New Connection Wizard dialog box, click the **Next** button. In the Network Connection Type dialog box, make sure the **Connect to the Internet** option button is selected, and then click the **Next** button to open the Getting Ready dialog box.

3. Click the **Use the CD I got from an ISP** option button, and then click the **Next** button. The Completing the New Connection Wizard dialog box opens.

4. Click the **Finish** button.

5. Insert the CD-ROM your ISP gave you in the CD-ROM drive of your computer. A Setup program should start automatically to help you connect to the Internet.

   TROUBLE? If a Setup program does not start, contact your ISP.

If you set up an Internet connection by using the CD-ROM your ISP provided, you can now use the connection to dial up to your ISP and connect to the Internet. See "Using the Network Connections Window" for details. If you did not set up an Internet connection in the previous steps, you will learn how to set up a connection manually in the following section.

Setting Up a Connection Manually

If you could not set up a dial-up connection to your ISP using an online service, an ISP from the Microsoft Internet Referral Service, or a CD-ROM your ISP provided, you can set up a connection manually. To do so, you use the New Connection Wizard to enter the phone number of your ISP and the user name and password for your account. You can add a desktop shortcut to the connection so you can easily access it when you're finished.

To set up a connection manually:

1. Start the New Connection Wizard.

   TROUBLE? To start the New Connection Wizard, click the Start button, point to Connect To, click Show all connections, and then click Create a new connection.

2. In the Welcome to the New Connection Wizard dialog box, click the **Next** button. In the Network Connection Type dialog box, make sure the **Connect to the Internet** option button is selected, and then click the **Next** button to open the Getting Ready dialog box.

3. Click the **Set up my connection manually** option button, and then click the **Next** button. The Internet Connection dialog box opens, asking how you want to connect to the Internet. In addition to using a dial-up modem to connect, you can also use this dialog box to connect using a broadband connection, which is a high-speed connection using either a digital service line (DSL) or a cable modem.

   TROUBLE? If your computer has more than one modem, the Select a Device dialog box opens. Click the modem you want to use and then click Next.

   TROUBLE? If you are using a broadband connection, see your instructor or technical support person for instructions on completing the New Connection Wizard.

4. Make sure the **Connect using a dial-up modem** option button is selected, and then click the **Next** button. The Connection Name dialog box opens.

5. Type a name for this connection, such as the name of your ISP, and then click the Next button. The Phone Number to Dial dialog box opens.

   TROUBLE? If the Connection Availability dialog box opens, click Next to continue to the Phone Number to Dial dialog box.

6. Type the phone number of your ISP, and then click the Next button. The Internet Account Information dialog box opens.

7. Type the user name and password for your ISP account. In the Confirm password text box, type the password again. As you type the password, bullets appear instead of the letters you type, as shown in Figure A-5. This is a security feature; you should keep your password secret, so that unauthorized users cannot access your account.

   TROUBLE? Refer to your ISP documentation for your user name and password. If you cannot find your user name in your documentation, it might be called the User ID, Member ID, Account Name, Login Name, or something similar.

Figure A-5   ENTERING ACCOUNT INFORMATION

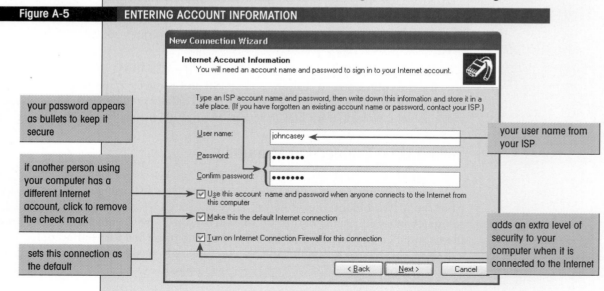

your password appears as bullets to keep it secure

if another person using your computer has a different Internet account, click to remove the check mark

sets this connection as the default

your user name from your ISP

adds an extra level of security to your computer when it is connected to the Internet

8. Click the **Next** button. In the Completing the New Connection Wizard dialog box, click the **Add a shortcut to this connection to my desktop** check box to select this option, and then click the **Finish** button.

The Connect dialog box opens. You could use it to connect to your ISP now by clicking the Dial button. For now, you can close this dialog box.

9. Click the **Cancel** button.

Now you can use your new dial-up connection to connect to your ISP and the Internet.

Using the Network Connections Window

Once you have established a dial-up connection, you are ready to use it to connect to the Internet or another network or computer. Windows XP will try to connect to the Internet automatically whenever you start a program that requires Internet access, such as your Web browser. If you have more than one ISP, Windows XP uses the one you set as the default connection.

Other ways of establishing your Internet connection would be to double-click the shortcut icon to your ISP on your desktop, or open the Network Connections window and then double-click the icon for your ISP. This window also provides tools to change your dial-up settings or any of your network connections (through your modem or local area network).

To connect to your dial-up service through the Network Connections window:

1. Click the **Start** button ⊞ **start**, point to **Connect To**, and then click **Show all connections**. The Network Connections window opens as shown in Figure A-6.

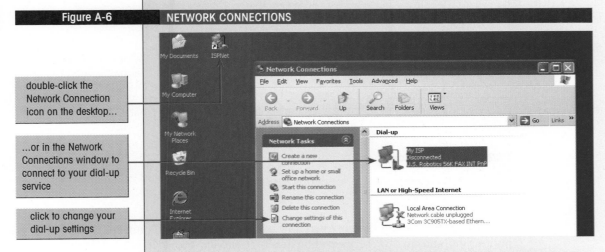

Figure A-6   NETWORK CONNECTIONS

double-click the Network Connection icon on the desktop...

...or in the Network Connections window to connect to your dial-up service

click to change your dial-up settings

You can have more than one network service, in which case multiple icons appear in the Network Connections window. One connection might provide your business Internet service, another might be for home or family use, and another might access your local area network.

2. Make sure your phone line is connected to your computer's modem.

3. Double-click the icon for your ISP.

The Connecting dialog box opens and identifies the steps of establishing a connection. First it uses your modem to dial the number, then it verifies your user name and password, and finally it establishes a connection. A ScreenTip may appear, indicating that you are connected to your ISP.

4. A connection icon 🖥 appears on your taskbar that indicates you are connected. You can now start your Internet browser to view Web pages, check your e-mail, or use any of the other Windows XP online communications features.

Your dial-up account will remain connected until you leave your computer idle for several minutes, in which case your ISP may automatically disconnect you, or until you disconnect from your account yourself.

To disconnect your dial-up account:

1. Double-click the Connection icon 🖥 on the taskbar. The Status dialog box opens, shown in Figure A-7.

| Figure A-7 | THE STATUS DIALOG BOX |

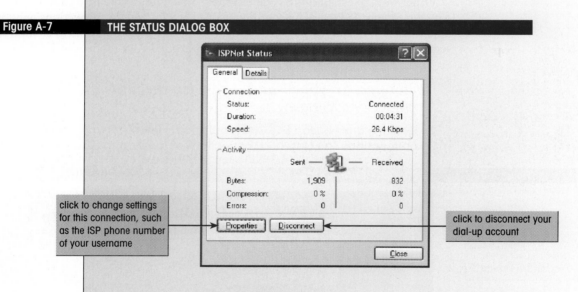

click to change settings for this connection, such as the ISP phone number of your username

click to disconnect your dial-up account

2. Click the **Disconnect** button.

3. Close the Network Connections window.

In this appendix you have learned how to set up an Internet connection using your voice phone line and an ISP service. The Internet service provider market is changing very rapidly, so make sure you compare prices and features before choosing the ISP that best suits your needs.

INDEX

TASK	PAGE #	RECOMMENDED METHOD/NOTES
Active Desktop item, add from Web Gallery	WIN 5.26	In Control Panel, click Appearance and Themes, click Change the desktop background, click the Customize Desktop button, click the Web tab, click the New button, click the Visit Gallery button, click the Add to Active Desktop button for the item you want, click Yes, click OK
Active Desktop item, close	WIN 5.29	Point to an item, wait for a title bar to appear, click ☒
Active Desktop item, delete from desktop	WIN 5.35	In Control Panel, click Appearance and Themes, click Change the desktop background, click the Customize Desktop button, click the Web tab, click the item you want to remove, click the Delete button
Active Desktop item, move	WIN 5.29	Point to an item, wait for the title bar to appear, drag the title bar
Active Desktop item, resize	WIN 5.29	Point to an item, wait for a border to appear, drag the border or the border corner
Active Desktop item, schedule an update for	WIN 5.34	See Reference Window: Scheduling an Update
Active Desktop item, synchronize	WIN 5.31	See Reference Window: Synchronizing an Active Desktop Item
Active Desktop item, view an update schedule	WIN 5.32	Point to an item, wait for a title bar to appear, click the down arrow in the upper-left corner of the title bar, click Properties, click the Schedule tab
Character, insert	WIN 2.07	Click where you want to insert the character, type the character
Control Panel, open	WIN 4.16	Click ⊞ start , click Control Panel
Desktop, access	WIN 1.14	Click ▣ on the Quick Launch toolbar
Desktop appearance, save as theme	WIN 4.28	In Control Panel, click Appearance and Themes, click Change the computer's theme, click the Theme list arrow, click My Current Theme, click the Save As button, type a filename, click Save
Desktop background, use HTML file for	WIN 5.38	In Control Panel, click Appearance and Themes, click Change the desktop background, click the Browse button, select the HTML file
Desktop color palette, change	WIN 4.34	In Control Panel, click Appearance and Themes, click Change the screen resolution, click the Colors list arrow, click the palette you want, click OK
Desktop document, create	WIN 4.04	See Reference Window: Creating a New Document Icon on the Desktop
Desktop document, open	WIN 4.06	Double-click the document icon
Desktop resolution, change	WIN 4.32	In Control Panel, click Appearance and Themes, click Change the screen resolution, drag the Screen area slider, click OK
Desktop, change appearance	WIN 4.29	In Control Panel, click Appearance and Themes, click Change the computer's theme, click the Theme list arrow, click a theme, click OK
Desktop, change background	WIN 4.20	In Control Panel, click Appearance and Themes, click Change the desktop background, select an item in the Background list, click OK
Device, select	WIN 3.08	Click the device icon on the Explorer bar of Windows Explorer

TASK	PAGE #	RECOMMENDED METHOD/NOTES
Disk, format	WIN 2.02	Right-click the 3½ Floppy icon in My Computer, click Format on the shortcut menu, click Start
Disk, quick format	WIN 3.24	In My Computer, right-click 🖫, click Format, click Quick Format, click Start
Explorer bar, view	WIN 3.04	In Windows Explorer or My Computer, click View, point to Explorer Bar, click the Explorer bar you want to open
Favorites folder, add a Web page to	WIN 5.20	See Reference Window: Adding a Web Page to the Favorites Folder
Favorites folder, organize	WIN 5.20	See Reference Window: Organizing the Favorites Folder
Favorites folder, view	WIN 5.19	In Windows Explorer, click View, point to the Explorer Bar, click Favorites
File or folder, delete	WIN 3.27	Click the file or folder icon, press Delete
File, copy	WIN 2.28	Use the right mouse button to drag the file you want to copy, release the mouse button, click Copy Here on the shortcut menu
File, copy from one floppy disk to another	WIN 3.20	See Reference Window: Moving and Copying a File
File, delete	WIN 2.30	Right-click the file you want to delete, click Delete on the shortcut menu
File, download from Web	WIN 5.23	In Internet Explorer, right-click the file you want to download, click Save As (or Save Picture As, or something similar), enter a location, click OK
File, locate by contents	WIN 6.13	In the Search Companion, click All files or folders, click the A word or phrase in the file text box, type the text you want to search for, click the Search button
File, locate by date	WIN 6.18	In the Search Companion, click All files or folders, click When was it modified?, select a date option, click the Search button
File, locate in a specific folder	WIN 6.14	See Reference Window: Searching for a File in a Specific Folder
File, move	WIN 2.28	Use the right mouse button to drag the file you want to copy, release the mouse button, click Move Here on the shortcut menu
File, move or copy from floppy disk to hard disk	WIN 3.23	See Reference Window: Moving or Copying Files with the Move To Folder and Copy To Folder commands
File, move or copy with Cut and Paste	WIN 3.20	See Reference Window: Moving or Copying Files with Cut, Copy, and Paste
File, open from My Computer	WIN 2.12	Open My Computer, open the Window containing the file, double-click the file
File, open from Search Results	WIN 6.10	Locate the file using the Search tool, double-click the file in the Results list
File, open from within a program	WIN 2.13	Start the program, click 📂, select the file in the Open dialog box, click Open

TASK	PAGE #	RECOMMENDED METHOD/NOTES
File, preview before printing	WIN 2.15	Click [icon]
File, print	WIN 2.15	Click [icon]
File, rename	WIN 2.29	Right-click the file, click Rename on shortcut menu, type new filename, press Enter
File, save	WIN 2.08	Click [icon]
File, select	WIN 3.15	See Reference Window: Selecting Files
File, select all but a certain one	WIN 3.16	See Reference Window: Selecting All Files Except Certain Ones
Files, locate by type or size	WIN 6.19-6.20	In the Search Companion, click All files or folders, click More advanced options, click Type of file list arrow, click file type, and then click the Search button
Files, view as large icons	WIN 2.21	Click the Views button, click Tiles
Files, view as small icons	WIN 2.21	Click the Views button, click Icons
Files, view details	WIN 2.22	Click the Views button, click Details
Files, view in list	WIN 2.21	Click the Views button, click List
Files, view thumbnails	WIN 2.21	Click the Views button, click Thumbnails
Floppy disk, copy	WIN 2.31	Right-click the [icon] icon in My Computer, click Copy Disk on the shortcut menu, click Start, insert the disk you want to copy from (source disk), then click OK
Folder, create	WIN 2.25	Click File, point to New, click Folder, type a folder name, press Enter
Folder hierarchy, move back in the	WIN 2.26	Click [icon]
Folder hierarchy, move forward in the	WIN 2.26	Click [icon]
Folder hierarchy, move up	WIN 2.26	Click [icon]
Folder options, restore default settings	WIN 2.23	Click Tools, click Folder Options, click the General tab, click Restore Defaults, (or click the View tab and click Restore Defaults), click OK
Folder rename	WIN 3.11	Right-click [icon], click Rename, type the new folder name
Folder, create	WIN 3.09	See Reference Window: Creating a Folder in Windows Explorer
Help, display topic from the Home page	WIN 1.30	In Help and Support, click Home in the navigation bar
Help, display topic from the Index page	WIN 1.31	In Help, click Index in the navigation bar, scroll to locate a topic or type a keyword, click the topic, click Display
Help, find topic	WIN 1.33	In Help, click in the Search box, type word or phrase, click [icon]
Help, start	WIN 1.29	Click [start], click Help and Support
History pane, display	WIN 3.34	In Windows Explorer, click View, point to Explorer Bar, click History

TASK	PAGE #	RECOMMENDED METHOD/NOTES
History pane, display objects by most visits	WIN 3.36	In the History pane, click View, click By Most Visited
History pane, display recently opened files	WIN 3.35	In the History pane, click View, click By Order Visited Today
Insertion point, move	WIN 2.06	Click the location in the document to which you want to move
Internet Connection Wizard, start	WIN A.04	Click **start**, point to Connect To, click Show all connections, click the Create a new connection link
Internet Explorer, start	WIN 5.06	See Reference Window: Starting Internet Explorer
List box, scroll	WIN 1.26	Click the list arrow for the list box to display the list of options; click the scroll down or up arrow; or drag the scroll box
Log file, create	WIN 4.06	In Notepad, type .LOG
Menu option, select	WIN 1.23	Click the option on the menu; for submenus, point to an option on the menu
My Computer, open	WIN 2.12	Double-click the My Computer icon on the desktop
Objects, display or hide in the Folders pane	WIN 3.06	See Reference Window: Displaying or Hiding Objects in the Folders Pane
Outlook Express, receive e-mail from	WIN 5.53	Click 🖂
Outlook Express, reply to e-mail from	WIN 5.55	Click 👤↵
Outlook Express, send e-mail from	WIN 5.50	See Reference Window: Sending an E-mail Message
Outlook Express, set up an e-mail account for	WIN 5.44	See Reference Window: Setting up an E-mail Account
Outlook Express, start	WIN 5.41	Click **start**, point to All Programs, if necessary, click Outlook Express
Panes, adjust width	WIN 3.11	See Reference Window: Adjusting the Width of the Exploring Window Pane
People, locate on the Web	WIN 6.30	In the Search Companion, click Search the Internet, enter search criteria, click the Search button
Program, close	WIN 1.12	Click ☒
Program, close inactive	WIN 1.15	Right-click the program button on the taskbar, click Close
Program, start	WIN 1.11	*See* Reference Window: Starting a Program
Program, switch to another	WIN 1.14	Click the program button on the taskbar
Properties, view	WIN 4.20	Right-click an object, click Properties
Results list, sort	WIN 6.16-6.17	In the Search Results window, display the file list in Details view, click the title buttons on the top of the file list
Screen saver, activate	WIN 4.30	In Control Panel, click Appearance and Themes, click Change the screen resolution, click the Screen Saver list arrow, select a screen saver, click OK

TASK	PAGE #	RECOMMENDED METHOD/NOTES
Screen, print	WIN 3.17	Press PrintScreen, start WordPad, click 📋, click 🖨
ScreenTips, view	WIN 1.05	Position pointer over an item
Start menu, open	WIN 1.06	Click 🔵 start
Search Companion pane, open	WIN 6.03	Click 🔵 start , click Search
Search the Internet	WIN 6.26	In the Search Companion pane, click Search the Internet
Search, locate file by name	WIN 6.05	See Reference Window: Searching for a File by Name
Send To command, copy files with	WIN 3.25	Right-click the file icon, point to Send To, select the destination of the file
Shortcut icon, delete	WIN 4.15	Select the shortcut icon, press Delete, click Yes
Shortcut, create	WIN 4.09	See Figure 4-9: Methods for Creating Shortcuts
Start Menu, add an item to	WIN 4.46	See Reference Window: Adding an Item to the Start Menu
Start Menu, remove an item from	WIN 4.50	See Reference Window: Removing a Start Menu Item
Subfolders, view or hide	WIN 3.07	Click ➕ or ➖
Taskbar toolbar, create	WIN 4.40	See Reference Window: Displaying a Taskbar Toolbar
Taskbar toolbar, modify the appearance of	WIN 4.42	Right-click the taskbar, click Properties, modify the properties that apply to the taskbar's appearance
Taskbar toolbar, remove	WIN 4.44	Right-click a blank area on the taskbar, point to Toolbars, click the taskbar toolbar you want to remove
Taskbar, move and resize	WIN 4.36	See Reference Window: Moving and Resizing the Taskbar
Taskbar, set properties	WIN 4.39	Right-click the taskbar, click Properties
Text, select	WIN 2.06	Drag the pointer over the text
Toolbar button, select	WIN 1.25	Click the toolbar button
Toolbars, control display	WIN 2.20	Click View, point to Toolbars, select the toolbar options you want
Web page, activate link	WIN 5.12	In Internet Explorer, click a link on a Web page
Web page, open with URL	WIN 5.09	See Reference Window: Opening a Page with a URL
Web page, return to previous	WIN 5.16	In Internet Explorer, click ⬅
Wildcards, use to find files by name	WIN 6.11	In the Search Companion, click All files or folders, type search string using ? in place of single characters and * in place of multiple characters
Window, close	WIN 1.12	Click ✖
Window, maximize	WIN 1.20	Click ◻
Window, minimize	WIN 1.20	Click ▬

TASK	PAGE #	RECOMMENDED METHOD/NOTES
Window, move	WIN 1.21	Drag the title bar
Window, resize	WIN 1.21	Drag ⊞
Window, restore	WIN 1.21	Click ⧉
Windows Explorer, start	WIN 3.02	Click **start**, point to All Programs, point to Accessories, click Windows Explorer
Windows XP, shut down	WIN 1.15	Click **start**, click Turn Off Computer, click the Turn Off button
Windows XP, start	WIN 1.02	Turn on the computer

Windows XP Level I File Finder

Location in Tutorial	Name and Location of Data File	Student Saves File As...	Student Creates New File
Windows XP Level I **Tutorial 1**	No Data Files needed		
Tutorial 2			
Session 2.1			Practice Text.txt
Session 2.2 *Note*: Students copy the contents of Disk 1 onto Disk 2 in this session	Agenda.rtf Beck.asx Holiday.bmp Iceberg.jpg Logo.bmp New Logo.bmp Proposal.rtf Resume.rtf Salinas Family.eml Stationery.bmp Vinca.jpg Practice Text.txt *(saved from Session 2.1)*		
Review Assignments and Projects *Note*: Students continue to use the Data Disks they used in the Tutorial. For certain Assignments, they need a third blank disk		Woods Resume.rtf	Letter.rtf Song.rtf Poem.rtf

Windows XP Level II File Finder

Location in Tutorial	Name and Location of Data File	Student Saves File As...	Student Creates New File
Windows XP Level II **Tutorial 3** Session 3.1	[16 files] Clients (folder) Advanced (folder) [4 files] Alpine (folder) [3 files] Ice (folder) [2 files] Sport (folder) [2 files] Basic (folder) [4 files] Gear (folder) [3 files] Guides (folder) [3 files]	[16 files] Clients (folder) Advanced (folder) [4 files] Alpine (folder) [3 files] Ice (folder) [2 files] Sport (folder) [2 files] Basic (folder) [4 files] Gear (folder) [3 files] Hardware (folder) Ropes and Harnesses (folder) Guides (folder) [3 files]	Gear (folder) Hardware (folder) Ropes and Harnesses (folder)
Session 3.2	*(Continued from Session 3.1)*	[4 files] Clients (folder) Advanced (folder) [4 files] Alpine (folder) [5 files] Ice (folder) [2 files] Sport (folder) [2 files] Basic (folder)	

		[13 files]
		Gear (folder)
		  Hardware (folder)
		  Ropes and Harnesses (folder)
		  [5 files]
		Guides (folder)
		  [3 files]	

Session 3.3	No Data Files needed		
Review Assignments and Projects			C:/My Documents/Advertise A:/All Clients
Tutorial 4			
Session 4.1	Same files used as in Session 3.2.		Phone Log.txt
Session 4.2	Logo.bmp		
Session 4.3	No Data Files needed		

Review Assignments and Projects			Classes.txt
			A:/Sally (folder)
			  Smith.txt
			  Arruga.txt
			  Kosta.txt
			A:/My Signature.bmp

Tutorial 5			
Session 5.1	No Data Files needed		Lake.jpg
Session 5.2	Highland.htm [15 supporting files]		
Session 5.3			Highland.htm [15 supporting files]
Tutorial 6			

Session 6.1	Alphabet (folder)
	  [25 files]
	Authors (folder)
	  [25 files]
	Comedy (folder)
	  [18 files]
	Images (folder)
	  [2 files]
	Social (folder)
	  [16 files]
	Topics (folder)
	  [19 files]		

Session 6.2	No Data Files needed		
Review Assignments and Projects	Same as Session 6.1		